On the Job

An Encyclopedia of Unique Occupations around the World

Margo DeMello

ABC-CLIO®

An Imprint of ABC-CLIO, LLC
Santa Barbara, California • Denver, Colorado

Library of Congress Cataloging-in-Publication Data

Names: DeMello, Margo, author.
Title: On the job : an encyclopedia of unique occupations around the world
  / Margo DeMello.
Description: First edition. | Santa Barbara, California : ABC-CLIO, an
  imprint of ABC-CLIO, LLC, [2021] | Includes bibliographical references
  and index.
Identifiers: LCCN 2020007298 (print) | LCCN 2020007299 (ebook) | ISBN
  9781440863509 (hardcover) | ISBN 9781440863516 (ebook)
Subjects: LCSH: Occupations—Encyclopedias. | Job
  descriptions—Encyclopedias.
Classification: LCC HF5382 .D45 2021 (print) | LCC HF5382 (ebook) | DDC
  331.7003—dc23
LC record available at https://lccn.loc.gov/2020007298
LC ebook record available at https://lccn.loc.gov/2020007299

ISBN: 978-1-4408-6350-9 (print)
       978-1-4408-6351-6 (ebook)

25 24 23 22 21   1 2 3 4 5

This book is also available as an eBook.

ABC-CLIO
An Imprint of ABC-CLIO, LLC

ABC-CLIO, LLC
147 Castilian Drive
Santa Barbara, California 93117
www.abc-clio.com

This book is printed on acid-free paper (∞)

Manufactured in the United States of America

Contents

Alphabetical List of Entries

Topical List of Entries

JOBS INVOLVING ANIMALS

Alligator Wrestler

Animal Talent Agent

Anthrozoologist

Bullfighter

Deer Urine Collector

Equine-Assisted Therapist

Geoduck Farmer

Guide Dog Trainer

Insect Farmer

Mahout

Panda Nanny

Pet Taxidermist

Ravenmaster

Roadkill Cleaner

Rodeo Performer

Sloth Nanny

Snake Milker

JOBS INVOLVING ART OR POPULAR CULTURE

Animal Talent Agent

Background Artist

Belly Dancer

Caricature Artist

Ethical Hacker

Facebook Content Moderator

Fortune Cookie Writer

Graffiti Artist

Griot

Instagram Influencer

Professional Television Watcher

Psychic

Rental Paparazzo

Rose Parade Float Builder

Sideshow Freak

Sugar Painter

World of Warcraft Gold Farmer

YouTube Celebrity

JOBS INVOLVING BODIES

Hand Model

Mohel

Organ Harvester

Porn Star

Sex Worker

Standardized Patient

Surrogate

JOBS INVOLVING BODILY FLUIDS OR WASTE

Bathroom Attendant

Crime Scene Cleaner

Deer Urine Collector

Ear Cleaner

Organ Harvester

Roadkill Cleaner

JOBS INVOLVING CRIME

Bounty Hunter

Car Watchman

Crime Scene Cleaner

Graffiti Artist

License Plate Blocker

Pirate

Polygraph Examiner

Sex Worker

Victim Advocate

JOBS INVOLVING DANGER

Alligator Wrestler

Bounty Hunter

Bullfighter

Pirate

Rodeo Performer

Saturation Diver

JOBS INVOLVING DEATH

Burial Bead Maker

Crime Scene Cleaner

Fantasy Coffin Maker

Ghost Hunter

Mourner

Organ Harvester

Pet Taxidermist

Psychic

Roadkill Cleaner

JOBS INVOLVING FOOD

Competitive Eater

Culinary Historian

Dabbawala

Food Taster

Insect Farmer

Sugar Painter

JOBS INVOLVING GARBAGE

Garbage Detective

Pallet Recycler

Roadkill Cleaner

JOBS INVOLVING RELIGION

Astrologer

Bruja

Exorcist

Feng Shui Consultant

Ghost Hunter

Psychic

Traditional Healer

Witch Hunter

JOBS INVOLVING SEX

Love Hotel Operator

Porn Star

Sex Worker

JOBS INVOLVING SPORTS

Competitive Eater

Golf Ball Diver

Rodeo Performer

Geographical List of Entries

GLOBAL

Anthrozoologist

Astrologer

Background Artist

Bathroom Attendant

Belly Dancer

Caricature Artist

Culinary Historian

Cult Leader

Equine-Assisted Therapist

Ethical Hacker

Executioner

Exorcist

Facebook Content Moderator

Food Taster

Ghost Hunter

Google Street View Driver

Graffiti Artist

Guide Dog Trainer

Hand Model

Insect Farmer

Instagram Influencer

Mime or Clown

Mohel

Mystery Shopper

Organ Harvester

Pallet Recycler

Pet Cemetery Operator

Polygraph Examiner

Porn Star

Psychic

Rickshaw Driver

Saturation Diver

Sex Worker

Surrogate

Traditional Healer

Ufologist

YouTube Celebrity

AUSTRALIA AND NEW ZEALAND

Crime Scene Cleaner

Professional Line Stander

Rodeo Performer

Sideshow Freak

Victim Advocate

EAST ASIA

Burial Bead Maker

Chicken Sexer

Ear Cleaner

Feng Shui Consultant

Love Hotel Operator

Matchmaker

Preface

One of the most common questions that children are asked by adults is, "What do you want to do when you grow up?" Once we do grow up, often the first question we are asked upon meeting someone new is, "What do you do?" Everyone knows what *do* means. It means what we do for work.

Work is critical to our survival (if we did not work, we would not eat), and it is important for our identities as individuals as well. The kind of work that we do, how much we are paid and valued for that work, who we work with, and the conditions in which we work all shape our identities, our values, and what we believe in. So it is not surprising that the first question we are asked by strangers has to do with what we do for a living. It is another way of asking, "Who are you and what are you about?" But what happens when the answer to that question is not "I am an accountant" or "I am a nurse" but "I am a gondolier" or "I am an Instagram influencer"?

This encyclopedia tries to answer the question by looking at jobs from around the world that are out of the ordinary and even crazy sounding. It covers culturally unique occupations around the world, from bike fishermen in the Netherlands to professional wedding guests in South Korea, and it gives the reader a sense of what doing that job is like. For example, how does one qualify to dress elephants for ceremonies in India? What would it be like to smell people's armpits all day? And we might ask, what kind of person would be good at breeding bugs?

This encyclopedia will help the reader to understand jobs that seem incomprehensible, and it may even lead some readers to explore a few of these jobs in further detail. Who knew, for instance, that you could work as a line stander in New York or as a train pusher in Tokyo?

What makes a job strange? The encyclopedia includes jobs that are unique for any of the following reasons:

- They might be dangerous.
- They might be dirty.
- They might be gross.
- They may involve working with unusual animals.
- They may reflect a particular cultural value or practice that is not readily understood outside of that cultural context.

- They may involve working with things that are typically taboo, such as dead bodies, vomit, feces, or blood.
- They may involve sex.
- They may be illegal.
- They may involve extraordinary skills or talents.

This encyclopedia is appropriate for general readers, high school students, and undergraduates. The reader will not only be exposed to unique occupations, but because of the cross-cultural scope of this work, readers will also explore other cultures through an especially unique lens.

All entries include a list of sources for further reading on the subject for readers who desire more information, and these are also included in a comprehensive bibliography.

There are ninety entries in this encyclopedia that cover occupations from alligator wrestler to YouTube celebrity. There are a great many entries from North America, but the encyclopedia also includes societies spanning the world. The encyclopedia entries focus on contemporary jobs, but it also includes twenty-five sidebars that highlight unique jobs from history to give readers a sense of how unusual (and often terrible!) some jobs once were.

Entries are listed in alphabetical order, and when a subject has multiple names, the most commonly used, or generic name (e.g., traditional healer) will be the name used for the entry.

Each entry defines the job, gives an overview, and provides the historical, social, and cultural significance of the job. The entry also includes where the job is located, how it came to be, how people get into the position, and what the future economic outlook is for each job. Because of the speed with which the economy changes, especially in postindustrial nations, there will doubtless be new unusual occupations that will have emerged following publication of this encyclopedia. Nevertheless, all attempts have been made to include the most relevant and up-to-date information.

Acknowledgments

This is the fifth encyclopedia I have produced for this company, and I am thankful to ABC-CLIO for giving me the opportunity to write these books. I also want to thank my editor, Kaitlin Ciarmiello, who has worked with me on the last few books and is patient and forgiving of my missed deadlines!

Finally, I want to thank my husband, Tom Young, who supports me as I write, and my parents, Bill DeMello and Robin Montgomery, who have always given me love and support throughout all my projects.

Introduction

Work, like taxes and death, is a universal aspect of culture. All people throughout history have worked. And if we define *work* more broadly than simply performing activities for wages, then all living creatures work, in that all animals engage in activities that keep them alive, including providing food for themselves, finding shelter, and maintaining safety. Human occupations are simply an extension of the basic need shared by all animals to do what is needed to keep ourselves alive.

All people work in some way, shape, or form. Most of us engage in wage labor, working in exchange for pay, but we also engage in domestic labor, which is—work that is done to keep a household running. Women also engage in reproductive labor—the work that is involved in producing and rearing children.

Even though all people everywhere share the same basic life needs, all societies do not do the same types of work, and, indeed, prior to the spread of capitalism and, later, industrialism throughout the world, how people made a living was often very different in different parts of the world.

Economic systems are made of three distinct components: production, distribution or exchange, and consumption. Production refers to how goods (which includes basics such as food, clothing, and shelter as well as every other product that people make and use) are produced via what economists call the means of production. The means of production includes labor, the focus of this book, and labor includes everything from wage labor to reproductive labor to subsistence labor. Besides labor, a system of production needs resources, which may include land, animals, plants, or minerals, and technology, which includes both the tools and cultural knowledge that are necessary to take a raw resource and turn it into a finished good. Finally, capitalist economic systems (which are now found in every society around the world), have a fourth element: capital—or money.

Anthropologists divide systems of production into six major modes: foraging, pastoralism, horticulture, agriculture, industrialism, and postindustrialism. These six modes refer to how the means of production are utilized to produce goods, and they differ based on the environmental conditions in which the systems are found and the different ways in which people exploit those conditions. For instance, foragers (also known as hunter-gatherers), who use the simplest system and the system that all humans utilized until the domestication of plants and animals during the Neolithic Revolution, gather wild plant foods and hunt animals for the majority of their diet. All members of the society, except for the very young and very old, work, and there is very little occupational specialization—most men hunt, most women gather, and most people make their own basic tools. These types of cultures, which only exist in a few locations today and now combine foraging with some sort of capitalist exchange, are mobile, and they depend on having access to large areas of undeveloped land. Because there are very few private possessions and no excess of goods, these cultures tend to be egalitarian, with no (or very little) social stratification.

Another system of production that is relatively rare today is pastoralism. Pastoralism developed after the domestication of plants and animals and was (and is) found in areas of the world that were not suitable for simple farming. Pastoralists herd ruminants, such as cattle, goats, reindeer, or sheep, and build their economic system around those animals. Traditionally, pastoralists were mobile, like foragers, moving their animals across large areas of land for the animals to forage, and, both in the past and in the present, they supplement their lifestyles by exchanging the products from their animals with goods from other cultural groups. Pastoralists have a strict division of labor based on gender, with men primarily herding the animals, but little occupational specialization.

After the domestication of plants and animals, which began about 12,500 years ago in a handful of locations around the world, horticulture and agriculture developed. Both systems involve planting crops for food, rather than gathering plants, and are generally supplemented with raising animals as well. The primary differences between both systems, according to anthropologists, have to do with the frequency of planting and the tools and energy needed to operate the system. Agriculture, which dominates around the world today, involves continuous planting (rather than shifting cultivation) and utilizes either animal labor (such as cattle that pull the plow) or modern technology (such as tractors) along with irrigation. Both systems differ from foraging and pastoralism in that farming allows people to settle in one location, and because farming is more productive than either foraging or pastoralism, is there is a surplus of goods; therefore not everyone needs to farm, so many people are freed up to engage in other kinds of labor.

Intensive agriculture, in particular, with its extensive occupational specialization, combined with a goods surplus has allowed for nonlaboring classes such as political and religious elites and, ultimately, the rise of systems of social stratification that continue to be central in the majority of cultures around the world. Without intensive agriculture, in which farmers support both nonworking classes and merchants and traders, it is doubtful that we would have modern state-level societies (what most of us call *civilization*) today.

In the mid–eighteenth century, the industrial revolution began, first in Great Britain and later in Europe and North America. *Industrialism* refers to the shift from home-based hand- or animal-aided production to mechanized production and the assembly line model of manufacture, in which tasks are broken down into small, simple steps, and workers and machines do this new, simplified, and often unskilled work. So instead of, for example, a shoemaker making a pair of shoes from scratch at his home workshop and selling or exchanging it directly with a customer, the process of making shoes is broken down into a dozen or more

simple tasks, and workers (often operating machines) each do a different specialized task at the shoe factory. Once the shoe is completed, it will be sold by a third
party to customers.

Industrialism radically increased the pace of production as well as the yield,
producing more goods at a far cheaper cost. This had incredible and far-reaching
social, economic, and political implications for the cultures in which industrialism
was embraced as well as those in which it was not.

For example, industrial economies became yet more stratified, with a new
super-rich class emerging and a massive unskilled labor pool leaving rural areas
(as mechanized agriculture replaced much of the human and animal labor on
farms) and migrating to the cities where the new factories were located. In the
early years of industrialism, these cities quickly became overcrowded, and they
developed a whole host of social problems, such as crime and the spread of communicable diseases. Work, too, moved from the home, where so much of production was once found, to factories and other work places, and because people could
afford to buy the cheaper products, more and more goods were produced, leading
to a leap in the scale of consumption. Population rates also exploded during this
period, leading to yet more overpopulation in the new industrial cities.

Workers, too, changed, as not only men were employed in the new factories but
women and children as well. (Of course women and children had previously
worked on family farms, but rarely for wages.) Eventually, worker protection laws
were passed in many countries, leading to the end of child labor in the developed
countries, but even today, children and young women are often the most preferred
factory workers; they can more easily be paid less and forced to work more hours,
and they are less likely to demand better pay or rights. In the West, industrial
workers began to experience higher wages and a greater standard of living in the
late nineteenth and early twentieth centuries, thanks in part to the rise of unions.

Countries without factories often provided (and continue to provide) many of
the resources necessary for industrial production as well as much of the low-cost
factory labor. The hyperconsumption that is necessary to support large-scale
industrial production has also led to the depletion of much of those resources. As
industrialism became globalized, with what are known as first world countries
exporting capital and technology to third world countries, which provide labor
and resources, the impact on the environment in those countries gets worse.

Finally, with the rise of industrialism around the world came the dominance of
the cash economy. Most people no longer engage in subsistence labor, producing
the goods on which their families or communities rely; instead, the vast majority
of people on the planet now work as wage laborers and use the cash that they earn
to buy the goods that they need.

Today, many of the societies that led the way in industrialism, as well as a host
of countries such as China that did not, have shifted to the final (thus far) system
of production, which is known as postindustrialism, the postindustrial age, or
sometimes informatics. The terms themselves move away from a focus on the
production of goods and refer to an economy in which goods production (including food production) is no longer the most important element of the economy.
Instead, in a postindustrial society, industrial and often even agricultural

production is outsourced to other countries, and the economy is instead based on the exchange of services.

What is unusual about this shift is the new emphasis on services over production in postindustrial economies. For most of human history, goods were produced by the very people who would ultimately consume them. Because production was for subsistence and was typically only exchanged (without the exchange of money) within the community, most people were closely connected to the goods that they consumed and to the people who produced them. Trade networks were close, made up of members of one's tribe or clan, and exchange was generally based on reciprocity and was used to reinforce social connections between trading partners.

Today, goods are produced in one part of the world by laborers who will never be seen or known by the consumers, who live in another part of the world. In the capitalist economy that we all share, cash acts as the medium of exchange, the payment, and the standard of value, and the relationship between trading partners is impersonal as is the exchange of cash. Another element of capitalism is the maximization of profits, which is the goal of the system itself. Capitalism has had a fundamental impact on workers because those who own the means of production (i.e., the companies that produce or distribute goods) are continually focused on producing profit, which means reducing the costs of either labor, technology, or resources—or all three. This explains the focus on low-skilled and low-wage laborers in so many industries today, which has led to a rise in migrant laborers (who may enter countries illegally to work), the rise in multinational corporations that set up shop in developing nations to employ low-wage laborers, the rise in structural unemployment in the former industrialized countries as whole sectors of jobs are outsourced to other countries, and the shift in many countries from full-time permanent work to part-time temporary work.

Today, foragers, where they still exist, have largely been incorporated into other economic systems. Their cultures have been incorporated into the state, and the land on which they depended has been taken over by government or commercial interests. Pastoralists, too, have experienced these changes. State governments have often forced them to settle and engage in farming or low-wage labor. Most horticultural cultures have also lost their land to more powerful parties, and they have been absorbed into the modern wage economy. Even smaller family farms in agricultural systems have started to disappear, with their land being bought by larger agricultural interests. Much of farm work today is no longer done by tenant farmers (the precapitalist model) or family farmers. Instead, it is primarily done by migrant workers who send their wages home (which is often in another country) to their families.

On the other hand, some former subsistence-based economies have started to revitalize elements of their former economies, often to exploit Westerners' interest in cultural tourism. For example, they sell traditional crafts to tourists or through international fair trade networks.

Another development of the global economy is the rise in multinational corporations and the concomitant rise in their economic and political power. According to Global Justice Now (2016), of the one hundred largest economies in the world, sixty-nine are multinational corporations. Multinational corporations, headquartered in first world nations such as the United States and Japan, exploit the loose environmental and labor laws in many third and fourth world countries to increase their profits and establish their factories in those countries. These corporations often wield an incredible amount of power in those countries, parlaying the economic benefits to the host country into the power to set (or veto) regulations and trade agreements that affect their businesses. The governments of many of these companies' host countries also set trade policy and pick international allies in part based on the needs of powerful multinational corporations, who often use the threat of outsourcing to gain leverage in first world countries.

Ironically, while the industrial revolution separated, for the first time, home and work for most people, many of us in postindustrial economies are finding that we are bringing work back home with us again. For example, many companies employ workers who telecommute—that is, those who work from home communicate with their coworkers and customers via video conferencing services such as Zoom or Skype. In addition, many workers in either managerial or creative positions find that they take home more and more of their work. With the ubiquity of mobile devices such as smartphones and tablets, workers are often expected to be available to their employers at all hours of the day and night—and weekends and vacations too. Women, in particular, often find themselves torn between the demands of work and their home lives and may find that the line between the two sectors becomes blurred.

Finally, many workers today (up to 24 percent of American workers in 2015, according to Smith 2016) work in what is called the "gig economy." This refers to work that is done on a temporary and often per-task basis, in which the workers often use their own equipment (computers, vehicles, or home) to complete the tasks they are expected to do. In some ways, this form of work hearkens back to much of the work that was done both before and after the industrial revolution, when many workers (often women) worked in their homes, sewing, making matchboxes, or engaging in other forms of piecework. Today's gig workers, on the other hand, whether they work for Uber, Lyft, Grubhub, or Uber Eats or run an Airbnb property or sell their goods on Etsy, rely on computer technology to do their work. These often mobile-enabled apps make jobs like these possible, and they were not even invented fifteen years ago, showing how quickly the economy can change because of technology.

Work is not only central to our lives, but given that almost all people live within deeply stratified (by gender, race, ethnicity, and often religion and other factors) societies, it should not surprise us to hear that work is also influenced by those factors as well.

For example, work is heavily gendered. According to the U.S. Department of Labor (2017), almost half (47 percent) of all workers in the United States are women, but women are paid far less than men; in the United States, they are paid eighty-one cents for every dollar a man earns, with other countries being better (Italian women are paid ninety-four cents for a dollar) or much worse (Korean women are paid just sixty-three cents). (There are signs to indicate that millennial women, on the other hand, are close to getting the same rate as millennial men

[Pew Research Center 2013].) One of the reasons for this phenomenon is that women tend to be employed in industries and occupations that are segregated by gender and dominated by women (Pew Research Center 2013), and those occupations and industries (which include, in the United States, health care, education, human resources, and the restaurant and hospitality industries), not coincidentally, pay less than those that are dominated by men because they are seen as "women's work." (Ironically, as men enter previously female-dominated occupations, pay tends to rise.) Another reason for women's lack of pay equity is the fact that most (70 percent) mothers work, and of those, 40 percent are not only single mothers but also the sole wage earners in the family.

In addition, women historically pay what sociologists call a "mommy tax," which means that mothers are paid less (about seventy cents to the dollar) than women without children (Crittenden 2002). Women also continue to engage in the majority of reproductive labor (bearing and raising children) around the world, and for the most part, this work is uncompensated.

"Pink-collar jobs" are service jobs that are performed primarily by women. They tend to involve little physical activity, but because they feature customer service, they involve what sociologists call "emotional labor," in which workers are expected to display certain emotions as part of their job: workers must appear cheerful, helpful, and delighted to assist the customer. Like all forms of work that demand skills that are thought of as "female," jobs that require emotional labor tend to be less well paid than other positions.

Dress and appearance codes, especially as they apply to female workers, are another way in which the demands and standards of the workplace are inscribed onto the body. Flight attendants, once called stewardesses (and once exclusively young, unmarried, and female), have long been subject to strict appearance codes, in which their weight, hairstyles, jewelry, and makeup are scrutinized by management. In addition, for years, minority and working-class women could not get hired as flight attendants because their hair and makeup norms were not acceptable to the airlines. Hooters waitresses, too, are expected to not only be cheerful (even in the face of blatant sexual harassment) to customers but also must maintain slim figures and dress in revealing clothing to show off their "hooters" to appeal to male customers.

Race and ethnicity also continue to play a heavy role in pay equity and workplace discrimination. In racialized countries such as the United States, occupations are not just segregated by gender but segregated by race as well. In fact, many sociologists argue that we have what is known as a dual labor market, whereby the primary market, where whites and men work, offers good wages, benefits, occupational prestige, job stability, job protection, and opportunities for promotion, while the secondary labor market, where minorities and women often work, lacks in all of these aspects. The result of this, as well as other issues contributing to the pay gap, such as unequal access to education, lower levels of inherited wealth, housing segregation, and simple discrimination, is that white males have the second-lowest unemployment rate (next to Asian males), have the second-highest representation in managerial positions (again, next to Asian men), and the second-highest rate of pay (next to Asian men). Except for Asians, non-whites continue to lag behind white men in the labor market.

Nonwhites also make up the majority of workers in the informal or underground economy. This refers to the segment of the economy that is unregulated, pay is under the table, and there are no job protections whatsoever. Some work in this sector of the economy is also illegal. This includes occupations such as sex work and drug selling, and it also includes babysitting, day labor, and domestic labor. Some of these jobs are also dangerous.

A great many of the jobs included in this encyclopedia include what sociologists call "dirty work" (see Hughes 1962 for the first use of the term). Dirty work is work that may be physically dirty as well as degrading, dehumanizing, or disgusting, for a variety of reasons. Dirty jobs may be physically or emotionally taxing; may involve blood, feces, or body parts; may be illegal; or may be thought to be immoral. The people who engage in dirty jobs are often stigmatized and socially isolated (see Davis 1984) and often have problems in forming a positive self-identity.

In 2005, the Discovery Channel began airing a new television show called *Dirty Jobs*, in which the host, Mike Rowe, takes on dirty, disgusting, or dangerous jobs. The show is entertaining for viewers because most of us cannot imagine doing the kinds of jobs that the show highlights. Some of the jobs featured on the series included pest extermination, pig farming, garbage collecting, septic tank cleaning, bat guano collecting, bridge painting, roadkill collecting, hot tar roofing, coal mining, and turkey inseminating. What links all of these jobs, besides the obvious fact that they involve dirt of some kind, is the fact that the vast majority of them are working-class jobs. In the opening to each episode, Rowe alludes to this by saying,

> My name's Mike Rowe, and this is my job. I explore the country looking for people who aren't afraid to get dirty—hard-working men and women who earn an honest living doing the kinds of jobs that make civilized life possible for the rest of us. Now, get ready to get dirty.

In fact, this is one of the primary distinctions between what we call blue-collar and white-collar jobs today.

Blue-collar jobs are performed by members of the working class and involve manual labor. The jobs are physical, often demanding, and can be both dirty and dangerous. They involve more workplace accidents, more environmental toxins and fumes, and a shortened life expectancy. They are called "blue-collar" because of the blue coveralls that are often worn in many of these jobs. White-collar jobs, on the other hand, are those that often require a college education and demand mental, rather than physical, skills. They are cleaner, safer, and involve no physical activity whatsoever.

The jobs featured in *Dirty Jobs* are dirty, for sure, and most middle-class Americans would never even consider doing them. When we look back in time, however, the working poor in medieval Europe were forced to take on far worse jobs, such as gong farming, which refers to the activity of cleaning human waste from privies and cesspits; executing people; catching rats; and burying those who have died of the plague. These jobs are covered in our historical sidebars.

Of course, in many places today, there are still horrible jobs that must be done, and those jobs are performed by the most marginalized people in those societies. Often called "untouchables," because they are considered less pure than other members of the society, these are the people who must engage in the jobs that are the most disgusting. Dalits, for example, the untouchable caste group in India, are responsible for handling corpses, cleaning human waste, skinning animal carcasses, and executing criminals. Because these activities are so polluting, the bodies of the Dalits are considered impure, which is why they are segregated from other members of Indian society and forbidden from sharing food, wells, temple space, or even burial grounds with them.

Quite frequently, dirty work involves animals (or their parts). In fact, animal studies sociologist Rhoda Wilkie (2015) shows that those people who work with animals and engage in dirty work as well as the academics who study them are tainted by the appellation because of the perceived physical and social dirtiness of the subject matter. It should not surprise us, then, that the largest category of odd jobs in this encyclopedia are those involving animals and that class, gender, and race all play a role in how these jobs, as well as other dirty jobs included here, are managed.

Work, while necessary to provide for basic human needs, has evolved in ways that go well beyond providing human sustenance. Work shapes our identities, is shaped by inequality, and is one of the most central and defining features of our lives. As children, we look toward the day when we are grown up and can begin our working lives, and as elderly citizens, we eagerly await our transition into retirement, if we can afford it.

Work—what we do, who we work with, whether or not we like it, and how much we get paid for it—is, next to family, the most important component of our lives, and for some, it is more important than even family. Understanding what we do for a living, including the unique jobs included in this encyclopedia, is central to understanding ourselves.

Further Reading

Allen, R. C. (2009). *The British industrial revolution in global perspective* (Vol. 1). Cambridge University Press.

Amott, T. L., & Matthaei, J. A. (1996). *Race, gender, and work: A multi-cultural economic history of women in the United States.* South End Press.

Arndt, S. W., & Kierzkowski, H. (Eds.). (2001). *Fragmentation: New production patterns in the world economy.* Oxford University Press.

Blau, F. D., Ferber, M. A., & Winkler, A. E. (2013). *The economics of women, men and work.* Pearson Higher Ed.

Crittenden, A. (2002). *The price of motherhood: Why the most important job in the world is still the least valued.* Macmillan.

Davis, D. S. (1984). Good people doing dirty work: A study of social isolation. *Symbolic Interaction, 7*(2), 233–247.

De Stefano, V. (2015). The rise of the just-in-time workforce: On-demand work, crowdwork, and labor protection in the gig-economy. *Comparative Labor Law & Policy Journal, 37,* 471.

Deane, P. M. (1979). *The first industrial revolution.* Cambridge University Press.

Firth, R. (Ed.). (2013). *Themes in economic anthropology.* Routledge.

Global Justice Now. (2016). *Controlling corporations: The case for a UN treaty on transnational corporations and human rights.* http://www.globaljustice.org.uk/sites/default/files/files/resources/controlling_corporations_briefing.pdf.

Hughes, E. C. (1962). Good people and dirty work. *Social Problems, 10*(1), 3–11.

Pew Research Center. (2013). *On pay gap, millennial women near parity—for now.* http://www.pewsocialtrends.org/2013/12/11/on-pay-gap-millennial-women-near-parity-for-now.

Simpson, R. (Ed.). (2012). *Dirty work: Concepts and identities.* Palgrave Macmillan.

Smith, A. (2016). *Gig work, online selling and home sharing.* Pew Research Center. http://www.pewsocialtrends.org/2013/12/11/on-pay-gap-millennial-women-near-parity-for-now.

Swedberg, R. (2009). *Principles of economic sociology.* Princeton University Press.

U.S. Department of Labor. (2016). *BLS report: Labor force characteristics by race and ethnicity, 2015.* https://www.bls.gov/opub/reports/race-and-ethnicity/2015/home.htm.

U.S. Department of Labor. (2017). *BLS report: Employment status of the civilian population by sex and age.* https://www.bls.gov/news.release/empsit.t01.htm.

Wilkie, R. (2015). Academic "dirty work": Mapping scholarly labor in a tainted mixed-species field. *Society & Animals, 23*(3), 211–230.

Alligator Wrestler (Southeastern United States)

An alligator wrestler is someone who wrestles American alligators for wages. (There are two species of alligator, American alligators and Chinese alligators, but there is no alligator wrestling in China.) Most alligator wrestlers are men, but some women engage in it as well. Today, alligator wrestling is primarily used as a tourist attraction, but it is also considered a sport by some of its practitioners.

Alligator wrestling, like rodeo sports, evolved out of a practical activity that was once common in areas where American alligators are common (the southeastern United States). Where rodeo sports such as bronc riding, steer wrestling, and calf roping grew out of activities that cowboys did in order to control cows and horses in the course of their work, alligator wrestling grew out of some of the activities involved in alligator hunting. Also akin to the rodeo, alligator wrestling is seen today as a cultural tradition, especially by the Seminole Indians who perform it. And finally, like rodeo sports, alligator wrestling is also used to demonstrate the performer's dominance of the animal—a particularly large and dangerous animal.

Alligator hunting has been practiced in the southeastern United States—particularly Louisiana and Florida—by indigenous Americans prior to the colonization of North America, by Anglo and Spanish conquerors, and by nonindigenous American hunters today. Alligators were traditionally hunted by Native Americans for their meat as well as for their hides. Today, the primary goal in alligator hunting is the hides, as well as teeth, which are sold and turned into boots, belts, bags, and other items.

Because alligators (unlike, for example, cattle, who are domesticated and thus easily caught and slaughtered) are wild animals who live in wetlands, they are harder to locate and, thus, harder to capture and kill (especially when hunted at night). This is one reason why alligator wrestling evolved among some of the tribes who hunted them; the young men needed to learn how to control the animals when killing them. (The Timucua of Northeast Florida, for example, disabled an alligator by shoving a long wooden pole down its throat and then flipped the animal over and killed him by spearing his belly with arrows.) After the arrival of white settlers, alligators were so heavily hunted (by this time, most people hunted them with guns) that they were listed as endangered in 1967; because of this, hunting alligators is now regulated by state fish and game departments in all the southeastern states except North Carolina, where their hunting is prohibited.

Alligator wrestling began to be treated as a distinct activity in the 1920s, when Seminoles and Miccosukee Indians began performing for tourists at roadside attractions and theme parks in Florida, such as the St. Augustine Alligator Farm,

---

Gladiator

A gladiator was a man (or, rarely, a woman) who performed in organized fights, called *gladiatorial games*, in front of a public audience in the late Roman Republic through the Roman Empire. Gladiators were introduced to Rome from the Etruscans in the third century BCE. They were typically slaves, prisoners of war, or convicted criminals, although sometimes free men volunteered for the position and were trained at gladiatorial schools throughout the empire. During a gladiatorial show, gladiators fought each other; there may also have been *bestiarii* (beast fighters), who were men who fought against large animals.

When a gladiator went down, the crowd played a role in deciding whether the loser lived or died, and the emperor, or the man in charge of the games, made the ultimate call. In regular games, gladiators could hope to survive the game if they beat their opponents or performed bravely. The games were also used to execute death sentences: condemned criminals could be made to fight other gladiators, or wild animals (sometimes without weapons), to their deaths.

Even though most gladiators did ultimately lose their lives in the ring, the job brought honor, fame, and sometimes even wealth and freedom to the best and most popular competitors. The games ended in 404 CE under the emperor Honorius.

Source: Dunkle, R. (2013). *Gladiators: Violence and spectacle in ancient Rome*. Routledge.

Florida's first theme park (which no longer offers wrestling today). And although alligator wrestling began as an outgrowth of Seminole hunting practices, its status as a stand-alone activity can be traced not to tradition but to economic needs. For example, alligator wrestling was not done during Seminole or Miccosukee rituals but was only performed for tourists.

During a typical wrestling match, the performer, who works with the alligator either in the water or on land, typically grabs the animal by the tail and then, once a safe hold on the animal is established, uses a variety of wrestling techniques and holds (such as holding the alligator's mouth open under the performer's chin) for the crowd, all the while trying to keep the animal's mouth (with over seventy-four teeth and a bite force that has measured up to 2,125 pounds per square inch of force) away from him (alligators can and do occasionally kill people). Besides the danger of being bit, wrestlers also have to worry about being hit by the tail, which has a tremendous amount of force as well, and the animal's sharp claws.

Some alligator wrestlers perform in traveling shows such as fairs or expos, but most perform on Indian reservations, such as the Miccosukee Indian Village (which closed in 2014 but later reopened); at alligator farms, such as Gatorland in Orlando, Florida; or at wildlife parks, such as Croc Encounters in Tampa. Rescue groups, such as the Gator Boys Animal Rescue (whose operators, Paul Bedard and Jimmy Riffle, were featured on the Animal Planet show *Gator Boys*), which operates out of Everglades Holiday Park in Fort Lauderdale, also offer wrestling to the public. Besides alligator wrestling and other alligator shows, many of these places now offer some education to their patrons as well, and some market what they offer as a form of ecotourism.

Most wrestlers simply learn from other wrestlers (on the reservation, many young men learn from their fathers), but some alligator parks, such as Colorado Gator Park in Mosca, Colorado (where alligators do not naturally live), and Everglades Alligator Farm in the Florida Everglades, offer classes in wrestling, although these are for tourists, not would-be performers.

Today, alligator wrestlers are still predominantly Seminole, although there are non-Indian wrestlers as well. In general, the practice is dying out (especially in the smaller, family-owned attractions) because fewer young people want to do it and because of the slow death of similar roadside attractions, which have given way to larger, more expensive, and more family-friendly attractions, such as Disney World. In addition, the Seminoles have, since the opening of a bingo hall in 1979, operated a number of financially lucrative casinos and racinos that have largely supplanted the need to make money through mom-and-pop alligator operations (these gaming houses may bring the tribe as much as $2.3 billion per year [Beckett 2017]). Finally,

Alligator wrestling at Gatorland in Florida. (Kphotos6411/Dreamstime.com)

animal advocates deplore the practice because of the perceived cruelty and the lack of any regulations or protections for the animals.

However, many Seminoles are keen to preserve wrestling because it is seen as a visible symbol of their cultural heritage and their connection to the Everglades. And like the rodeo, it represents the strength, bravery, and masculinity not only of the performers but of the entire Seminole tribe. Of course, the tradition of alligator wrestling is only about a century old, and although it evolved out of older traditional practices associated with hunting alligators, it was developed in the twentieth century as a means for financial gain.

See also: Rodeo Performer.

Further Reading

Beckett, S. (2017). *Florida Seminole casinos generating massive revenues for tribe.* Casino.org. https://www.casino.org/news/florida-seminole-casinos-generating-massive-revenues-for-tribe.

Ogden, L. A. (2011). *Swamplife: People, gators, and mangroves entangled in the Everglades.* University of Minnesota Press.

Salamone, F. A. (Ed.). (2012). *The Native American identity in sports: Creating and preserving a culture*. Scarecrow Press.

West, P. (1998). *The enduring Seminoles: From alligator wrestling to ecotourism*. University Press of Florida.

Animal Talent Agent (United States)

An animal talent agent is a person who handles the careers of animal actors and, increasingly, internet animal celebrities.

Humans have been watching animals perform in a variety of venues for thousands of years. From the animal acts in ancient Rome to juggling bears in Medieval Europe to the rise of the performing circus animals in the nineteenth century, animals have long played a role in the entertainments of humans.

In the abovementioned cases, when the animals were trained, they were trained by either the person who owned the animal or an animal trainer hired by, for example, the circus that owned the animals. However, with the rise of film in the twentieth century, this began to change. Specialized individuals who owned and trained animals emerged, and they rented out their animals to film and television productions. Later, a new industry would emerge modeled on the professional agencies that represent human actors for film, theater, and television: animal talent agencies.

(Human) talent agencies emerged during the nineteenth century to represent stage actors in Europe and the United States. One of these early agencies was the William Morris Agency, which originally represented New York theater actors and, as the silent film industry began to rise in the 1920s, early film actors, including Charlie Chaplin and the Marx Brothers. With the rising popularity of television in the 1950s, talent agencies began to encourage some of their performers to work in this new medium as well.

Finally, in the early twenty-first century, with the rise of new social media platforms such as YouTube (2005) and Instagram (2010), a new population of individuals began to seek representation. Unlike earlier generations of performers, these new parties were not trying to get hired to perform on television or film; rather, they were looking for assistance in monetizing their social media platforms. In other words, they were hoping to gain sponsors and advertisers.

One could perhaps argue that P. T. Barnum (1810–1891), of Barnum & Bailey Circus fame, was the first animal talent agent. As a showman who ran dime museums and later circuses, he displayed both human "freaks" and exotic animals (the most famous of which was Jumbo, an African elephant) and used his skills as a promoter to showcase his attractions.

In the twentieth century, with the rise of film, specialized animal trainers who bought or bred animals (either exotic or domesticated) and then trained them themselves and hired them out to Hollywood productions began to emerge. Some of the first of these agencies were Gentle Jungle, which began during the silent film era and now provides trained wild animals to film and television, and Hollywood Paws, which bills itself as the world's first animal talent agency. Prior to the rise of these agencies, the first animal used in a film was a dog named Blair, who was featured in the 1905 film *Rescued by Rover* and was owned and trained by the film's director, Cecil Hepworth.

Today, some animal talent agents continue to operate under the older animal trainer model, with the same person or company owning, training, and promoting his or her own animals. (In California, thanks to the importance of the film industry, animal trainers, whether or not they act as agents, belong to a union, as do others who operate in Hollywood.) For example, All Creatures Great and Small is a New York-based agency that still trains and provides their own animals. Founded in 1956, they are one of the oldest such agencies still operating on the East Coast.

Some animal agencies that still own and train their own animals, such as Hollywood Animals, rent out animal actors (including elephants, lions, tigers, bears, leopards, and panthers as well as domestic animals) for use at private parties, promotional events, and in film. Other companies, such as Have Trunk, Will Travel, which provides elephants for films, television, weddings, and parties, promote themselves as conservationist organizations by breeding elephants "to ensure that our grandchildren will have the chance to see and appreciate these amazing animals" (from the archived version of the old Have Trunk, Will Travel website).

Newer agencies, however, simply represent the animals. As animal internet celebrities begin to dominate the industry, it is more likely that the newer model of animal agent will continue to rise, as most animal internet celebrities are privately owned. In fact, for those people seeking advice on how to break into show business with their especially cute or talented animal, the advice is typically to make sure that the animal is well trained and then to seek out an agent to represent them.

Today, there are over forty animal talent agencies in the United States, some of which only represent animals within one region and others who send talent out to national and international jobs, although most can be found in either New York City or Los Angeles.

Some talent agents specialize in particular media. For example, William Berloni, who runs Theatrical Animals (and who owns and trains his own animals), primarily works with theater companies, either in New York or elsewhere. But the growth rate in today's industry is clearly from agencies that represent internet animal stars.

The agents who work for these companies do not own or train the animals themselves. Instead, they represent the human owners of these animals, who are overwhelmingly companion animals, such as dogs and cats, and help them to gain sponsorships and advertising opportunities. Some especially popular animal stars, such as the late Lil Bub or the late Grumpy Cat (who was worth well over $1 million at the time of her death in 2019), have also gained significant income through public appearances, advertising campaigns (usually for pet food or product companies), and books, films, and television shows, all of which are made possible through talent agents. Grumpy Cat, for example, sold Friskies, Honey Nut Cheerios, two books, calendars, a video game, and apps and starred in both a documentary and a feature film, which aired on the Lifetime Network in 2014, called *Grumpy Cat's Worst Christmas Ever*.

Even animals without the astronomical fame of a Lil Bub or Grumpy Cat can make significant amounts of money through advertising and sponsorship deals.

These animals, also known as animal influencers, have gone from appearing only in marketing campaigns for pet products, like Grumpy Cat, to being featured in fashion campaigns, hotel advertisements, and even the Super Bowl.

To help an animal influencer gain fame and income, animal talent agents rely not only on the animal's inherent cuteness (talent being no longer that important for this genre of stars) but also on the popularity of the animal on Instagram or YouTube. Today, Instagram is the most important place on the internet for animal or human influencers, and to even consider representing someone, the agent has to see that the number of followers on the influencer's account is high enough to generate interest from advertisers. An animal with a minimum of tens of thousands of followers is an animal with the potential to bring in money for his or her owner.

Agents are also looking for personality in their clients. As crowded as the influencer market is becoming, cute animals are not enough for the kind of fame that generates income. In addition, agents ensure that the owners/managers of the animals do most of the heavy lifting. They are responsible for photographing their animals, posting their pictures (with funny or cute captions) regularly (at least daily), and engaging with their followers.

One prominent animal talent agent today is Loni Edwards, the founder of the Dog Agency, a New York-based agency that only represents internet dogs, which Edwards says is the first such agency. Edwards got into animal talent representation through her own dog, Chloe, a French bulldog who died in 2017. Chloe had over 150,000 Instagram followers and a thriving influencer business before her death. Edwards now represents other dogs and has been able to generate business for her clients through companies such as Barneys, Purina, Google, and Nikon. Prior to starting her company, as a lawyer, Edwards realized that other pet influencers were unsure of how to navigate the world of corporate partnerships and began helping people to negotiate contracts. At the time of this writing, Edwards's agency is expanding and hiring a junior talent relations manager to work with clients and brands to create relationships and marketing campaigns. In the case of such influencer agencies as the Dog Agency, the job is not to help make the animal famous. Instead, already famous animals use agencies to monetize that fame. As with human influencers, the amount of money that can be earned by animal influencers depends almost entirely on the number of followers the animal has.

Some internet animal celebrities do not have outside agents representing them. For instance, Mr. Winkle, a small Pomeranian mix who was rescued by photographer Lara Jo Regan in 1996 (and died in 2019), gained his celebrity thanks to his adorable looks and the talent of Regan, who photographed Mr. Winkle to highlight his best characteristics (such as his huge eyes, bear-shaped ears, and perpetually hanging tongue) and promoted him on her own website. In the years before social media, Regan's work was so effective that she not only got a three-book deal from Random House, countless television appearances, and an appearance on an episode of *Sex and the City* (where he upstaged star Sarah Jessica Parker at a book signing), but he was also named the first Internet Celebrity of the Year by Time in 2002. Like other owners of internet celebrity animals, Regan ended up devoting much of her career to promoting Mr. Winkle and selling his merchandise (also designed by Regan) on her own website. Maru, a Scottish fold cat who lives in Japan and loves boxes, is another famous celebrity without outside representation. His owner (known only as mugumogu) is responsible for his promotion and fame, which is all the more remarkable considering that she does not speak English.

In the United States, the Animal Welfare Act (first enacted in 1966 and updated multiple times over the ensuing years) regulates the use of performing animals on television or in film and provides them some minimal protection. However, there are no such laws that regulate the use of animals on the internet.

See also: Instagram Influencer; YouTube Celebrity.

Further Reading
Giles, D. C. (2013). Animal celebrities. *Celebrity Studies, 4*(2), 115–128.
Pschera, A. (2016). *Animal internet: Nature and the digital revolution.* New Vessel Press.

Anthrozoologist (Global)

An anthrozoologist is a person who studies the relationships between humans and other animals. Anthrozoology, also known as human-animal studies (HAS), is a relatively new, multi- and interdisciplinary field of study that looks at the many ways in which humans interact with, represent, and use other animals, whether in the past or present and whether or not those interactions are real or virtual. The field traces its scholarly roots to the publication of two major philosophical works on animals, Peter Singer's *Animal Liberation* (1975) and Tom Regan's *The Case for Animal Rights* (1983), which led to an explosion of interest in animals among academics, animal advocates, and the general public. The 1980s saw the very first journal dedicated to anthrozoology, *Anthrozoös*, which was published in 1987 by the International Society for Anthrozoology (ISAZ); ISAZ was the first organization dedicated to this new field.

Beginning in the 1990s, the field began to grow, and major new works were published throughout the decade from scholars in fields as diverse as history, sociology, anthropology, social work, geography, criminology, feminist studies, and more. Since these early days, there are now dozens of degree programs in anthrozoology or a related field around the world, dozens of book series and journals devoted to the field, and scholarly conferences at least a few times per month.

Although anthrozoology began in the English-speaking world—primarily the United Kingdom, North America, Australia, and New Zealand—it has recently spread into Asia, most of Europe, parts of Africa (primarily South Africa and a handful of northern African countries), and parts of Central and South America.

What an anthrozoologist does differs greatly according to one's training and interests. For example, anthrozoologists with a background in criminology, psychology, or social work may be interested in studying the relationship between violence toward humans and violence toward animals. Policy implications of this important area of research have led to, for example, the development of programs and facilities for battered women where they can bring their companion animals so that they do not have to leave them at home when they flee their batterer and programs that train veterinarians, social workers, and law enforcement professionals to detect the signs of abuse in a home—whether that abuse is aimed at animals or humans. These scholars may help develop diversion and intervention programs for animal abusers and can provide the courts and law enforcement agencies with information about how to detect signs of abuse.

Animal-caused violence is another area that has been studied by HAS scholars. Dog bites and dog attacks are two of the most heavily researched areas. Scholars have looked at the risk factors for dogs who bite and have analyzed the legislation and social policies that have been enacted in communities as a result of so-called dangerous dogs. This research has found that dogs who are chained, dogs who are bullied, and dogs who are neglected are more likely to bite than dogs who are well treated, regardless of the breed. This research suggests that dangerous dog legislation—legislation banning breeds of dogs, such as pit bulls—cannot truly solve the problem of dog bites.

Another important application of anthrozoological research deals with animals in shelters. At least four million animals per year are euthanized at animal shelters in the United States, and this is an important issue both in terms of the deaths to animals and the trauma to animal care workers. It is an important economic issue as well. It costs millions of dollars each year for animal care workers to catch, care for, and ultimately euthanize these animals.

Research that looks at the factors associated with the breeding, abandonment, and adoption of companion animals can be an important factor in alleviating this enormous problem. Some scholars have looked at issues such as temperament testing for domestic cats, the factors that lead to people abandoning animals at shelters, and whether dog training classes or other shelter support programs can lead to permanent placement of animals in homes. Other scholars have focused on animal shelter workers, who have the difficult job of caring for animals thrown away by the general public. Other studies have looked at how movies and television shows contribute to fads in pet ownership, such as the rise in Dalmatian purchases after the Disney movie *101 Dalmatians* or the rise in Chihuahua purchases after the *Beverly Hills Chihuahua* film or the Taco Bell television commercials featuring a talking Chihuahua.

Until the last few years, this field did not exist, and even after it emerged and began to gain some legitimacy, there was still no way to train to be an anthrozoologist. Instead, practitioners came to the field from a variety of disciplines in the social sciences, humanities, and, more recently, the natural sciences. However, students can now get a bachelor's degree in anthrozoology (again, often called human-animal studies or even animal studies) at about a dozen universities around the world as well as a master's or PhD at another three dozen universities. With a master's or a PhD in anthrozoology or, as is still most common, another discipline, a scholar can teach at the university level, do research, and write.

Today, anthrozoologists can be found in mainstream academic departments in universities around the world as well as in the newer anthrozoology departments. They are working for humane organizations, zoos, animal shelters, sanctuaries, and policy-making organizations. They may work with nurses, veterinarians, ranchers, animal laboratory technicians, animal shelter workers, soldiers and military veterans, or prosecutors and judges—anyone who works with animals whose job involves dealing with animal issues or whose work can be improved via animals. Anthrozoologists who work in a university setting can expect to make the same salary as others with their degree, publishing background, and other credentials.

Most anthrozoologists end up in the field because of their passion for animals. But that does not mean that anthrozoology is the same as animal rights. While it is true that, today, many younger scholars who enter the field define themselves as animal activists or are otherwise involved in animal welfare or animal rights work, this does not cover all anthrozoologists. For example, not all anthrozoologists are vegetarian or vegan, although many are.

Anthrozoology is one of the fastest-growing academic disciplines in the world. But because the field is relatively new, because it is focused on animals, and because of its association with animal rights, it continues to carry a stigma. As some scholars have written, the field is "tainted" (see Wilkie 2015; O'Sullivan, Watt, and Probyn-Rapsey 2019) by its association with animals, who are still considered unworthy of study in much of academia. In addition, like the mainstream animal protection movement, anthrozoology is dominated by women, which serves to further stigmatize the field. However, even with these challenges, the field continues to grow, and in the one published survey of practitioners so far, participants found their work to be satisfying from an intellectual standpoint as well as from a moral standpoint.

See also: Equine-Assisted Therapist; Guide Dog Trainer.

Further Reading
DeMello, M. (2012). *Animals and society: An introduction to human-animal studies.* Columbia University Press.
O'Sullivan, S., Watt, Y., & Probyn-Rapsey, F. (2019). Tainted love: The trials and tribulations of a career in animal studies. *Society & Animals, 27*(4), 361–382.
Wilkie, R. (2015). Academic "dirty work": Mapping scholarly labor in a tainted mixed-species field. *Society & Animals, 23*(3), 211–230.

Astrologer (Global)

An astrologer is a person who practices astrology and creates astrological charts for a living. Astrology is an ancient system of foretelling the future and interpreting the events of the present by mapping the stars. Although astrology is considered to be a pseudoscience today, it was thought to be a science for much of its history.

The history of astrology is intertwined with the history of astronomy. All cultures have, to a greater or lesser extent, learned to read the stars (including planets, moons, and other celestial objects) to help with navigation and agriculture and to track the passage of time. However, when the early astronomers developed the science of astronomy, the field was interwoven with religion, as the job of interpreting the stars was often vested in the religious leaders of a society. So it should be no surprise that while the stars (especially the travels of the sun and

---

Phrenologist

A phrenologist was a practitioner of the pseudoscience of phrenology, which claimed that the shape and size of the skull are physical representations of personality or character. Phrenology dates to the eighteenth century, when physician Franz Joseph Gall first proposed that different areas of the brain had different functions. Gall believed that the brain was broken into twenty-seven sections, or what he called *organs*, each with a function, for example, a tendency toward murder, pride, or religiosity. Further, each organ corresponded with a section of skull, so looking at the bumps on a person's skull (which were believed to have conformed to the different organs in the brain) could give insight into that person's abilities and character.

Phrenologists, who often called themselves *professors*, came from both within and outside of the medical profession and were generally self-taught in phrenology, advertising their services to the public at large and giving public lectures to attract new business. The profession attracted both men and women. Customers sought advice on finding spouses and making hiring decisions (phrenologists provided character references to employers) or asked for help with their unruly children.

Phrenology reached its height of popularity in the nineteenth century in Great Britain, the United States, and Europe. However, even as it began to decline, it was still practiced; in 1931, Henry Lavery developed a machine called a *psychograph* to measure the skull and provide a number of possible personality traits associated with its findings.

Source: Van Wyhe, J. (2017). *Phrenology and the origins of Victorian scientific naturalism.* Routledge.

---

moon) could be useful in, for example, developing agricultural calendars, they could also be used to direct and shape other aspects of human life. For instance, astro-theology, or astrolatry, refers to the association between planets and stars with gods and other deities, and it has been practiced in many ancient cultures, from the Mayans to the Sumerians to the Greeks. Astrology goes further than astro-theology, in that it suggests that the celestial bodies can shape the lives of humans and can be used to understand and predict human activities.

Astrology rests on the principle of "as above, so below," which means that the individual, and in fact all life on earth, is influenced by the activities of the planets and signs in the heavens. Astrology has been practiced for thousands of years; the earliest known culture to have developed a system of astrology, primarily for predicting the future, was the Babylonians, at least four thousand years ago. The Egyptians had a native system of astrology as well; it incorporated Babylonian elements as well as Greek practices. It was the Greeks, who inherited their traditions from the Babylonians, who shaped Western astrology into the practice that we know today.

From about the fourth century BCE, this new form of astrology would become the model for Western astrology into the present day, moving from the Hellenistic world to the Roman and, from there, west into medieval Europe and east into the Muslim world. Different forms of astrology were also practiced in India and China, and, in the New World, it was practiced by the Aztecs and, most notably, the Mayans. All forms of astrology are based on a geocentric model of the universe that understands the earth to be the center of the universe, with the sun (and the planets) appearing to rotate around the earth. This is contrasted with the heliocentric model of the solar system in which the sun is in the center with the planets traveling around it.

E. SIBLY, M.D. F.R.H.S.
Member of the Royal College of Physicians in Aberdeen.

Ebenezer Sibly, a British astrologer. (Wellcome Collection)

Western astrology uses the zodiac as well as the horoscope as the basis of its practice. The zodiac is the circular band of twelve constellations that can be seen just above and just below the ecliptic, the path that the sun appears to move on in the geocentric model of the universe. Those twelve constellations, or signs, which each occupy thirty degrees, or one-twelfth, of the zodiac, serve as the basis for the system, and they are interpreted as representing the twelve basic personality types. Many of the constellations are named after animals (Aries the goat; Leo the lion, Taurus the bull, etc.); in fact, the term *zodiac* comes from the Greek words meaning "circle of little animals." In Western astrology, which uses the tropical zodiac, Aries, which begins on March 21, or the spring equinox, is the first sign. Each sign is ruled by a planet and is ascribed characteristics based on that planet. The twelve signs can also be grouped by fours into three categories: cardinal, fixed, or mutable. Further, each sign is assigned to one of four elements—air, fire, earth, and water—such that the three earth signs, for example, Taurus, Capricorn, and Virgo, will all share some characteristics in common.

The horoscope, on the other hand, is a visual representation of the sky—including the signs of the zodiac as well as the planets—at a particular moment in time. Using a horoscope that marks out the planets and signs at the time of a person's birth allows the astrologer to make predictions about the life of that individual. (Horoscopes can also be used to understand world events or to help leaders predict the best time to engage in a war or other important activity.)

Casting a horoscope—also known as a natal chart, as it is a picture of the sky at a person's birth—is the first thing that an astrologer will do for a client. This involves collecting the exact date, time, and place of birth. In the past, the astrologer would then consult an ephemeris, an extensive chart listing the locations of the stars and planets at the time, date, and location of one's choosing (for a natal chart, this means choosing the time and location of a person's birth), and then do a number of calculations to ensure the correct placement of the elements. This information would then be plotted on an empty horoscope template—a large circle broken into twelve quadrants. Today, however, astrologers can use free programs online that include all the planetary information and calculations necessary to create a horoscope.

The twelve quadrants of the circle are known as houses, and they cover the spheres of life, such as self (house 1), money (house 2), relationships (house 7), and career (house 10). The chart always begins with the first house on the left center side of the chart and continues counterclockwise from that position. Each house is traditionally ruled by both a sign and a planet. The signs are then added to the houses, one sign per house, based on the astrologer's calculations. The planets, which themselves represent basic human impulses, such as aggression and war (Mars) or love (Venus), are then plotted within the houses. The planets initially included the known planets in the classical world (Mercury, Venus, Mars, Jupiter, and Saturn) as well as the sun and the earth's moon, but as astronomers discovered Neptune, Uranus, and Pluto, those were also added. Today, the planets in Western astrology include the ancient planets, the sun and the moon, and the more recently discovered planets, including Pluto (even though Pluto is no longer considered to be a planet), and many astrologers add Ceres, a dwarf planet discovered in the nineteenth century.

Once the astrologer has plotted a client's horoscope, he or she must do the main job, which is interpreting the chart. The astrologer will look at the whole picture of the chart to see broad patterns. For instance, perhaps most of the planets are clumped into one section of the chart, or perhaps there are an unusual number of planets in the air signs, or perhaps a house has no planets in it at all. All of these first impressions can give an overall sense of who the client is and what main challenges may be in that person's life.

After the whole picture has been discussed with the client, the astrologer will go through the chart and cover all the details, including the placement of the signs in the houses, the planets in the houses and signs, and the aspects, or angles, between those planets, which is measured in degrees and is represented visually on a horoscope by means of colored lines linking planets. For example, planets that are found to be in conjunction (where the angle between the planets is less than 10 degrees) are thought to exert a significant force over one another as well as over the individual client. The trine angle, indicating an angle of 120 degrees between planets, represents harmony between the elements, and a square, which represents an angle of 90 degrees, indicates conflict. One important feature of each chart is the rising sign—the sign found in the first house. Even the direction of a planet is important; if a planet is retrograde, meaning that it appears to be moving backward in the sky from the perspective of the earth, this has important repercussions in a person's chart. Other celestial bodies and elements are included in a chart as well, including the moon's nodes and the transits of the planets.

Astrology began to fall out of favor in the West during the Enlightenment, although other forms of astrology remained popular in other areas of the world, especially Asia, where Chinese astrology was absorbed into Japan, Korea, and much of Southeast Asia. But even in the West, astrology has experienced a number of resurgences, such as during the 1960s, and is still quite popular today.

Chinese astrology, like Western astrology, uses twelve signs that are not based on constellations but on an ancient myth that tells the story of a race featuring all the animals of the world: the first twelve animals to finish the race became the Chinese zodiac. So while both the Chinese and Western systems are called *astrology*, the Chinese system has nothing to do with the stars. Each of the Chinese signs corresponds to the year in which one is born (as opposed to the monthly system in the West), with new years beginning in February. Like the Western system, those signs (which are all based on animals) each represent a basic personality type. Chinese astrologers also look at the month and date of a person's birth to provide more detail about a person than can be found through just looking at the sign of their birth year. Chinese astrology is still important in many Asian countries today.

Indian astrology is another ancient practice that continues in the modern world. Unlike Chinese astrology, Indian astrology was influenced by the arrival of Greek thought in the subcontinent in the fourth century, during which the Western signs were imported into the Indian system. Because of this cultural exchange, modern Indian astrology works like Western astrology, in that the movement of the planets and other heavenly bodies influences the direction of human lives on earth. Indian astrologers use charts to help customers determine the best dates for important events such as weddings. Astrology continues to be taught today in Indian universities.

Becoming an astrologer is not nearly as taxing today as it was just twenty years ago. Would-be astrologers must devote a great deal of time learning the principles and elements of astrology, including how to interpret a chart, but they no longer need to learn how to calculate a horoscope, as that is handled by modern technology. But there is still a great deal to learn. Many astrologers are self-taught; others learn by working with experienced practitioners. There are also online courses that students can take to prepare oneself for a career in astrology. Those who wish to learn can also study charts that have been prepared and interpreted by others and may also choose to have their own chart read by multiple professionals. Most new astrologers create and interpret charts for family and friends before looking for paying customers. Finally, some organizations, such as the American Federation of Astrologers and the Organization for Professional Astrology, provide certification.

Once acquiring the needed training, most astrologers work on their own, advertising their services online or through community forums and charging anywhere from one hundred to many hundreds of dollars for a reading. Online readings are typically cheaper than in-person readings, as in-person readings involve more interpretation on the part of the astrologer.

Another job for a trained astrologer is to write the daily horoscope columns for newspapers or magazines. This does not require constructing a horoscope. Instead, it involves looking at what the planets are doing on a given day (for instance, in what signs the planets are traveling) and determining how that planetary activity may shape the lives of those whose suns are located in particular signs; the daily prediction for Sagittarius, for example, is aimed at those who were born in the month when the sun was in that constellation. These predictions are very general, as can be expected since they are aimed at millions of people who were born in any given month.

See also: Psychic; Traditional Healer.

Further Reading

Baigent, M. (1994). *From the omens of Babylon: Astrology and ancient Mesopotamia.* Arkana.

Beck, R. (2008). *A brief history of ancient astrology* (Vol. 4). John Wiley & Sons.

Curry, P. (1989). *Prophecy and power: Astrology in early modern England.* Polity Press; B. Blackwell.

Lewis, J. R. (2003). *The astrology book: The encyclopedia of heavenly influences.* Visible Ink Press.

B

Background Artist (Global)

A background artist, background actor, or extra is an actor who performs in non-speaking roles in films and television shows.

Most movies and television shows use a casting director, or work with a casting agency, to find the actors to use in the production. The casting director first works with the director and sometimes the producer to determine the acting needs and what the director envisions for the talent. The casting director then approaches a talent agency that represents actors; the agent will then suggest some of the agency's clients for the job, based on the actor's resume, headshots, and demo reel (which is a series of clips from the actor's previous appearances). (Actors without agents can also look for audition opportunities through the industry trade magazine, *Backstage*.) Those actors must then audition with the casting director to get a spot. For larger productions, or important roles in the production, there will be more than one audition; the process could include multiple meetings, and sometimes multiple auditions, with costars, the producer, the director, or others involved in the making of the film or show. Ultimately, an actor only gets hired for a job when the director has given his or her approval.

There are two kinds of actors in most film and television productions. The actors that most of us think about, and that casting directors hire, act in speaking roles. These are known as principal actors. To get hired as a principal actor on any union project, one must be a member of the Screen Actors Guild–American Federation of Television and Radio Artists (SAG-AFTRA), the major union for actors.

The second type of actor is the background actor or extra. He or she cannot speak on camera (although it is possible to get "promoted" while on set to a speaking role) and does not need a union card to perform. Instead, background actors join a talent agency for extras; most major metropolitan areas have such agencies, as many productions are filmed outside of Hollywood.

Background extras are used to fill in scenes. If a film includes a shot of a busy street, a battle, a concert, or any other public or private event that requires other people to be present outside of the principal actors, extras are used to make the scene appear realistic. (Background performers can also be hired in stage productions, such as plays or operas, but jobs are far more plentiful in television and film.)

Background casting agencies, and especially those working in busy cities, need to have a stable of performers that they can call on for any type of production. They seek people from every ethnic background, age, weight, height, and appearance. Applying is as simple as visiting the website of a background casting agency and filling out the application form. These forms ask for detailed information on physical appearance (including sizing for wardrobe), augmentations (such as tattoos or piercings), special abilities (such as juggling, guitar playing, or karate), any languages spoken (or accents used), and experience. The good news is that a background artist can be hired with no acting experience at all, although experience also benefits a candidate because it proves to directors that he or she can accept direction and understand what being on a set is like.

Once a background casting agency has been approached by a film production with the details of the types of extras needed, the agency will look at its database of registered performers and forward the details for appropriate performers to the casting director, who ultimately makes the hiring decisions.

Background actors must be punctual, reliable, and able to take direction well. Many shoots start very early in the day (sometimes as early as 5:00 a.m.), and some do not end until well into the night; therefore, the actors must be willing to work long days, often from before dawn to after dusk. They must also be ready to take a job on very short notice, as they will often be notified the night before a shoot that they will be needed on set.

The job itself is not strenuous; in fact, many performers consider much of the time that they spend on set as boring. (Most extras bring something to read to pass the time.) Actors often have to be on set for the entire day, starting at dawn, even if the scene is short. Extras do get fed on set, so they do not have to worry about bringing lunch.

The pay for an extra is quite low compared to principal actors; rates are hourly, and, in the United States, background actors are generally paid minimum wage. They can make more if they are asked to do more in the role, such as dancing or fighting. In addition, the agency takes a percentage of each actor's pay. Background actors are usually asked to bring their own clothing to the set (and do their own hair and makeup), although period films and other films with specialized plots will provide wardrobe. For films that require extras to be dressed for a business meeting or a cocktail party, it helps if the extras own that type of clothing, which they can bring with them. Most extras do the work on a part-time basis, as it is difficult to put together enough background jobs to make a living.

Once on the set, extras will wait in a holding area until they are called for their scenes. A scene may require dozens or even hundreds of background actors to walk around in a mall or on a city street while the principal actors perform their scenes. Because scenes often take multiple takes, the background actors will be asked to perform their tasks over and over until the director has the shots he or she needs. Once a scene is complete, the extras are sent back to the holding area to await the next scene that they will be used in.

The fact that extras are not principal actors is made clear on many sets; background actors are asked to not speak to principal actors, and they eat at separate tables (or in an entirely different area) from the principal actors.

Extras can "graduate" to becoming a principal actor. Sometimes a director will make an on-the-spot call and give an extra a speaking line or two, which automatically means that the actor has been upgraded to principal, will get paid more, and can join SAG-AFTRA, which makes the actor eligible for principal work. Extras can also join the union if they accumulate union vouchers, which are provided when a background artist works on a union set. After receiving three vouchers, they are eligible to join SAG-AFTRA.

Extras do not need to live in Los Angeles to work. Some of the major locations that host movie and television productions include Boston, Albuquerque, Chicago, New York, Austin, Atlanta, Miami, New Orleans, San Francisco, and Toronto, Canada.

See also: Animal Talent Agent.

Further Reading

Benedetti, J. (2012). *The art of the actor: The essential history of acting from classical times to the present day.* Routledge.
O'Neil, B. (2010). *Acting as a business: Strategies for success.* Vintage.

Bathroom Attendant (Global)

A bathroom, or washroom, attendant is a person who works in a public restroom, typically in a fancy restaurant or nightclub, and keeps the room clean and well stocked.

Public bathrooms have existed for centuries, with the earliest known public bathrooms being found in the ancient world. Remains of public toilets have been found in South Asia (the oldest being in Mohenjo-daro, now Pakistan, dating to the twenty-sixth century BCE) as well as other locations, but the most well-known and commonly used was the Roman latrine. However, early forms of toilets were usually found in private homes and consisted of chamber pots, holes or pits in the ground, outhouses (over holes or pits in the ground), and, starting in the thirteenth century, close stools (boxes or chairs that enclosed a chamber pot).

Roman public toilets, or *foricae*, probably date to the second century BCE. (These toilets, and the aqueducts that served them, certainly borrowed technologies from other ancient civilizations, such as the Minoans and the Mesopotamians.) Roman engineers built aqueducts throughout the Roman Republic, and later the Roman Empire, to bring water directly into cities and towns, giving Roman citizens not only public fountains, baths, and water for farming but also sewage systems as well. The first such aqueduct was built in the fourth century BCE, and hundreds of years after the collapse of the Roman Empire, many still exist today. The Roman sewers, which were served by the aqueducts, were used to flush water from the many public bathrooms, or latrines, throughout the Roman world.

The Roman latrines were essentially long benches, either wood or stone, with keyhole-shaped holes cut into them every few feet. They were built over trenches that emptied into the sewer system, which had water running through it to help move the waste through the sewers and into rivers or other bodies of water. In addition, water from the aqueducts flowed through a second smaller trench that was located at the users' feet. The Romans would use the latrine and then pick up a tersorium (a sponge attached to a wooden stick), wipe themselves, and then rinse the sponge in the running water. The tersorium was then left for the next person to use (unless the user brought his or her own). These latrines, found in public baths, military forts, and amphitheaters, were most likely open to both men and women (although some scholars feel that women were excluded or at least had separate facilities) and had no privacy whatsoever. After the fall of the Roman Empire, the

---

Groom of the Stool

The groom of the stool, or the groom of the privy, was a position in the Tudor court, beginning with Henry VII. The groom's job was to attend the king while he was on his privy, or "close stool," which was the commode into which the king urinated and defecated. The groom of the stool's main job was to undress and dress the king prior to sitting down and to wipe the king's bottom, but the groom also assisted with the king's meals and provided general companionship. The position was highly respected and sought after because the groom of the stool was with the king during his most intimate moments and could hope to sway his opinion or gain favor during these times. Under the reign of Henry VIII, the groom of the stool also controlled the king's finances.

The groom of the stool was a member of the gentlemen of the privy chamber, the men who kept the king company, dressed and undressed him, and entertained him. The position lasted through the reigns of Henry VII, Henry VIII, and Edward VI, but grooms were not used by Queen Mary or Queen Elizabeth; instead, they employed gentlewomen of the privy chamber. The job did make a brief return for the short tenure of James I, after which it evolved into the lord or groom of the bedchamber and, still later, into the groom of the stole, a job that was finally discontinued for good under the reign of Edward VII.

Source: Hoak, D. (1987). The secret history of the Tudor court: The king's coffers and the king's purse, 1542–1553. *Journal of British Studies, 26*(2), 208–231.

---

latrines fell out of use and were replaced by outhouses, chamber pots, and other devices that were used in the home (or just outside of it).

The use of public toilets of any kind began to decline in the Middle Ages but emerged again in the nineteenth century in Europe. Prior to that time, there were sometimes temporary public toilets available in particular situations, such as at balls, fairs, and other public events. Even when they did reemerge, however, they did so for men before women: women were often confined to the private sphere and were thought to not need these facilities like men did. Because women had so little access to public facilities, they often used the cover of their large skirts to go to the bathroom in the public sphere. The first public pay bathrooms with toilets that flushed (known as monkey closets) were found in the Crystal Palace, the huge glass building that was built to house the Great Exhibition of 1851 in London, and they quickly spread after that.

By the 1920s, public bathrooms, segregated by gender, were common in the United States and Europe and were found in workplaces, entertainment venues, and other public spaces. Some were pay and some were free, although from the nineteenth through the twentieth centuries, a variety of laws were passed to ensure that free bathrooms were available to people who needed them—especially in the workplace.

These public bathrooms continued to evolve, with specialized rooms known as rest rooms, ladies' rest rooms, or restroom lounges emerging in the nineteenth century that provided women with not only a space to use the bathroom facilities but also to rest while shopping, visiting civic buildings, or attending theaters. (Some of these early rest rooms did not actually have bathroom facilities but were intended specifically to provide women a private space when outside the home.)

These rooms were responsive to the gendered and privacy norms of the era, but they also responded to the fact that women's clothing at that time was large and cumbersome, necessitating more space to dress and undress than men needed. Today, some public women's restrooms continue to have the parlor or lounge area outside of the bathroom proper, complete with couches to rest on. Many of these early restrooms, or comfort stations, had bathroom attendants to serve the largely white, upper- and middle-class clientele.

Probably the earliest type of bathroom attendant was the gong farmer, gong monger, or night soil man who was paid (typically by the municipality) to clean latrines, outhouses (also known as privies), and cesspits in medieval England. Unlike modern bathroom attendants, gong farmers did not work while the user was using the bathroom; instead, they typically performed their duties at night, when they would not be seen by the public. Another early type of bathroom attendant was the person known as the groom of the stool (or stole), who attended the king (or queen) of England while on the toilet starting in the Tudor era. These grooms helped the king with dressing and undressing for the toilet and also with wiping himself.

But the bathroom attendants that we think of today emerged in the nineteenth century in Europe and the United States, just as public restrooms were taking off. At that time, Europe, and later the United States, was experiencing a boom in high-end restaurant and hotel construction, which appealed to upscale customers who expected luxury and service. Much of what we know about bathroom attendants from this era comes from Victoria Hughes, an Englishwoman who worked as a bathroom attendant (what she called a "loo lady") in a public restroom in the first half of the twentieth century in Bristol and wrote about it in her memoirs.

Bathroom attendants are an example of people who worked in subordinate service roles, jobs in which people of a lower class perform services for others who are of higher status than them. Because the users of many public bathrooms from the nineteenth century to the mid–twentieth century were primarily middle- and upper-class white people (a situation reinforced in the United States by the development of Jim Crow segregation that restricted African Americans (and often Latinos, Native Americans, and Asians) from using public spaces deemed the domain of whites), it was primarily people from the lower classes—and often African Americans—who did these jobs. For years, being a bathroom attendant was one of the only jobs available for African Americans. Oscar-winning actress Hattie McDaniel (who won the Academy Award for Best Supporting Actress for her work in *Gone with the Wind* in 1939), even after starting a career as a singer, songwriter, and performer, ended up having to take a job as a bathroom attendant during the Great Depression.

So what does a bathroom attendant actually do? The job primarily involves maintaining the cleanliness of the bathrooms and ensuring that toilet paper, paper towels, soap, and other supplies are available. But because bathroom attendants have become more rare, and because they are primarily located in upscale facilities, the attendant may offer more premium services as well, such as turning on the water for customers to wash their hands, handing them a towel, or offering items such as perfume or lotion. Unfortunately, bathroom attendants are also responsible for caring for drunk patrons, cleaning up vomit, and dealing with rude customers or the theft of the supplies that they have purchased.

Today, as in the past, bathroom attendants are a relatively low-status job. As in the past, bathroom attendants typically service customers of a higher status than themselves, and simply having a bathroom attendant in service can reinforce the status differences between the customer—who is served in the most intimate of spaces—and the attendant, whose job it is to help customers with their toilet needs. Although the pay is good at certain establishments, many bathroom attendants only make minimum wage and depend on tips to make enough money to survive. (Others only make tips and are not paid a wage at all.) Some even purchase the toiletries they offer to customers out of their own pockets.

The job also involves emotional labor. Bathroom attendants are expected to not only be polite and helpful to their customers but also to comfort them when they are down and to build up their egos by complimenting their clothes, makeup, or hair. Studs Terkel, in his 1972 book *Working*, interviewed a bathroom attendant at an upscale Chicago hotel. The attendant told him that the biggest part of his job was to make the clients feel important.

Today, bathroom attendants are a dying profession. According to the U.S. Bureau of Labor (2019), there are 15,990 bathroom, coatroom, and dressing room attendants, a number that has been declining for years. While they once reinforced an elegant evening for a customer out for a nice meal and a show, today, they often make the younger generation of customers uneasy. In addition, as gender-neutral bathrooms have become more common, the idea of having a man or a woman standing in such a bathroom, attending to customers of both sexes, has become awkward. Finally, the younger generation is much less concerned with formality or status distinctions, and many do not carry cash (which was once used to tip restroom attendants). On the other hand, many nightclubs, whether or not they serve an upscale clientele, are now using bathroom attendants to keep drug use in the bathroom to a minimum.

See also: Roadkill Cleaner.

Further Reading

Hughes, V. (1977). *Ladies' mile*. Abson Books.

Molotch, H., & Norén, L. (Eds.). (2010). *Toilet: Public restrooms and the politics of sharing* (Vol. 1). New York University Press.

Terkel, S. (2011). *Working: People talk about what they do all day and how they feel about what they do*. New Press.

U.S. Bureau of Labor Statistics. (2019). *Occupational employment and wages, May 2019: 39-3093 locker room, coatroom, and dressing room attendants*. https://www.bls.gov/oes/current/oes393093.htm.

Belly Dancer (Global)

A belly dancer is a person who practices belly dancing to make a living. *Belly dancing*, also known as Oriental or Middle Eastern dancing, is a broad term that refers to any dance that ostensibly originated in the Middle East that involves body isolations and sinewy movements as a basic principle. The dance is centered around the movements of the hips, abdomen, chest, and arms.

The term *belly dance* is derived from the French term *danse du ventre*, or "dance of the stomach," and was first used at the Chicago World's Fair in 1893 when a group of dancers, brought over from Egypt by an entrepreneur named Sol Bloom, performed as part of an attraction called "A Street in Cairo" on the Midway to the delight, consternation, and shock of the American audience. (It was also referred to as the "hoochie coochie," a derogatory term coined by moralist Anthony Comstock, referring to the midriff-bearing costumes and suggestive movements of the dancers.) These performances took place during the height of imperialism, when it was com-

A tribal belly dancer performing. (Darkbird77/Dreamstime.com)

mon for Westerners to see other cultures as either primitive and backward or irresistibly exotic. Called "Orientalism" by Edward Said (1978), this way of seeing Eastern cultures tended to exaggerate the differences between Eastern and Western cultures and to emphasize the superiority of the West. It also continued to shape Westerners' views of Middle Eastern dance for decades. (Ironically, most belly dancers today are white, making belly dancing problematic for some cultural critics who see Western belly dancing as a form of cultural appropriation, especially during a time when people from the Middle East are being demonized in the West.) The version of belly dancing that was popular for years in the West derived from this period of time and was seen as a vulgar, sexualized form of dancing that was unsophisticated compared to Western forms of dance such as ballet. Even today, belly dancing continues to be treated as a lesser form of dance by many dancers trained in Western dance traditions, although this is beginning to change.

Many Western feminist practitioners believe belly dancing dates back to societies that worshipped a goddess figure, and they are "reclaiming" this ancient and feminine tradition. (This may be because belly dancing reemerged in the West in the 1970s, which was during the rise of the second-wave feminist movement.) Whether or not Middle Eastern dance forms emerged from some pagan feminist

Castrato

A *castrato* is usually defined as a castrated man who sings opera. From at least the seventeenth century, women were not allowed to sing in the church (following the Apostle Paul's order [I Corinthians 14] that women keep silent in church), so men needed to sing any parts that women would normally sing. Castrati became so popular that they were used for shows, particularly operas, that were not held in churches, such as traveling shows or shows performed in the courts of Europe. However, their popularity had risen even before Pope Innocent XI's edict banning women in 1686 from singing in church; they were first admitted into the papal choir in 1599, and the use of castrated male singers goes back to the Byzantine Empire.

By castrating a boy (via the cutting of the spermatic cords, without anesthesia, allowing the testes to wither) at the age of eleven or twelve, the release of dihydrotestosterone was suppressed, allowing the boy's vocal chords to remain small (and also resulting in a lack of facial and body hair, unusual tallness, and extra body fat) and his voice to remain high through adulthood.

In 1878, Pope Leo XIII banned the use of castrati by the Catholic Church, although women were still not allowed to sing female roles, which now went to boys. The last known castrato, Alessandro Moreschi, died in 1922.

Source: Barbier, P. (1996). *The world of the castrati: The history of an extraordinary operatic phenomenon.* Souvenir Press.

prehistory, it is clear that dancing has been a part of social gatherings and public celebrations (especially weddings) throughout West Asia and North Africa for hundreds, if not thousands, of years. It is likely that the dance traditions of Turkey (with its folkloric traditions) and Egypt (with its cabaret tradition) were the most influential in respect to the development of modern belly dancing. With the British control over Egypt from the 1890s through the 1950s, British travelers and expatriates visited nightclubs to watch dancers perform. The dancers of this era, whose performances evolved based on the preferences of foreign viewers, developed what would become known as Egyptian belly dance, or *raqs sharqi*, which is performed on a stage by dancers wearing an outfit made of a bra, skirt, bare midriff, and lots of beads or coins. (Today, most dancers who perform for tourists in Egypt are themselves foreign.)

It was not until the 1970s when belly dancing was rediscovered by Western audiences and exploded in popularity. Since that time, a huge variety of belly dance styles have been popularized or newly developed, including cabaret, Egyptian, *beledi* (or *baladi*), folkloric, ghawazee, Turkish, goddess, Gothic, and tribal. The tribal styles, which include American tribal style, international tribal style, and tribal fusion, are among the most popular new styles of belly dancing today.

In most cultures, Middle Eastern dance was a female activity, but in some areas, such as Egypt, men also danced. It took many years for male dancers to be accepted in the West, as Western audiences only wanted to see women.

Belly dancers primarily dance to Middle Eastern styles of music, either traditional or contemporary, live or recorded, although some dancers, especially those who perform belly dance fusion styles, use other music as well. Today, belly dancers dance in Middle Eastern restaurants and nightclubs, and they may also perform at festivals, stand-alone performances, and other social gatherings. Depending on the dance style, dancers may perform choreographed routines (alone or in a troupe), improvised solo dances, or group improvisations in which group members follow the leader's moves (this is most popular in tribal forms of the dance).

Becoming a professional belly dancer involves years of training. Belly dance classes can be found in almost any moderately sized city in much of the world, although the chances of training with a well-respected professional dancer go up in the larger cities. Although there are countless opportunities to learn to dance without working with a teacher (YouTube alone offers over five hundred thousand video tutorials), becoming a professional dancer involves attending classes, workshops, and private lessons. These classes do not stop once a dancer starts getting paid; professional dancers take classes and build on their skills throughout their lives. Many belly dancers have a background in other forms of dance before they begin belly dancing, but this is not necessary.

Belly dance training involves learning the fundamental moves in a particular style, understanding Middle Eastern music rhythms, dancing to live music, choreography, improvisational techniques, floor work, costuming, the playing of cymbals or other instruments, working with props, such as veils, swords, canes, or even snakes, and more.

Belly dancers are independent contractors who are hired for individual performances at restaurants or shows. They are responsible for buying or making their own costumes (which can be very expensive, especially the cabaret-style outfits) and props. Besides classes, many belly dancers also go to belly dancing festivals, where they perform in front of other dancers, network, buy new costuming materials, and learn new skills. To make a living, it is critical that belly dancers have their own websites and that they promote themselves via social media to develop opportunities and attract students.

Unlike other forms of dance, such as ballet or jazz, belly dancers can be seen performing almost anywhere. While ballet dancers must compete for a limited number of positions in ballet companies, belly dancers can more easily find ways to perform and make money. Most belly dance teachers have their own troupes that offer their students performing opportunities, and skilled dancers can transition from amateur performances to paid performances. In addition, belly dancers have a much longer career trajectory than many other dancers. Most dance careers last no more than twenty years and often end well before then because of injuries, but belly dancers can dance well into their senior years. In addition, although a professional belly dancer is a highly trained athlete, the dance form allows for a wide variety of body types.

Belly dancers can make money in a variety of ways. Besides performances, which may pay $50–$200 for a typical restaurant performance, virtually all professional belly dancers teach. Dancers charge about $10–$15 per class, so a class of ten students can generate $100–$150 for an evening. The better-known dancers travel internationally to give workshops around the world, and they charge much more for those workshops. Others offer private classes that also command higher fees. Some offer classes through DVD sales, and others operate YouTube channels where they upload performances and instructional videos. Finally, some belly dancers will do private performances at parties or sell costumes, accessories, music, and other supplies.

See also: Mourner; Wedding Guest; YouTube Celebrity.

Further Reading

Said, E. W. (1978). *Orientalism*. Pantheon.
Shay, A. (2005). *Belly dance: Orientalism, transnationalism and harem fantasy*. Mazda Publishers.
Ward, H. D. (2017). *Egyptian belly dance in transition: The Raqs Sharqi revolution, 1890–1930*. McFarland.

Big Man (Melanesia, South America)

A *Big Man* is an anthropological term for a type of political leader that is found in tribes and particularly in those tribes that are found in horticultural societies. Big Men are most commonly found in Melanesia and South America.

Tribal groups with Big Men are defined by anthropologists as those that maintain nonintensive food production (i.e., horticulture) as a subsistence system, typically combined with the raising of small animals and hunting wild animals. These types of tribes are ranked, in that there are status differences between different kinds of people based on individual accomplishment as well as by gender, but the societies are not stratified like contemporary nation-states, even though all tribes today are incorporated into a nation-state. There is no formal centralized government that holds the whole tribe together; instead, in the case of Big Man organization, villages, or groups of villages, are led by men (Big Men are virtually always men) who make important decisions and mediate conflicts for those groups.

Unlike a tribal chief, the Big Man does not have formal power. Instead, his position, which is temporary, is maintained through persuasion. He can push, harangue, or encourage people to do as he says; however, no one is forced to obey the Big Man, and they do not have to follow him either. One does not inherit the position of Big Man, and there are no elections. Instead, the position is acquired by gaining respect and status within the community through the person's abilities in warfare, oration, the organization of tribal events, or other important skills.

One example of a culture with a Big Man leadership system is the Yanomami, first described in detail by anthropologist Napoleon Chagnon in the 1960s (see Chagnon 1983; 2013). The Yanomami are a horticultural tribe found in the jungles of Venezuela and Brazil, and each village has its own village headman, or Big Man. The society, which has about thirty-five thousand people with a shared language and culture, is organized through patrilineal descent, which means that lineage is traced and inheritance works through the male line, and after marriage, women move to the husband's village (known as patrilocal postmarital residency). Villages are primarily connected through trade, warfare, and marriage.

Like other tribes, the Yanomami traditionally have no centralized government or ruler. Instead, the Big Man gains his status through his skills in warfare and then maintains it through displays of violence. Because the Big Man cannot control members of the village through formal authority, the Yanomami Big Man persuades or influences others to do as he wishes. But if he has a large following, made up first of his patrilineal male kin, this adds to his ability to control others. Another factor that is important in creating and maintaining alliances is having a large number of daughters who are then traded with important members of other groups, creating permanent alliances with those groups. The Yanomami are polygynous, meaning a man can have multiple wives, so the Big Man will typically be able to produce multiple daughters through his wives.

As in other Big Man societies, the Yanomami Big Man must be seen to be generous and not simply fierce. He throws feasts for other villages in which foodstuffs and other goods are distributed to those participating, and this causes those people to be obligated to him. The more he gives away, the more people the Big Man can cultivate to become his allies and followers.

Like other tribal groups around the world, the Yanomami have suffered in recent decades from the effects of colonization and the loss of their land and culture to developers, miners, ranchers, and the governments of Brazil and Venezuela, all of whom have displaced them from their land. Since the early 1990s, however, the remaining Yanomami have lived on protected land.

Most of the tribes of Papua New Guinea are horticultural with a Big Man system. One such group is the Kawelka of the Mount Hagen region of the country, who were first described by anthropologist Andrew Strathern (see Strathern 1988; Godelier and Strathern 1991). The Kawelka grow sweet potatoes to eat and trade, and they raise pigs, primarily for trade. Many Kawelka also now participate in the cash economy of Papua New Guinea by growing or picking coffee.

Like the Yanomami, the Kawelka have no centralized government (since independence in 1975, Papua New Guinea has been ruled by a prime minister combined with a parliament); instead, the tribe, like other tribes in the country, is made up of a number of politically unintegrated descent groups; each group maintains its own authority and has its own Big Man. The Kawelka are patrilineal, and they maintain patrilocal postmarital residences. They are also polygynous.

Like the Yanomami village heads, the Kawelka Big Men do not inherit their positions (although many Big Men do have fathers who were Big Men) and do not control people or exert power in any formalized manner. Rather, they are able to influence the actions of those who follow them through persuasion, the power of their personality, bravery, and through gift giving. A Big Man gains and maintains his position through commanding respect from others and compiling a large number of obligations. The best way to do this is by giving away women for marriage and by throwing large ceremonies, to which another tribal group will be invited and given gifts. Traditionally, the most important items, besides women, that can be given away in these ceremonies, known as *Moka*, are pigs. Pigs were used to pay bride-price, to pay off debts incurred through intertribal violence, and to create alliances—both within and between the tribal groups. By demonstrating generosity through the giving of gifts at the Moka, and at other times, the Big Man takes the surplus that he has encouraged his wives and others in his community to create, and parlays that generosity into prestige and obligations. Big Men only maintain their positions for as long as people follow them; once they lose the respect and admiration of others, they will be challenged by a more popular man for the position.

Today, Papuan Big Men still play a role in both local and national politics. Members of Parliament, who are often Big Men, continue to be beholden to the tribal groups from which they come, and, given the shifting nature of local political alliances, this creates instability on the national level. In addition, because women have not been able to attain the Big Man position, it is equally difficult for them to become elected to Parliament. It is thought that as long as the Big Man remains an important feature of Papuan society, women will never be able to achieve political power in the country.

See also: YouTube Celebrity.

Further Reading

Chagnon, N. A. (1983). *Yanomamö: The fierce people.* Holt, Rinehart and Winston.
Chagnon, N. A. (2013). *Noble savages: My life among two dangerous tribes—the Yanomamö and the anthropologists.* Simon and Schuster.
Godelier, M., & Strathern, M. (1991). *Big men and great men: Personifications of power in Melanesia.* Maison des Sciences de l'Homme.
Sahlins, M. D. (1963). Poor man, rich man, big-man, chief: Political types in Melanesia and Polynesia. *Comparative Studies in Society and History, 5*(3), 285–303.
Strathern, M. (1988). *The gender of the gift: Problems with women and problems with society in Melanesia* (Vol. 6). University of California Press.

Bike Fisherman (Netherlands)

A bike fisherman is someone who retrieves abandoned bicycles from the canals of Amsterdam.

The Netherlands is a small, densely populated nation, which, like most European countries, is concerned about the impact of human activities on the environment. The Dutch are especially concerned about air and water pollution as well as crowding on the nation's roads. Cycling is one way that the Dutch help to alleviate these problems.

After the end of World War II, car ownership exploded in the Netherlands, and the country began updating its road infrastructure to make room for more vehicles, which not only displaced many cyclists from the city streets but resulted in the deaths of thousands of cyclists, especially in the older cities where streets are narrow. With the oil crisis in the early 1970s and the resulting spike in gasoline prices, there was further incentive for the Dutch government to deal with the problems caused by cars.

One of the first steps to address the vehicle problem was the introduction of car-free Sundays in the Netherlands' cities, followed by the banning of cars in many city centers. By 1975, the government was building protected bike lanes. All of these measures resulted in a steep decline in car ownership and driving rates and a hike in cycling. The Dutch have implemented further policies since then that provide financial and other disincentives for vehicle use, and these have made the use of bicycles even more attractive.

Rusty bicycles pulled out of a canal in Amsterdam. (Kimbobo/Dreamstime.com)

Thanks to all of these policies, the Netherlands is now the most bike-friendly country in the world. (The fact that the Netherlands is one of the flattest countries in Europe helps as well.) In 2016, 27 percent of all transportation in the Netherlands was done by bicycle, and the country has more bicycles (23 million) than people (17 million). (See Harms and Kansen 2018 for more information.)

Amsterdam is one of the world's most cycling-friendly cities thanks to decades of government policy combined with Amsterdam's narrow streets and flat roads. Seventy-eight percent of all residents own at least one bike, and the city has 881,000 bikes. All these bikes can also cause problems. Bicycle theft is extremely high, with approximately 200 bikes per day being stolen in the capital city.

Another problem has to do with the city's canals. Amsterdam, like Venice, is a city of canals. Originally built in the Middle Ages to aid with water management and the city's defense, the canals ended up being an important way to transport goods into and out of the city. In the seventeenth century, as Amsterdam became a global trading powerhouse, more canals were built, expanding the size of the city and allowing for ever greater quantities of goods to be transported to and from the city. These canals were filthy, filled with the city's garbage. In the mid–twentieth century, about half of all the city's canals were filled in to provide roads for the growing numbers of cars, but the city still has over one hundred kilometers (or about sixty-five miles) of canals, which make up about a quarter of the city's surface. While the canals are much cleaner today, there is still one major problem associated with them: bicycles.

The city's canals are filled with bicycles. Some of these bicycles may have fallen into the water (people will often park their bicycles along the canals, and the city is notoriously windy), but many, if not most, are thrown into the canals by vandals, thieves, or people who no longer want their old bikes.

To deal with this problem, Waternet, which oversees the city's water services, began hiring people to find and recover the bicycles in the 1960s. These people, known colloquially as bike fisherman, ride along the city's canals in a barge specially fitted with a crane that operates a giant hydraulic claw. The claw works like the big toy claw machines that are found in video arcades, bowling alleys, movie theaters, and other places where children congregate. The bike fisherman operates the claw from the barge and uses it to lift bikes from the bottom of the canals. The bikes are then dropped onto a second boat, which hauls them away. Some go to metal recyclers, who take them apart and recycle the parts, and some go to bicycle wholesalers, who repair the bikes that are in the best shape and resell them. It only takes about three hours of dredging to fill a boat with bikes. According to Waternet, its employees, who patrol the waters daily, retrieve about fifteen thousand bikes per year. (Some cyclists who lose their bikes in the canals will retrieve them themselves, but without the aid of the claw. Instead, they fish the bikes out with poles or other makeshift tools.)

Bike fishermen, who are full-time employees of the city and work in teams of two (one to drive the barge and the other to operate the claw), also occasionally remove cars, shopping carts, refrigerators, and sunken boats from the canals, but the majority of objects found at the bottom of the water are bikes.

See also: Golf Ball Diver; Gondolier; Scooter Charger and Retriever.

Further Reading

Harms, L., & Kansen, M. (2018). *Cycling facts*. Netherlands Institute for Transport Policy Analysis/KiM, Ministry of Infrastructure and Water Management.

Pucher, J., & Buehler, R. (2008). Making cycling irresistible: Lessons from the Netherlands, Denmark and Germany. *Transport Reviews, 28*(4), 495–528.

Bounty Hunter (United States)

A bounty hunter, or bail enforcement agent, is a person who locates and captures people who have paid bail and missed a court appearance. The job is only found in the United States because it is specific to the U.S. court system and is illegal in the rest of the world.

Bounty hunters emerged in the western United States in the nineteenth century, in a time and place when law enforcement was much more informal than it is today. As American colonists traveled west during the period of westward expansion, opening the frontier to new territories and, eventually, new states, there was little in the way of law enforcement. As the frontier pushed westward, the U.S. military established forts along the way, providing some measure of federal oversight to the new territories. However, these forts could not prevent most crime. The lawmen who did exist at this time—primarily sheriffs elected at the local level—could not do the job on their own. If they knew of a person who was wanted for a crime, they often lacked the resources to find the suspect. This resulted in one of the most famous symbols of the Old West: the wanted poster. Sheriffs, or sometimes vigilance committees formed in lawless communities, put up posters with an image of the suspect and the amount of money offered for his or her capture. This led to regular citizens tracking down and bringing in these suspects for a fee, at which point the suspects were tried and sentenced. This was the origin of the modern bounty hunter. Today, bounty hunters still bring in criminal defendants, but the process is more formalized.

In the United States, when someone has been arrested and charged with a crime, one of the first hearings that is scheduled for that person is a bail hearing. This is when the defense attorney for the accused asks for bail, arguing that his or her client is trustworthy, is not a danger to the community, and will not flee prior to his or her trial. Bail is essentially a form of promissory note: by paying the court a substantial amount of money, which will be forfeited if the accused does not return for trial, the accused is promising to return. If the judge agrees with the defense and sets bail, the client is released from prison after paying it. After the trial is over, assuming the suspect has appeared at all of the required hearings, the bail bond is returned. However, if the suspect does not return for trial, he or she not only forfeits the bail that has been paid but a warrant will be issued for his or her arrest. If rearrested, he or she will most likely not get bail again. In addition, failure to appear, also known as bail jumping, is also a crime in many jurisdictions, so the suspect, called a "skip," can be charged with a new crime upon his or her rearrest.

Although the American bail system is based on cash deposits paid to the court, it originally developed out of the medieval English system of bail, wherein the accused was expected to pay the victim compensation for the crime that he or she committed. To demonstrate to the court that the victim would be compensated, the defendant chose another person who guaranteed that he or she would, if needed, pay the compensation. This was changed in the United States to a system whereby defendants pay the court, rather than the victim, to demonstrate their willingness to return to trial.

Each state has its own bail laws that determine the conditions under which bail can and cannot be granted as well as guidelines for the amounts that can be charged and other terms. (New Jersey and Alaska no longer have cash bail systems.)

In most American states (and the Philippines), the accused does not need to pay the bail bond himself or herself. Instead, he or she can use the services of a bail bondsman to pay the majority of the bond. Generally, the accused only pays a 10–15 percent fee to the bondsman, with the bondsman paying the remainder to the court. The suspect must also try to make up the rest of the bond in collateral, which usually takes the form of the defendant's (or the defendant's relatives) property, such as a home, vehicle, or jewelry. Using a bail bondsman makes it easier for the accused to get out of jail prior to the trial, but it also means that he or she no longer has as great a stake in attending the trial because only 10 percent of the bail will be lost. However, if a suspect does not appear in court, that means that the bail bondsman has forfeited the money that he or she has paid. (In those states that have prohibited the use of commercial bail bond companies, the suspect still only pays 10 percent of the bail but does so directly to the court.) The only ways to get that money back is to collect on the collateral offered in the initial agreement or to make sure that the suspect is taken into custody. This is where the bounty hunter comes in.

Bounty hunters work for or contract with bail bondsmen. Once a suspect has jumped bail, and usually after a thirty-day grace period, a bounty hunter is assigned to find and recapture the suspect. The bail bondsman will provide the bounty hunter with information on the defendant, including addresses, phone numbers, social security number, type of vehicle, and date of birth. The bounty hunter may dig through trash, trace phone calls, and interview (or even bribe) associates of the suspect to get additional information.

Bounty hunters are paid per suspect and are generally paid a percentage of the bail amount. (In states that have prohibited the use of bounty hunters, bail bondsmen must try to catch the suspects themselves.) Bounty hunters who work regularly can make $50,000 or more per year, and those with a lot of experience and a good track record of arrests can command higher rates.

Once a bounty hunter has found the skip, he or she is legally allowed to arrest the person. When getting a bail bond through a commercial service, defendants sign a contract that promises they will show up to court. The contract also stipulates what will happen when they do not: a bounty hunter can be dispatched to arrest them, and their loved ones can be approached to pay back the bond with the collateral that they promised. The defendant who signs a bail bond contract also waives state (but not federal) extradition: if found by the bounty hunter in another state, he or she can be legally transported to the state where the crime occurred for prosecution.

Bounty hunters do not need an arrest warrant to make an arrest (although a few states do require a court order), nor do they need to read the suspect his or her Miranda rights. They can also enter private property without permission. The fact that a bounty hunter can do things that are constitutionally prohibited for police makes bounty hunting problematic from a civil rights perspective, which is why it is not legal in all states (and is illegal in the rest of the world). When an arrest is made, the suspect is driven by the bounty hunter to the jail where he or she was originally arrested.

Bounty hunting is a dangerous profession. Bounty hunters work with criminals, or people involved in crime, and are expected to locate and apprehend people who may be armed and dangerous. (Realistically, however, it is rare for extremely dangerous people to be released on bail.) In addition, the hours can be long, as part of the work involves staking out locations for hours at a time. It also means a lot of computer research to find up-to-date addresses. Bounty hunters should be familiar with the areas where criminals hang out, and they spend a lot of time in poor or dangerous neighborhoods.

Bounty hunters typically enter the job through formal training programs, which can be found at both colleges and private institutions. Some have a police background or a degree in criminal justice, but it is not necessary for the job. They should be patient, discreet, and resourceful, and they must know and abide by the law. (One of the most famous bounty hunters today, Duane "Dog" Chapman, was arrested trying to apprehend a skip in Mexico, where bounty hunting is illegal, although charges against him were later dismissed.) They should also be physically fit, as the job may demand running, climbing over fences, crawling through windows, or overpowering a suspect. Bounty hunters must be licensed in most states and insured, and if they want to carry a firearm, they must have a separate license for that. They must buy all their own equipment, which may include cameras, binoculars, a bulletproof vest, a taser or pepper spray, and handcuffs. Bounty hunters typically have other training as well, such as weapons training, self-defense training, and training in computer investigations. Some would-be bounty hunters may also apprentice with an experienced professional. Finally, as the jobs come through bail bondsmen, it is critical that bounty hunters create relationships with the bail bonds professionals in their area.

See also: Crime Scene Cleaner.

Further Reading

Burns, R., Kinkade, P., & Leone, M. C. (2005). Bounty hunters: A look behind the hype. *Policing: An International Journal of Police Strategies & Management, 28*(1), 118–138.

Burton, B. (1990). *Bail enforcer: The advanced bounty hunter.* Paladin Press.

Bruja (Latin America)

A *bruja* (female) or *brujo* (male) is a magic user in Latin America. *Brujería* (the Spanish word for "witchcraft") is the tradition of magic use in Latin America, especially in Mexico, Cuba, and Puerto Rico, as well in immigrant communities along the Mexico–United States border—particularly Southern California, Arizona, and Texas.

In cultures around the world, there are beliefs in either sorcery, witchcraft, or both. Anthropologists typically distinguish between what they call *witches* and what they refer to as *sorcerers*. Sorcerers are people who use herbs and other tools to harm or heal other people and to benefit themselves or their clients. Witches, on the other hand, are thought to be individuals who are born with the supernatural ability to harm others; sometimes this skill is involuntary, and sometimes the alleged witch does not even know that he or she possesses such a skill. In most cultures that have both a witch figure and sorcerers, sorcerers do not have inherent supernatural powers but have developed abilities that they can use to cause harm. They can be hired by someone who wants to have someone harmed, and most sorcerers use folk magical practices, herbs, and folk remedies to harm and to help people.

In other cultures, the figure of the witch and the sorcerer are combined into one person, as in the case of brujería. Because a bruja or brujo uses spells, rituals, and tools to manipulate the spirit world and cause change in this world, he or she fits the anthropological definition of a sorcerer. But some brujas are thought to have inherent magical or psychic abilities (some are even thought to have the ability to shapeshift, a classic sign of a witch), and the term "witch" is the most commonly used translation for *bruja* or *brujo*. Consequently, brujería can be thought of as a mixture of both witchcraft and sorcery.

Latin America—made up of the Spanish-, Portuguese-, and French-speaking countries of North, South, and Central America, plus the West Indies—is predominantly Catholic, as the modern-day nations of Latin America were colonized by Catholic countries. Yet, there are dozens of different religious traditions that are also practiced in Latin America, often alongside traditional Catholicism. These syncretic traditions, which blend elements of different religions together, have borrowed elements from the many indigenous traditions practiced in the pre-Columbian Americas as well as features from Central and West African religions brought over by African slaves. These religions are practiced by indigenous peoples, Afro-Latin Americans (i.e., Afro-Cubans, Afro-Haitians, etc.), and the wider mestizo populations.

Brazil, colonized by the Portuguese in 1500, has a number of such traditions, including Candomblé, Santo Daime, Umbanda, and Quimbanda, and Cuba, colonized by Spain in 1511, has the practices of Santería, Vodú, Abakuá, and Palo, among others. Virtually every other country in the region that experienced European colonization combined with African slavery has similar traditions, with perhaps the most well-known being Haitian voodoo. (New World nations colonized by Protestant countries, such as England, also developed their own syncretic traditions, but they look very different from those in the Catholic countries.) Thanks to immigration, many of these traditions have moved into new countries over the centuries.

Mexico, which never developed a slave-based economy like, for example, Brazil or the United States, nevertheless has a long history of Africans (both slaves and free people) living in the country since the earliest days of the Spanish colony in the sixteenth century. As in the other countries, these Africans brought over their own religious traditions, which then merged with traditions already present on the continent. In addition, as in the other countries in the New World, thanks to the constant flow of people from one country to the next, these traditions continued to develop as new elements continued to be incorporated into the religious practices of everyday citizens. For this reason, Santería and Palo, both from Cuba, are currently practiced in Mexico. These religions join other syncretic traditions popular in Mexico today, including the veneration of the Virgin of Guadalupe (who is a combination of the mother of Jesus and Aztec goddesses), the celebration of the Day of the Dead, and the cult of Santa Muerte, the Mexican goddess of death.

Brujería, or Mexican witchcraft, is another example of a syncretic religious tradition that remains popular in Mexico today. Like other countries with a belief in witches and sorcerers, Mexico's brujería tradition is based on a belief that humans can, with aid from saints, gods, or ancestors, control the natural world through supernatural means, or the use of magic. Equally important is the belief that these same supernatural figures can and do influence people's daily lives. Just as traditional healers, such as the Latin American *curandero*, will borrow Catholic elements for their healing, such as holy water and the images of the saints, and combine them with practices from indigenous and sometimes African traditions, the bruja also crosses religious and cultural borders in his or her practice.

According to anthropologist Ruth Behar (1987), it was Catholicism, and the hostility of the Spanish colonizers to indigenous and African religious practices, that led to the rise of brujería and other syncretic practices in Mexico. Because the Spanish were so focused on wiping out the "superstitions" of the Mexican people, those who continued to practice any forms of traditional, or syncretic, religions were pushed further to the margins of Mexican society, resulting in an explosion of unorthodox beliefs and practices.

A bruja can be hired to hurt someone by casting spells that can cause the person to experience bad luck, develop an illness, lose his or her mind, or die. He or she utilizes sympathetic magic to do this. Sympathetic magic is based on two laws: the law of similarity and the law of contagion. The former law, used in imitative magic, assumes that items that look the same can exert an impact on each other. The law of contagion, on the other hand, which is used in contagious magic, assumes that items that are in contact with each other can influence each other. A voodoo doll, for example, is a form of imitative magic, in that the doll is created by the bruja to resemble the subject of the spell. Adding some nail clippings or bits of hair from the subject to the doll involves the use of contagious magic; because the hair and nails were once connected to the subject, the doll will be more powerful. Both these forms of magic are used to give people control over the world around them and to mitigate anxiety.

But they can also help people. Brujas are often hired to counteract what a client thinks is a curse, a spell from another bruja, or another form of spiritually based bad luck. Here, the bruja will use the same forms of magic—imitative and contagious—to reverse the black magic. For example, if someone believes that he or she has been cursed by a bruja with the evil eye, a simple spell to counteract that is to rub an egg over the victim and then dispose of the egg. Thanks to the law of contagion, the egg will absorb the evil from the victim, curing him or her. Another simple cure for a curse is an amulet or talisman, either worn on the person or displayed in the home, to ward off the evil. The bruja may even cast a spell against the original bruja or brujo who caused the client the harm if other methods do not do the trick. And, of course, clients can visit a bruja to gain something good—money, luck, success in marriage or a job, or good health. The most popular issue, however, is love, with customers from both sexes using brujas to find it.

Today, both men and women continue to practice brujería, drawing clients from across the socioeconomic spectrum. They perform both "black magic" and "white magic," referring to magical practices that are intended to either harm (or kill) or help. Some brujas (known as *brujas blancas*) only perform white magic, while others do both. (Brujas blancas are relatively indistinguishable from curanderos. The difference is that where the curandero or curandera is brought in to cure a physical illness, using a combination of natural and supernatural means, a bruja is used when there is a spiritual problem that must be solved—such as a curse. In addition, *curanderismo* does not carry the same stigma that brujería carries today.)

A bruja or brujo needs a vast amount of supplies to service clients; many of these are purchased at shops called *botanicas* (and sometimes *candle shops* in the United States). Here, brujas can purchase candles, sprays, powders, dolls, oils, herbs, animal parts, gold dust, graveyard dirt, images and statues of Catholic saints and African gods, and all manner of amulets and talismans to be used in both white and black magic. The public can also visit these stores, where, for a fee, the bruja can perform a spell. Adherents of the Santa Muerte cult can also purchase offerings and supplies at these same shops. In addition, brujas in Mexico City can shop at the Mercado de Sonora, a large public market that sells, in addition to all manner of secular merchandise, a wide array of herbs, magical items, and items related to syncretic religions such as Santería and the cult of Santa Muerte. The market also sells live animals for sacrifice.

There are no universities that offer degrees in brujería, although most universities offer classes, as part of their anthropology offerings, in the academic study of witchcraft, magic, and sorcery. Brujas, like other magic users and healers in other cultures, learn their profession either through their parents (typically either a mother or father being a practicing bruja) or through mentoring with someone. And while there are both academic books and practical manuals on brujería today, most of the knowledge has been passed down orally, from practitioner to practitioner.

In early written accounts of brujería practices by the Spanish, it was described as a form of devil worship, as were most indigenous traditions that the Spanish did not understand. Interestingly, while both men and women practice brujería, in colonial Mexico, it was brujas who were typically prosecuted for engaging in witchcraft, especially during the Mexican Inquisition of the eighteenth century. One of the reasons for the criminalization of women's activities was that many of the prosecuted women were accused of engaging in sexual magic, which was an especially threatening form of magic to men in a time when women had no legal rights at all, and thus magic was often their only option to assert some control over their own lives.

Today, both brujería as well as the worship of Santa Muerte are very popular with members of the illegal drug gangs that flourish throughout Mexico and produce and transport drugs into the United States. Santa Muerte, for example, is said to protect her worshippers from violence and can provide favors for those who make the proper offerings.

In 1989, an American college student from Texas named Mark Kilroy, who was visiting the northern Mexico town of Matamoros while on Spring Break, was kidnapped and ritually sacrificed by members of a drug cartel who followed a Cuban American immigrant named Adolfo Constanzo, who had learned Palo Mayombe and Santería as a teenager. Constanzo had begun his work as a brujo by casting spells and sacrificing animals to bring good luck and protection to his clients. Eventually, he joined a drug cartel run by two brothers, and he promised the members of the cartel that if they followed him, they would gain great power. He ran the group alongside a Mexican American named Sara Aldrete, a bruja who the group members referred to as the "godmother." In addition, once they began sacrificing humans as well as animals on Constanzo's recommendation, the cartel members were promised that they would be immune not only from bullets and other forms of violence but also from detection by the police. The group ritually killed (and tortured, sexually assaulted, and dismembered) at least fifteen (and probably many more) people before they were caught.

Brujería is also experiencing a resurgence today among younger Latinx, who, like Wiccans in many countries, are reclaiming this once demonized form of religious practice and embracing it as a form of feminized and indigenous power in a patriarchal, postcolonial society.

See also: Exorcist; Psychic; Traditional Healer; Witch Hunter.

Further Reading

Behar, R. (1987). Sex and sin, witchcraft and the devil in late colonial Mexico. *American Ethnologist, 14*(1), 34–54.

Devine, M. V. (1982). *Brujeria: A study of Mexican-American folk-magic.* Llewellyn Publications.

Endredy, J. (2011). *The flying witches of Veracruz: A Shaman's true story of indigenous witchcraft, devil's weed, and trance healing in Aztec Brujeria.* Llewellyn Worldwide.

Nutini, H. G., & Roberts, J. M. (2019). *Bloodsucking witchcraft: An epistemological study of anthropomorphic supernaturalism in rural Tlaxcala.* University of Arizona Press.

Toohey, J. V., & Dezelsky, T. L. (1980). Curanderas and brujas—herbal healing in Mexican American communities. *Health Education, 11*(4), 2–4.

Zavaleta, A., & Salinas A., Jr. (2009). *Curandero conversations: El niño fidencio, shamanism and healing traditions of the borderlands.* AuthorHouse.

Budtender (United States)

A budtender is a person who sells marijuana products at a legal marijuana store. According to the Marijuana Policy Group, there were approximately thirty thousand Americans working as budtenders in 2016.

Marijuana is a drug that comes from the cannabis plant, which is a close relative of the hop plant (which is used in beer), and is indigenous to Tibet. Today, marijuana is most well known for its psychoactive properties—thanks to the compound THC as well as other cannabinoids—but it has been used ritually and medicinally for thousands of years. It is used, both legally and illegally, by over 219 million people around the world and generates almost $17 billion in annual revenue.

Marijuana was first used in Central Asia at least five thousand years ago, but other uses of the cannabis plant (such as hemp for rope and paper) were known even earlier. Since that time, the drug has been used for a variety of purposes (including food, as many people once ate cannabis seeds) throughout Central and East Asia and had spread into Europe and East Africa on the Silk Road by at least the first century.

The first known use of marijuana specifically for its mind-altering qualities was found at an ancient cemetery in the Pamir Mountains in far western China on the Tajikistan border. Archaeologists tested the burnt remains of marijuana that were found in wooden braziers and noted that the remains had much higher levels of THC than had been found at earlier sites. The archaeologists have postulated that the Sogdian peoples (or perhaps just priests) who lived in the region most likely burned the marijuana as part of their funeral rites. Other early indications of the drug were found in a 2,400-year-old Scythian tomb (which held both opium and cannabis), and there are references to the use of the drug in China as early as

---

Ale Wife

An ale wife was a woman who brewed beer in medieval England. The job emerged out of the traditional domestic tasks of an English wife at that time; women were tasked with making ale (which is a drink made of fermented grains and water, but without the hops that beer contains) along with their other daily household chores. Eventually, some women began selling leftover ale to people outside of the family, and the ale wife position emerged. It remained, for most women, an activity that brought supplemental income to the family, as ale was rarely produced in commercial quantities—and not by women alone—in that period. In the early modern period, as beer production overtook ale production, beer production came to be dominated by the new brewers' guilds, which were made up of men, and domestic ale production, as well as ale wives, became a thing of the past.

Source: Bennett, J. M. (1986). The village ale-wife: Women and brewing in fourteenth-century England. In Barbara A. Hanawalt (Ed.), *Women and Work in Preindustrial Europe* (pp. 20–36). Indiana University Press.

2700 BCE. It has been referred to in ancient texts from China, Persia, and India and was mentioned in the Talmud and by ancient Greek scientists as well.

Today, marijuana is consumed in a variety of forms, the oldest of which (and still the most efficient) is smoking it through a pipe, cigarette, bong, or other device. But marijuana can be eaten (when it is cooked into candies, snacks, and baked goods), drank (as a tincture, syrup, tea, or soda), vaped (inhaled through an electronic device), and even sprayed in the mouth through a THC spray.

For most of the history of marijuana use around the world, marijuana was neither criminalized nor regulated. In fact, the notion of criminalizing psychoactive substances was relatively unknown around the world until the last two centuries, but it was not unheard of. Alcohol, for example, is a substance that has been prohibited by a number of religions, including Islam, which first banned its use in the seventh century, and even coffee has been subjected to similar prohibitions, first being banned in the Ottoman Empire in the seventeenth century (a prohibition that was rescinded shortly afterward). The first attempt to ban opium was in the fourteenth century in Thailand, and again in the nineteenth century by China, although that ban was revoked by the British (who profited from the import of opium into China by the British East India Company) after winning the Opium Wars against China. Marijuana, however, had only once been prohibited by authorities prior to the twentieth century, when Napoleon found that French soldiers brought back the practice of smoking marijuana from Egypt and banned its use in 1798.

Cannabis plants first arrived in the New World in the seventeenth century, when they were planted by French and British colonists (in fact, King James I mandated that American colonists grow cannabis for hemp); African slaves also brought the plant to Brazil, where they planted them in the sugarcane fields. While initially the cannabis plants in North America were used for hemp, Americans began using the plant for other purposes as well, and hashish (which is made from the resin of the cannabis plant) became popular in the eighteenth century, when Europeans also began smoking the substance. Both Europe and the United States saw a major fashion in hash smoking, usually in "tea pads" or hash parlors, from the eighteenth to the nineteenth centuries. At this time, marijuana, cocaine, and other drugs could be easily purchased through pharmacies and general stores as well as doctors' offices.

The first modern drug laws emerged in the nineteenth and early twentieth centuries in Europe and the United States, and they succeeded in curbing the use of the prohibited drugs, which included opium and opiates, cocaine, and marijuana. Marijuana was first regulated in 1906 when it was included in the list of drugs to be regulated by the Pure Food and Drug Act. It was first criminalized in 1913 in California after concerns that Mexican immigrants were using the drug. The prohibition spread throughout the Southwest until 1937, when Congress passed the Marihuana Transfer Tax Act, which effectively banned marijuana use, distribution, and production throughout the country.

During the second half of the twentieth century, and especially with the emergence of the U.S. War on Drugs, laws against a variety of drugs—including marijuana—became stricter, both in the United States and elsewhere. Mandatory sentencing laws, for example, were passed in the 1950s, which provided for mandatory minimum sentences and fines to be imposed for illegal drug use; the penalty for a first-time marijuana user was two to ten years in prison and a fine of $20,000. After the repeal of the Marihuana Transfer Tax Act, marijuana was added to the brand-new Controlled Substances Act of 1970. Finally, in the 1980s and 1990s, mandatory minimum sentences, which had been repealed in 1970, were reinstated as well as a number of other new drug laws, many of which targeted marijuana users. Many other nations also passed their own laws banning marijuana. In 1961, the Single Convention on Narcotic Drugs was passed by seventy-three nations that attended the United Nations Conference on Narcotic Drugs, and it included marijuana on the list of drugs to be banned for nonmedical use.

Since the mid-1990s, countries around the world, as well as a number of states in the United States, have repealed their marijuana prohibitions by decriminalizing the drug (which means users may not be prosecuted but manufacturers and dealers will), legalizing it for medical use, or legalizing it entirely (albeit under certain conditions) for recreational use. As of late 2019, four countries and eleven states plus the District of Columbia have legalized marijuana for recreational use, and twenty-one countries and thirty-three U.S. states have legalized it for medical use.

With the rise of legal (either for medical or recreational use) marijuana came the rise of marijuana dispensaries, where marijuana can be legally sold in states and countries where the drug is legal. In the United States, which borrowed its model from the "coffee shops" of Amsterdam, the dispensaries are regulated by the state and do not allow consumption or children on the premises. The workers in these dispensaries are known as budtenders.

Budtending is an entry-level job, in that it does not require the kind of technical knowledge that would be necessary to work in other areas of the industry (such as growing plants), but would-be budtenders still need to be more knowledgeable than the general public. This is important not only because of the vast array of products offered by marijuana dispensaries but also because they are providing information both to recreational customers as well as medical customers, so they need to have a deep knowledge of both the physical effects of each strain and product that they sell and their medicinal benefits. As the science of marijuana cultivation and product creation continues to develop, budtenders need to be on top of the emerging body of knowledge so that they can effectively help their customers.

Budtenders are retail employees, so customer service is a major part of their job, just as it would be in a coffee or clothing shop. (The major difference is that budtenders are selling a recently legalized product that still carries a great deal of taboo.) Budtenders must talk with customers, make product recommendations (which often means finding out intimate aspects of their customers' physical, emotional, or mental health issues), make sales, set up and restock product displays, roll joints, trim marijuana buds, and more. They must be able to talk knowledgably about the industry and be able to provide information to people who may know little to nothing about legal marijuana. They must know about the different consumption methods and the dizzying array of products used for marijuana consumption. They must understand, at least at a minimal level, the science involved in creating many of the products because most people are confused by the various processes, acronyms, and terms (CBD, CBN, THC, Sativa, Indica, wax, shatter, terpenes, etc.) and need help understanding how everything works. (Even people who smoked marijuana in college twenty or thirty years ago do not understand the complicated marijuana industry of today.) They need to know the most popular strains, what they do, and what other customers say about them. They must know about other dispensaries in the area and the products they carry so that they can advise customers on, for example, the best deals. They even must know about the latest research on medical uses of marijuana so that they can continue to advise their medical customers properly. And because their customers range from life-long stoners to first-time users to elderly people looking for help with sleeping or pain, budtenders need to be able to positively work with all types of people.

To get a job as a budtender in a country or state where dispensaries exist, the candidate must demonstrate his or her customer service and sales experience as well as a vast knowledge of cannabis. The pay is typical for other entry-level customer service jobs—about $13–$16 per hour—but for people who are passionate about marijuana and want to help people, budtending is a very good job opportunity. In addition, many dispensaries offer customers a discount. At the same time, it is getting to be a highly competitive profession as the industry expands.

As marijuana continues to be decriminalized around the world and marijuana use rises, marijuana dispensaries will become more common, and, consequently, budtenders will become more common as well. "Universities" that offer training, either in person or online, to those who want to get involved in the marijuana industry are also new to the industry. Courses are offered for budtenders, growers, would-be dispensary owners, and for other positions in this rapidly growing industry. There are even companies that help recruit cannabis workers.

See also: Graffiti Artist.

Further Reading

Geluardi, J. (2016). *Cannabiz: The explosive rise of the medical marijuana industry.* Routledge.

Light, M., Orens, A., Rowberry, J., & Saloga, C. W. (2016). *The economic impact of marijuana legalization in Colorado.* Marijuana Policy Group.

Bullfighter (Spain, Portugal, Latin America, France)

A bullfighter, known as a *matador* in Spanish, is someone who professionally fights bulls for a living. Besides the matador, there are other professionals who participate in the fight as well, including the *banderillero* and the *picador*, who, with the matador, are collectively known as *toreros*. Other people who assist these fighters include the *monosabio*, the *mulillero*, the *arenero*, and the *rejoneadore*. Bullfighting should be distinguished from bull wrestling (sometimes also called bullfighting), which is found in countries as diverse as Turkey, India, and Japan.

Bullfighting traces its roots to bull sacrifice among ancient religions in the Middle East and was found in the cultures of Mesopotamia, Egypt, Crete, Greece, and Rome, among other places. Rome strongly influenced the growth of bullfighting not only through its cults that venerated the bull but also through its organized animal fighting and killing shows that were held in public stadiums throughout the Roman Empire; in the medieval period, these led to a variety of blood sports in which animals were harassed, fought, and killed for entertainment. But it was

A bullfighter fights a bull that has banderillas protruding from his body. (Christian Martinez/Dreamstime.com)

one Roman province in particular, Hispania (now modern-day Spain and Portugal), that saw the development of the modern sport of bullfighting in the first century CE. Later, the Spanish exported bullfighting to its colonies, where it still survives in a handful of countries today.

Like medieval jousting tournaments, which involved knights performing to celebrate important events in front of the king in other European countries, bullfighting began as a highly prestigious activity and was reserved for the nobility. Originally, noblemen fought bulls on horses, mimicking the warrior practices of medieval knights, but by the eighteenth century, bullfighters were fighting on foot. Today, however, and especially with the change from fighting on horseback to fighting on foot, people from all classes can become bullfighters.

Modern-day bullfighting is a highly ritualized sport, with every aspect—from the type of arena to the kinds of weapons used to the costumes of the participants—being symbolically important. Although each country, and even each region in Spain, has its own distinctive practices, for the most part, modern bullfights take a very similar form.

The modern Spanish bullfight, or *corrida*, takes place in a specially built arena, or bullring, in which the fighters and the bull compete on a sand surface. After the initial parade that opens the fight, there are three distinct parts to each corrida, and these involve different types of fighters. In the first part, the matador, or primary bullfighter, uses a colorful cloak, called a *capote*, to tease the bull, after which two people, known as picadors, enter the ring on horseback and, armed with lances, attempt to stab the bull on the back of the neck. This weakens the bull for the matador, provides the matador with information on how the bull fights, and also ensures that the bull's head (and horns) are lower during the later stages of the fight.

In stage two, three banderilleros enter the arena and attempt to stick barbed weapons known as *banderillas* into the animal, which, if they are successful, further weakens the bull.

In the third stage, only the matador returns to the arena, armed with a wooden sword and a second, but smaller, cape—which is always red—known as a *muleta*. Eventually, after performing numerous dance-like passes with the cape, wearing the bull down, and getting as close to the bull as possible, the performer exchanges his wooden sword for a steel sword (known as the *estoque de verdad*, or "real sword") and stabs the bull, sometimes killing him outright but at other times only wounding him; sometimes the matador uses other weapons to make the job easier. As with Roman gladiatorial games, the audience can sometimes demand that the bull, if they think he has fought well, be spared from death.

Spanish and Latin American bullfights end with the public death of the bull (and the awarding of the ears or tail to the matador if he performed well), but Portuguese bullfights do not. Instead, mounted Portuguese bullfighters stab the bull with *banderas* (the Portuguese word for what the Spanish call banderillas) in the first stage, and in the second stage, fighters confront the bull with no weapons at all. After the fight is over, the bull is killed, but off stage, by a butcher. As with the Spanish, a bull will occasionally be spared this death.

Bullfighting is also practiced in southern France, where they follow the Spanish tradition, although there is another form of bullfighting in France that does not include the death of the bull and does not derive from the Spanish practice. There is also a form of bullfighting performed in North American rodeos, but as with other rodeo practices, the bulls are not killed. In Latin America, Spanish-style bullfighting is still practiced in Mexico, Columbia, Venezuela, Ecuador, and Peru, and in these countries, the bull is, or can be, killed as part of the fight. (Costa Rica also practices bullfighting, but the bull is neither stabbed nor killed there.)

Animal welfare and animal rights activists have been protesting bullfighting for decades as an unacceptable form of entertainment. They have had some important victories, such as the banning of bullfights in Catalonia, the Canary Islands, and dozens of Spanish towns. Mexico, too, has seen bullfighting banned in three of its thirty-one states, and it has been permanently banned in Argentina, Uruguay, Panama, the Philippines, and Cuba. However, in Spain, where bullfighting has been practiced the longest, conservative politicians and members of the public are especially strong defenders of bullfighting, viewing it as part of the country's national and cultural heritage.

To become a bullfighter, one must be extremely physically fit and can expect to train for the position for years. The job is physically demanding and very dangerous (while death is rare, injuries are very common), but because it is seen in most countries that practice it as an art form rather than a sport, the bullfighter must simultaneously be an athlete, a fighter, and a dancer.

Women can also become bullfighters, but this is a new development. Female bullfighters only emerged in the twentieth century, with Spain formally allowing them as of 1974. Even today, there are only a handful of female bullfighters, and they face a great deal of public opposition.

One of the reasons for female bullfighters' difficulty has to do with the way that masculinity is a central feature in the bullfight. Symbolically, the bull represents, at least in some readings, nature, and the bullfighter represents civilization and the conquering of the wild. Because women have long been symbolically associated with nature, it would not make sense in this traditional understanding for women to act as the conquerors.

To become a bullfighter, one needs to put in thousands of hours of training over approximately seven years—alone, with other students, and, eventually, with live bulls. Today, most would-be bullfighters attend one of a number of bullfighting training schools; there are at least fifty in Spain alone and another dozen in Mexico. Before working with actual animals, the students sit in a classroom before graduating to train with capes, mock bulls (typically made of wood and straw), and horns. Once they begin working with animals, they start with calves and only graduate to larger bulls when they are ready. They must learn how to read the bull, how to use their bodies effectively, and, eventually, how to develop their own personal style, as without that, the bullfighter will never achieve fame or glory. Bullfighters must also develop the confidence and poise to face large, dangerous animals who are terrified and angry. Students start out as young as five, and after graduating, they become a *novillero*, or semiprofessional novice bullfighter. In Spain, a novillero cannot kill a bull until turning sixteen. Many incoming bullfighters have bullfighters in their family.

Besides paying to train (which includes paying for the costs of the hundreds of calves and bulls that a fighter will kill during training), student bullfighters must also pay for their elaborate costumes and their weapons. The matador also pays the assistant bullfighters, such as the banderillero and the picador, and in some countries, new fighters must also pay for the right to fight in the arena. (Once a performer becomes well known, he or she can seek sponsors to help with some of these costs.)

Although bullfighting remains an important part of many Spanish- and Portuguese-speaking countries' cultural heritage, it is also declining in popularity. According to the Spanish Ministry of Culture, bullfighting attendance in Spain has dropped from almost 10 percent visiting a bullfight in 2008 to 7 percent in 2015. Part of this has to do with the power of the animal rights campaigns against the practice, but another part has to do with younger people not being interested in bullfighting. This loss of interest translates to a decline in the number of corridas each year and a corresponding loss of income for the industry. As opportunities decrease for bullfighters (and each town or region that bans it worsens the problem), many training bullfighters leave their own countries to seek better opportunities elsewhere.

And, finally, the pay has dropped as well. Bullfighters make less today than they did even forty years ago, and they are also less venerated today than in the past, when successful bullfighters were the rock stars of the era. While the most famous of all the bullfighters can make tens of thousands of dollars (or even hundreds of thousands) for one big event, most bullfighters will never reach that level of fame nor fortune, and most only earn a few hundred dollars per event. Because it is neither an easy occupation nor a well-compensated one, bullfighting tends to attract people who have a passion for the practice.

See also: Alligator Wrestler; Rodeo Performer.

Further Reading

Marvin, G. (1994). *Bullfight*. University of Illinois Press.
McCormick, J. (2017). *Bullfighting: Art, technique and Spanish society*. Routledge.
Pink, S. (1997). *Women and bullfighting: Gender, sex and the consumption of tradition.* Berg Publisher Ltd.

Burial Bead Maker (South Korea)

A burial bead maker is a person who makes burial beads—also known as death beads—which are beads made out of the cremated remains of the dead.

All human cultures take care of their dead in some way by burying, burning, embalming, or otherwise treating the bodies. In addition, all human cultures mourn the dead in some way, providing some sort of cultural event or ceremony to say goodbye to the dead. Sometimes the body is preserved after death via embalming and mummification. For instance, the ancient Egyptians embalmed the bodies of the dead by removing the organs and bodily fluids and preserving them in pots, where they would be reunited with the dead in the afterlife. After embalming, the corpses would be mummified, preserving them for posterity.

In the contemporary West, bodies are also embalmed in preparation for burial, but not for mummification. The exception to this practice is found among Jews and Muslims, who do not embalm their dead; instead, they bury them as soon as possible after death. In some cases, bodies are embalmed but not buried. For instance, both Vladimir Lenin and Joseph Stalin were embalmed so that their bodies could be placed on permanent display. Lenin's can still be seen in Moscow today, but Stalin was eventually buried in 1961.

Today, cremation is an increasingly popular option for people who do not want to burden their loved ones with the costs of burial or who do not like the idea of their remains rotting in the ground. For others, cremation is a more environmentally friendly way to dispose of a body, as it eliminates the need for embalming (with its toxic chemicals), does not require elaborate coffins, and does not take up the land that burials take. Cremation is generally performed in crematories, where the body, in a simple wooden or cardboard coffin, is burned in a furnace. The loved ones then receive the "cremains," or pulverized bone fragments, which they can display at home in an urn or box, store in a columbarium (usually associated with a cemetery), or, within some legal limits, scatter.

Although a number of religions—such as Judaism, Eastern Orthodox Christianity, and Islam—forbid cremation, it is an important practice in a number of other religions. For instance, almost all Hindus cremate their dead and then dispose of the ashes in the Ganges River. Other Indian religions, such as Jainism, Sikhism, and Buddhism, also practice cremation, which is seen as the best way to allow the spirit to disengage from the body. Among the Yanomami of South America, the dead were once cremated and the remains mixed with banana paste and then eaten.

Cremains can also be made into a variety of objects, which allows mourners to keep their loved ones near them. Ashes can be mixed with planting soil, placed into a stuffed animal, or mixed with dye and made into a portrait or even tattooed into the skin. You can even have cremains made into a pencil. The most well-known modern use of cremains is in memorial jewelry. A small amount of cremains can be encased inside of a locket or other tiny urn that can be worn as a necklace, or the ashes can be made into a diamond that can be worn in a ring or pendant. But in South Korea, over the past ten or so years, a new tradition has emerged in which ashes are turned into burial beads—small, smooth stones that look like river rocks.

Cremation has become extremely popular in South Korea in recent years, but especially since a 2000 law that mandates that all new burials must be dug up after sixty years to preserve space. South Koreans now cremate 60 percent of their dead, with only 30–40 percent being buried in a cemetery. With the rise in cremation came both old and new ways to deal with the cremains, from scattering the ashes, to burying them under a tree (where the ashes are wrapped in traditional Korean paper), to keeping them in an urn at home, to storing them in an ossuary niche. Cremation was also commonly practiced in ancient Korea, prior to the arrival of Confucianism from China in the fourth century (but especially after the fourteenth century), when Korea was still a largely Buddhist country. Under Buddhism, cremation was thought to aid the journey of the dead into paradise. After the rise of Confucianism, cremation was primarily reserved for those who had died a violent death.

Most Koreans still use public or private cemetery ossuaries, one of the oldest ways of storing ashes to house (and visit) loved ones' cremains; however, burial beads have emerged as the latest and most distinctively Korean way of storing those remains. Burial beads are produced in specially made machines that use extremely high temperatures to melt the ashes into small beads. These beads, which are usually a seafoam green in color, but can be black or pink as well, can be worn on a necklace, although that is not how they are normally used (unlike similar beads made from the ashes of dead pets, which are common in the United States and usually worn by the dead pet's owner). Instead, they are typically displayed in a bowl or other container. The process to produce the beads only takes about two hours, and the cost is in the hundreds of dollars.

The use of cremation instead of burial and the development of burial beads demonstrate a major change from the way that death has long been observed in Korea. Korea's traditional death practices were informed by a blend of religious traditions—including Confucianism (which teaches that deceased ancestors remain forever within the family and thus must be cared for in perpetuity), Buddhism (which teaches that the dead are eventually reborn into other lives), Shamanism, and, in recent years, Christianity.

In addition, death rites in South Korea in particular have been transformed by economic changes and, as mentioned earlier, demographic changes that have led to a lack of land for burial. Other changes have been urbanization and industrialization, both of which have, since the mid to late twentieth century, led to a separation of people from the graves of their family members, which also led to a decline in care for graves. This was a highly problematic situation, as Confucianism demands that the dead ancestors must be cared for.

These changes have been part of an overall modernization of the country, with the "inefficient" use of land for burials being seen as something premodern, irrational, and to be overcome. In fact, cremation, which under the Confucian system was thought of as a "second death" for the deceased, has been redefined today such that burial now carries the stigma and cremation is seen as environmentally and economically sound. Burial, on the other hand, is now reconceived by government officials and cremation proponents as dirty, old-fashioned, expensive, and wasteful. Finally, the fact that many South Koreans die in hospitals today—a stark contrast to the home as both the traditional site of death and funeral—has also changed funerary rites, as many hospitals now offer both funeral and cremation (but not burial) services.

Even though the burial beads represent a marked change from the funerary practices mandated by Confucianism, they also offer Koreans a modern way to keep close to their ancestors. For many urban South Koreans, maintaining the graves of their ancestors is becoming increasingly difficult, and the beads, which are typically kept at home, allow people to demonstrate their filial care to their family members.

See also: Mourner.

Further Reading

Horlyck, C., & Pettid, M. J. (2014). *Death, mourning, and the afterlife in Korea: Ancient to contemporary times*. University of Hawai'i Press.

Kastenbaum, R. (2001). *Death, society, and human experience* (7th ed.). Allyn & Bacon.

Prébin, É. (2012). Cremation's success in Korea: Old beliefs and renewed social distinctions. In N. Aveline-Dubach (Ed.), *The Invisible Population: The Place of the Dead in East Asian Megacities* (pp. 138–164). Lexington Books.

Car Jockey (Indonesia)

A car jockey is someone who is paid by private car drivers to ride with them so that the driver can ride in the country's carpool lanes. The job only emerged in 1992 and then ended in 2016, when a change in the law rendered the practice unnecessary.

Indonesia is a rapidly growing country, especially in the Jakarta region, the nation's largest city. In 2019, the population of the country was estimated at 270 million, with over 14 million of those living in Jakarta and 30 million living in the metropolitan region. Jakarta is the largest city in Southeast Asia and, according to a 2019 *USA Today* report, has a population density of 27,138 people per square mile (compared to New York City, the United States' most populous city, with a population density of 26,403 people per square mile). As the country has rapidly undergone development, more Indonesians are purchasing cars than the country's roads (most of which are quite narrow, having been built before the current explosion of vehicles) can comfortably handle. In addition, the density (and corresponding traffic) gets worse every day as millions more enter the city from the wider region for work. Consequently, the traffic entering Jakarta is terrible (it can take two to three hours to drive twenty-five miles from the suburbs into the city) as is traffic in the city itself.

One of the problems that Indonesia is facing is found in other older but rapidly developing cities and countries. The major cities were not built with cars in mind, nor were they built with the kinds of subway systems that other major cities have. In addition, owning a car is seen as a sign of status, so for those who can afford to buy a car, driving is far preferred over other means of transportation.

In 2003, to help alleviate the problem, city managers implemented a carpool policy that mandated that all drivers who wish to use the main streets in the central business district during business hours must travel with three or more people in the car. Drivers got around this rule by using car jockeys to make up the remaining passengers, which allowed them to drive into the city.

Each day, as millions of Jakartans went to work (by motorcycle, bus, train, motorcycle taxi, or private car), car jockeys went to work as well. In the morning, men, women (sometimes with young children, who were also counted as riders, in tow), and entire families lined up on the side of the road just outside of the "three-in-one" zone made up of carpool roads, where they would indicate with their hands that they were interested in a ride. Drivers who wanted to enter the city simply pulled over, negotiated a fee (usually around a dollar), and picked up as many jockeys as needed to meet the carpool minimum. The practice was illegal, as it allowed drivers to skirt the carpool rules, but the law was not regularly enforced. After entering the city, the car jockeys typically took a bus home. According to cultural anthropologist Rusdi Muchtar (see Onishi 2009), many commuters saw the use of car jockeys as an informal form of social security: they felt good that the fees (and often tips) that they paid were helping the poor to earn a living for their families.

The goal of the three-in-one zone, as in any city where high-occupancy lanes are used, is to reduce the number of cars traveling on those roads. If every car filled with a single commuter were replaced by a car filled with three commuters, that should, in principle, reduce the number of cars on the road by two-thirds. Because so many commuters picked up car jockeys, who did not otherwise need to travel into the city, the three-in-one zone did not appear to be working.

Ultimately, the carpool lanes were eliminated in 2016, leading to the evaporation of the car jockey position. However, according to a 2017 study (see Hanna et al. 2017), it turns out that even with the use of car jockeys, the carpool lanes did, in fact, reduce traffic. The authors, who compared traffic delays before and after the law was changed, found that traffic worsened considerably immediately after the three-in-one zone was discontinued.

See also: Car Watchman; License Plate Blocker.

Further Reading

Hanna, R., Kreindler, G., & Olken, B. A. (2017). Citywide effects of high-occupancy vehicle restrictions: Evidence from "three-in-one" in Jakarta. *Science, 357*(6346), 89–93.

Lee, D. (2015). Absolute traffic: Infrastructural aptitude in urban Indonesia. *International Journal of Urban and Regional Research, 39*(2), 234–250.

Onishi, N. (2009, May 12). Finding a detour to earn a living in Indonesian traffic jams. *New York Times.* https://www.nytimes.com/2009/05/13/world/asia/13indo.html.

Car Watchman (Costa Rica)

A car watchman, or watcher, is a person who is paid to watch someone's parked car. In Spanish, they are called *cuidacarros* (from the Spanish *cuidar*, "to take care of," and *carro*, "car") or *guachiman* (from the English word *watchman*).

Costa Rica is the most popular country in Central America for international tourism, having almost three million visitors—mostly from the United States—in 2016. Many tourists visit the country to participate in one of the many ecotourism opportunities; Costa Rica has more national parks and protected natural areas than any other nation on earth, and visitors eagerly arrive to see sloths, monkeys, tapirs, turtles, and other animals. Costa Rica is also an attractive country to visit because it has one of the highest standards of living in Latin America, making tourists feel better about traveling there. (Medical tourism is also growing in the country, as is sex tourism.) It is also a relatively safe country, with a murder rate of 11.7 per 100,000 people (as of 2018). This compares favorably to other Latin American countries, such as Mexico (with a murder rate of 25.8 per 100,000), Jamaica (47 per 100,000) and Venezuela (81.4 per 100,000). (See Dalby and Carranza 2019.) In comparison, there are around 5 murders per 100,000 people in the United States.

However, there is crime, and tourists in particular worry about crimes that target them, which include theft, assault, rape, and murder. One area where tourists can protect themselves from crime is through the use of car watchers.

Car watchers, or watchmen, work in the country's major cities, especially in the nation's capital of San José. They approach cars (often targeting tourists) and typically first offer their assistance to help the driver find a spot, or even park, after which they offer to watch the car for a fee. The fee is typically $1 or less, and by paying it, the tourist can feel confident that the car will not be broken into or stolen.

Car watchers offer their services to people who have parked on the street as well as to those who have parked in parking lots. In the latter case, tourists are often confused because they do not realize that if they pay the watcher, they must also pay the fee to park in the parking lot. In general, many tourists think that paying a stranger to watch their car is a scam, but it is common in many other places, such as Brazil. (Paying a person while parking, however, will often result in the watcher simply taking the money and leaving; that is why it is recommended that watchers be paid after the driver has returned to the car.) Sometimes the driver does not even know that his or her car has been watched until returning to find a watcher asking for a fee. Some watchers will give the driver a small ticket that lists the amount of the fee that is being requested. Many American expatriates who live in Costa Rica see paying watchmen as part of their daily living expenses, as choosing not to pay could result in the car being damaged or stolen.

Because car watchers are independent contractors, and there is no agency that regulates where each car watcher can work, they work out among themselves which streets and parking lots "belong" to a certain watchman to cut down on competition and conflict. Some cities provide training to their local watchmen to ensure that they abide by the laws and do not threaten tourists; the cities of Cartago and Coronado even provide identification cards for watchmen to carry, giving them more legitimacy. Other than this, there is no training or requirements for the job.

See also: Car Jockey; License Plate Blocker.

Further Reading

Dalby, C., & Carranza, C. (2019). InSight Crime's 2018 homicide round-up. *InSight Crime.* https://www.insightcrime.org/news/analysis/insight-crime-2018-homicide -roundup.

Wallerstein, C. (2010). *Culture shock! Costa Rica: A survival guide to customs and etiquette.* Marshall Cavendish International Asia Pte Ltd.

Caricature Artist (Global)

A caricature artist is a person who draws caricatures for a living. Caricatures are simple drawings that are intended to represent an individual by highlighting or exaggerating one or more of the person's distinctive physical traits, such as big ears, a prominent nose, bushy eyebrows, wild hair, or buggy eyes. While today's caricature artists can be found working on boardwalks or at carnivals or amusement parks, they have primarily been used as a form of political commentary and are the source of the modern political cartoon.

The use of caricature as a form of political commentary developed in London in the eighteenth century, although artists had been representing people with exaggerated qualities for some time before that. For example, Leonardo da Vinci enjoyed drawing people he saw who had unusual heads or faces and drew them in such a way as to emphasize their unique physical features. Other artists, such as Monet and Daumier, also drew such portraits. Caricatures were used as an entertaining parlor game by the royal classes of France and Italy during the seventeenth century, but in the middle of the eighteenth century,

A caricature artist at work. (Jurby Jumawan/ Dreamstime.com)

English artists such as James Gillray began using caricatures to satirize political figures and the English royal family. This practice soon spread to the rest of Europe and ultimately the Americas and the rest of the world.

Caricatures, as they became used in eighteenth-century England, became a form of "unmasking," whereby the artist, through highlighting a few key features of the subject, was able to make the internal character of the subject visible on the face. By highlighting a person's large nose or bushy eyebrows, a talented caricature artist can shed some light on the personality and temperament of the subject. The art form is related in part to the science of physiognomy, which is the science of reading character traits from facial features. The word itself was first used by the seventeenth-century philosopher Thomas Browne, who was a proponent of physiognomy. Interestingly, while da Vinci did draw what we would consider to be caricatures, he was not a proponent of physiognomy. Other artists, on the other hand, such as the eighteenth-century portraitist Joseph Ducreux, used physiognomy in their work.

It is not surprising that caricatures emerged during the rise of Democratic movements in Europe and around the world; the people were clamoring to understand more about the politicians who were often deciding their fate. Through distortion of the physical, the internal is supposedly revealed. Most commonly, political caricatures were negative and often grotesque; they were created to high-light the moral failings of the powerful, and the nose, lips, eyebrows, and jaws could be used to create portraits of greed, lust, sloth, or avarice. Caricatures and the new art of political cartoons became an effective way to reveal the supposed character or authentic self of politicians, but for the readers of these images, they became an important weapon to attack the wealthy, politicians, celebrities, and even an entire nation or belief system.

For example, Napoleon Bonaparte was glorified in official portraits, but royal-ists used caricature to lampoon his character and to challenge his legitimacy as emperor. After Napoleon's reign, later in the nineteenth century, Charles Philipon, an artist and the owner of *La Caricature* magazine, was repeatedly jailed for his caricatures of King Louis-Philippe of France, whom he represented as a pear. Philipon's work became so popular that the pear ultimately became the most long-lasting symbol of Louis-Philippe and his regime. Another result was that France passed a law banning political caricatures.

In the United States, political caricatures had a long-lasting impact as well; cartoonist Thomas Nast's images shed light on, and ultimately helped bring down, the corruption of New York City's Tammany Hall political machine. Nast also cre-ated the Republican elephant and the Democratic donkey, two of the most iconic political images in the United States.

Caricatures quickly became harnessed to racial ideologies in Europe and espe-cially the United States. In the eighteenth, nineteenth, and twentieth centuries, artists have used caricatures to build on racial and ethnic stereotyping and to cre-ate new stereotypes, many of which have had long-lasting repercussions. For instance, caricatures of African Americans were common in American newspa-pers from the antebellum era through Jim Crow and into the civil rights era. Those caricatures drew on a number of common stereotypes about African Americans, featuring wooly hair, inky black skin, grotesque lips, and bulging white eyes. They also often included watermelons, alligators, and other items associated with blacks in the popular imagination. Pickaninnies, Uncle Toms, mammies, and Sambos were all variations on this theme, combining distorted imagery with ste-reotypical behavior patterns, and all served to portray blacks in a negative light and either support the institution of slavery or, in the postwar era, maintain racial segregation.

Other racial groups have also been visually stereotyped in this way. Asian Americans, for instance, whether Chinese, Japanese, or from other countries, are usually represented with two primary physical traits: large buckteeth and thick glasses. While it is not common to see such images used today, they were popular for so long that they are firmly cemented in the American imagination.

With the election of the first African American president, we have seen a resur-gence of racially charged caricatures. Although Barack Obama is most often represented with a super skinny neck and big ears—both features of the former president—he is also represented with classic racial stereotypes associated with blacks, such as big lips; he is also occasionally represented as a monkey or ape. Political cartoons are supposed to be provocative, and even offensive, but cartoon-ists tread a fine line between being provocative and openly racist. Racist individuals and organizations, on the other hand, have no qualms about this and openly create and share such racist material.

Today, the use of caricatures to satirize politicians, the wealthy, and celebrities is common around the world and is found in all countries where there is a free press. However, in recent years, there has been a conflict between the democratic notion of freedom of the press and cultural and religious ideals about how far caricature should go. The most inflammatory example of this controversy occurred in 2005 when the Danish newspaper *Jyllands-Posten* published a number of cartoons in which Muhammad was represented as a form of political commentary about the fear in many Western nations about criticizing Islam. Much of the Muslim world erupted in protests; in Islam (especially among Sunnis) depictions of Muhammad are said to be prohibited, and the images were perceived as being disrespectful in the way that the Prophet was treated; in one cartoon, for instance, he was represented as a dog, and in others, he was holding bomb. Many newspapers refused to reprint the images, but others chose to do so, citing freedom of expression as an important democratic concept; they refused to censor themselves to appease a religious group. Ultimately, dozens of people were killed in the protests, and a number of death threats were issued against the cartoonists and those responsible for publishing, or republishing, the images.

Becoming a caricature artist, like any other artist, requires natural artistic talent as well as training. Having artistic talent—in particular, the ability to draw—is critical, but on top of that, the caricature artist must quickly assess the overall appearance of a person so that, within a relatively short period of time, he or she can create a portrait that both looks like that person and also conveys something of the personality or essence of the person. That is what makes a good caricature. In addition, caricature artists use humor in their portraits, whether they are creating a drawing for a fairgoer or are creating a political cartoon for the editorial page of the *New York Times*. And they must do this quickly (often in under five minutes!) and as efficiently as possible. Finally, a good caricaturist must develop his or her own distinctive style. For what seems like a simple line portrait, creating a caricature is actually quite a difficult task.

Caricature artists, like other artists, may go to school for specialized art training or be primarily self-taught. To work as an editorial cartoonist, however, an art degree is generally required. (The Center for Cartoon Studies offers specialized certificates, workshops, and a master of fine arts [MFA] degree for artists who want to specialize in cartoons.) More important than a degree, however, is experience. Caricature artists, like all artists, create a portfolio that can be viewed by potential employers or those who would like to commission a portrait.

Caricatures are still heavily used by political and editorial cartoonists, who use easy-to-recognize caricatures of public figures to provide a commentary on social, cultural, or political events.

In addition, freelance caricature artists hire themselves out to work at parties, fairs, corporate events, and other public and private events, where they offer their services for a fee. In some events, the artist will be paid for his or her work at the event (with rates being in the ballpark of $100–$200 per hour), or they may instead charge per portrait, with rates starting at about $20 per portrait. In addition, many freelance artists now offer their services online; anyone can purchase a caricature of a person or even a pet from countless artists through Etsy, dedicated caricature websites, or WhataPortrait.

See also: Graffiti Artist.

Further Reading

McPhee, C. C., Orenstein, N. M., & Orenstein, N. (2011). *Infinite jest: Caricature and satire from Leonardo to Levine.* Metropolitan Museum of Art.
Richmond, T. (2011). *The mad art of caricature: A serious guide to drawing funny faces.* Deadline Demon Publishing.

Chicken Sexer (Japan, Great Britain, United States)

A chicken sexer is an agricultural worker who determines the sex of baby chicks in a commercial hatchery for the egg industry.

Chickens were first domesticated in South and Southeast Asia for meat and for eggs about eight thousand years ago. For thousands of years, and indeed for most of the chicken's history with humans, chickens were raised in a relatively simple manner, on family farms, where they were raised with other animals large and small. They were controlled (if they were controlled at all) in a penned-in area, and their eggs were collected by the women or children who were largely responsible for the care of small animals. Eventually, they were slaughtered for meat. There was no distinction between a "meat" chicken and an egg-laying chicken. Even as late as the early twentieth century, chickens were still being raised on family farms with very little human intervention over their lives (until their deaths, that is).

Things were different in the ancient classical world, however. We know that the ancient Egyptians invented an incubator to raise chicks, which freed up hens to lay more eggs, and Romans learned that by castrating roosters, the animals would become fatter and thus the meat better tasting; they also fattened chickens by feeding them fattening foods. The Romans also developed large commercial farms where they raised chickens in greater numbers to feed the Roman Empire. In fact, the Romans loved chicken so much that a law was passed in the second century BCE that limited the number of chickens to be consumed at one per meal; the law further stated that the chickens could not have been overfed prior to slaughter.

In the twentieth-century United States, however, a series of changes emerged that changed the way that chickens (as well as other farmed animals) are raised, slaughtered, and consumed. The first major innovation with respect to modernizing livestock production in the United States was the expansion of the railroad into the South and West and the development of the refrigerated railroad car. The expansion of the railroad and the refrigerated railcar allowed locally produced eggs and meat to be transported from agricultural communities to markets farther away, increasing meat consumption among Americans.

Besides the railroad, the single greatest development with respect to modern animal-raising techniques in the early part of the twentieth century was the introduction of methods drawn from a rapidly industrializing Western world, which can be summed up as large-scale, centralized production and intensive animal rearing. This concentrated animals into small spaces and controlled food, water, and temperatures; enabled easier health monitoring; and controlled "unnecessary" and "inefficient" animal movements. With this step, chicken production became more efficient and much less expensive, and in the United States, chicken moved from a luxury meat to one of the least expensive meats.

Chickens are now housed in large facilities known as concentrated (or confined) animal feeding operations (CAFOs), where all aspects of the animals' lives are completely controlled and human-made: there is no outside air, no dirt, no sunlight, and no capacity for natural movement or activities such as grooming, play, exercise, unaided reproduction, or the like. Ironically, the same social behaviors that allowed these animals to be domesticated in the first place are eliminated because the animals' social structure must be subverted in favor of total confinement, either alone or crowded together into nonkin groupings, thus the importance of practices such as debeaking to keep down aggression.

Chickens are now separated by the final product that will be consumed; egg-laying chickens (layers) and meat-producing chickens (broilers) are raised in different situations. Laying hens, nearly three hundred million of whom are raised and slaughtered in the United States every year, experience the most extreme example of not just intensive confinement but complete control over the animals' lives. Over 90 percent of eggs worldwide are now produced in "battery" conditions, where tightly packed and stacked cages of birds are kept in a large facility with light, temperature, food, and water tightly controlled and a steady stream of antibiotics is used to keep the birds healthy. This phenomenon developed in the 1920s but has accelerated in the last thirty years. This system is so efficient that one person can care for as many as thirty thousand birds. Broiler chickens are kept in a similar environment, but because they are slaughtered much earlier than layers (at six to seven weeks of age as opposed to a year or two), the effects on their bodies from this kind of confinement are lessened.

For egg-laying hens, life begins in commercial hatcheries that produce millions of chicks. Once the eggs hatch, chicken sexers sort the chicks, collecting the females for shipment to egg producers. Because the egg industry has no use for male chicks, they are killed almost immediately; the hatcheries usually gas them, grind them up, or simply discard them in dumpsters to suffocate or dehydrate. It is estimated that six billion newborn male chicks are killed and discarded every year around the world.

Smaller hatcheries and family farms that cannot afford to hire a chicken sexer must wait until the chicks have reached adolescence, when some of the secondary sex characteristics appear; males, for example, develop a longer comb than females, and females' tails are longer. Males and females will begin to show behavioral differences as well, with males becoming more aggressive than females. Waiting to sex a chick has considerable disadvantages, as the farmer is spending money feeding chicks who will not be able to produce eggs and then the chicks must be killed while they are no longer day-old babies.

After they are hatched, baby birds are dropped onto a conveyor belt that moves past the chicken sexers, or sorters. They quickly grab each chick and try to determine whether the chick is a male (a cockerel) or a female (a pullet). They do this through a variety of means: some hatcheries train their chicken sexers to look for the subtle color differences between males and females in certain crossbreeds of chickens. Some breeds have greater sexual dimorphism than others, with different features that show up on males or females, such as feather shape and length; hatcheries that use this method specifically breed their chickens to develop these feather differences. Another common method is vent sexing, in which the sexer picks up a chick, turns the chick upside down, and squeezes open the anal vent, releasing a small amount of feces, to see the genital organ. All of these methods are not 100 percent foolproof, and sometimes male chicks get placed with the females.

The chicken sexer has a monotonous job. The sexer either stands or sits in front of the conveyor belt and picks up and examines thousands of chicks per shift; good sexers can sex a thousand chicks an hour. Some are paid with a salary, and others are paid piecemeal, per sexed chick.

Unless the hatchery uses specially bred chickens to produce chicks that are visually distinct, the job of chick sexer is a difficult one and involves years of training to reach an expert level. But many people who take the job do not stay long enough to gain this level of expertise, so hatcheries are continuously looking to hire new sexers.

The art, or skill (depending on who is asked), of vent sexing was developed in Japan in the 1920s, when a Japanese scientist realized that by inspecting the vent of a chick, one could accurately determine the sex. The first (and last) of its kind chick-sexing school, the Zen-Nippon Chick Sexing School, trained novice sexers by having them work with master sexers for a two-year course. In traditional Japanese training, intuition is emphasized as well as the ability to internalize the hundreds of tiny differences in chick vent shapes so as to know, in less than a second, which ones are which. In the 1930s, Japanese trainers began teaching non-Japanese how to sex chicks, first in Great Britain and then in the United States. The first chick-sexing school in the United States, the American Chick Sexing Association, was founded in 1938 and eventually came to be dominated by Japanese American sexers who taught a new generation of American workers.

Chick sexers, in the heyday of the industry in the mid–twentieth century, were once independent contractors who hired themselves out to different hatcheries, but they now work for the hatcheries. The mystique of the job has given way in recent years to the job being seen as no more than the butt of jokes, as specially bred chickens are produced that allow untrained sexers to determine the sex based on color or feather differences, and as the poultry industry, like the meat industry, is seen very differently to modern eyes than it once was.

The job of the chicken sexer, and the slaughter of millions of male chicks per year, may soon end. The U.S. egg industry hopes to have in place a method to determine the sex of a chick while it is still in the egg, which would allow for male eggs to be diverted into the commercial egg market, eliminating the need to kill male chicks. However, it is unknown how those eggs will be sexed or whether specialized individuals will be needed for that process.

See also: Geoduck Farmer; Insect Farmer.

Further Reading

Clinton, M., Haines, L., Belloir, B., & McBride, D. (2001). Sexing chick embryos: A rapid and simple protocol. *British Poultry Science, 42*(1), 134–138.

Horsey, R. (2002). *The art of chicken sexing* (University College London Working Papers in Linguistics No. 14).

Weissmann, A., Reitemeier, S., Hahn, A., Gottschalk, J., & Einspanier, A. (2013). Sexing domestic chicken before hatch: A new method for in ovo gender identification. *Theriogenology, 80*(3), 199–205.

Competitive Eater (United States)

A competitive eater is a person who makes a living by participating in eating competitions. Competitive eating contests have been part of rural fairs, festivals, and other events for many years. In addition, restaurants will often host their own contests, in which they invite the public to try to eat a specific, very large food item. Usually, the person who succeeds in eating the food is rewarded by not having to pay for the food and perhaps winning the right to have his or her photo displayed at the restaurant.

It was not until Nathan's Hot Dog Eating Contest became popular in the 1990s that the activity exploded in popularity, leading to not only a variety of competitive eating contests around the world but also the rise of professional eaters. No one knows when Nathan's, a hot dog stand on Coney Island, began hosting hot dog eating contests on Independence Day (Nathan's claims it began in 1916, the year the hot dog stand first opened, but this story was made up for publicity), but the first recorded event was held in 1972. By the 1990s, the contest was becoming well known, and by the 2000s, a handful of regular winners, such as Takeru Kobayashi and Joey Chestnut, began to develop international fame, helping to popularize competitive eating as a sport. Competitive eating is considered a sport today, and professional eaters are represented by such organizations as Major League Eating, which represents the big stars in the field, such as Kobayashi.

At a competitive eating event, the competitors stand in front of a table piled with the foods that they will be eating—hot dogs, waffles, matzo balls, or even deep-fried asparagus. There is also water available, which many eaters use to make the food go down easier. The food is either weighed beforehand (chicken wings), counted (hot dogs), or measured by volume (chili). The winner is determined by counting what is left, weighing the remains of the food, or determining the volume of the food remaining. (Some eaters specialize in certain kinds of contests, as training differs depending on whether the food is countable, must be weighed, or is primarily liquid and must be measured by volume. Others specialize in a type of food, with only certain eaters participating in spicy food contests.)

Most events are timed, with participants being judged strictly on how many twinkies, burritos, or other foods that they can consume in the amount of time while following the contest rules (such as no vomiting). If there is food remaining in the contestant's mouth when time is called, they are permitted to swallow it.

A young man competes in a hot dog eating contest. (Russ Ensley/Dreamstime.com)

(Many contestants exploit this rule by "chipmunking," which means stuffing as much food as possible into one's mouth in the seconds before time is called and swallowing it afterward.) Contest times usually range from three to fifteen minutes. An emcee provides commentary, calls out times, and keeps the crowd excited throughout the competition, and a panel of judges ensures that the rules have been adhered to and certifies the winner.

The biggest contests are televised live; ESPN aired its first competitive eating contest, the Nathan's event, in 2004. When events like this are televised, the competitions are treated just like any other sport, with play-by-play announcements and color commentators.

To be a competitive eater, it is not simply a matter of having a big appetite. (And it does not help to be fat; the top competitive eaters come in all body shapes and sizes, but most are on the thinner side.) While the only real requirement to participate in most contests is to be eighteen, there is more to competitive eating than just eating.

Eaters train for competitions in different ways: by eating larger and larger amounts of food (or water) to stretch the stomach, eating one large meal per day, or chewing gum to build jaw muscles. Just prior to an event, many competitors restrict their diet to liquids. They also practice eating the food that will be featured at their next event, as the technique for consuming hot dogs is very different from the technique for eating bowls of mayonnaise, including holding their own time trials. (Practicing at home can be dangerous, however, as there are no medical professionals available in case the eater begins to choke.) Every competitive eater must develop control over his or her gag reflex; vomiting during an event means automatic disqualification. Finally, competitive eaters must also control their breathing so that it does not get in the way of eating.

Each eater also has his or her own technique for consuming the most food in the shortest amount of time. Kobayashi, for example, developed a method for eating hot dogs quickly: he broke each hot dog in half so that it could fit into his mouth more easily, eating both halves together, and then dipped the bun into water and stuffed it into his mouth whole. This became known as the "Solomon Method," and is sometimes also called "Japanesing." Some big stars have their own trainers to help them with both training and technique.

The sport has its own governing body that sanctions, regulates, hosts, and markets professional eating events. Founded in 1997 as the International Federation of Competitive Eating and now known as Major League Eating (MLE), it hosts dozens of events per year, both in the United States and internationally, including its flagship event, Nathan's contest. MLE not only host events but also acts as the main professional league in the sport today, representing the top competitive eaters. To participate in an MLE event, eaters must sign a contract stipulating that they will not participate in non-MLE events, which led to the sport's founding star, Kobayashi, ending his participation in the Nathan's event in 2010.

Competitive eaters earn money by winning contests, which can pay hundreds or thousands of dollars; the winner of the Nathan's contest wins $10,000. But most competitors will never earn enough to make a real living. Competitive eating may sound easy, but it is difficult to reach the level of accomplishments and fame that the leading eaters have. Most eaters start by attending local non-MLE contests, where they can determine their capacity and whether they have what it takes to be a professional eater. Once they have graduated to the big MLE-sanctioned events, they can start to make money, but now they will be competing against the leaders in the sport. There are only so many events per year, so the chances of most eaters earning enough to survive is slim. (It has been estimated that Joey Chestnut, the current top-ranked eater in the world, has earned $800,000 throughout his career since 2004.)

The job can be dangerous; a half dozen people have died from choking during competitive eating competitions over the last decade, and every competitive eater is at risk for problems such as stomach perforation and ulcers. In addition, some eaters will purge immediately after a contest; repeated vomiting can result in damage to the teeth and esophagus. Even without these health risks, competitive eating is painful. Like other athletes, eaters learn to push through the pain while training and competing.

See also: Food Taster.

Further Reading

Fagone, J. (2006). *Horsemen of the esophagus: Competitive eating and the big fat American dream.* Crown Books.

Johnson, A. R. (2011). The magic metabolisms of competitive eating. In P. Williams-Forson & C. Counihan (Eds.), *Taking food public: Redefining foodways in a changing world* (pp. 279–292). Routledge.

Nerz, R. (2006). *Eat this book: A year of gorging and glory on the competitive eating circuit.* St. Martin's Griffin.

Corporate Anthropologist (United States)

A corporate anthropologist, or business anthropologist, is an applied anthropologist who works for a corporation or who acts as a consultant, offering his or her services to corporations. They work in a variety of industries, including health

care, technology, the automotive industry, the travel industry, and the retail industry, among others.

Anthropology is the study of humanity. It is one of the social sciences and is
distinguished from other disciplines because of its holistic four-field approach.
Archaeological anthropology, one of the subfields, for example, studies past cultures through an analysis of the material remains of those cultures. Biological, or
physical, anthropology looks at our species from the perspective of biology and
asks questions such as these: How did humans evolve? What is the nature of the
biological diversity within the species? Linguistic anthropology, the third of the
subfields, is devoted to an understanding of language within particular cultural
and social contexts. Finally, cultural anthropology is the study of living human
cultures, especially through the use of ethnography, the field's key method.

Most anthropologists work in an academic setting, conducting research, teaching, and writing. But there is also a fifth subfield of anthropology, known as
applied anthropology, which involves anthropologists from the main four subfields
working outside of academia in industry, government, the nonprofit world, or
another setting.

Corporate anthropologists are people trained in cultural anthropology who do
applied work in the business world. They use the methods, theories, and perspectives of cultural anthropology to answer questions about how employees utilize
technology, how consumers identify with brands, and how corporate culture may
hinder productivity. Since the late twentieth century, corporate anthropology has
become an important new career path for anthropologists.

Corporate anthropologists use ethnography, or participant observation, to study
and understand the corporate world. Participant observation involves carefully
and systematically observing a social situation while also participating in that
environment to understand the social and cultural dynamics. Traditionally, anthropologists lived with the community that they studied, but in the corporate world,
they simply insert themselves into the culture of the corporation, integrating
themselves as much as possible into that world to better understand it as both an
outsider and, ideally, as an insider.

Corporate anthropologists, just like their colleagues working in other field sites,
interview subjects to try to get to an understanding of how and why people do
what they do. But the goal is different because a corporate anthropologist, unlike
other anthropologists, is hired by the corporation to, typically, improve efficiency
among its employees. (Other companies are seeking to improve their organizational culture, but creating a positive work environment for employees is often
secondary to the goal of improving productivity.) That changes the role of the
anthropologist from his or her traditional role, which did not involve actively
intervening in the lives of subjects.

Where an anthropologist will typically spend a minimum of a year in the field
to try to understand the culture being studied, corporate anthropologists will work
in a shorter timeframe. (Most companies will not want to wait that long to see
results.)

So what does an anthropologist working within a corporate environment do?
Anthropologists study the behaviors and practices of those in a business setting as

well as their values and beliefs. It is not enough to know that someone does something in a certain way. It is also important to know why they behave the way that they do. Behaviors are visible and observable. But the values and beliefs that underlie those behaviors are not. Anthropologists are specially trained to get at these invisible, but important, aspects of culture.

A cultural anthropologist's basic unit of analysis is culture. Every organization has its own organizational or corporate culture, which is often invisible to employers and employees alike, as it is difficult to detect the workings of culture when we are a part of it. An anthropologist, on the other hand, by focusing on behavior patterns among employees, can see elements of the corporate culture emerging and can offer suggestions for how to improve any negative aspects of that culture. For instance, anthropologists, and especially those with a background in gender anthropology, can see whether a particular work environment is female friendly. Are management practices organized in such a way that all employees have the same opportunities, or are promotions tied to employees, for example, socializing after work in such a way that mothers cannot participate? Even if a corporation has tried to ensure that its written policies promote equality in the workplace, there could still be elements of the corporate culture that work against it.

Corporate anthropologists are an important part of market research today. Just as corporations use a variety of professionals to evaluate how consumers use their products, anthropologists will not only interview users but also observe them working with those products. Do employees use the product as it was intended, are they using it differently because the instructions are hard to understand, or does the product not work the way that it should? The anthropologist can make recommendations to the company that produced the product on improving it to better meet real-world working conditions.

A corporate anthropologist can also make recommendations with respect to communication within the company. All cultural anthropologists have at least some training in linguistics, so they have skills to understand the communication styles within a company and how those play into social relationships. Anthropologists can also participate in crafting advertising messages that reach consumers the way that the company intended; sometimes a lack of awareness about the beliefs and values of the targeted consumer can result in an advertising campaign that offends customers.

Like anyone who wants to work in anthropology, an advanced degree is required. Most working anthropologists, either in academia or in the applied world, have a PhD, but a master's degree is often adequate. (Applied archaeologists, for example, may find work with a master's degree, and most community colleges do not require PhDs for their teachers.) However, many universities do not offer courses in corporate anthropology, and some do not even offer courses in applied anthropology. So much of the learning in this relatively new field happens in the field.

Another important reason for having a corporate anthropologist on staff is to help companies that have or want to develop a global reach. Companies that work with international partners or who sell their products internationally have a vested interest in understanding how to best communicate with, work with, or appeal to international markets. Anthropologists can provide information to management to help them develop culturally sensitive methods of reaching out to foreign markets and partners.

Corporate anthropology is a growth field, especially in the technology sector, where the major companies have their own in-house anthropologists. As technology continues to transform our lives, anthropologists can help to make sense of this and point to new directions in product development.

Salaries for corporate anthropologists are determined by a number of factors, including the anthropologist's degree and years of experience and the environment in which he or she works. The salary range can start as low as $30,000 and go as high as $100,000 per year.

See also: Anthrozoologist.

Further Reading
Denny, R. M., & Sunderland, P. L. (Eds.). (2016). *Handbook of anthropology in business.* Routledge.
Jordan, A. T. (2012). *Business anthropology.* Waveland Press.

Crime Scene Cleaner (United States, Canada, Australia, Great Britain)

A crime scene cleaner is a person who cleans up crime scenes or scenes where someone has died alone. Crime scene cleaning is also known as bioremediation, biohazard remediation, or trauma scene restoration. Crime scene cleaners are hired by victims or their loved ones, property managers, business owners, and those who have experienced either a dead body or traumatic injury on their property.

If a person has been a victim of a crime or has a loved one who has been a victim of a crime, there are countless traumas and stressors that may affect that person—especially if the crime was a violent one, and especially if the crime was murder. Victims and their loved ones may experience physical trauma, emotional pain, or loss of income and property, and many undergo victimization all over again as they move through the criminal justice system, which may or may not offer them any closure for the crime. They may be worried about their physical safety in the aftermath of the crime, and besides medical attention, they may need counseling or mental health care. They may be seeking compensation from the perpetrator of the crime. All of this is stressful for the victim and the people around him or her. What many crime victims and their family and friends do not anticipate, on top of the other forms of trauma, is having to clean up the scene of the crime. (In fact, many people think that this is the police's responsibility.) This becomes especially difficult if the crime involves the death of the victim.

When someone has been murdered or a person has committed suicide, the body will begin to decompose. In addition, the body of a person who has died alone and whose body has been left there unnoticed will also undergo decomposition. Decomposition begins just a few minutes after death; the internal organs begin to break down, and the process accelerates over the next few days. In just a few days after death, depending on the environment in which the body has lain, fluids will begin to leak from the body. Within a week, organs, skin, and muscles will liquefy, and the body will become infested with insects. Finally, if a person has been murdered, has committed suicide, or has even experienced a serious accident or injury, there may also be blood and bodily tissue at the scene. All the fluids that have escaped the body will be released into the environment in which the body was found. If the body is indoors, the flooring under the body may be ruined, and the underlying floor may be damaged as well.

Cleaning up a scene like this unpleasant, but it is also traumatic for the victim or victim's family. It is also traumatic when a person has died away from home— at a business or other public space. In these cases, the owner or manager of the scene of the death is responsible for cleaning the scene. On top of this, cleaning up a crime scene can be hazardous as well. For all these reasons, crime scene cleaners emerged as a new industry in the 1990s, and by 2012, it was a $350 million industry in the United States.

Crime scene cleaners are not just professional cleaners. Cleaning a crime scene, the scene of an unattended death, or the scene of a bloody death or accident involves more than just the cleaning up of bodily fluids (blood, semen, vaginal secretions, vomit, and other fluids can also contain blood-borne pathogens). It also involves decontamination and disinfection because the fluids (and any materials exposed to those fluids) could potentially be infected with HIV, hepatitis, or other serious infectious agents, such as Ebola. The cleaner may be working in a home, a hotel room, or a vehicle, but he or she must be prepared for any type of situation.

Once the first responders have handled the scene of the crime or death, the owner or manager of the scene can hire a crime scene cleaner to take care of the cleanup. Crime scene cleanup involves first finding every location at the scene where blood, other fluids, or tissue have made contact, as sometimes these areas can be small or hard to detect. (Most companies use a hydrogen peroxide–based product that foams when it comes in contact with blood.) Each substance requires a different cleaning product; blood requires different products than brain matter,

---

Scullery Maid

A scullery maid was a member of the domestic staff of a manor house who was responsible for washing dishes, assisting the cook, and doing other jobs as assigned. Scullery maids, who were typically young women or girls, were found in large, wealthy households in Great Britain and the United States from the early nineteenth through the early twentieth centuries. Scullery maids also worked in public restaurants, teahouses, and boardinghouses. The scullery maid was often the lowest, or among the lowest, of the household servants. She woke up before everyone else and typically went to bed after everyone else. She was responsible for lighting the fires first thing in the morning, stoking the kitchen fires, boiling water, cleaning the "downstairs" areas of the house where the servants lived and worked, emptying female servants' chamber pots, prepping for meals, and fetching things for other servants. The work was terribly hard and the pay low, but some scullery maids were promoted to higher-ranked jobs, such as maid, cook, or housekeeper.

Source: Meldrum, T. (2014). *Domestic service and gender, 1660–1750: Life and work in the London household.* Routledge.

for example. The cleaners have to ensure no cross contamination occurs between the scene of the crime or death and the rest of the property. Once the cleaning has been completed, the scene must be disinfected and deodorized using a variety of products.

Cleaners may have to destroy property as well; it is not uncommon for a portion of flooring to have to be cut away and replaced with fresh flooring, and when a person dies in bed, the mattress and bedding will typically have to be tossed out. If a person dies in a bathtub, part of the plumbing system may need to be dismantled to fully remove the tissues and fluids. Anything that needs to be disposed of must be handled properly; a bloody mattress cannot simply be put out for curbside trash pickup. After the process has been completed, many companies offer property managers who need to rent or sell the property to new tenants a certificate that demonstrates that the property has not only been cleaned but also deodorized and disinfected and is now safe for new people to occupy it.

The tools of the trade include the same types of cleaning products used by janitors and house cleaners—mops, buckets, and sponges—plus scrapers, shovels and other implements as well as highly specific medical- or industrial-grade products for removing all traces of bodily fluids from the scene. In addition, cleaners will often utilize machines for controlling odor and moving the air around in a confined space.

If someone died alone and the body was not found for some time, there may also be a deceased pet or one that was left unattended. Therefore, the scene may also be contaminated by pet urine or the body of the dead pet.

Even though most people who know about this profession continue to call it crime scene cleanup—in part because of the publicity the job has received through the television show *Grim Sweepers* or the 2008 film *Sunshine Cleaning*—crime scene cleanup is not the major source of work. In fact, unattended (accidental or natural) deaths and suicides make up the bulk of a crime scene cleaner's work.

Cleaners must be trained (usually by the company that hires them) and should ideally be certified and licensed. Because they are in contact with potentially dangerous substances, cleaners should undergo training in blood-borne pathogens, hazard assessment, the use of protective equipment, and the disposal of medical and hazardous waste products (which is usually outsourced to a medical or hazardous waste disposal company), and they must learn how to use the right chemicals for each substance. Companies must also hold permits to dispose of (usually through incineration) or transport hazardous waste. Many companies will stage crime scenes, using theatrical blood or animal blood, to teach their employees the process of cleanup and decontamination.

In the United States, crime scene cleaners must abide by a host of state and federal regulations through such agencies as the Occupational Safety and Health Administration (OSHA) and the Environmental Protection Agency (EPA). Other countries that regulate crime scene cleaners, such as Australia, Canada, and the United Kingdom, have similar governmental agencies that provide oversight and regulations for the industry.

In addition to the training required, crime scene cleaners need to have the ability to work in environments that most people would avoid. Even though they are protected with biohazard suits, gloves, face masks, and sometimes respirators, they are still exposing themselves to substances that are gross, smelly, and often dangerous. They need to have physical stamina, as the job can be taxing, and they must be trustworthy because they are often working in private homes. They also need emotional stamina, as they will be dealing with situations that most people spend their lives avoiding. A good crime scene cleaner must also be compassionate. Their customers are dealing with a stressful situation, and many of them are grieving as well. Many crime scene cleaners come into the field with a background in criminal justice or in the medical field. This type of background, in which the employee has already been exposed to death, can make the job easier.

The costs for cleanup vary tremendously, based on the size and complexity of the scene, the amount and types of hazardous material, and the amount of structural damage present, and can run into many thousands of dollars. Companies generally charge at least $250 per hour for their services. Home and property owners often find that the service is covered under their property insurance, but renters are not so lucky and must pay for the services themselves if their landlord does not handle the cost. Crime scene cleaners make about $40,000 per year, although owning one's company can drastically increase the salary.

Since the 1990s, violent crime rates in the United States have been on a steep and steady decline, which means that, at least in the United States, crime scene cleaners need to diversify their work. Besides scenes of death or serious injury, some crime scene cleaners clean up other areas as well, such as sites of industrial or chemical spills, methamphetamine labs (which is among the most dangerous scenes to clean), chemical attacks, animal hoarding cases, or contagious disease outbreaks.

See also: Victim Advocate.

Further Reading
Emmins, A. (2009). *Mop men: Inside the world of crime scene cleaners.* St. Martin's Griffin.
Freckelton, I. (2018). *The trauma cleaner: One woman's extraordinary life in death & disaster.* St. Martin's Press.

Culinary Historian (Global)

A culinary historian, or food historian, is a person who researches the history of food. Culinary history, or food history, is a relatively recent interdisciplinary field that looks at the history of food, cuisine, food preparation, and food styles. While social and cultural historians have always written about food, it was not until the last two decades that the specific field of food history has emerged.

Food historians look at the development and movement of foods, recipes, and cooking styles over time and through place. They may specialize in the Columbian exchange of foods between the Old World and the New World after the fifteenth century, how the Silk Road transformed European diets, the history of cookbooks, the ways that race and class shape diet, the impact of famines on political change, or the symbolic importance of the turkey to the American

Thanksgiving holiday. Food historians can end up writing about religion, science, nutrition, parenting, art, or agriculture. They may focus on how people prepared foods, or they may look at how table manners developed.

Many food historians have chosen to focus on a single food or ingredient, tracing a broad cultural history of that food. One of the better known such histories is by Sidney Mintz. His book *Sweetness and Power: The Place of Sugar in Modern History* (1986) traces the history of the sugar crop and its impact on global diets while also uncovering the role that African slavery played in sugar's spread. Mintz is an anthropologist, not a historian, demonstrating that food history is often done by nonhistorians.

Many culinary historians do practical research as well as historical research. Creating foods based on ancient recipes (using only period techniques, ingredients, and tools) is one way that a food historian may try to better understand how people cooked and ate in the past; other historians may develop their own recipes to try to recreate historical dishes. It is not a requirement of the job to be able to cook, but many food historians like experimenting with historical cooking techniques and ingredients.

Food historians typically have a degree in history, but some come from a background in culinary arts or nutrition; others may have a degree in archaeology with a specialty in food or cooking. To teach in a university setting, a PhD is typically required, but many food historians work outside of academia, within a museum, archive, or even corporate environment, such as working for a food company. Others write and do research on their own. Food historians often work at living history museums, where they discuss foodways and cook historical foods for the visiting public. Others write articles, books, and blogs, and some teach about food history outside of the university environment. Better-known food historians can also be seen cooking and talking about food on historical television programs. Some become food critics, while others become consultants, helping to ensure, for example, that the food prepared and presented in a historical film is accurate.

Culinary historians have a passion for food. The other major requirements are an ability to do research (sometimes in dusty archives, other times through interviews with chefs or informants, and sometimes through participant observation in a kitchen or on a farm) and to write.

Today, there are dozens of college programs for those with an interest in the broader field known as food studies. Some of these programs focus on history; others focus on nutrition, gastronomy, food science and technology, public health, or the anthropology of food. New York University (NYU) offers students a degree in food studies and laboratory sciences, which combines courses in the science of food with courses focused on writing about food, food in art and culture, and theoretical perspectives on food.

Students can achieve a bachelor's degree, a master's degree, or a PhD from these programs, although most programs are aimed at master's students (which require a bachelor's degree in a related subject). Those with a PhD can expect to make at least $60,000, but salaries for culinary historians, no matter what the degree, are highly dependent on both background and type of work. The organization for the field is called the Association for the Study of Food and Society (ASFS), but there are dozens of other organizations and journals that service the field.

See also: Food Taster.

Further Reading

Colas, A. (2018). *Food, politics, and society: Social theory and the modern food system.* University of California Press.

Mintz, S. W. (1986). *Sweetness and power: The place of sugar in modern history.* Penguin.

Pilcher, J. M. (2017). *Food in world history.* Routledge.

Cult Leader (Global)

A cult leader is a man or a woman who leads a cult. Although we do not typically think of leading a cult as a type of job, no one who leads a cult sees their religion as a cult. Instead, cults, which are typically small, nonmainstream religious groups, are led by religious leaders similar to pastors, priests, and reverends.

Cults are dissident religious groups with a theology that is both novel and in opposition to those found in mainstream religions within the culture. The members are devoted to a specific cause or leader and are organized into a tight community in great tension with the larger environment. Cults tend to be emotionally intense, and they often develop within and coexist uneasily with an established mainstream religion.

Most mainstream religions started out as cults. They were founded by a charismatic leader whose ideas were new and somewhat threatening to members of the established religion. Most cults tend to die out if they cannot attract enough members or if their message is not successfully spread throughout the larger society. Those that survive, however, often grow to become mainstream, established religions themselves. If this occurs, the cult generally loses much of what made it so novel and threatening to begin with, and the theology, control of the members, and other elements generally become more conservative.

Christianity is an example of a mainstream religion that began both as a sect of Judaism and as a cult in terms of its structure and evolution. As most people know, it started with Jesus of Nazareth, a Jewish teacher and prophet who lived at a time when the area now known as Israel was controlled by the Roman Empire. Jesus preached a vision of the world and the afterlife that was in conflict with the messages of mainstream Judaism, and while Jesus's intention was not to create a new religion, his followers, after his death, ultimately did create a new religion centered on Jesus's life and teachings. Jesus's followers, both during his lifetime and after his death, traveled throughout the Jewish and, later, the Roman worlds, spreading the message of Jesus to new followers. Because of the radical nature of the message, the early Christians were persecuted by both the Jewish leadership of the time as well as by Roman authorities, both of whom saw Christianity as a threat. It was not until the conversion of the Roman emperor Constantine in 312 that the Roman Empire ended its persecution and embraced Christianity as the religion of the Empire.

As it became more widespread and established, Christianity lost some of the urgency that it had in the days of Jesus, and it also became more mainstream in its preaching and practices. Jesus, for example, preached an imminent end of the world, but by the time the Gospels were completed at the turn of the first century, that message, which is found in the Gospel of Mark (the first Gospel that was written), had largely disappeared. Because Jesus was alive, and the Gospel of Mark was written, during a time of intense religious persecution, it is not surprising that the early messages offered followers relief with the coming Kingdom of God.

Early Christians were largely antisocial, unwilling to participate in regular Jewish (or Roman) social life and rituals. Because they did not worship or sacrifice to either the Roman gods or the Jewish god, following ancient Jewish practice, they tended to be scapegoated for all manner of unfortunate events, such as the Great Fire of Rome in 64. Christians did not, for example, circumcise their sons, and they practiced baptism and began observing the Sabbath on Sunday instead of Saturday. And, of course, Christians, unlike Jews, saw Jesus as the divine son of God. In addition, while the early Christians had originally focused Jesus's message toward Jews, they eventually began to focus their efforts on converting Romans (and later other pagans), which caused the further separation of Christianity from Judaism.

Most cults, unlike Christianity or Mormonism, another religion that began as a cult, do not attain mainstream success. Although many cults are successful, at least initially, in recruiting new members, once the cult has survived long enough that children have been born and grown up in it, these children often leave the cult to rejoin normal life. In addition, because the teachings of cults are sometimes so out of the ordinary, they often come up against not just the norms but also the laws of mainstream society, resulting in the leader's arrest, as in the case of Shoko Asahara of Aum Shinrikyo ("The Supreme Truth") in 1995, after cult members killed thirteen people on a Tokyo subway, and Warren Jeffs of the Fundamentalist Church of Jesus Christ of Latter-Day Saints, who was arrested in 2006 for rape. Once a cult leader has been arrested and the views of the cult exposed through media to the wider society, the group often falls apart.

Jesus was a charismatic leader, and leaders of this type continue to be found leading religious cults today. Most of us have heard of Jim Jones, David Koresh, and Marshall Applewhite as well as the cults (People's Temple, Branch Davidians, and Heaven's Gate, respectively) that those men led. Men like this were charismatic in that their personalities and personal intensity were the focus of the cult and drew in many of the followers. Many of these cults were and are millennial, in that they preach a major confrontation that will develop between the cult and the wider society that will end in the destruction of humanity or earth and the development of a new society of true believers (a Kingdom of God). In particular, when this message is translated in such a way as to demand that the cult participants kill themselves, as in the cases of the People's Temple and Heaven's Gate (it is still debated whether any members of the Branch Davidians killed themselves), the leader's personal charisma is key to the success of the mission.

Cult leaders command respect and obedience from the members of the cult, and they do so through the use of scripture, through demanding adherence to strict rules and regulations, and sometimes through force or violence. Cult leaders may control what members eat, who they marry or have sex with, whether or how much they can contact their family and friends outside of the cult, and even their clothing, hairstyles, and names. In cases where the cult leader's influence over the members is absolute, these cults are known as totalistic cults. Cults often employ mind- or body-altering activities and substances, such as meditation, prayer, trance, or hallucinogenic drugs, to keep the members controlled. Cult leaders may or may not adhere to the rules that they have established for cult members, and because they often see themselves as divine or semidivine individuals, they may believe they are even outside of their groups' laws. The laws and norms of the greater society are typically not adhered to. Instead, conformity to the group's rules and norms is demanded.

Cult leaders do not typically inherit their positions; instead, they create their own religion via their own preaching and through developing a following. They open their own churches, temples, or other facilities of which they will be the leaders. Cult leaders are paid through the disciples' contributions to the group, which may be financial or may come in the form of personal property. Some cults demand or expect that their members give away their personal belongings, with the cult being the recipient; this was the case with the People's Temple.

While all cult leaders are charismatic, many are also messianic, in that they see themselves, or represent themselves, as a messiah to their members. Some consider themselves to be the only person who can communicate with God, and thus members have no choice but to put their trust into that person.

Cult leaders often recruit new members through oppressed groups. The socially or economically dispossessed and the otherwise vulnerable tend to gravitate toward cults, which offer them a new home, a new family, and feelings of unconditional love that they did not feel they had received outside of the cult. Cults also tend to be more popular during times of major social and economic stress. The Ghost Dance movement emerged and gained popularity among Plains Indians during the nineteenth century while Indians were undergoing a period of deep loss. In Melanesia, new religious cults known as cargo cults emerged during the nineteenth and twentieth centuries during times of colonial strain.

New members are converted to the ideologies and practices of the cult through a process of resocialization, during which the recruits' former identities are broken down, their ties to their former lives are severed, and they are showered with love and support from the leader and other adherents. Sometimes cults offer candy, cake, and other sugary and "childish" foods as a way to help break down the convert and keep them in a perpetual childlike state, with the leader as father or mother.

Although relatively rare, women have also led cults. Anne Hamilton-Byrne, for example, led the Family, an Australian cult that was active in the 1970s and 1980s. Hamilton-Byrne maintained that she was the reincarnation of Christ, and she preached to her five hundred followers that the end of the world was near. Her followers were primarily children who she controlled through hallucinogenic drugs, violence, and fear. She was arrested in 1993 and charged with fraud and perjury, but she was not charged with or convicted of abusing her followers.

Many cult leaders began their careers as leaders of mainstream religious groups, only founding their new religions after finding dissatisfaction with the mainstream groups. The Reverend Jim Jones of the People's Temple, for example, began as a Methodist pastor, and David Koresh of the Branch Davidians was active in the Seventh-day Adventist Church (until he was expelled for bad behavior).

But whether or not the leaders began in a mainstream religion or simply started their own religions, cult leaders, like most mainstream religious leaders, make a living through their congregations. Some do so via tithing—a mandated amount of money or percentage of income that members must donate to their church. For example, Herbert Armstrong, the founder of the Worldwide Church of God, demanded that members donate 30 percent of their income to the church. Some groups expected that their members work specifically to support the church; this was common among People's Temple members. Other groups had their members panhandle from the public, as with the Hare Krishnas. Still other cults encourage their members to donate their wealth (after selling all possessions) to the leader; this is especially common in apocalyptic movements that are anticipating an immediate end of the world. And other groups run businesses alongside of, or as a front for, their religious groups.

Even those who ran cults that did not preach the end of the world were able to make huge amounts of money from their followers. For instance, Bagwan Shree Rajneesh, known later as Osho, the founder of the Rajneesh movement, made millions of dollars from his international followers and was known for owning ninety-three Rolls-Royces. Swami Bhaktipada, the founder of the Hare Krishna movement, made over $10 million through the group, and Sun Myung Moon, the founder of the Unification Church, made billions of dollars through his church and associated businesses. Perhaps most notoriously, L. Ron Hubbard, founder of the Church of Scientology, was worth over $26 million at his death, and his organization continues to make hundreds of millions of dollars per year through charging people to take classes or buy materials. In all of these cases, as long as the cult is recognized as a legitimate church (in the United States), the group can claim tax-exempt status, allowing the leader to become even richer.

The term *cult* is generally used to refer to new religious movements, but it can also be used to refer to nonreligious groups in which charismatic leaders control the minds and behaviors of their followers. Using this broadened definition, Charles Manson (the Manson Family), Osama bin Laden (al-Qaeda), and Lyndon LaRouche (the LaRouche Movement) all qualify as cult leaders.

See also: Exorcist; Traditional Healer.

Further Reading

Atkins, G. G. (2014). *Modern religious cults and movements* (Routledge Revivals). Routledge.

Dawson, L. L. (2006). *Comprehending cults: The sociology of new religious movements.* Oxford University Press.

Weber, E. (2000). *Apocalypses: Prophecies, cults, and millennial beliefs through the ages.* Harvard University Press.

Dabbawala (India)

A *dabbawala* is a person who delivers boxed lunches in Mumbai, India, and other regions. Mumbai (formerly Bombay) is one of the world's largest and busiest cities and had a population of almost 18.5 million people in 2017. It is India's wealthiest city and is home to the entertainment, commercial, high-tech, and financial industries of the country. Because the city is so crowded, driving private cars is a poor option; instead, most people use one of the city's many public transportation systems to get around. For the city's workers, one option for getting lunch, instead of going home to eat or to local restaurants, is to call one of Mumbai's many lunch box delivery services.

Unlike many American cities, where workers regularly go out to eat for lunch, eating at restaurants is not normative for Indian workers. And it is not common for office workers to eat at food stalls, as it is in Mexico. Instead, middle-class Indians typically enjoy eating the food that they are used to, which was likely prepared by their mother or wife. In addition, because Indians belong to such a variety of religious, geographic, and caste groups, dietary differences can be difficult to negotiate when eating food that someone else has cooked. By eating food that was cooked at home, office workers and others who commute into the city to work maintain a connection to home that can be lacking for many people today.

At about ten in the morning, one set of delivery drivers, or dabbawalas, pick up the home-cooked lunches, which are packed in two- to four-tier tin boxes called *dabbas* or *tiffin tins*, from houses throughout the city, where workers' wives or mothers supply

A Dabbawala at work in Mumbai, India. (Fagianella/Dreamstime.com)

them. The dabbas all generally carry the same type of lunch; rice is in the bottom of the three containers, with a curry in the middle, and bread or dessert in the top. Women prepare the lunches after their husbands have left for work in the morning and leave them at the front door for the dabbawalas to pick up. Some women will also place a note in the box for their husband to read.

The lunches are taken by handcart to one location for sorting, and after sorting, they are loaded onto a train from which they are delivered to spots around the city, where other dabbawalas pick them up and deliver them, via bicycle, to their customers at work or school. Because of the size of the city and the complexity of the routes, one box, or dabba, may be handled by as many as twelve men. In the afternoon or the next day, the dabbawalas return to the customers to pick up the empty boxes, and the boxes are delivered back to their original homes via the same system of trains and bicycles.

Because many of the dabbawalas are illiterate, the boxes are marked with an alphanumeric code that indicates where they are to be delivered. Even with that system, which is extraordinarily complex and relies upon a deep knowledge of the neighborhoods within a dabbawala's route, the dabbawalas must memorize the details about their various deliveries so that they know when and where to drop some off and to pick up others, and there is no computer, or even written, system to guide them. For the deliveries to be on time, all the participants must be organized and punctual, and the trains must run on time as well. The dabbawala system also rests upon a traditional Indian division of labor: women make the food for their husbands and sons, and men deliver (and eat) it. (There are a handful of female dabbawalas now, and female workers are becoming more common in the workplace, which will ultimately shift this traditional gender system.)

The dabbawala system is the oldest lunch delivery system in the world. It started in 1890 under British colonial rule after banker Mahedeo Havaji Bachche asked someone to bring him a meal from home one day. The man he hired was from the Varkari religious sect from the state of Maharashtra, and that group, whose families are typically small farmers, continues to provide the bulk of all dabbawalas to this day.

Mumbai has four thousand to five thousand dabbawalas who deliver up to two hundred thousand lunch boxes each day. The charge for these deliveries amounts to around eight hundred rupees per month. Dabbawalas work in cooperatives and are all paid the same amount, approximately twelve thousand rupees per month. They must use their own bicycle; purchase their own white uniform (with Gandhi cap), which is the traditional outfit for peasants in Maharashtra; and must provide a box or crate to transport the dabbas. All dabbawalas belong to the Mumbai Tiffin Box Supplier's Association, a trade organization that regulates services, mediates conflicts, and fires troublesome people; they must return a portion of their earnings to the association. (The association also cares for the families of deceased dabbawalas.) Dabbawalas are so well known, both within India and, in recent years, internationally, that they command a great deal of respect.

New dabbawalas are always linked by kinship to an older dabbawala, who takes them on, trains them, and cares for them until they are able to work independently.

Some dabbawalas, known as *muqaddam*, control a certain region of town and have other dabbawalas and trainees working for them.

One newer aspect of the dabbawala system is called Share My Dabba. Workers who do not finish their lunches can now place a sticker that reads "share" on top of their tiffin; when it is picked up and returned to the sorting point, the dabbawalas are met by volunteers from the Happy Life Welfare Society, who quickly remove the food from the share boxes and deliver it to Mumbai's slum children.

Today, dabbawalas have a few new forms of competition: Uber Eats, which was founded in the United States in 2014 and launched in India in 2017, allows people to order restaurant food to be delivered by Uber drivers on an on-demand basis. Two local food delivery companies, Swiggy and Runnr, also provide on-demand food from restaurants. Only the dabbawalas provide home-cooked food, which is still preferred in India, even as the country grows more cosmopolitan by the day. Whether it will remain that way in the future remains to be seen.

In response, the dabbawalas have begun expanding their services. They are working with a handful of companies in India to provide new items, such as juices and health foods, to customers.

See also: Rickshaw Driver.

Further Reading

Roncaglia, S. (2017). *Feeding the city: Work and food culture of the Mumbai dabbawalas.* Open Book Publishers.

Thomke, S., & Sinham, M. (2010). *The dabbawala system: On-time delivery, every time.* Harvard Business School.

Deer Urine Collector (United States)

A deer urine collector is a person who collects and sells deer urine to deer hunters.

According to the U.S. Fish and Wildlife Service, about 11.5 million Americans hunt, or 3 percent of the population. American hunting developed, in part, as a response to the English tradition of hunting. In England, hunting was an aristocratic tradition, and the concept of "public lands" did not exist; in other words, only wealthy landowners and their friends could hunt on private property. Because hunting was mostly reserved for the wealthy, the public considered wild animals as the property of the rich to the exclusion of the poor. Hunting, then, was not only a sign of prosperity and status but also demonstrated mastery over nature and the lower classes as well.

Hunting in the United States did not begin as an aristocratic tradition but as a democratic one. It has never been restricted to privately owned lands. At least in the early colonial days, most land was "public" because Americans did not think Native Americans had any ownership rights to land. Hunting was an important part of the diet of many Americans, especially for those living on the frontier— however it was defined at the time. At the turn of the twentieth century, many Americans, even those living in the West, no longer needed to hunt for their food, as they had moved to a lifestyle more dependent upon farming. Many others

Saltpeter Man

A saltpeter man was a person who collected potassium nitrate, known in England as *saltpeter*, one of the major components of gunpowder. Although gunpowder was invented by the Chinese in the tenth century, it was not used as a propellant in cannons and muskets in Europe until the end of the thirteenth century. At that time, it could be found on the ground in certain areas of the world or in caves where bats roosted, but where it was not naturally available—in England as in most of Europe—it was produced by mixing straw or hay with stale urine and ash. The ideal conditions for producing saltpeter often occurred naturally in old houses and barns, which had large quantities of old urine, straw, and manure built up on the floors.

By the seventeenth century, saltpeter was in such high demand in Europe, because of the frequency of wars during the period, that King Charles I mandated that families collect the urine of their livestock and provide it to the saltpeter men as well as the night soil men. Soon after, the English Parliament passed a law allowing saltpeter men to dig in "all Pigeon-houses, Stables, Cellars, Vaults, empty Ware-Houses and other Out-houses, Yards and places likely to afford that earth." A similar law was passed in France as well. Anyone who refused to allow the saltpeter man to dig on their property (or even within a church) would be punished.

Saltpeter men often dug out the floors of the buildings to such an extent that the buildings collapsed, so one clause in the new ordinance mandated that they repair any damage to the buildings that they had caused. A number of countries also had laws that mandated that each municipality erect purpose-built buildings specifically to allow for the formation of saltpeter on their floors; in addition, farmers were prohibited from building barns with any sort of paving.

Because of the privileges given to saltpeter men, the job could be quite lucrative. Today, potassium nitrate is produced in a lab and is no longer collected.

Source: Cressy, D. (2013). *Saltpeter: The mother of gunpowder.* Oxford University Press.

moved from rural areas into cities. Hunting turned into a sport, attracting a much smaller portion of the population and drawing the wealthiest Americans.

Of the 11.5 million American hunters, 9.2 million hunt big game. Of the big game hunters, the most popular animal by far to hunt is deer, with the two most popular species for hunters being white-tailed deer and mule deer. Hunters are more likely to come from the middle and upper middle classes, and big game hunters are even more likely to have higher incomes. (For more statistics, see U.S. Fish & Wildlife Services 2018.) Today, most also hunt on private property, a big change from the past. Some deer hunters eat the meat of the animals they have killed, but others hunt for the trophy (the stuffed and mounted head, or complete body, of the animal, which is put on display).

Deer hunters use a variety of methods to hunt deer. Deer hunting can be done with a firearm or crossbow, and the simplest method is to walk through the woods looking for prey. Some hunters will use dogs to track deer or to find a wounded deer after a hunter has wounded, but not killed, the animal. The use of dogs is subject to state legislation, however; some states only allow a leashed dog to track a prey animal, while others allow dogs to track animals, wounded or not, with no regulations. Some states do not allow dogs in hunting at all. Hunters can also hunt with another hunter: the first hunter drives the deer to one spot, where the second hunter is waiting to kill the deer. (Other hunters hunt in a group with dogs; the dogs drive the animals into a spot where the hunters can kill them.) Another method to hunt deer is called spot and stalk, and it involves a hunter standing in one location with a set of binoculars. Once the deer is spotted, the hunter will either shoot from that distance or try to approach the deer to shoot from a closer spot.

Some hunters use a deer blind, which is an enclosure made of camouflage material that hides a hunter on the ground while waiting for prey. Finally, many hunters use stand hunting. The hunter uses a tree stand or deer stand, a platform built onto a tree. The hunter takes a position on the stand, typically wearing camouflage, and waits for deer to approach. Because there is no way to guess when a deer might show up, many stand and blind hunters also use bait to attract animals to the stand.

Some hunters install a deer feeder at the blind or stand to attract the deer with foods that deer like, such as cracked corn, acorns, peanut butter, or apples. Other hunters use commercially made attractants made from the urine of deer; these are especially used to attract male deer who are looking to mate with a female. Many states and counties ban any use of deer attractants, but other states allow them, although typically with restrictions as to the time of year they can be used; some states allow the use of bait until a period of time prior to hunting. Sometimes these laws are used to keep deer hunting from turning into canned hunting, whereby wildlife are kept in fenced corrals for hunters to kill, but sometimes, as with the recent law banning the use of attractants in South Carolina, it is because the urine can be taken from diseased deer, which may then spread to wild deer.

So how do deer urine collectors, or deer scent makers, as they are often called, collect the urine that they use? They do so by raising deer themselves. On a typical deer scent farm, which can contain hundreds of deer, the deer live outdoors in large pens but are fed in a barn over a floor with grates installed in it. While the deer eat, their urine drips into a collection pan beneath the floor, where it is collected by the farmer. One animal can produce a half gallon of urine each day, and most farmers collect the urine of females, to attract males; the urine from does in heat commands the highest price. The urine goes into a refrigerator, where it will keep for up to sixty days, and can be sold as is to other hunters or combined with other ingredients into a commercial product. Some companies add preservatives to deer urine to keep it from going bad, but others have found that preservatives kill the pheromones in the urine. Deer urine can also be freeze-dried, which removes the moisture and keeps the urine from going bad. (The hunter will later reconstitute the freeze-dried urine with water.) The hunter sprays the urine around the deer blind or tree stand to attract bucks. The urine also helps to mask the scent of humans, making it doubly effective for hunters.

Deer urine collectors are typically deer hunters themselves; most go into the business because they are interested in helping themselves and hunters like them to better attract deer. Today, this is a multi-million-dollar business, as deer hunters make up the largest percentage, by far, of all hunters in the United States. A Google Shopping search for "deer urine attractant" generates hundreds of products, from 100 percent pure urine produced by female deer in estrus to products that mix urine with other ingredients, which can be sprayed, scattered, or poured around the environment (or even on the clothing of the hunter) or can be added to the food provided in the feeder. Some hunters soak a rag in urine and drag it behind them while walking to their stand. There are also synthetic deer urine products on the market, but those who sell real urine maintain that those products are ineffective.

Deer urine collectors can sell their products directly to hunters or wholesale to large hunting supply companies, which will either sell it as is or use it as an ingredient in their other products. Some deer urine farmers also sell their deer to private game ranches where hunters pay to kill big game animals at close proximity.

See also: Food Taster; Geoduck Farmer; Insect Farmer.

Further Reading
Dray, P. (2018). *The fair chase: The epic story of hunting in America*. Basic Books.
U.S. Fish & Wildlife Service (Eds.). (2018). *2016 national survey of fishing, hunting and wildlife-associated recreation*. U.S. Fish & Wildlife Service.

E

Ear Cleaner (India, Japan, China)

An ear cleaner is a person who cleans ears for a living. All humans—and many nonhuman animals—have wax in their ears. Earwax, or cerumen, is produced naturally by glands within the ear canal, and it helps to lubricate the ears, to protect them from infection and from foreign objects getting inside, and to keep the ears clean. For the most part, ears do not need to be cleaned because they are self-cleaning, with the movement of the jaw helping to keep the earwax moving. In addition, cleaning the ears leads to the ear producing more wax! However, many people produce too much earwax or just have the desire to remove the wax from their ears.

Even though most doctors advise against putting anything into the ear canal, there are a variety of methods that people have used around the world to remove earwax, including candling (in which one end of a candle is placed into the ear with the other end lit), pouring a homemade mixture into the ears, inserting a cotton swab, squirting water into the ear canal, and using a steel or wooden pick, loop, or curette to scrape out the wax. Some of these methods are quite ancient: Roman texts cover the use of ear syringes to squirt liquid into the ears, and candling was used in ancient Egypt, China, Greece, Tibet, and pre-Columbian America. All of these methods can cause problems because they are ineffective, can push the wax further into the ear canal, or can damage and even perforate the ear drum. However, this does not make them any less popular.

In addition, there are two kinds of earwax in humans, a dry type and a wet type, which are determined by a single gene. The wet type of earwax, which is the dominant and "original" trait, is more common among Europeans and Africans, whereas the dry type of earwax is more common among Asians and Native Americans, most likely developed through a mutation in Asia tens of thousands of years ago. Because of the different types of earwax, it should not be a surprise that cleaning methods differ from one region of the world to another or that Asia developed practices unique to that region of the world. In particular, the most common tools used by Asian ear cleaners—ear scoops and ear picks—are especially useful for removing dry wax. (The loop-type of ear scoop is a good example of a tool with limited value to customers with wet wax but that works perfectly for dry wax; the cotton-tipped swabs that are common in the West are better for wet wax.)

Most people who feel the need to clean the earwax out of their ears do so themselves with one of the methods previously mentioned, and others with severe problems may visit a medical professional to have their earwax removed. But in some cultures, dedicated ear cleaners developed to meet this need.

China's traditional ear cleaners do not have offices, nor do they have medical degrees. Instead, ear cleaners work on the streets, selling their services to passersby. The practice, known as *cai er* ("ear picking") or *tao er* ("ear scooping"), dates back to at least the Ming Dynasty (1368–1644 CE) and perhaps as far back as the Song Dynasty (960–1279 CE), when ear cleaners visited teahouses to solicit customers. While ear cleaners now work on the streets and use a headlight to better see into the ear, the bulk of the job has changed very little in hundreds of years.

The tools of the trade—a variety of picks, tweezers, scoops, and scrapers made of steel or plastic, with some topped with goose down and all with different functions—have changed very little. The cleaner determines what tools will be needed for the customer based on his or her ear shape, the amount of wax, and other conditions and then goes to work. The process of cleaning only takes about twenty minutes and costs under $10. Some Chinese health spas and salons now offer ear cleaning services where customers can get the traditional ear picking or can have their ears cleaned via candling. These services last longer than those on the street and cost more as well.

Regardless of medical doctors' views on ear cleaning, it remains a popular practice in China, where many people believe that ear cleaning (which simulates acupressure points within the ear canal) is good for the entire body and, along with bathing and foot massage, should make up a part of basic hygiene. Even so, ear cleaning is more popular among older generations (and today's foreign tourists); many young people no longer visit ear cleaners. Some people worry that this ancient practice may begin to decline with younger generations being less likely to visit ear cleaners. In fact, a group of ear cleaners in Chengdu, which has the oldest and strongest ear scooping tradition in China, has been trying to get the government to classify ear cleaning as a cultural heritage.

India also has a long tradition of street ear cleaning. India's ear cleaners, known as *kaan saaf wallahs*, advertise their wares on the street and are marked not only by their distinctive tools but also by the red head coverings that many wear. The cost for such a service is just a few dollars (or less) and involves not just picking but also the use of oils. As in China, most Indian ear cleaners inherited their trade from their fathers. This is unsurprising because in India the caste system regulates traditional occupations such as ear cleaning as well as marriage, status, and social interaction. Many Indian ear cleaners belong to the Kanmailia (*Kan* means "ears," and *malia* means "dirt" in Hindi.), or Shaikh, community, a Muslim occupational caste. Because caste groups are typically endogamous, meaning that people marry within their caste group, this helps keep the occupation within the caste. Members of the Kanmailia community are among the poorest in India.

As in China, younger Indians are no longer choosing to get their ears cleaned by street cleaners, so the customer base has shrunk to older people and tourists—many of whom are very leery of having sharp, unsterilized instruments stuck into their ears.

In Japan, the traditional method to remove earwax involves a small steel or bamboo tool with a curved tip called a *mimi kaki*, or "ear rake." The rake (which has many iterations, just like the Indian tools) is inserted into the ear and is used to scrape out the wax. As with other methods, doctors oppose the use of tools like this (they can perforate the eardrum if used improperly), but ear cleaning (known as *mimi souji*)—whether done at home or by professionals at a spa—remains very common in Japan. Many Japanese grew up with their mothers cleaning their ears at home, so the practice carries warm and maternal connotations to many adults today. In fact, many Japanese visit salons that have tools with LED lights on the end, and tiny video cameras are inserted into the ears to help the cleaner locate the wax. The cost for the service starts at about $30, but it can go much higher, depending on the type of salon, the length of the visit, and any other services involved.

Unlike in India and China, many ear cleaners in Japan are women, so the process of getting one's ears cleaned in a Japanese salon mimics, for many customers, the feeling of having one's mother clean one's ears as a child. In addition, many ear cleaning salons are less like health spas and more like a traditional Japanese teahouse, where young beautiful women provide social services to men. The primary customers are Japanese men as well as some tourists.

Becoming an ear cleaner, no matter the country, involves a great deal of training. Ear cleaners practice using their tools to do very delicate tasks, such as peeling off the skin of a boiled egg or removing debris from a burning candlewick, which helps them to navigate the delicate work of ear cleaning. They must practice for many hours to develop the precision needed to handle such a delicate task. Many ear cleaners (most of whom are male, as are the majority of customers) come from a family of ear cleaners, having learned the trade from their fathers.

Many people visit ear cleaners, but not just because they feel the need to clean their ears. The sensation of having someone touching and cleaning one's ears can be highly satisfying, and some have compared the experience to watching an autonomous sensory meridian response (ASMR) video, which, via the use of certain audio triggers, such as whispers or light tapping, makes the viewer feel tingly and satisfied. Some Chinese cleaners insert a vibrating tuning fork into the ear at the end of the cleaning, which mimics the feeling one gets from watching an ASMR video.

See also: Sugar Painter; YouTube Celebrity.

Further Reading

Frembgen, J. W. (2011). Itinerary ear-cleaners: Notes on a marginal profession in urban Muslim Punjab. *Anthropos, 106*(1), 180–184.

Wang, D. (2000). The idle and the busy: Teahouses and public life in early twentieth-century Chengdu. *Journal of Urban History, 26*(4), 411–437.

Equine-Assisted Therapist (Global)

An equine therapist is a person who works with horses in a therapeutic context, either for physical or mental benefits. It is a form of animal-assisted therapy.

Animal-assisted therapy (AAT) uses specially trained animals to help with the mental, physical, and emotional care of patients with a variety of complaints. The animals used in AAT are known as therapy animals and are chosen because of their gentle temperaments and their ability to help patients heal. They include

An equine-assisted therapist works with a child. (Donna Kilday/Dreamstime.com)

dogs, cats, rabbits, horses, birds, guinea pigs, and dolphins. Unlike service dogs, who live with the person with the disability or condition, therapy animals typically live with handlers (and sometimes at facilities) who train them and bring them to meet patients. Very often, these animals are companion animals as well as therapy animals.

AAT officially began during World War II, when a little dog named Smoky accompanied a military doctor on his rounds; his presence was found to make the wounded soldiers feel better. It is likely that this sort of occurrence has been going on for as long as humans have lived with animals; for instance, dogs were used in some Greek temples to help heal the sick and wounded, and in ninth-century Belgium, animals were sometimes used to help the disabled cope with their conditions—but it was not until this time that animals were formally recognized as playing a role in human healing. The idea that animals could play a role in psychiatric treatment did not develop until the 1960s, when a New York psychotherapist brought his dog Jingles to work and found that patients would communicate with Jingles present but not in his absence.

AAT has exploded in the last thirty years, with new organizations and college programs emerging to both study the roles animals play in human healing and to promote the use of therapy animals. Today, therapy animals are used in hospitals, nursing homes, orphanages, and hospices. Therapy animals are also used in a rehabilitation setting to improve physical health by improving motor skills and balance for the disabled or injured and those with neurological disorders.

Therapy animals are also used in areas where the healing is entirely emotional or psychological rather than physical. For example, therapy animals are used at prisons and juvenile detention centers, at schools and libraries, and with people suffering from autism, speech disorders, Parkinson's, dementia, schizophrenia, and a whole host of other conditions. Because of the documentation demonstrating that the presence of animals can lower stress in people, animals are now starting to be used in courtrooms when children are asked to testify in stressful court cases.

Finally, the use of therapy animals has been shown to increase social health by facilitating verbal interaction, increasing attention skills, decreasing loneliness,

Fuller

A fuller is a person who cleans woolen cloth. Fullers have been practicing their craft since the development of weaving in the Middle East about six thousand years ago, and it was an especially important occupation in medieval England, given how important wool was to the English domestic and foreign economy. It was English wool that fueled the cloth production industries in the low countries and Italy during this time.

In the ancient world, fullers cleaned newly woven cloth by submerging it in human urine and pounding it for hours with their feet or wooden mallets; urine was used because of ammonia's effectiveness in removing oils. During the Middle Ages, fulling moved from being conducted by individuals working cloth in urine baths to the cloth being worked in a water mill with mechanical agitation and hammering; the goal was to both clean and thicken the fibers in the cloth. Still, fullers remained the least skilled and lowest status of the cloth-producing professions.

Source: Oldland, J. (2014). Wool and cloth production in late medieval and early Tudor England. *Economic History Review, 67*(1), 25–47.

and increasing self-esteem. Using animals in an educational setting can help children increase vocabulary skills, improve reading, and assist with memorization. Therapy animals provide comfort, someone safe to talk to, and a feeling of safety and security, and they can bring withdrawn children and adults suffering from PTSD out of their shells. It is not uncommon for patients who are uncommunicative and withdrawn to open up and begin talking after receiving a visit from a therapy animal. Some facilities, such as nursing homes, are adopting their own cat, rabbit, or dog to live in the facility so that the patients can have access to an animal all the time. Even substance abuse treatment can benefit from the participation of animals in therapy sessions.

Equine-assisted therapy (EAT) is a subfield of AAT; it refers to the use of horses to benefit children and adults with physical or mental problems. EAT includes two types of therapy. First, equine-facilitated psychotherapy (EFT) is used for patients with psychiatric problems and does not typically involve riding horses. For people with anger control problems, for example, learning to care for a horse without expressing anger is one benefit. And second, therapeutic horse riding, or hippotherapy, is the use of horse riding as a form of therapy for physically and emotionally disabled people or for people recovering from conditions such as stroke. Equine therapists, depending on their training, may do either form of therapy.

There are a number of organizations and colleges that provide training and certification in EAT. Students can get an AAS degree in equine studies at the University of Montana–Western, and social work students at Bethany College can receive a minor in EFT. With the degree from Bethany, participants can gain a certification from the Professional Association of Therapeutic Horsemanship (PATH) or the Equine Assisted Growth and Learning Association (EAGALA). Other colleges offer degrees in AAT with a specialization in equine interventions. Because there are two different organizations that certify equine therapists and both have different ideas regarding therapeutic models, safety, and training, there are no universal standards for the field. This means that equine therapists, even if they have a certification from one of the two organizations, may operate in very different ways. To engage professionally in the field, students must have an advanced degree in their basic field, such as counseling, plus the additional training and certification (which may involve hundreds of hours) in working with horses in a therapeutic context. Most people who work in equine therapy have been riding and working with horses for much of their lives.

Unlike other forms of animal-assisted intervention, where the animal is often a pet and participates in the counseling session within a normal therapy office, equine-assisted therapists must take their patients to the stable where the horses are. Equine therapists typically work as part of a team, with different team members handling different parts of the care for the human and for the horse. Sessions usually only last from thirty to sixty minutes so as not to overly tax either the patient or the horse. Patients (or clients) are directed to observe, touch, and work with the horses in a variety of ways, and how they are asked to interact with the horses often depends on the problems that the patient has.

Equine-assisted therapists, like most animal-assisted therapists, do not make a lot of money in their jobs. But most people who are attracted to this profession do so because they love horses and also want to help people, and in this job, they can do both.

See also: Anthrozoologist; Guide Dog Trainer.

Further Reading

Fine, A. (Ed.). (2000). *Handbook on animal-assisted therapy: Theoretical foundations and guidelines for practice.* Academic Press.

McCormick, A., & McCormick, M. (1997). *Horse sense and the human heart: What horses can teach us about trust, bonding, creativity and spirituality.* Health Communications.

Trotter, K. S. (Ed.). (2012). *Harnessing the power of equine assisted counseling: Adding animal assisted therapy to your practice.* Taylor & Francis.

Ethical Hacker (Global)

An ethical hacker, or white hat hacker, is a computer hacker who works on behalf of a business to locate and sometimes fix any weaknesses in the computer system that might allow an outsider to hack that system.

With the development of computer technology in the 1960s and 1970s, the term *hacking* was coined to refer to someone using an unauthorized shortcut to do something on the computer. The term eventually evolved to refer to the practice of gaining unauthorized entry into a computer or computer system to disrupt that system, profit from it, or, sometimes, so that the hacker can claim bragging rights over the hack.

As hacking became more prominent and more destructive in the 1980s, the first laws were passed to criminalize computer hacking. But with the rise of the Internet in the 1990s, hacking became even easier and potentially much more destructive. Hackers target major corporations, stealing credit card and social security information, banking information, e-mail addresses, and other private

A hacker at work. Criminal hackers carry out unauthorized entry into computer systems to cause damage, steal information, or engage in other illegal activities, while ethical hackers work to protect those systems. (Dan Grytsku/Dreamstime.com)

information from millions of consumers at a time, which they then sell on the black market. One of the first major hacking cases was in 1995, when a Russian software engineer hacked into the Citibank website, transferring millions of dollars from the bank into other bank accounts.

Other hackers launch cyberattacks to disrupt the activities of the targeted company; in 2000, a teenage hacker from Canada launched a denial-of-service attack (in which the server is overloaded and shuts down) against major companies such as Yahoo!, Dell, CNN, and eBay, causing them over a billion dollars in lost income. And some hackers, known as "hacktivists," illegally hack into the computers of businesses, governments, or prominent individuals to bring about social or political change. Anonymous is the most well known of all hacktivists operating today.

Hackers have also targeted government servers and the servers of major political parties and figures to use hacking as a form of espionage. For instance, in 2015 and 2016, Russian hackers got into the computers of the Democratic National Committee in the United States and stole information that was used to help elect Donald Trump to the American presidency.

One way that government agencies and large corporations have employed to fight the threat of hacking is to hire ethical hackers. These specialists attack the security system of the agency that hired them to identify any vulnerabilities. These planned attacks are known as penetration tests. Sometimes a company will have its own hackers on staff, while other companies bring them in as consultants when a threat arises. And some hackers, known as "gray hat hackers," hack into a company's systems without its permission to find weaknesses; they then inform the company (who may or may not pay them).

Ethical hackers must be highly competent computer security specialists. Some have computer science degrees, but many are self-trained with no college whatsoever. (Some of the most dangerous hacks have been perpetrated by high school students.) Once they are hired, ethical hackers are expected to identify any threats facing the company's computer system, and they must maintain complete confidentiality. Besides the technical skills needed to do the job, being trustworthy is the most important requirement.

Some countries offer certification to hackers who want to work professionally. In the United States, the International Council of Electronic Commerce Consultants (EC-Council) offers a certified ethical hacker certification that can be taken by computer specialists with at least two years of experience. This makes them more attractive to hire. Hackers will be tested on creating Trojan horses, worms, and viruses and launching denial-of-service attacks, among other tasks.

Interestingly, hackers who have previously been prosecuted for criminal (or black hat) hacking can still gain work as ethical hackers; their highly specialized skills are sometimes more important than their criminal background. On the other hand, some companies will not hire a hacker with a criminal background, arguing that this makes them untrustworthy.

Like other highly specialized computer professions, ethical hacking can pay very well, with entry-level jobs sometimes paying $50,000 per year, and the most experienced hackers can command high incomes because their work can potentially save the companies that hire them millions—or even billions—of dollars. Hackers who are seeking employment should look for jobs with "computer security" or "network security" in the title, as many companies will not hire hackers outright.

As cybersecurity becomes more important and cyberattacks more destructive, the demand for ethical hackers will continue to grow.

See also: World of Warcraft Gold Farmer.

Further Reading
Caldwell, T. (2011). Ethical hackers: Putting on the white hat. *Network Security, 2011*(7), 10–13.
Radziwill, N., Romano, J., Shorter, D., & Benton, M. (2015). *The ethics of hacking: Should it be taught?* arXiv preprint arXiv:1512.02707.

Executioner (Global)

An executioner is a person who executes people on behalf of the state. Today, the position is relatively rare in developed industrial countries, as most have ended the practice of capital punishment. But prior to the mid-twentieth century, most cultures around the world used the death sentence for people convicted of the worst crimes.

In the Middle Ages and the early modern period, when the death penalty was used for crimes big (murder, rape, and treason) and small (theft and adultery), executions were common in European cities and towns; most executions were done in public so as to act as a deterrent to future would-be criminals and to reinforce the power of the state. Animals were also subject to execution for their crimes. They were tried in the same courts as humans and were executed by the same executioners via the same methods (usually hanging or burning). In addition, even when people were convicted of crimes, animals were often punished as well. For example, bestiality typically resulted in the human and the animal being killed. When a person was convicted of a particularly heinous crime, he could be hanged alongside two dogs who were also hanged for his sins.

Executions in Europe reached their height in the eighteenth century, when England's "Bloody Code" was underway. Execution methods at that time included beheading, hanging, being drawn and quartered (reserved for the worst of all crimes), being burnt alive, and garroting.

The premodern executioner was sometimes a traveling executioner who went to where the work was. Other times, he was a resident specialist, working for the court or the municipality. If there was no specialist available, the job could be conducted by an officer of the court or the city. Eventually, with the rise of modern prisons, executioners usually worked for the prison.

The executioner began each job with a warrant that authorized him to execute the prisoner. He typically worked with one or more assistants, who helped him assemble his equipment, aided in dressing the convict in his execution apparel, and bound the prisoner's hands. When executions were public, the executioner and his assistants walked with the condemned man or woman from the holding cell to the place of execution. During the procession, the executioner was responsible for maintaining order among the crowd and ensuring that the scene proceeded with some dignity. During the execution itself, his goal was to execute the prisoner as cleanly and efficiently as possible; for executions by the sword, for example, the executioner hoped to kill with just one stroke. Because the job of killing people could be traumatic, many executioners drank to help them cope. Unfortunately, being drunk while on the job was often the cause of a botched execution. In Germany, after the execution, the executioner would turn to the judge and ask, "Lord Judge, have I executed well?" Finally, it was the executioner and his assistants who were responsible for cleaning up the scene and disposing of the dead.

Today, executions can be conducted by a variety of people. Within the military, soldiers are responsible for executing other soldiers. For instance, during World War I, hundreds of French and British (including Commonwealth) soldiers who were accused of desertion or cowardice were shot by a firing squad made up of their comrades. Today, in the United States, there is no single executioner position anymore. The people involved in executions are members of the prison staff who are called upon to participate in executions. The person who oversees the process and directly executes the sentence is often the warden, the superintendent, or another senior prison officer. Along with the lead executioner, other staff members help to prepare the death chamber, rehearse and test the process ahead of time, and, on the day of the execution, help to prepare and tie down the prisoner.

The person carrying out the execution is hidden from view behind a curtain or partition to ensure that witnesses do not see him.

In the U.S. states where executions are conducted by lethal injection, a method that has risen in popularity since the late twentieth century, medical professionals may be hired to perform some of the tasks associated with killing someone for the state; these can include doctors, nurses, and anesthesiologists, all of whom perform their services anonymously and are paid in cash. Because the American Medical Association frowns upon doctors helping to kill people, it is not always easy for prisons to find qualified medical professionals to participate. Because medical personnel may or may not want to participate (and most states do not require it), prison officers often do the work that would typically be done by someone with medical training: inserting the needles into the veins, preparing the drugs, securing the IVs, and injecting the drugs.

Some people who have executed prisoners have experienced some level of stress, guilt, or anxiety associated with their work. People who participate in executions in the United States may suffer from posttraumatic stress disorder (PTSD) because of their participation (see Bohm 2010). Others, however, do not seem to carry anything negative about their jobs at all, and still others engage in a variety of techniques aimed at justifying their work to themselves and warding off feelings of guilt (Osofsky, Bandura, & Zimbardo 2005). Some prisons offer psychological counseling to those who participate in executions; other prisons offer financial incentives for those who participate. Besides the stress of the job, in many countries, executioners are stigmatized by their communities because of their work and are typically drawn from the lower classes.

By the mid-eighteenth century, a movement to abolish the death penalty emerged and began to grow both in Europe and the United States. It was not until the mid-twentieth century, however, that most countries began to ban their death penalties.

Today, China is the country with the greatest annual number of executions (while Iran has the greatest number of per capita executions), although the exact number of executions is unknown. China has used execution as a method of punishment for at least four thousand years, and, today, the person who executes the condemned is a member of the police. China executes some prisoners in public, as the state says, as a form of education.

Today, only fifty-seven countries and in thirty-one U.S. states continue to sentence people to death. Public executions are even rarer still and are only carried out in four countries: North Korea, Iran, Saudi Arabia, and Somalia. Execution methods used include hanging, the firing squad, lethal injection, gas, beheading, and electrocution.

See also: Bounty Hunter; Victim Advocate.

Further Reading

Bohm, R. M. (2010). *Ultimate sanction: Understanding the death penalty through its many voices and many sides.* Kaplan.

Evans, E. P. (1906). *The criminal prosecution and capital punishment of animals.* William Heinemann.

Laurence, J. (1963). *A history of capital punishment*. Citadel Press.

Merback, M. B. (1999). *The thief, the cross, and the wheel: Pain and the spectacle of punishment in medieval and Renaissance Europe*. University of Chicago Press.

Osofsky, M. J., Bandura, A., & Zimbardo, P. G. (2005). The role of moral disengagement in the execution process. *Law and Human Behavior, 29*(4), 371.

Exorcist (Global)

An exorcist is a person, usually a priest, who attempts to remove, or exorcise, a demon or other negative spirit from a person. The idea that there are spirits who can possess people is ancient and probably universal. Spirit possession refers to the practice whereby a person is possessed or taken by a spirit—either involuntarily or voluntarily. When we look at cultures around the world where spirit possession is known, spirits may be good, neutral, or evil, and the belief system and practice can be culturally institutionalized or considered deviant.

In shamanism and in many African and Afro-Caribbean religions, such as Haitian voodoo, spirit possession is not just a normal part of the culture; adherents will voluntarily undergo possession. In these circumstances, a believer goes into a trance, often brought on by chanting, fasting, drugs, or lack of sleep, and during the trance, the person is possessed by the spirit. When possessed, or as the Haitians say, when "mounted," the possessed will behave in ways very differently than normal and in accordance with the norms of the particular spirit. In shamanism, the spirits can be asked to aid the living with a variety of problems—health, luck, protection, or divination.

In some cultures, marginalized or dispossessed people, often women, may join what anthropologists call cults of affliction, where multiple people become possessed, often at once. Through participation, their marginal status is temporarily reversed, and the victims can make demands that would otherwise go unanswered. Sometimes, if the afflicted become particularly good at managing their spirits, they can become shamans themselves and help others.

Spirit possession is typically viewed negatively in Christianity, but in the United States, it does occur in some Pentecostal traditions. In this case, a person can be possessed by the Holy Ghost, which manifests itself when the person exhibits glossolalia, or speaking in tongues.

The idea that someone can be possessed without his or her consent by a demon, ghost, or evil spirit is commonly found in cultures and religions around the world. For example, in the Islamic world, people can become possessed by dangerous spirits called jinns, which can be exorcised by anyone who has read the entire Koran. Muslim exorcisms usually involve the use of prayer, holy water, and the recitation of verses from the Koran. Exorcism is also used in Jewish mysticism, where it is believed that people can be possessed by a ghost called a dybbuk. Rabbis trained in the Kabbalah, a twelfth-century mystical text, are used to cure the victim.

In much of India, ghost possession is typically associated with stress and anxiety; for example, young girls and women who are about to be subject to an arranged marriage will often become possessed by a ghost beforehand. That ghost may speak through the victim, giving voice to the victim's anxieties. While most victims of ghost possession in India improve on their own, some do visit Hindu temples, where exorcisms are performed on both Hindus and Muslims. Indians can also visit the village of Malajpur, in the state of Madhya Pradesh, where a festival has taken place each year since at least the eighteenth century in which the possessed (mostly women) are cured by being beaten with brooms to chase the ghost away.

Possessions typically manifest themselves by the victims behaving erratically and in direct conflict with the culturally specific norms expected of them. They may withdraw from social contact, not recognize friends or relatives, or behave violently. In the Christian tradition, a possessed person will react violently toward any sign of Christianity, such as a cross or holy water, and some may not be able to enter a church.

Many Catholics, and some Protestant sects, also believe in demonic possession, where the devil or demons possesses a person; in that case, an exorcist must be brought in to remove the demon or demons from the person's body. Anglicans and members of the Eastern Orthodox Church also practice exorcisms today.

In Catholicism, only ordained priests with special training can perform exorcisms for demonic possession. Although the Catholic Church does have a set of guidelines, which originally dates to the seventeenth century but was updated in 1999, that an exorcist must follow, the actual exorcism ritual itself can vary tremendously, depending on the priest, the victim, and the context. Today, Catholic exorcists must make sure that the victim has been evaluated by a doctor before proceeding with an exorcism to ensure that he or she is not suffering from a physical or mental illness. This has resulted in most cases of potential possession being dismissed as illness. Even so, the need for exorcisms within the Catholic Church has been on the rise in recent years (after a few centuries of decline).

Today, the Vatican requires that every diocese has a trained exorcist. The priests who are chosen for this task are picked by a committee of bishops that meets every two years at the Vatican. To become an exorcist, a Catholic priest must be an experienced clergy member who has proven himself to be both pious and trustworthy. Priests can take a two-month course at the Athenaeum Pontificium Regina Apostolorum, the official college of the Vatican, and they are encouraged to take courses in psychology to get a better understanding of mental illness, which is often interpreted by family members as a sign of possession. After consulting with at least one medical doctor, it is the church (and specifically the bishop of the diocese) that ultimately makes the determination that a person is possessed and in need of spiritual help. (The Vatican also offers annual weeklong courses that are open to members of other faiths as well as Catholic priests.)

A Catholic exorcism, known in the church as a "major exorcism," involves the use of prayers; the cross and other holy symbols and figures; relics if possible; holy water; and commands for the demon to leave the body. It can take hours or days to complete. The priest is dressed in his cassock, surplice, and a violet stole, demonstrating the solemnity of the occasion. All Catholic exorcisms are performed in the name of Jesus. Although popular culture shows exorcisms taking place at the home while the victim is in bed, most Catholic exorcisms take place in a church.

Most Protestants do not believe in or practice exorcism. However, this is not the case in the smaller evangelical and Pentecostal sects and especially not within the Pentecostal churches of Africa and Latin America, where traditional beliefs in spirit possession combine with charismatic Christianity to create a strong belief in the power of demons. In these groups, where hierarchy is much less present than in the Catholic Church, almost anyone who professes the ability can perform an exorcism. Pentecostalism is the fastest growing type of Christianity in the world, so exorcism will no doubt continue to rise in importance.

A possessed person may scream, curse, soil himself or herself, or act violently. Unfortunately, the symptoms associated with mental illnesses such as schizophrenia and bipolar disorder and diseases such as epilepsy and Huntington's disease are often mistaken as symptoms of possession. Even depression can trigger in a believer the belief that a person is possessed. For this reason, people who need medical or psychiatric treatment are often brought to exorcists, who sometimes use violent methods of treatment and restraint for dealing with victims who are indeed suffering from a physical or mental condition.

There are numerous accounts from all over the world of people dying during exorcisms. Some have been drowned, some beaten to death, and some asphyxiated, either during the ritual itself or while being restrained. The most well-known of these cases is the case of Annaliese Michel, a German woman who died of malnutrition and dehydration in 1976 after having undergone dozens of exorcisms through the Catholic Church. Most deaths today do not stem from Catholic exorcisms, however, thanks in part to the (since 1994) mandate that an exorcist must first rule out a preexisting mental or physical condition. Instead, they are found in the Protestant sects that lack this requirement and allow laypeople to perform exorcisms. In addition, many exorcism-related injuries and deaths occur with children. One of the most recent cases involved a child of six who was killed by his father in October 2019; the father poured hot water down his throat.

See also: Bruja; Cult Leader; Traditional Healer; Witch Hunter.

Further Reading

Amorth, F. G. (2015). *An exorcist tells his story*. Ignatius Press.

Goodman, F. D. (1988). *How about demons? Possession and exorcism in the modern world*. Indiana University Press.

Young, F. (2016). *A history of exorcism in Catholic Christianity*. Palgrave Macmillan.

F

Facebook Content Moderator (Global)

A Facebook content moderator, known at Facebook as a community operations specialist, is a person who is hired by Facebook, either as an employee or an independent contractor, to search through Facebook posts, looking for illegal or inappropriate content.

In 2017, Facebook came under public pressure to deal with a rise in posts in which people engaged in violent acts—suicides, animal cruelty, child abuse, assaults, and even murders. The company faced extra criticism when it was reported that a Cleveland man named Steve Stephens uploaded a video that showed him murdering a man; the video was live on Facebook for two hours, even after it was reported through Facebook's official system multiple times. These types of posts, along with those using hate speech or sexual content, are not allowed on Facebook, as they violate the company's community standards. However, there is no automated system that will detect posts like this, which resulted in a commitment from Facebook to make reporting inappropriate or dangerous content easier and to hire thousands of additional moderators. Moderators are part of the Community Operations division at Facebook and are responsible for applying and enforcing Facebook's community standards across the platform.

Requirements for this job include investigative abilities, customer service skills, conflict management skills, and an ability to handle traumatic and offensive content. Facebook's content moderators must be tech-savvy and have a bachelor's degree, a detailed understanding of Facebook and its policies, and experience in a similar online work environment. Language abilities are a plus, as Facebook's users come from a variety of countries and speak a variety of languages. Facebook currently uses moderators that speak fifty languages.

Some Facebook moderators work directly for Facebook at one of their many offices around the world, but the vast majority are independent contractors, known as community operations contractors, who are hired through outside companies such as Accenture, Cognizant, and PRO Unlimited. Contractors do not work at Facebook offices but at the offices of the contractors. They are paid around $15 per hour and receive none of the perks associated with working for Facebook. Training is provided on-site by Facebook managers.

Facebook's fifteen thousand moderators, who work at fifteen different content review sites around the world, are exposed to some of the worst behaviors that human beings are capable of. Users upload videos featuring violence of all kinds, graphic pornography, and racist and sexist content, and it is up to other users to report that content. Moderators do not search for such content; users upload three hundred million photos alone per day, and there is no way that this amount of content can be policed. Instead, moderators respond to the abuse reports that come in daily from around the world and must determine whether the reported posts violate Facebook's community standards.

Facebook's employees and independent contractors alike must sign nondisclosure agreements when they begin working for the company, but in 2018, a number of workers broke their agreements and went public with information about their working conditions. In particular, they told reporters about the emotional toll that seeing such content every day does to them, which has resulted, for many, in posttraumatic stress disorder (PTSD). Some moderators reported that after watching so many conspiracy videos, they have come to embrace some of those views themselves.

Understandably, the job has a very high turnover rate, not only because of the difficult content but also the high quotas that contractors must observe. In addition, although contractors are under pressure to evaluate hundreds of posts per day, whether a post violates community standards is not always clear, so they must double-check the guidelines (which are updated daily), look at the context surrounding the post, and confer with colleagues to make the best decision, all of which takes valuable time. For instance, are racist jokes always prohibited? What if the user is black? Each moderator's work is audited on a weekly basis by Facebook managers who determine whether the moderator is "correctly" handling his or her posts.

Because of the publicity surrounding the traumatic experiences of many Facebook moderators, contractors are now providing counselors, called wellness coaches, for their moderators. In 2019, it was reported that one firm, Accenture, was demanding that counselors disclose the content of their sessions with contractors, violating those workers' privacy (a charge the company denied).

Since the 2016 American presidential election, when Facebook was accused of allowing inaccurate news, much of it from Russia, to proliferate on its site, possibly impacting election results, Facebook has also stepped up its efforts to stop the proliferation of "fake news" on its site. One way that they have done this is through the creation of a Misinformation Process team, whose employees work to control and prevent the spread of misinformation on the site.

See also: Ethical Hacker.

Further Reading

Kirkpatrick, D. (2011). *The Facebook effect: The inside story of the company that is connecting the world.* Simon and Schuster.

McNamee, R. (2019). *Zucked: Waking up to the Facebook catastrophe.* Penguin Press.

Fantasy Coffin Maker (Ghana)

A fantasy coffin maker is a person who makes elaborately decorated coffins for funerals in Ghana. There are specialists in other countries who make unusual decorated coffins as well, but no country or culture has the tradition that Ghana does.

Death is one of the most significant life changes that all humans—and indeed all animals—will experience, so it should not surprise us to see the wide variety of rituals that have been developed to help people navigate that transition. The funeral is a universal rite of passage: all cultures have some sort of ritual that allows a community or family to say goodbye to a loved one, to help usher the deceased into the afterlife, and to help those who are left behind to cope with the loss of that person.

In sub-Saharan Africa, as in all places, the form that funerals take is a reflection of the cultural, religious, social, and economic conditions within that community. Most African cultures have elaborate and lengthy mourning practices—of which the funeral only plays a part—which often include dancing, drumming, singing, ritualized wailing, drinking, and eating that can last for days. Funerary practices are not just about saying goodbye to the dead and helping the living; they are also a way to express the status and social concerns of the dead and his or her family. In addition, in small-scale communities, a death affects more than a small group of family and friends; the death affects the entire community, so the entire community is expected to participate in the funerary events. Finally, because so many African cultures believe that one's dead ancestors continue to play a role in one's life after death, funerals are also a way of acknowledging the importance of that connection and of helping to guide the dead into the new world of the ancestors.

Because of all these issues, funerals in Africa are lavish affairs that can cost huge amounts of money and involve months of planning. Because of the ability of mortuaries to keep bodies frozen, funerals can now be delayed for months or even years after a death to ensure the best possible funeral. (The cost of these

Fantasy coffins from Ghana. (Askme9/Dreamstime.com)

funerals has long caused a considerable amount of hand-wringing among African politicians, preachers, and other observers, who consider them to be examples of waste and a demonstration of people's unseemly concern with showing off status.) Another factor that has allowed funerals in Africa to grow so large is migration. Many Africans have migrated to other countries, but they will return for the funeral of a family member. They can use the money earned elsewhere to help pay for a more lavish ceremony—including a more lavishly decorated coffin.

The coffin is, in many ways, the central element of a funeral. As the bearer of the body of the deceased, the coffin not only contains the body but also acts as a virtual stand-in for the body. In many cultures, masks made up to look like the face of the deceased were placed on a body before burial to remind the mourners of the person who has departed and to protect the body against evil spirits. In some cases, as in ancient Egypt, the mask also allowed the deceased's spirit to recognize the body in the afterlife, and because the facial features of the mask

---

Resurrection Man

A resurrection man, or grave robber, was a person who stole bodies from graves to sell to medical professionals. Prior to the modern era of body and organ donations, doctors, barber-surgeons, and anatomists, from about the seventeenth century, needed access to bodies to train themselves and their students, and when those bodies were not easily available—people did not at that time donate bodies to science because they believed that one could not enter heaven unless their body was intact—nefarious means were often employed to get them. Until 1832 in the United States and 1836 in England, the only legal means to get dead bodies was to acquire the bodies of executed murderers (one form of capital punishment in Europe involved hanging followed by mandatory dissection). To get around this limitation, doctors hired resurrection men, who worked in gangs, to dig up bodies for them. Because the sentences for grave robbing were relatively light (and in some cases, it was not even illegal), doctors sometimes procured the bodies themselves or had their students do it.

During the height of the practice, resurrection men could steal anywhere from twenty to thirty bodies per year. Not only would they make money from the sale of the body, but before they bundled the body up for delivery to the medical school, they removed the teeth for sale to dentists, who would pay up to 60 pounds for a full set of teeth that they could make into dentures. The bodies were often of poor men and women; those who could afford it were interred in tombs that could not be easily entered. In the United States, the bodies of dead slaves were also dug up and removed for this purpose.

In the early nineteenth century, two English grave robbers, William Burke and William Hare, ended up killing poor people to sell their bodies to anatomists once they realized how much money they could make from it. When the public heard about these crimes, the people responded with outrage. In the United States, there were a number of "anatomy riots" at the end of the eighteenth and beginning of the nineteenth centuries.

The era of the resurrection men was largely ended by the passage of laws in the United States and Europe that allowed doctors to use unclaimed bodies from local morgues.

Source: Bailey, J. B. (1896). *The diary of a resurrectionist, 1811–1812: To which are added an account of the resurrection men in London and a short history of the passing of the Anatomy Act* (Vol. 1). Library of Alexandria.

were correlated to those of important gods, the wearer could travel safely to the afterlife. Viking death masks were made of the bones of animals, such as wolves and goats, and were intended to signify a warrior's strength and virility and to protect the wearer from demons after death.

In Ghana, in the 1940s, a new tradition emerged of paying woodworkers to create elaborate coffins that were not decorated to look like the dead but to represent the interests, values, and even employment of the dead. These caskets, called *abebuu adekai* ("boxes of proverbs"), are brightly painted and carved into fantasy shapes, such as a shoe, a Coca-Cola can, a lion, or a fish. The idea for these coffins may have evolved from the fancy wooden litters that were used to carry Ga royalty; the Ga, one of Ghana's many ethnic groups, are well known for the production of fantasy coffins.

These coffins visibly demonstrate the wealth and status of the deceased and his or her kin. Even if the family could not have afforded such a coffin when the deceased was alive, by putting together the money to buy it and throwing a lavish funeral, the family can ensure that the community sees that they really do have money and status. In addition, the coffin tells the deceased how much the family cared about him or her, which helps to ensure that the deceased will treat them well as an ancestor.

The coffins are made by hand by a handful of well-regarded Ghanaian woodworkers and a team of apprentices, who will serve their apprenticeships for years until they become master woodworkers themselves. They are hired by the family of the dead and can take up to six weeks to make a coffin, during which time the body will remain frozen. Some of these coffin makers are now so well known that they have had their work displayed at art museums and galleries around the world and have been featured in a number of television programs. Western art collectors are now buying these coffins for themselves and can even buy them on the Internet. Locally purchased coffins cost about $500 and are made of lighter wood, such as white wood, for burial. However, coffins purchased for export are made of hardwoods such as mahogany and can cost up to $15,000. They are promoted by one company as "antiques of the future."

See also: Burial Bead Maker; Mourner.

Further Reading

Griffiths, H. R. (2000). *Diverted journeys: The social lives of Ghanaian fantasy coffins* (No. 83). Centre of African Studies, Edinburgh University.

Jindra, M., & Noret, J. (Eds.). (2013). *Funerals in Africa: Explorations of a social phenomenon.* Berghahn Books.

Feng Shui Consultant (China, United States)

A feng shui consultant is someone hired to ensure that someone's home or business is designed and decorated in accordance with the principles of feng shui. Feng shui is an ancient Chinese system that dates back thousands of years and was originally used to design and orient buildings and city streets in a way that will bring luck and success. Feng shui specialists determined this by looking at the natural world around them, including the heavens, using astronomical devices such as the astrolabe and, later, the compass. (The compass was invented two thousand years ago by the ancient Chinese for its use in feng shui; it only later became a required tool for naval navigation. Today, the magnetic compass remains the main tool for determining orientation.) Feng shui's focus is to provide a way to best harmonize individuals with their physical environments through the proper placement of buildings and objects within the natural environment.

The goal of feng shui is to ensure that the buildings and the objects within and surrounding them do not negatively impact the people who live or work there. One way that they do this is through the use of the *bagua*, which means "eight areas." A bagua is an "energy map" of a space that claims that certain areas of the home are connected to certain areas of life, such as love and marriage, children, wealth, career, health, or spiritual growth. To determine the right bagua for a space, the consultant uses either the traditional system, which is based on compass readings, or the Black Sect Tantric Buddhism (BTB) system, most popular in the West, which is based on breaking the home into eight equal parts around a center and assigning each of those parts to one of the eight areas.

Today, feng shui is used to ensure that buildings, their exteriors (such as the garden), and their interiors are built, decorated, and oriented in such a way that they have good energy, known as qi. Many architects, landscape designers, and interior designers use feng shui in their work.

Feng shui fell out of favor in China after the revolution in 1949, but it never really disappeared, although today it is most commonly used by members of the older generations. It is also still practiced in Taiwan and Hong Kong. However, it has become globalized through the immigration of Chinese people to other countries, such as the United States and Australia, and U.S. president Richard Nixon's visit to China in 1972 allowed for the import of a variety of little-known Chinese cultural practices into the United States.

In the United States, feng shui is not used by architects, home builders, or public planners. Instead, it is primarily used within the realm of interior design. Feng shui consultants (who need not, and probably will not, be of Chinese descent) offer their services to homeowners, home buyers, or those looking to redecorate their homes. For home buyers, a consultant will look at the floor plan and layout of the home, and once the home has been purchased or moved into, the consultant will determine the best ways to decorate the home to ensure good energy and "flow." Western feng shui consultants can charge hundreds or thousands of dollars per assessment, which includes meeting with the client, visiting the property, and making recommendations for improvement.

To become a feng shui consultant, most Westerners take courses at one of the many schools that provide either in-person or online training. Many of these schools, such as the Feng Shui Institute of America and the International Feng Shui School, offer certification in feng shui. However, there are no national or international standards for the field, so training methods and philosophies may differ greatly. Students learn the basics of feng shui and the various theories behind it. They use a compass, conduct a consultation, use the I-Ching, clear a space of negative energy, use the five elements (wood, metal, fire, water, and earth), use yin and yang, and diagnose problems; one program even teaches dowsing. After finishing such a course, which may take a few months to complete, the student is ready to offer his or her services as a feng shui consultant. One program, however, offers an abbreviated training program that just lasts four days. Another program, Feng Shui Designs, takes students to China as part of the training. Training can cost thousands of dollars. One can also take courses in feng shui at mainstream art and design schools. Some students also mentor with older professionals, but taking coursework is the primary way that Western feng shui consultants gain their knowledge. Finally, feng shui consultants can join a guild, such as the International Feng Shui Guild, through which customers can find them.

Western feng shui consultants come from a variety of backgrounds, including interior design and alternative medicine, and some have an interest in other pseudosciences, such as astrology.

See also: Astrologer.

Further Reading

Lim, G. D. J. T. (2017). *Feng shui and your health: A guide to high vitality.* Partridge Publishing Singapore.

Wu, S.-J. (2019). *Feng shui: A comparison of the original concept and its current Westernized version* [thesis]. Rochester Institute of Technology. https://scholarworks .rit.edu/theses/10226.

Food Taster (Global)

A food taster is a person who tastes food for a living. Food tasting has its roots in the royal courts of the world. It dates to a time when courtiers and royal servants were expected to put aside their own health and safety to protect the monarch and royal family from assassination. It was especially common for monarchs and other elites to have food tasters during times when poison was a popular method of killing someone, such as in imperial Rome. Food tasters, or praegustators, in Rome were chosen from the rank of household servants and slaves, but in Greek courts, they were typically fellow aristocrats. Food tasters were so common in Rome that they formed a collegium with a head, called the procurator praegustatorum. Macedonian food tasters, or *edeatroi*, served Greek leaders, which was a highly honorable position. Alexander the Great's taster was the general Ptolemy, who would eventually take over Egypt after Alexander's death, founding the Ptolemaic Dynasty that would last for over three hundred years.

A leader was only as safe as his or her food tasters were trustworthy. It has long been rumored that the murder of Emperor Claudius was facilitated by his food taster, Halotus, who served the emperor a dish of allegedly poisoned mushrooms on behalf of Agrippina, the emperor's wife.

Although food tasters have typically been people, the task has occasionally been performed by animals; Napoleon used a golden retriever–spaniel mix to taste his food for him, and the dog eventually became a beloved companion. His stuffed body is displayed next to Napoleon's tomb at the Hôtel des Invalides in Paris.

Food tasters have been used in more recent years by political leaders; Adolf Hitler and Joseph Stalin both used food tasters, as did Iraq's Saddam Hussein decades later. Most modern world leaders no longer employ food tasters (or they do not acknowledge that they do) because of the high degree of security that is typically employed in modern state kitchens and because of the security clearances that staff who work for state leaders typically undergo. However, both Russia's president Vladimir Putin and Turkey's president Recep Tayyip Erdoğan still employ food tasters, and it has been rumored (but denied by the U.S. Secret Service) that U.S. presidents dating to at least Ronald Reagan have employed them. It is known that the White House provides "screeners" for U.S. presidents while traveling overseas, but it is not known what they do. It is assumed that they ensure that the food prepared for a president meets White House standards in terms of the president's personal food preferences, any allergies, and any other issues that may come up. In addition, food tasters have been used at international events to ensure the safety of the food provided to international guests, such as at the 2008 Beijing Olympics, where mice were used to screen the food that was provided to the athletes.

Today, food tasters are employed in the food industry, as well as the pet food industry, to taste foods as they are being developed—not to ensure its safety but to make sure that it looks, smells, feels, and tastes appealing.

It is sometimes hard to imagine how much the diets of most humans on the planet have changed in the last one hundred years. For most of human history, people were hunter-gatherers, or gatherer-hunters, eating only foods that were collected from the wild, with very little human transformation of those foods. After the Neolithic Revolution, after which many parts of the world transitioned to either farming, raising animals, or a combination of the two, food collecting moved to food production. This radically transformed not just human diets but human cultures around the world, leading to the development of settled communities and, eventually, to the rise of cities, states, and empires. Domesticating ruminants alongside plants increased crop productivity and provided dairy products, and occasionally meat, to the farmer's diet. With the rise in cereal crops, which were prepared by boiling grain into a porridge or grinding and baking it into bread, the human diet changed again, with long-lasting implications for human health and culture.

As early civilizations developed new ways for both growing new varieties of crops and for transforming raw ingredients into food, food became, at least for those at the middle and upper ends of the socioeconomic scale, more diverse. Technology continued to improve, leading to new ways of growing, harvesting, preserving, and preparing foods. As trading developed, especially in the Old World, foods, spices, and other ingredients moved across Asia, Europe, and North Africa, further transforming the diets of the people in those regions. With the age of exploration, followed by the developing European colonies, food practices changed even more, as goods such as sugar, tomatoes, and potatoes transformed European, and later global, diets.

With the industrial revolution, food transformed even further. New chemical preservatives and leavening agents were introduced; new techniques were developed, such as canning; and new machinery was invented that allowed for the faster processing of foods such as grains. (With canning, families could preserve their own vegetables and fruits, and the invention also allowed for the provisioning of Napoleon's armies with transportable, safe food with no danger of spoiling.)

In the twentieth century, food changed even more drastically. In the first two decades of the twentieth century, modern food science emerged, allowing for the development of prepared products that would make cooking and meal preparation easier for American housewives (especially when combined with new refrigerator and freezer technologies); later, these innovations would spread around the world. Because of the invention of canning in the nineteenth century, for the first time in history, food was prepared at factories rather than in the home. American fast food emerged midcentury, and by the end of the century, it had spread across the world, wiping out many traditional foodways in the process. Food is now cheaper to purchase than ever before; however, and not coincidentally, the changes that allowed for food to be produced so cheaply have also been implicated in making it less healthy.

Food and drink companies today have large staffs of scientists who are employed to develop new products and refine existing products. The goal is to make food cheaper, tastier, safer, easier to transport, (sometimes) healthier, and more attractive to consumers. Chemists, biologists, engineers, and nutritionists are employed by massive corporations such as Nestlé and PepsiCo as well as smaller companies to develop new flavors, odors, colors, and textures to appeal to consumers and new additives and technologies to make the foods safer and more appealing.

With all this new technology, someone needs to ensure that the new foods taste good. If the food does not appeal to consumers, it does not matter how healthy it is. To taste foods, food tasters are used along with survey panels using potential customers. The food tasters typically work within food companies and taste new ingredients and products, providing feedback to the scientists on how the food item tastes, feels, and smells and where the product can be improved.

Professional food tasters do not need any special training for the job. Instead, they must have a strong sense of taste and smell, no food allergies, a sensitive palate, and the ability to discriminate between multiple flavors within a single food or drink item. The ability to distinguish whether a product has too much, or too little, fat, salt, acid, or sugar is also useful. They must be willing to taste a wide variety of foods and drinks. Food tasters also evaluate the appearance of a product and thus cannot be color blind. If it does not look good, it will not appeal to the consumer.

Because a food taster must be able to give intelligible feedback to the scientists about the food, they must be able to speak about taste, mouthfeel, and smell using language that is specific enough for the scientists to understand. There are no universities that provide training courses, but companies do provide on-the-job training and, depending on the type of food or drink being produced, may provide their food tasters with additional training to capture the nuances of the products. (There are, however, a handful of related and relevant college programs, such as a certificate program in applied sensory and consumer science at the University of California–Davis.) Chocolatiers, winemakers, and other producers of high-end goods will expect their tasters to understand the entire process of producing their products to better help them to do their job. All tasters are expected to take a test that evaluates the sensitivity of their taste buds and how well they can identify what they are tasting.

Some food tasters have job responsibilities that extend well beyond tasting products. Some companies employ tasters, or sensory scientists, to not only taste food but also to participate in product development and product launches, to organize taste-testing panels, and to make suggestions about production to improve the final product. These professionals typically have a degree or background relevant to the field of food science, nutrition, or culinary arts.

To protect their palates, food tasters typically abstain from smoking, wearing perfume (especially while on the job), and eating especially spicy foods. Like a hand model who protects her hands during off times by wearing gloves, food tasters ensure that their private diet does not interfere with their work. Professional food tasters continue to develop their palates by trying new foods.

Food tasters, like wine tasters, do not eat large quantities of the foods or ingredients they are tasting. Instead, they take small bites and often spit the food out after evaluating it. After tasting one product, the taster will drink water or even gargle before trying the next one.

Whether or not a food company employs its own tasters, before a product is released on the market, it will first be tasted by panels put together by the company. The panels are staffed by members of the public who are paid a small amount of money to participate on an as-needed basis. Some companies may also outsource its food tasting to market research companies that organize testing panels for new products. Other companies use a combination of human testers and machines that were developed to test the products. For instance, Beyond Meat, the maker of the Beyond Burger, has one machine that "smells" food by isolating the molecules in the product. It has another machine that measures the density and chewiness of its burgers.

Professional food tasters with degrees in food science or related fields can make a good salary, depending on the company and the responsibilities of the job. Food scientists in general make at least $65,000. For food tasters who participate in panels or who lack the degree of a food scientist can expect to make much less and will usually be paid by the hour. One place to find these less-qualified jobs is to look at the large market research companies that work in the food industry, as these companies hire large numbers of tasters.

In late 2019, one of the biggest trends in the packaged food world was the explosion of alternative meat, or "alt-meat," products. Although these have been a staple of vegetarian and vegan diets since commercially produced plant-based burgers and hot dogs were introduced in the 1980s, the end of the second decade of the twenty-first century has seen dozens of new companies emerge and the most "meaty" alt-meat products enter the market. Many of the major fast-food companies and "fast casual" restaurant chains now offer such products as the Impossible Burger and the Beyond Burger, with other companies testing their own plant-based products. In this environment, the role of the food taster is even more critical, as one of the goals of these companies is to create products made from plants that appeal to meat eaters. Food tasters are used in these companies to ensure that the new burgers not only taste good but also smell, look, and even act like burgers made from animal flesh. Tasters must evaluate how juicy these new burgers are, how chewy they are, and even how much they "bleed," an effect created through the use of beet juice or, in the case of the Impossible Burger, a molecule called heme.

Pet foods also need to be tested before they are sold to consumers. Pet food testing works differently than human food testing because of the different levels of regulation that apply to the pet food industry and because the food is produced for animals rather than humans. For example, prior to the release of a new pet food, flavor, or ingredient to the market, many large companies hold feeding trials. These trials, or feeding protocols, are done in a laboratory setting with animals who have been bred to be laboratory animals. While the animals are eating the food, they live their lives in cages, where they will also die. The animals are used to test flavor as well as nutritional adequacy, so the laboratory animals continue to be monitored throughout the trial.

Another aspect of pet food development is the use of human tasters. This job is typically performed by the food scientists tasked with developing new products. One part of their research involves actually tasting (and smelling) the food.

See also: Competitive Eater.

Further Reading

Butler, E. (2018). Tasting off-flavors: Food science, sensory knowledge and the consumer sensorium. *Senses and Society, 13*(1), 75–88.

Johnston, C. E. (2013). *Beware of that cup. The role of food-tasters in ancient society* [master's thesis]. University of Otago.

Potter, N. N., & Hotchkiss, J. H. (2012). *Food science.* Springer Science & Business Media.

Fortune Cookie Writer (United States)

A fortune cookie writer is a person who writes fortunes for fortune cookies. Fortune cookies are a crisp cookie that has a small slip of paper with a message on it tucked inside. They are served as dessert in Chinese restaurants (mostly in the United States). A fortune cookie is made from a flattened circle of cookie dough that is baked. While the cookie is still soft, a fortune is pressed into the middle of the circle, and, at the same time, the cookie is folded into its distinctive butterfly shape. After the cookie hardens, it is packaged in plastic.

The messages in the fortune vary depending on the company that produces them. Fortunes may include compliments ("You are a kind friend"), encouragement ("Believe in yourself and others will too"), sayings ("An inch of time is an

A typical fortune cookie. (Ekaterina79/Dreamstime.com)

inch of gold"), prophecies ("You will meet a handsome stranger today"), translations of Chinese words, or lottery numbers.

Fortune cookies are most likely derived from a savory Japanese cookie called *tsujiura senbei*. The cookies came to the United States with Japanese immigrants and were first introduced to an American audience in San Francisco at the turn of the twentieth century. They were called Japanese tea cakes at this time.

In California, in the early part of the twentieth century, many of the Chinese restaurants at the time (which were known as chop suey restaurants) were owned by Japanese Americans, some of whom served cookies with their meals. During World War II, with most Japanese Americans confined to internment camps, Chinese immigrants took over both the production of fortune cookies and the running of the chop suey houses. With the invention of the fortune cookie machine in the 1960s, production was easier, and fortune cookies became even more firmly associated with Chinese restaurants in the United States. Most fortune cookies today are made in the United States, where most of the cookies are consumed. (Some Chinese restaurants outside of the United States now offer fortune cookies to their customers, but those restaurants are rare.) There are approximately three billion cookies produced each year.

So, who writes fortune cookie fortunes? Donald Lau (on top of his regular job as chief financial officer) has written the fortunes for the largest fortune cookie producer in the world, Wonton Foods, for the last thirty years, since the company purchased a fortune cookie company. Wonton now has a database of over ten thousand fortunes from Lau, freelance writers, and members of the public who submit ideas as part of corporate-sponsored contests. Another large company, Yang's Fortunes, has five thousand fortunes.

Most companies use freelance writers, who send in their fortunes in exchange for a fee per fortune. The pay is not great, less than a dollar per fortune, but for young writers who want to test their writing skills, it may be a good way to gain experience.

See also: Sugar Painter.

Further Reading

Liu, H. (2015). *From Canton restaurant to Panda Express: A history of Chinese food in the United States*. Rutgers University Press.

Yin, J., & Miike, Y. (2008). A textual analysis of fortune cookie sayings: How Chinese are they? *Howard Journal of Communications, 19*(1), 18–43.

G

Garbage Detective (Germany, Switzerland, Wales)

A garbage detective (*Mülldetektiv* in German) is a person who works for a municipal agency and sorts through trash, either the personal trash of citizens or trash that has been dumped in a public area.

Like many European countries, both Germany and Switzerland are concerned about trash and its impact on the environment. One of the reasons for this has to do with the size of European nations as compared to, for example, the large size of the United States or Australia. Smaller nations have less space, and with less space, they must be more sensitive about how much they discard and where it goes. In addition, Europeans are typically more focused on the collective than the individual, while the opposite holds true for Americans, whose values are centered around individual freedom and choice. Europeans, then, tend to enact laws that may restrict the freedoms of individual citizens but increase the public good. One way that we see this happening is through laws mandating, or encouraging, recycling.

For example, Germany has the world's highest rates of recycling. Germans recycle about 65 percent of their waste, according to the Organization for Economic Co-operation and Development (compared to 35 percent for Americans). Throwing away recyclables is not illegal in Germany, but it is both stigmatized and financially disincentivized. To encourage Germans to recycle, recycling refund deposits are added to the price of many items; the deposits are returned to the consumer when the packaging is returned to a recycling center or automated machine. (Laws also mandate that manufacturers are ultimately responsible for creating packaging that avoids waste and is easy to recycle; a new 2019 law mandating even stricter packaging requirements will fine manufacturers up to 50,000 euros if they do not comply. Manufacturers must also pay the government to get a green dot, which indicates that the packaging is recyclable, to use on their products; this system is used in twenty-five European countries.)

All Germans are provided with a set of six color-coded bins for paper, plastic, clear glass, colored glass, compost, and trash, and all must presort their trash into these bins. If the trash has not been properly sorted, it will not be picked up.

For those who choose not to recycle, and thus forfeit their deposits, there are other ways in which German citizens pay for recycling. One way is through paying more to have their trash picked up. Trash is charged by weight, so there are financial incentives built through the system to ensure compliance with recycling demands. For users who still do not want to recycle and are happy paying steep fees for garbage pickup, trash collectors will sort through the trash on the back end to remove the recyclables out of the waste. Trash in Germany is only picked up once per month (as opposed to weekly in many parts of the world), so without sorting out the recyclables, which are picked up weekly, a family's trash can build up over the course of the month.

Germans recycle so many goods that the complicated rules on how trash should be sorted can be intimidating for foreigners traveling or living in Germany. (There are also public recycling bins, sorted by color, throughout the country, typically right next to the trash cans, to make it easier to recycle while away from home; but here again, users must sort out their trash ahead of time.)

Some Germans try to get around the various regulations and just dump their trash (especially large items like mattresses or other items that would be expensive to have picked up) on the side of a road, down an embankment, or in any other public spot. Municipal trash collectors are responsible for picking up those items, but they are accompanied by trash detectives who will sort through the trash to determine where it came from so that the perpetrator can be charged.

One place where German authorities have really cracked down on trash is in public parks, which during the summer months can become littered by the trash produced by picnics and barbecues. In recent years, some German cities began employing security guards to patrol parks and ensure that people pick up their trash. Those who do not can be fined.

Although Switzerland cannot boast about being the world's top recycler (with a 54 percent recycling rate), the country is working to encourage even higher rates of compliance. Like Germany, Switzerland's waste management model is based on the idea that the polluter should pay to stop pollution (rather than the consumer, the model that is used in the United States), so there are various regulations in place that manufacturers and distributors must follow. In addition, private and business trash pickup must be paid for, but recycling is free for Swiss citizens, which encourages the Swiss to recycle.

In Switzerland, garbage must be placed in special trash bags purchased through the state, or they must buy stickers to affix to nonofficial bags. The bag tax was instituted in 2012 and is intended to ensure that people recycle, as citizens now have to pay for their nonrecyclable waste; more waste means more bags and more fees. Because not everyone wants to pay for their trash pickup, garbage detectives who work for the city go through trash bags that do not have a sticker and bags not placed in a collection point to determine whose trash it is; when a perpetrator has been identified, he or she is given a "polluter's fine." Unfortunately, unlike in Germany, many people do not get recycling pickup and must drive their recyclables to a facility, where they can dispose of their items for free.

For those Swiss who do not want to pay for their trash bags or do not want to sort out their recyclables to reduce the amount of trash they produce, they often opt to dump their trash illegally. Because of the heavy fines that the Swiss authorities charge, some residents of border towns cross the border into neighboring France or Italy (but not Germany!) and dump their trash there. If caught, they will be fined by the authorities of that country and sent back to Switzerland with their trash.

Great Britain, with a recycling rate of approximately 43 percent, lacks many of the specialized garbage laws found in Switzerland and Germany, but its citizens are still encouraged to recycle by providing color-coded recycling bins (up to nine in some locations) and offering trash pickup only twice per month. In Wales, the number of bags that people can use has been reduced, and people who do not recycle properly are fined. Welsh trash detectives, who often work for local councils, which are mandated to reduce the trash levels in their regions, have started searching through trash bags put out for pickup to determine whether there are recyclables inside that should have been sorted out. Authorities will give each individual three warnings, but if they do not sort out their recyclables, they will receive a fine. Wales' new crackdown on recycling scofflaws has resulted in the country's above 60 percent recycling rate.

See also: Bike Fisherman; Golf Ball Diver; Pallet Recycler.

Further Reading

Halvorsen, B. (2012). Effects of norms and policy incentives on household recycling: An international comparison. *Resources, Conservation and Recycling, 67*, 18–26.

Stokes, R. G., Köster, R., & Sambrook, S. C. (2013). *The business of waste: Great Britain and Germany, 1945 to the present.* Cambridge University Press.

Geoduck Farmer (United States, Canada)

A geoduck farmer is a person who farms geoducks for a living. A geoduck (*Panopea generosa*) is a large burrowing bivalve clam indigenous to the Pacific Northwest coast of North America, from Washington to Alaska; the name comes from the Nisqually (a tribe who lives in western Washington) word *gweduc* and means "dig deep." Geoducks weigh about two and a half pounds (but can be as large as

A geoduck spout in the sand at a geoduck farm. (Burningmine/Dreamstime.com)

fourteen pounds) and must be dug out of the sand at the bottom of the ocean. They are so big that the neck of the geoduck extends well outside of its small shell. They can live for over a hundred years (the oldest ever found was thought to be 168 years old, based on the rings on its shell) but can be harvested at any time of their lives.

Geoducks were eaten by the people of the Pacific Northwest for hundreds, if not thousands, of years, and they still play an important part in the diets of many Northwest tribes. However, geoducks are now a popular food in China, where demand is much higher than can be met through traditional methods of harvesting, which is regulated to prevent overharvesting. It is also a popular food in Korea and Japan as well as in Asian communities around the world.

Since the 1990s, when geoduck aquaculture emerged as a viable enterprise, geoducks have been farmed in large outdoor underwater farms from Oregon through Alaska, but especially in Washington's Puget Sound, where they sell for more money, by weight, than any other sea creature—wild caught or farmed—in the region. They are also being successfully farmed in British Columbia. Geoduck farming is an $80 million industry.

To farm geoduck, the process begins with collecting wild adults and breeding them in a spawning tank to produce the baby geoducks, known as "seeds" in the industry. Divers use a pressure hose to loosen the sand at the bottom of the sea and then dig into the ocean bottom to pull out the animals. Because there is no way to know the sex of the geoducks, the wild-caught individuals are just put into the tank with the expectation that there will be enough males and females to produce young.

When they get big enough, the seeds are transferred to a floating bin that is anchored to a barge in the bay. The babies remain in the bins for one to two years, until they grow large enough to be transferred to their final beach location, where they are "planted" into little nooks in the sand surrounded by a protective piece of PVC pipe covered with mesh. As the geoduck grows, it digs itself deeper into the sand. The pipe will be removed after a couple of years; removing the pipe too soon can result in hundreds of thousands of young geoducks being eaten by predators. The geoduck will then use its foot to dig into the sand, where it will remain, three to four feet deep, for about five years (unless it is found first by a poacher, a major threat to the geoduck farming industry). Harvesters will then dig through the sand to find the animals, using a pressure hose to blast water into the hole to make it easier to reach them. The dirtiest and most difficult part of the process of farming geoducks is the harvest. Even after using a hose to loosen the sand, workers must shove their arms shoulder deep into the cold, wet sand to retrieve the animals.

Once the geoduck has been removed, the harvester places a large rubber band around the shell to keep it from opening up. The geoducks are then shipped alive to their final destination, often across the Pacific. In Washington, geoduck farmers own about two hundred acres of tidelands where the animals are raised, and the state is currently running a test program that would allow farmers to farm on state-owned land.

Most people who get into geoduck farming come from families with a long history of fishing, shellfish collecting, or the breeding of shellfish, but it is also possible to go to college to earn a degree in aquaculture. Farmers must be physically fit, as the work is demanding. Other workers may be required to have diving experience or boating experience.

Geoduck farming takes years between the initial breeding of the wild geoduck to produce seeds and the final harvesting, but it is a lucrative business. A single geoduck can sell for up to $100, based on size, and the largest growers can make hundreds of thousands of dollars per year. Geoduck farmers only provide about 10 percent of the geoduck market, with wild-caught geoduck making up the bulk of the industry, so there is plenty of room to grow. However, the industry is threatened by increasing levels of complaints about the potential environmental impact of so many hatcheries on vulnerable tidelands as well as the loss of public beaches to farming, all of which make geoduck farming a somewhat risky venture.

See also: Insect Farmer.

Further Reading

Gao, Y., Colby, R., & Ikeda, G. (2014). The feasibility and economic potential of geoduck aquaculture in Neah Bay, Washington. *Journal of Agricultural Science and Technology. A, 4*(4A), 291–299.

Gordon, D. G. (1996). *Field guide to the geoduck*. Sasquatch Books.

Ghost Hunter (Global)

A ghost hunter, also known as a paranormal investigator, is someone who looks for ghosts. Because ghosts are viewed with fear by most people who believe in them, some people who feel that they have a ghost haunting their home or workplace may call a ghost hunter to both confirm that a ghost is present and to, hopefully, cause the ghost to leave.

Ghosts are the spirits of the dead and may be, depending on the belief system, visible or invisible. Invisible ghosts make their presence known through noise, moving objects, or even changes in temperature or air pressure. Although the term can be used to refer to animal spirits, it is most commonly used to refer to dead people. Almost every culture and religion around the world has beliefs about ghosts that explain why some people, after death, continue to play a presence in human lives.

Ghosts relate to the religious practice commonly known as ancestor worship, but this is better defined as ancestor veneration. It is the belief that a person's deceased ancestors continue to participate in the lives of the living, watching over their descendants and sometimes offering assistance. In these cultures, the living care for their dead relatives by showing them respect, offering them gifts, caring for their grave, and honoring them in other ways. The Mexican holiday Día de Muertos is an expression of these beliefs.

Where ghosts differ from ancestors is that ghosts are not defined as family members of the living, and their presence among the living does not mean that they are there for a positive reason. Instead, ghosts are spirits of the dead who, for some unhappy or unnatural reason, are not able to move toward a "regular" afterlife and instead must remain among the living. Because ghosts are usually not related to those they haunt, and because they may be angry about how they died (or how they were treated during life), they are viewed by the living with fear. In addition, a belief in ghosts can exist even where other religious beliefs are lacking. Modern Norway, for example, is primarily secular but is experiencing a rise in beliefs about spirits and ghosts.

Where ancestors remain connected to the world of the living through the descendants of the dead, ghosts are tied to the living through the place where they are found. The English word *haunt*, which refers to a ghost's presence in a physical place and its involvement with the people who live or work there, is related to the German word for home (*heim*), emphasizing the importance of place in the life history of a ghost. Unfortunately, the connection between place and the ghost is usually a negative one. Most cultural beliefs about hauntings assume that the ghost haunts a location because that is where the living person lost his or her life.

In Europe and the Americas, beliefs in ghosts and other spirits skyrocketed during the nineteenth and early twentieth centuries, when spiritualism was popular. The spiritualist movement claimed that the spirits of the dead not only continued to exist but also could communicate through the living via people with special abilities known as psychics or mediums. Generally, the medium would speak to the dead during séances, where a handful of people sat around a table and watched as the medium contacted the spirit and channeled his or her message to the participants. This movement attracted massive numbers of people—including Mary Todd Lincoln, the widow of Abraham Lincoln—who yearned to speak to their dead loved ones. In addition, a number of prominent spiritualists believed that the dead could provide important information to the living. This era also saw the beginnings of scientific inquiry into ghosts and other types of spirits, with the Society for Psychical Research being founded in 1882. (The group still operates today.)

Today, a belief in ghosts, for most people, is a matter of faith. (According to market research firm YouGov, 45 percent of Americans believed in ghosts in 2019.) Like other matters of faith, the existence of ghosts cannot be proven or disproven. There is no scientific proof of the existence of ghosts (nor of the existence of an afterlife in general), but that does not mean that there are not professionals who have been trying to amass such proof. Those professionals generally call themselves ghost hunters. Although ghosts (or a belief in them) can be found everywhere, ghost hunters are primarily located in Europe, North America, Australia, and New Zealand.

So, what does a ghost hunter do? Most investigations start with an e-mail or a phone call to a ghost hunter by a property owner who is concerned about some unusual occurrences on his or her property. The investigator typically speaks to the person over the phone or in person first to determine whether there is a basis for an investigation, followed by a visit to the property. After that initial visit, a date is set for an investigation.

Investigators use a variety of equipment, such as digital still and video cameras, including night vision cameras and thermal cameras (which render hot spots visible on camera); accelerometers (which measure vibrations); EMF meters (ghosts are thought to interfere with the electromagnetic field); audio recorders; a tablet to take notes; and digital thermometers to capture differences in temperature. Some ghost hunters also use Geiger counters, compasses, and homemade equipment. And as a less-complicated tool, some ghost hunters use dowsing rods (which are traditionally used to find water) to help them to find ghosts. Although most of these items can be bought online at a variety of retailers, a company called Ghost Hunters Equipment (which provides the equipment for the television show *Ghost Adventures*) offers all of these items plus even more specialized equipment, such as the Paranormal Music Box, a coffin-shaped item that plays music when a ghost is present.

The investigation, which typically takes place at night, can take many hours to complete. Some investigators bring a Bible or other object to act as a form of spiritual protection. After setting up the equipment, the investigators turn off the lights and wait. The investigators keep an eye on the equipment and make note of any unusual occurrences or sightings. Indications of a ghostly presence include cold spots, apparitions, and glowing balls of light known as orbs. They also monitor the various electronic devices (the Geiger counter may click, demonstrating radiation) and attempt to determine what might be causing any disturbances. But these occurrences can be rare, or even entirely absent, leaving the investigators to sit in the dark for nothing. Most investigations are relatively straightforward (as straightforward as ghost hunting can be), but ghost hunters occasionally report dramatic, violent, or even physically dangerous situations that occurred because of alleged malicious or vengeful ghosts.

Most people who work as ghost hunters are self-taught or have learned the skills of the job through working with experienced ghost hunters. Some are psychics (or feel that they have psychic abilities), and others just have a strong interest in the paranormal. Most come to the job with a broad knowledge of paranormal phenomena acquired through reading, joining a paranormal society, or visiting allegedly haunted locations on their own.

Regardless of training or psychic abilities, ghost hunters need to have a number of characteristics. Ghost hunters must be patient, as much of the job involves waiting for a ghost to make an appearance. They must be observant to tiny, almost imperceptible changes in the environment, which may indicate a ghost. They must have an open mind toward paranormal activity (in fact, most are believers), but at the same time, they should be critical thinkers.

An investigator cannot simply accept that a building is haunted without gathering some proof. That "proof" is generated through the use of specialized equipment that is aimed at capturing the existence of a ghost. Most ghost hunters try to rule out the logical, rational, or natural explanations for an unexplained phenomenon first; when those explanations are lacking, then the explanation may be supernatural. As one might expect, ghost hunters should not fear ghosts or the unknown. (They should, however, be alert to danger, as some haunted locations, which tend to be in older buildings, may have hazards in them.) Finally, to be a ghost hunter, one must be able to handle criticism and even ridicule.

Today, would-be ghost hunters can take a variety of classes on the subject, either through online course companies or even local community colleges. As of this writing, there are four different community colleges in the United States that offer courses in ghost hunting and other forms of paranormal investigation. In addition, a company called Imagine Spirit offers courses as well as certification for ghost hunters (and for mediums and spirit guides). These courses provide information on equipment and conducting research. (Conducting research refers to both paranormal research and regular research: ghost hunters investigate the history of the home or property to find out whether a violent crime has occurred there, which may explain who might be haunting the building and why.) The courses also provide practical information. For instance, students are encouraged to never hunt ghosts alone and to always ask permission before entering a property.

Ghost hunters are hired by customers to investigate haunted properties and, where possible, clear them of ghosts. Most ghost hunters, however, do not charge for visits to homes (although they will ask for travel expenses) but only charge businesses. That means they need to make their money in other ways. Unfortunately, ghost hunting is an expensive job, as each ghost hunter must purchase his or her own equipment. Ghost hunters who have achieved a level of fame for their work may capitalize on that by writing books, teaching classes, giving talks, or putting up YouTube videos. Ghost hunters can also offer tours of haunted locations, sell equipment to other ghost hunters, or even publicly debate skeptics. Celebrity ghost hunters—such as those who have been featured on television or who have large followings on YouTube—can command much more money.

Ghost hunting is extremely popular today, thanks in part to the many media portrayals of ghost hunters in the last decade, such as the Syfy channel program *Ghost Hunters*, which has run from 2004 to present; the Travel Channel shows *Ghost Adventures* (since 2008) and *The Holzer Files* (since 2019); and the 2013 film *The Conjuring*. In addition, earlier films such as *Ghostbusters* (1984) and *Poltergeist* (1982) have been remade in recent years.

See also: Exorcist; Psychic.

Further Reading

Auerbach, L. (2010). *Ghost hunting: How to investigate the paranormal*. Ronin Publishing.

Hanks, M. (2016). *Haunted heritage: The cultural politics of ghost tourism, populism, and the past*. Routledge.

Potts, J. (2004). Ghost hunting in the twenty-first century. In J. Houran (Ed.), *From shaman to scientist. Essays on humanity's search for spirits* (pp. 211–232). Scarecrow Press.

Golf Ball Diver (United States)

A golf ball diver is a person who is employed to find golf balls in bodies of water on golf courses.

In golf, a hazard is an intentional obstacle on a golf course that provides a challenge to golfers. One type of hazard is the water hazard: a stream or a pond located between the hole, which the golfer is trying to reach, and the teeing ground, where the player begins each hole. The player tries to avoid the hazards during play. In some hazards, the player can retrieve the ball and continue to play (following certain rules), but in other hazards, the ball is no longer easily reachable by the player. (Although most hazards are relatively shallow, they can be as deep as fifty feet; many golfers do not want to get wet and will not enter a shallow hazard to retrieve their ball.) In that case, the player uses a new ball and begins play again.

So, what happens to the estimated one hundred million balls that end up in American water hazards each year that are not easily retrievable? Golf ball divers retrieve them.

Golf ball divers are primarily independent contractors who travel from golf course to golf course to retrieve balls from water hazards. They are not hired by the golf course; in fact, they are not paid at all and actually must pay the golf course a fee for the privilege of diving on their property. However, they can keep all the balls that they find, which they then sell to golf ball companies, other retailers, and golf courses, who repackage and resell them. (Because modern golf balls are waterproof, they are not damaged by water.) For people who enjoy diving, golf ball diving is a great way to do what they love and make money at the same time.

To gain access to a course, a diver first talks with the owner or manager of a gold course to get permission to dive, to pay any fees, and to negotiate any other terms. (Some divers may pay their fees in recovered balls rather than cash.) Depending on the golf course and the number of ponds (which range from four to twelve per course), some divers can find thousands of balls in a single day. It may take a single diver multiple days to finish diving a course, although that time can be shortened if the diver works with a crew. In a typical crew, a couple of divers work in the pond, collecting balls by hand, and pass the balls to another crew member on land. Other divers use a roller, a wheeled device that grabs balls as it moves through the water while the crew members guide it.

Divers sell the balls for just a few cents apiece. But finding five thousand balls in one day, which may sell for ten cents per ball (and resold for $2 per ball), can net a diver $500 for a single day's work. Depending on how many days the diver works, he or she can make anywhere from $48,000 per year on the low end (working just twice a week) to $100,000 or more for a full-time diver. Special balls—such as those used in tournaments or those made by top brands such as Titleist—can fetch higher prices than other balls. Divers can also sell other things that they find, such as golf clubs or other items.

Divers store the balls in a storage unit, warehouse, or other facility with the space to hold many thousands of balls until they can be sold. They must also be processed. That means cleaning, counting, and sorting balls into different groups based on condition, brand, or special status.

Because golf ball divers are self-employed, they can work as frequently or infrequently as they like. Some specialize in the area where they live, but others travel from golf course to golf course, making travel another perk (or demand, depending on one's perspective) of the job. Most successful divers have contracts in place with multiple golf courses, which ensures that they will have work.

The requirements to become a golf ball diver are similar to those of other divers, although the conditions are typically (but not always!) safer than other divers face. They need to be at least eighteen, must be physically fit and able to carry from fifty to one hundred pounds, and must have a basic certification from an organization that certifies underwater divers. The certification needs to include low-visibility diving, as they will not be working in the clear waters surrounding Hawaii. Divers must also provide their own liability insurance. Some young divers may apprentice with an experienced golf club diver to learn how to do the job from a professional. They provide their own transportation (which must be large enough to hold thousands of balls packed into large bags) and their own diving equipment, so there are some overhead costs to be incurred by the diver. (In addition, independent contractors are responsible for paying their own income taxes.) Some divers invest in a counting rack to make the job of counting the balls easier. Beyond that, however, there are not a lot of other requirements to do the job.

In addition to the demands inherent in diving, the work is physically demanding, as the divers end up carrying bags of balls that can weigh up to one hundred pounds each. Because of the nature of golf course water hazards, it is difficult to see under the water (even when very shallow), so divers must use their hands to feel along the bottom of the pond for balls. Many divers accustomed to diving in clear, beautiful waters realize very quickly the diving in golf course ponds is very different.

The job can also be dangerous, especially to divers working the courses in southeastern states such as Florida; besides golf balls, the ponds may contain alligators, snapping turtles, leeches, or poisonous snakes. Some divers have drowned

---

Mudlark

A mudlark or mudman was someone who scavenged in the River Thames in the nineteenth century. The mudlarks were very poor children or, less commonly, adults, who waded down the banks of the river at low tide in search of anything that could be sold for even a little bit of money. They were a common site in Victorian London and were marked by their filthy appearance. Some of the children were orphans, but others gave the money they made to their parents.

Mudlarking was one of a number of jobs that emerged in the years after industrialization, when London was besieged by poor people who arrived in the city from rural areas looking for work. Mudlarking required no specific tools or equipment—usually just a stick with which to poke into the mud and a basket or bag to carry the goods. The kinds of objects that mudlarks could find included pieces of coal dropped from passing barges, pieces of iron, and bits of rope, all of which were sold to people who could use them. Some mudlarks supplemented their income through theft and were thus not well liked by the police or better-off citizens.

With the development of the London sewer system in the late nineteenth century, a new type of mudlark emerged called the *tosher*. Toshers explored the tunnels of the sewer for small items of value that had been dropped down drains. Today, there are still people who mudlark in London; they receive a license from the Port of London Authority and use a metal detector. Because the river is now much cleaner, they find very different types of goods. In fact, most are seeking historical treasures rather than cheap items for resale.

Source: Picard, L. (2005). *Victorian London: The tale of a city 1840–1870.* Macmillan.

on the job from getting trapped in the water by fishing line or other hazards that can disable a diver wearing a heavy tank. Because the ponds are typically so murky, a diver may not see any of these dangers until it is too late. Ponds may also be contaminated with chemicals; golf courses are notoriously high users of herbicides, insecticides, and fungicides, all of which are toxic to humans and end up in the water hazards. Getting a cut or a scrape in such a pond can lead to serious or even debilitating infections. Most divers use oxygen tanks while diving, but some choose to forego them and consider it safer to dive in these conditions without a tank.

Another problem for divers is competition—both legal and illegal. While professional divers operate in cooperation with golf course operators, paying fees to dive on the property, other divers, known derisively as nighthawks or nighthunters, climb over golf course fences at night and surreptitiously collect as many balls as they can, cutting into the legitimate market. Finally, online golf ball retailers sell balls for less than golf clubs do, which means that they pay less for the balls retrieved by divers.

Golf ball divers can work anywhere where there are golf courses, but opportunities are more easily had in areas with good weather and a large population of retirees, such as Arizona, Florida, and Southern California. Because the work tends to be seasonal, many divers work part-time and either supplement their income with other jobs or use the income from golf balls to supplement their regular income.

Golf ball diving helps golf courses keep their water hazards cleared of balls, helps divers make a living, and helps the planet, as the retrieved balls get recycled back into play.

See also: Bike Fisherman; Geoduck Farmer; Pallet Recycler.

Further Reading
Machat, U., & Dennis, L. (2000). *The golf ball book*. Sport Images.
Pereira, N., Ribeiro, F., Lopes, G., Whitney, D., & Lino, J. (2012). Autonomous golf ball picking robot design and development. *Industrial Robot: An International Journal, 39*(6), 541–550.

Gondolier (Italy)

A gondolier operates a gondola for a living, usually in Venice, Italy. (At the Venetian Hotel and Casino in Las Vegas, which is designed to evoke the feeling of being in Venice, gondoliers take tourists on gondola rides through an artificial canal. In addition, a few cities outside of Italy with major rivers have borrowed the gondolier tradition, offering gondola rides to tourists.)

The city of Venice is composed of a series of islands in the Laguna Venezia, just off the Adriatic Sea, which are divided by a network of over 150 canals that were deepened, lined with stone, and widened over time to be more accessible to ships. Eventually, Venice became a city-state and an important center for commerce, with its canals crammed with commercial and private boats. Because Venice has very few streets, most people get around the city by boat. The locals tend

A gondolier in Venice, Italy. (Jan Skwara/Dreamstime.com)

to use water buses and taxis today, but tourists prefer the traditional Venetian gondolas.

A gondola is a flat-bottomed keelless and rudderless boat used to navigate the canals of Venice. The boats are operated by gondoliers who stand (rather than sit) and use a long oar to vertically row the boat, which propels the boat forward. The oar, which is affixed to the boat using a unique style of oarlock called a *forcola*, is also used to turn and stop the boat. This style of upright, forward-facing rowing is called the *voga alla veneta*, or Venetian style rowing.

Gondoliers have been operating on the canals for at least a thousand years, and they once worked exclusively for the city's wealthiest families, transporting them from place to place. During the Renaissance, there were many thousands of gondolas operating throughout the city.

In the sixteenth century, the city mandated that only black gondolas could be used, and in the seventeenth century, a sumptuary law was passed that mandated that all gondoliers wear black to match their boats. After World War II, however, many gondoliers began wearing black-and-white striped shirts, which evolved into the modern uniform. Today, gondoliers wear navy blue or red striped T-shirts, often combined with a red bandana worn around the neck or the waist, and a straw hat.

Historically, gondoliers inherited the position from their fathers and learned to navigate the canals as children. Gondoliers often teamed up to own boats together, in groups of four. Today, however, anyone can become a gondolier, although there are quite a few requirements for the position.

A gondolier owns and must maintain his own boat. Today, almost all gondolas in Venice are owned by gondoliers and are used to transport tourists. Next to owning a boat, an ability to row in the Venetian style is the most key requirement. This part of the training must be gained privately through working with an experienced gondolier. Gondoliers must also know how to swim, the basics of first aid, and because the gondolier's customers are tourists, he needs to have basic proficiency in other languages (especially English) in addition to customer service and hospitality skills. Once an applicant has passed these basic requirements, he undergoes a lengthy training program that lasts four hundred hours and takes anywhere from twelve to eighteen months to complete, during which time he learns about the history and geography of Venice as well as additional techniques for rowing. After the training program, only those students who pass the final exams (which test rowing skills, knowledge about the city, foreign language skills, and navigation) can work as gondoliers. Gondoliers must register with the local chamber of commerce and then put in a year as an apprentice or substitute gondolier to gain on-the-job training at one of the gondola stations in the city, where they begin by ferrying customers across the Grand Canal.

As in the past, all gondoliers are members of a guild that oversees the profession and limits the number of gondoliers who can operate in the city by restricting the number of licenses that can be given. All gondoliers must be licensed by the city of Venice; the license gives the gondolier the right to operate out of a specific gondola station and can be passed down from generation to generation. Today, there are approximately four hundred licensed gondoliers working in the Venetian canals. Women can also work as gondoliers in the city, but it is still rare to see them; the first woman was only licensed in 2010.

Although gondolas are no longer used by locals, they remain the most iconic form of transportation in the Venice and are extremely popular with tourists today. Gondoliers, while no longer responsible for ferrying the wealthy elites, are still members of a highly respected and highly paid profession. With gondola rides costing a minimum of 80 euros per person, a good gondolier can earn up to 100,000 euros per year.

Gondoliers show off their skills by competing with each other in a major annual tradition called the Regata dei Gondolieri, which takes place in April as part of the Festa di San Marco, and at smaller regattas held throughout the year.

See also: Rickshaw Driver.

Further Reading
Davis, R. C., Marvin, G., & Garry, M. R. (2004). *Venice, the tourist maze: A cultural critique of the world's most touristed city.* University of California Press.
Vallerani, F., & Visentin, F. (Eds.). (2017). *Waterways and the cultural landscape.* Routledge.

Google Street View Driver (Global)

A Google Street View driver is a person who drives a car for Google Maps and takes photos of the streets and surrounding environment while they drive.

Google Maps is an online mapping tool first launched by Google in 2005 for desktop users and in 2008 for mobile users. Users use Google Maps on their

The Google Street View car at work. (Cineberg Ug/Dreamstime.com)

smartphones, on their in-car GPS systems, or on other mobile devices to navigate from place to place. Besides the navigational functions, Google Maps also provides traffic conditions, overhead photos taken by satellite, and photos of streets taken by drivers in Google Maps Street View cars. Even though Google Maps came onto the market a decade after the first such company, MapQuest, Google Maps is now the most used navigational app in the world.

Google Maps gathers information from a variety of organizations, such as the U.S. Forest Service and the U.S. Geological Survey, as well as road sensors, private data providers, transportation departments, and user contributions through associated apps such as Waze (which Google now owns) and Google Earth to build its maps and provide real-time traffic data to users.

Google also relies on an army of drivers who are paid to drive down every street, alley, and road in every country in which it is allowed. These drivers drive cars equipped with special 360-degree cameras that take panoramic photos of streets, homes, businesses, people, and animals, and those are uploaded to Google Street View, providing a visual representation of the world one street at a time. (Google's software automatically blurs human faces and will blur out any houses if the owners put in a request to the company.) Google Street View images are also taken by people on boats, snowmobiles, bicycles, and on foot.

Besides the use of drivers, Google also relies on users to take their own photos of their surroundings, which must meet Google image requirements. Those photos can then be uploaded through the Google Street View app.

Google Street View was launched in the United States in 2007, followed in 2008 by the United Kingdom, Australia, Spain, France, Italy, New Zealand, and Japan, and is now available in over one hundred countries on every continent, although many countries only allow images to be of places such as businesses or public landmarks. As of 2017, Google had mapped ten million miles in eighty-three countries.

The Google car is brightly colored with a tall camera (which is actually seven or eight separate cameras) mounted on top. Inside, the car is equipped with a large screen and keyboard on the passenger side of the car plus a computer in the back. Once the driver is ready to start, he or she turns on the system and presses record; the system then alerts the cameras to start recording. The cameras take continuous rapid-fire images that are automatically uploaded to the server, where Google technicians combine the photos to create a 360-degree view of an area.

In the last few years, as Google Maps has rolled out new products, the company has expanded its Street View program to include underwater photography, walks on hiking trails, and indoor tours of businesses, offering additional opportunities for those wanting to work.

In 2009, Google introduced the Street View Trike, a tricycle with a computer and camera system built in, which has been used to capture images from hard-to-reach places such as Stonehenge. Google also has a backpack called the Street View Trekker backpack that it loans out to groups or individuals who want to use it to take photos of inaccessible locations.

Because the Google Street View car is so distinctive, drivers find that they are followed by people who would like to be included in the photos uploaded to Google Maps, which makes the job more difficult for drivers. In addition, when the conditions are poor because of weather, traffic, or construction and the driver's photographs do not turn out well, the driver, who can either watch the images being captured while he or she is driving or can more safely review them while stopped, is expected to revisit that area and capture better images.

Google hires its drivers through staffing agencies such as Adecco, and the employment is temporary and short term. Sometimes the jobs are advertised as Google Street View drivers, but other times the position title and job description are more vague; the workers only find out what they will be doing when they get hired. Working as a Google Street View driver requires, at bare minimum, a driver's license, a clean background and drug check, and a clean driving record.

Drivers are typically hired for a limited period, one to three months, and will be asked to cover a particular area. Through the course of the assignment, the driver will be expected to drive every street in the target area. If there is any travel outside of the driver's local region, the company will pay for lodging and, if needed, airfare. The company also provides a day of training for each new hire, which covers using the technology, maintaining the equipment (as well as the car), and following Google's rules. During the period in which the driver works for the company, he or she is responsible for maintaining the equipment and car and troubleshooting any problems. Drivers work alone and should, ideally, enjoy driving, as that is the primary requirement. To make the job more interesting, most drivers listen to music, audiobooks, or podcasts. The pay is $15–$16 per hour, and as the work is temporary, it is a good job for college students or others wanting to make some extra money. For a four-month job, assuming the driver works forty hours per week, the pay will be over $10,000 (minus taxes). Drivers who perform well may find that their contracts are renewed after they are up, providing them additional work, but there is no guarantee.

See also: Car Jockey.

Further Reading
Anguelov, D., Dulong, C., Filip, D., Frueh, C., Lafon, S., Lyon, R., . . . & Weaver, J. (2010). Google Street view: Capturing the world at street level. *Computer, 43*(6), 32–38.
Yin, L., Cheng, Q., Wang, Z., & Shao, Z. (2015). "Big data" for pedestrian volume: Exploring the use of Google Street View images for pedestrian counts. *Applied Geography, 63*, 337–345.

Graffiti Artist (Global)

A graffiti artist, or street artist, uses graffiti to make art, usually in public. Graffiti artists paint or draw on public surfaces, usually walls, and usually illegally. It is unknown when graffiti developed, but archaeologists have found numerous examples of early graffiti, including crude sexual drawings and expressions in the ruins of Pompeii, an advertisement for prostitution in the ancient Greek city of Ephesus (now in Turkey), and a Viking signature ("Halfdan carved these runes") in the Hagia Sophia. These ancient forms of graffiti are similar to modern forms in that they feature political commentary, displays of love, and sexual comments and drawings.

Many people see graffiti as an urban issue and associate it with gangs, but graffiti can be found in almost every culture. New Mexico's El Morro National Monument is a sandstone butte in the central part of the state that is covered with historical graffiti. Known as Inscription Rock, it features petroglyphs from the ancestral Puebloans who lived in the area until the twelfth century, graffiti carved

A grafitti artist paints bright colors on a concrete wall in Venice Beach, California. (Joe Sohm/Dreamstime.com)

Scribe

A scribe was someone who copied books and other documents in the time before the invention of the printing press. Prior to the mid-fifteenth century, all books and documents were printed by hand (or by a laborious use of wooden blocks), and those people who did the printing were highly trained men who could both read and write. In the classical world, merchants and wealthy people were literate, and people wrote on papyrus, parchment, wood, or wax tablets. Literature, laws, and other materials that were produced for public dissemination needed to be copied for distribution; it was the job of the scribe, who was typically a public clerk, to do this. These scribes were also employed to take dictation and record speeches and were employed by the nonliterate to write out, for example, business transactions or letters.

In Europe, after the fall of the Roman Empire, most people, including the wealthy, could neither read nor write. In some areas of the former empire, the only people who were literate were monks. So the early Christian monasteries trained monks to transcribe existing works of theology and, later, secular works as well, both classical literature and new works, such as Bede's *Ecclesiastical History of the English People*, written in 731. It is thanks to these monks that we have retained much of the literature from the classics today.

Source: Parkes, M. B. (1991). *Scribes, scripts and readers: Studies in the communication, presentation and dissemination of medieval texts.* Hambledon Press.

---

into the stone by the Spanish conquistadores who traveled through the area from the seventeenth to nineteenth centuries, and graffiti from Anglo-American settlers in the nineteenth to early twentieth centuries.

What many people think of as modern graffiti—simple drawings and writings on urban walls, often by members of gangs—emerged in the 1960s in Philadelphia and spread from there to New York City, where graffiti proliferated, especially on the subway trains. On the West Coast, this period also saw the emergence of gang graffiti in Los Angeles, where it developed out of the rivalry between the Crips and the Bloods.

Another development in the 1960s was the use of graffiti to express political sentiments. During the anti-war, civil rights, and student movements of the period, activists used graffiti as a form of political protest. As the 1960s gave way to the 1970s, punks also used graffiti to express antisocial sentiments.

By the 1970s, hip-hop developed as a distinct movement in New York City, and the graffiti of the city quickly began to express the flavor, rivalries, and styles of this emerging movement. Also, graffiti artists, who still operated underground in big cities such as New York, were refining their techniques and developing personal styles and unique tags that made them stand out from their peers. This was the beginning of the development of graffiti into an art form and of the elevation of a handful of street graffiti artists, such as Jean-Michel Basquiat, into respected artists. The 1980s saw a number of influential art galleries display graffiti art, first in New York and later around the world.

At the same time that graffiti was becoming recognized by the art world, it was being cracked down upon by authorities. Graffiti—and especially what the public saw as "gang-style" graffiti—became linked in the popular imagination with crime and became a subject of much public discussion and hand wringing.

By the 1980s, a new theory of crime had developed called the broken windows theory, which claimed that visible indications of disorder, such as graffiti, boarded up windows, and vandalism, encourage the proliferation of more serious kinds of crime. Politicians who promoted the broken windows theory, such as New York City mayor Rudy Giuliani in the 1990s, developed a number of zero tolerance policies to clean up their cities, with the assumption that dealing with petty lifestyle crimes such as graffiti would discourage the development of more serious crimes.

Although graffiti is still associated with gangs and crime, it is now seen as a legitimate form of art. Graffiti artists can command huge fees for their work, and they have been hired to create elaborate, colorful murals around the world.

Today, graffiti artists use spray paint, chalk, permanent markers, stencils (since the 1980s), and, occasionally, stickers or other supplements to create works of art, to comment on social problems and political issues, and to challenge authority. Most graffiti artists are self-taught, taking their own artistic skills and combining them with techniques learned through trial and error or by watching other graffiti artists work. Successful and well-known artists will develop their own distinctive style. Some graffiti artists go to art school to further develop their artistic skills, although it is by no means necessary. Another way to learn is by watching artists who have filmed their work on YouTube.

Most graffiti artists will not get paid for their work. To make money as a graffiti artist, the artist must be hired by a business or municipality to create a project or sell the works that they create (which means working in a studio, like other painters, and producing work that can be transported and sold, usually on canvas). Typically, only the most talented street artists rise to the level of fame where they can sell their own work this way, either through galleries or through websites such as Deviant Art. Many artists work on commission and have been hired to paint cars, trains, or private homes.

Big companies now hire graffiti artists to decorate their buildings or to create artwork for their advertising campaigns, demonstrating how far graffiti has come, especially since the 1960s; as it has moved from being a tool for political protest to being just another commercial art form. Municipalities have also hired graffiti artists to create large works of public art (which may, ironically, be tagged or defaced by other graffiti artists), recognizing the value of both giving artists room for self-expression and also having such artistic and often politically charged pieces as part of a community. Ironically, in recent years, a number of graffiti artists have filed lawsuits against large corporations for stealing their work and using it for their own products or advertising materials.

Some graffiti artists use their experience as street artists to transition to other forms of art. Graphic artists with a background in graffiti art, for example, can design logos, T-shirt graphics, and posters.

In most countries, it is illegal to mark or paint on public walls or other surfaces or on private surfaces without the property owner's permission. Some countries have offered special zones to graffiti artists where they can practice their craft without interference, but others have chosen to crack down on graffiti by arresting perpetrators and punishing them with steep fees or prison sentences. Some countries do not allow children or teenagers to buy spray paint as a way of discouraging graffiti. In the United States, law enforcement agencies track graffiti tags and styles in a database so that they can better find and prosecute the artists.

See also: Caricature Artist.

Further Reading

Austin, J., & Hobbs, C. H. (2001). *Taking the train: How graffiti art became an urban crisis in New York City.* Columbia University Press.

Ganz, N. (2004). *Graffiti world: Street art from five continents* (T. Manco, Ed.). Thames & Hudson.

Ross, J. I. (Ed.). (2016). *Routledge handbook of graffiti and street art.* Routledge.

Griot (West Africa)

A griot (or griotte for a female), also known as a jeli, is the name for a traditional storyteller in many West African nations. Griots use song, musical instruments, oral history, and poetry to tell the history and stories of their people. The griot tradition emerged during the Mali Empire of the thirteenth century, which spanned parts of the modern countries of Mali, Senegal, Mauritania, Guinea, Ivory Coast, Sierra Leone, and Burkina Faso.

Griots did much more than perform. They were and are the keepers of local history, and they told stories about gods, heroes, important leaders and battles, and other historic or mythological events. Prior to the nineteenth century, when Europeans brought their own languages and systems of writing to Africa, all West African history was transmitted by griots. Even today, many people in West Africa do not read or write, so oral history remains an extremely important

---

Town Crier

The term *town crier* refers to a public servant whose duty it is to announce important news to the public. In ancient Rome, the town crier, also known as the newsreader or senate crier, was responsible for delivering important news on market days. In England, since the Middle Ages, that duty belonged to a member of the English court, sometimes called a *bellman*, who notified the public of news involving the royal family, new taxation, foreign wars, and the like. He also performed other duties, usually involving public proclamations, such as charges against a condemned person. In other countries, the town crier, who also notified the public about deaths, births, and marriages, may have been employed by the city or village.

The need for a town crier began to disappear with the rise of newspapers, starting in the seventeenth century, and with the declining importance of the public space, although they survived in some places until the turn of the twentieth century. Today, many localities have brought the town crier back as a quasi-ceremonial position.

Source: Doig, J. A. (1998). Political propaganda and royal proclamations in late medieval England. *Historical Research, 71*(176), 253–280.

method of preserving and transmitting culture. Griots were employed by royalty to record and transmit court history and were tasked with learning the genealogy of the royals. They also served an important advisory function in the court of the king.

Most communities had a griot family within the village that was responsible for the activities within that village. Because of the importance of inheritance in the griot tradition, griots are seen as almost a different caste, with highly specialized roles and expectations.

Griots were so well respected that another role that they played was as an informal community diplomat; a griot may have been called in to mediate a conflict between families, to make important community announcements, or to officiate at royal events. Sometimes griots also doubled as healers, and they were also thought to be able to carry messages between the living and the dead. Griots performed at weddings, baptisms, and funerals and were expected to track all the births, marriages, and deaths of their community. There is a common expression that affirms the past importance of griots: "When a Griot dies, it is like an entire library is burning to the ground."

Griots were also expected to speak truth to power. Their stories and songs were not only a retelling of history but also a way of commenting on political or social injustice.

Typically, griots were not paid in cash but with gifts. Many griots were once supported by local elites (in a similar way to how composers in Renaissance Europe were sponsored by the wealthy).

Griots inherited the position from one or both of their parents, who taught their children singing, public speaking, instruments, community history, and much more. Because griot songs and stories were not written down (although many are being recorded and written down today) and often involve extensive genealogies or complicated histories, griots had to have an incredible memory. Some epic tales can take hours or even days to recite. After years of training, a griot would typically apprentice with a master performer. Griots also learned throughout their lives as they traveled from place to place, meeting other performers and learning from master griots.

Griots tend to learn and play the instruments associated with the art, such as the kora, a twenty-one-stringed harp; the balafon, a xylophone made with gourds; and the ngoni, a lute. Griottes typically focus on singing and do not play instruments, while griots play the instruments and use spoken word as well as singing. Griottes are popularly found at weddings and other celebrations, where they may sing the praises of the celebrants or use their songs to prepare a young bride for her life as a wife.

West African slaves brought the griot tradition with them to the New World, where it merged with other performance styles from other African communities and evolved into some of the earliest forms of Afro-American music.

Today, a person with an interest in becoming a griot can train to do so at special schools that teach oral storytelling, vocal techniques, musical performance, and the roles that griots plays in their communities. Some master griots travel, performing to crowds well beyond those of their community and training young people. Others have become popular musical stars, performing in front of international audiences and teaching non-Africans about traditional African arts. Others perform on television or radio, and many make and sell their own CDs.

Griots are still an important part of many West African cultures, although many of their traditional functions have declined in importance in favor of a focus on entertainment.

See also: Mourner.

Further Reading

Hale, T. A. (1998). *Griots and griottes: Masters of words and music.* Indiana University Press.

Okagbue, O. (2013). *African theatres and performances.* Routledge.

Tang, P. (2007). *Masters of the sabar: Wolof griot percussionists of Senegal.* Temple University Press.

Guide Dog Trainer (Global)

A guide dog trainer is a person who trains dogs to work as assistants for people who are blind.

Dogs were the first animal to be domesticated, between fifteen thousand and forty thousand years ago (and some scholars suggest this happened as long ago as ninety thousand years). Dogs were not domesticated to be food animals but to assist humans. The dog was man's first nonhuman partner and was initially brought into human culture to provide assistance with hunting in exchange for a

A guide dog trainer and guide dog in training. (Belish/Dreamstime.com)

share of the kill. It is easy to imagine that the dog's hunting skills were not all that were valued by Mesolithic-era humans. The dog's ability to protect, his playful nature, and his social qualities probably all came into play very early, and early hunter-gatherers most likely benefited from all of them.

With the domestication of plants in the Fertile Crescent about ten thousand years ago, human reliance on animals increased. Crops, and especially stored grain, would have attracted mice and rats, so human communities encouraged cats to take up residence in and around villages to control the rodent population. But the most fundamental shift in the human-animal relationship came with the first animals domesticated not as partners but as food. Goats, sheep, and cattle were the first animals to be used in this way, but in all cases, the animals had more to offer than just meat. Goats and sheep offered wool and milk, and cattle, most importantly, offered labor (as well as milk and meat). The cow, domesticated about eight thousand years ago, was the first animal to be used as a draft animal, and its ability to pull a plough would have a monumental impact on the development of human culture. Thanks to the plough, agricultural communities could significantly increase their crop yields, feeding far more people and producing more surplus foods, which in turn were used to support nonworking classes, to provide goods for trade, and to allow cultures to expand.

With the industrial revolution in the nineteenth century, dogs, cattle, and horses, the most important working animals, saw some of their traditional activities supplanted by machines in industrialized nations. Cars and trains replaced horse-drawn carriages, tanks replaced horses in battle, and tractors replaced the plough. Guard dogs were replaced by fences and electronics to guard property, and even cats were partially supplanted by chemical or electronic products that killed or repelled rodents. But that does not mean that humans stopped using other animals as workers or partners.

A special type of working animal is the service or assistance animal. Assistance animals are animals who have been trained to provide physical assistance to people with disabilities or other impairments. Some of these animals are rescued from shelters, but it is now more common for them to be specially bred and trained by assistance animal organizations and then given to people who need them. Training is extensive and involves the agency involved, typically a foster family who does the initial training, and then a final period of advanced training with the new owner so that the animal learns to work specifically with that person. The animal also has to undergo extensive training to be comfortable in the public and to not get distracted by the attentions of strangers. Training can cost up to $60,000 for a single animal.

In the United States, as in many nations, there are federal laws (in this country, the Americans with Disabilities Act) that protect the rights of people with disabilities to access public and private facilities, prohibit discrimination, and allow for disabled people to lead normal lives. These laws allow for people with documented disabilities to live and travel with service animals.

The oldest form of service animal is the guide dog for the blind—dogs who are trained to help those with visual impairments to get around, to cross streets safely, and to otherwise negotiate daily life. Guide dogs have been used in Europe for hundreds of years and were introduced into the United States after World War I (when thousands of soldiers were blinded from exposure to poison gas) through an organization called the Seeing Eye; this is why guide dogs are often called "seeing eye dogs." Helen Keller, for example, was given a guide dog in the 1920s. But the idea of dogs guiding humans is much older than this; in the mythologies of many cultures, dogs serve as the guide for the dead to enter the afterlife. The first guide dog was a German shepherd, and although there are other dogs who serve as service animals today, such as golden retrievers and Labradors, they remain very popular still.

Other types of service dogs include dogs who assist people with physical impairments or conditions such as Parkinson's disease. These dogs can push or pull wheelchairs, open doors, pick up dropped objects, and turn lights on and off. Some can even do the laundry, help their owners to dress, and help with grocery shopping. Importantly, service dogs, especially guide dogs, must be able to ignore their handlers' commands when it is apparent that following those commands would lead their owners into danger.

Dogs can be trained to assist the deaf or hard of hearing by alerting their handlers to such sounds as car alarms, door bells, smoke alarms, and cries. Some dogs can even alert their epileptic owners that a seizure is imminent so that they can sit down and take their medications before the seizure strikes. However, thus far it has not been possible to train specific dogs to do this. Seizure response dogs, on the other hand, are trained to provide help to a person once a seizure has occurred.

Guide dogs go through an extensive and rigorous training process in two stages. As puppies, they are raised by foster families whose job it is to socialize them and get them used to different people, different sights and sounds, and different situations. After they go through this introductory training, they go through their real training to become guide dogs.

Guide dog training involves teaching dogs how to negotiate the kinds of obstacles that blind people encounter in their daily lives, such as traffic lights, low-hanging branches, and curbs and stairs; how to avoid being distracted by loud sounds, busy crowds, and cats or other animals; and other skills. They learn how to walk in a straight line without stopping to sniff things, to enter and exit public transportation, and to rest quietly when their owner is at a restaurant, at work, or someplace else where they are not active. These dogs also receive specialized training that teaches them to disobey the commands of their new caretaker when the command would put the person in jeopardy. For example, guide dogs need to know to never cross a street with traffic coming, even when a person tells them to do so. The dogs' training begins at about six months and lasts for eighteen months to two years on average.

Guide dogs are trained by people who also have specialized training. Guide Dogs for the Blind (GDB), one of the most well-known organizations that provides and trains these dogs, employs trainers who work at their San Francisco Bay Area or Portland locations. GDB's guide dog trainers go through a three-year apprenticeship program with senior guide dog trainers. To qualify for the apprenticeship, they must first have extensive experience in dog training. The Seeing Eye, the oldest continuously operating guide dog training agency in the world, offers a similar apprenticeship. Other agencies look for service dog trainers with both a college degree and a certificate in service dog training from one of the many colleges and agencies that offer such training, such as the Certification Council for Professional Dog Trainers or Bergin University, which offers, besides a certificate, an associate of science degree in assistance dog studies. Some states also demand that service dog trainers get a license to engage in this work. Because there are so many agencies that offer training, there is no universally standardized curriculum or standards for trainers.

Training for a guide dog trainer involves learning about dog behavior, positive enforcement training methods, behavior modification, animal husbandry, operant conditioning, dealing with behavior problems, ethics, client counseling, and animal learning theory. Training programs cost thousands of dollars, and dog trainers can expect to make anywhere from $25,000 to $45,000 per year.

A guide dog trainer is responsible for both training the dog as well as instructing the blind people who are adopting the dogs in how to work with their new dogs. (They also train apprentice guide dog trainers.) At GDB, approved adopters live on campus for two weeks to undergo their training, which covers dog handling, bonding, traveling with a dog, and caring for guide dogs. Trainers also try to match the right dog to the person, ensuring that their personalities and communication styles mesh.

If the owner's condition changes, assistance animals can adapt to those changes; for instance, patients with conditions such as Parkinson's disease and multiple sclerosis will often experience a decrease in abilities, which the animal adapts to. Service animals both live with their owners and accompany them outside of the home. Only about 1 percent of all people in the United States with disabilities live with service animals. One reason for this low number is that, at this point, the demand for these highly trained animals is greater than the supply.

Service animals do not work for their entire lives. A typical service dog only works eight to ten years on average and is then retired, either to live with the family that they have served, but now as a pet, or a new family. When working, service animals wear brightly colored vests that identify them as service animals. These markers serve two purposes. They notify the public that the dog (or other animal) is a service animal, which means that in the United States, for example, they can be admitted into buildings not normally open to animals. But they also notify the public that the dog is working. This is important because when people in public see a dog, their first impulse is often to pet the dog, which is often very distracting to the working animal. But when these dogs get home after a long day, their owner takes the vest off, and they are allowed to relax, play, and be a dog again.

Over the last twenty years, other animals have entered the assistance animal world, including miniature horses and capuchin monkeys. In all these cases, the animals perform important functions for their owners, but they also provide companionship, which could be considered just as important given the social isolation that many disabled people experience in society. Studies show that people with disabilities who live with service animals have greater self-esteem, less anxiety, and are less socially isolated than those who do not live with service dogs. In 2010, the Americans with Disabilities Act was amended by the Department of Justice to narrowly define "service animals" as dogs and, in some cases, miniature horses who assist people with physical disabilities. This means that all other service animals, including psychiatric service animals, do not have ADA protection, and public and private facilities no longer need to admit them.

See also: Equine-Assisted Therapist.

Further Reading

Pfaffenberger, C. J., Scott, J. P., Fuller, J. L., Ginsburg, B. E., & Biefelt, S. W. (1976). *Guide dogs for the blind: Their selection, development, and training.* Elsevier Scientific Publishing Company.

Sillitoe, A. (2016). *Leading the blind: A century of guide book travel.* Open Road Media.

H

Hand Model (Global)

A hand model is a person who is hired to show his or her hands (or a portion of one or both) in print and television advertising campaigns.

The modeling industry developed in the mid-nineteenth century when fashion designers began having women wear their designs to social events as a form of advertising and at dressmaker shops in front of potential customers. These early women were the first "live mannequins" in the fashion industry. English designer Charles Frederick Worth was credited with being the first such designer to hire women to wear his clothing in this manner.

With the development of photography came the first advertisements featuring men or women who posed or modeled for the camera to sell a variety of products, including, but not limited to, fashion. The term *model* was originally used to refer to the dress that was worn for display by one of these early women; it was a model design and not intended to be purchased and worn by a customer. Later, the term began to be used to refer to the people who were hired to wear those dresses, and it ultimately expanded to incorporate anyone who is hired to demonstrate or advertise a product of any kind. Another kind of model was used to walk down a runway at public events or at department stores; these early events were called "mannequin parades" and evolved into the catwalk shows that we now expect at fashion shows.

While models originally worked directly for the design houses, in the 1920s, the first American modeling agencies were formed, which allowed models to work for different designers. It was not until the 1970s, though, that models began earning more money and the first models began receiving contracts to model for makeup companies and designers; these contracts could be quite lucrative. And finally, the 1990s saw the emergence of the "supermodel": well-known and highly paid models who are used by the major designers around the world, hold exclusive contracts with some of the most elite companies, and are in many cases better known than the designers that they work for.

Hand modeling is a subfield of the modeling industry. Hand models are hired by a variety of agencies and companies that want to demonstrate a product, such as an iPhone or a candy bar, in someone's hand; that need to advertise a piece of jewelry to be worn on a hand; or that are advertising nail polish, hand lotion, or some other product made specifically for the hands or fingers. Sometimes hands are used in print or television ads in a way that is not intended to sell a specific product; a hand seen touching a face, for example, may be used to convey a feeling of love.

To get work, regular models need to meet the demands of the company that hires them. For most print fashion campaigns, this means that the model must be beautiful (or handsome if male), must be a particular size (most female fashion models are tall and slender), and must be able to pose well for the camera. Models used in television must know how to act as well.

Hand models are hired to only show their hands, so it does not matter what the rest of the model's body, or even his or her face, looks like. Hand models have hands that are smooth, clean, and hairless (for women and sometimes for men); without wrinkles, discoloration, or blemishes; and with attractive, well-cared-for fingernails. Photographers tend to prefer long fingers, small knuckles, and long nail beds, but depending on the product and the shoot, other hand types may be preferred. Shots for high-end products demand a different type of hand than those of domestic products.

Because advertisements using hand models are typically shot in close-up, the hands must be extremely well cared for. Hand models protect their hands from anything that could possibly injure them. The most well-paid and sought-after hand models wear gloves every day and do not engage in many of the daily tasks that most people engage in, such as preparing food, gardening, house cleaning, washing dishes, and even opening cans or windows. Many hand models cannot keep a pet because of the danger that they will be scratched or bitten. Broken nails, paper cuts, hangnails, and bruises can significantly impact, or even end, a hand model's career. Others are not quite as protective, but they still must ensure that their hands do not suffer any injury. Regular moisturizing and manicures are a necessary part of a hand model's beauty routine.

Many models get discovered by photographers or others who work in the modeling or advertising industries when they see someone who has especially nice hands. But anyone can approach an agency or send in photographs. If the agency likes the photos, an agent will ask the person to come in for an interview. Hand models get work through parts agencies that only work with hand models, feet models, and other specialty models (such as lips, legs, or eyes) or with hand-only agencies. They get signed by agencies the same way as other models: through compiling a portfolio of professional photographs, in this case of their hands, in a variety of settings, light conditions, and with a variety of props.

There is no formal training to become a hand model, but models do have to go through casting, like other models, and could be rejected by the casting director if their hands do not meet the demands of the particular shoot. In addition, some shoots demand very specific types of hands; a director may be looking for an ethnic hand, a hairy hand, an older hand, or a small hand (which could be provided by a child or a woman with small hands). Because hand models get called on to pour drinks, chop vegetables, and do other tasks, some models will practice those tasks on their own or even take classes to make sure they can do what they are asked to do on camera.

Most hand modeling shoots are for products that relate to the hands. But sometimes ahand model is hired to be a hand double for another model or actor who does not have nice enough hands. The work is not physically demanding, although it can be tiring to keep one's arm or hand elevated for a long period of time or to maintain an unusual arm or hand position. Hand models, like all models, need to be able to follow the directions of the photographer or director and must know how to use the lighting correctly, be able to create and hold dozens of different poses, and hit their cues.

Most hand models cannot make enough money to make a living from hand modeling alone; they are not paid a salary but, like most models, are paid by the company that hired them, and fees can range from hundreds to thousands of dollars per shoot, depending on the demands of the shoot, how and where the ads will be seen, and whether it is a high-end product, among other factors. Hand models usually have another job that they do, with hand modeling providing supplemental income.

Both men and women are hand models, and while modeling is known to be an industry dominated by youth—younger hands are preferred just like younger faces and bodies—older models can still get work for products that are used by any age group, such as food, medicines, household products, and more. Children can also be hand models.

See also: Background Artist.

Further Reading
Kellett, O. (2017). *Hand jobs: Life as a hand model.* Hoxton Mini Press.
Quick, H. (1997). *Catwalking: A history of the fashion model.* Hamlyn.

Insect Farmer (Global)

An insect farmer is a person who raises insects for a living.

Humans evolved as omnivores, eating both plants for food as well as animal flesh. But for most of human history, in most cultures around the world, meat only made up a small part of most people's diets. Meat consumption has long been a luxury item reserved for special occasions or for the elites, who could afford to eat meat regularly and did so, in part, to demonstrate their status to others. (Even today, the very wealthy demonstrate their wealth by consuming exotic, expensive, and even endangered animals; this is just another way that their conspicuous consumption is used to elevate their status.)

In both traditional farming and pastoral societies, livestock have been raised for thousands of years—years in which the animals were not fed but allowed to graze on pasture, a system that was both simple, economically efficient, and good for the environment. Animals were only rarely slaughtered for food, often for ritual purposes, and the only cultures that ate meat on a daily basis were those that

Crispy cooked insects in a food market in Bangkok, Thailand. (Jedynakanna/ Dreamstime.com)

Leech Collector

A leech collector or leech finder was a person—often a woman—who caught wild leeches to be used in medical procedures. Leeches (*Hirudo medicinalis*) were used in medicine in ancient India, Egypt, and Greece and remained popular through the mid–nineteenth century. Leeches were primarily used in bloodletting because physicians thought that releasing blood had therapeutic benefits for a variety of illnesses. Today, we know that bloodletting is not helpful; however, leeches can be successfully used in certain procedures because of the anticoagulants that are injected through a leech bite.

To find leeches, European collectors had to wade through muddy, swampy areas where leeches live. They then used their own legs and arms, or the legs of an old horse, to attract the leeches; once they latched onto the body and filled with blood, the collector removed them and put them into a bag. Leech collectors could become sick after collecting because of the blood loss, compounded by any diseases they may have picked up. A busy collector could catch several dozen in just a few hours. Once the leeches were caught, they were kept in jars filled with moist earth; sometimes these were stored in buildings called *leech houses* or *leacheries*. So many leeches were caught in the nineteenth century to supply the pharmacists, barber-surgeons, and doctors who used them that leech populations suffered. Today, leeches are no longer collected but are purpose bred for medical use.

Source: Whitaker, I. S., Rao, J., Izadi, D., & Butler, P. E. (2004). *Hirudo medicinalis*: Ancient origins of, and trends in the use of medicinal leeches throughout history. *British Journal of Oral and Maxillofacial Surgery, 42*(2), 133–137.

---

subsisted largely on fish and populations such as the Inuit, who lived in environments with very little plant food.

It was not until the nineteenth and twentieth centuries that meat consumption became a daily activity in the West, especially the United States, thanks to major changes in how livestock were raised and how meat was produced. Changes in production patterns then resulted in vast changes in consumption, and rising rates of consumption in turn fueled the drive to find more efficient ways of increasing production that were drawn from industrial assembly methods. This new demand for animal products increased to a point where it could no longer be satiated by the family farm system that emerged thousands of years ago. Confined animal feeding operations, also known as factory farms, now produce the overwhelming majority of meat, dairy, and eggs today.

The modern system of industrial agriculture that produces the majority of the meat that is consumed today consumes vast amounts of resources: water to feed the animals and clean up the waste, chemicals to pump into the animals to keep them healthy, oil to run the factories and power the trucks that transport the animals, and grain that would normally be eaten by humans but is now fed to the animals. This heavy resource consumption results in severe environmental strain: the U.S. Department of Agriculture (USDA) estimates that animals raised for meat produce 1.5 billion tons of waste each year that pollutes both water and air and is a major contributor to global warming. In addition, intensive meat production results in deforestation, land degradation, and a loss of biodiversity.

The rapid industrialization of the meat industry, and its accompanying environmental and animal welfare implications, has led to concerns about meat consumption and a rise in vegetarianism and veganism. At the same time, however, the ability for the meat industry to produce meat on such a large scale has allowed for an increase in meat consumption in countries such as China and India, both of which have experienced a steep rise in meat consumption since the 1990s because of rapid economic growth and the rise of a new middle class. Even in the United States, where the debate around climate change and meat production has been growing, meat consumption is at an all-time high. Ultimately, as the world's population grows (it is projected to reach nine billion by the year 2050), people will need more food, and because much of the world is shifting to an American-style, meat-heavy diet, they will want more meat, which takes more resources to produce than grains or vegetables.

So, how will we meet this demand? If we continue on our current path, we will meet it by constructing more factory farms and diverting more land and resources to raise livestock in worsening conditions. However, a number of entrepreneurs are moving in a different direction, toward producing animal protein in a very different way. One of these ways is insect farming.

Most human cultures have eaten insects for most of human history, and insects were probably an important part of the diet of our prehuman ancestors. In fact, it is the rare culture (excepting the United States and much of Western Europe) that does not include insects as part of its cuisine. The most popular insects for consumption have been ants, grubs, beetles, crickets, and grasshoppers, all of which were traditionally scavenged directly from the wild. In the first decades of the twenty-first century, however, a number of scientists and entrepreneurs have borrowed some of the same methods of industrial farming that allowed for wide-scale meat consumption and are now using these methods to raise insects.

Insects, like other animals, provide protein, carbohydrates, vitamins, minerals, and even fat, and insect farming, even on a large scale, is thought to be a sustainable alternative to other forms of animal agriculture. In particular, insects can not only be raised in a much smaller space than traditional livestock such as pigs, cows, and even chickens, but they also require far less food. For example, it takes twelve pounds of grains to produce a single pound of beef, but insects can convert plant matter to protein anywhere from four to ten times more efficiently than this. They also require far less water, produce more young, produce less waste, and grow to full size more quickly. In addition, insect production does not produce greenhouse gases. And finally, because raising insects requires so little space, insects can be raised around the world, including in cities, which will reduce the fossil fuels that are required today to get meat from the farm to the consumers. Assuming large-scale production methods, all these factors should allow for insect protein to be produced at a much lower cost than other livestock.

Farmers raise insects in tanks, plastic bins, or other storage containers, where the insects are cared for until they reach maturity or the stage at which they will be eaten (for many species, insects are consumed in their larval form). They are killed by freezing, and then they are freeze-dried and either ground up into flour or packed whole.

Raising insects does not require the investment in land, supplies, equipment, or education that raising other animals does. Although it does take a commitment— like any other animal, they must be fed regularly, but unlike other animals, neglecting to feed insects may result in them cannibalizing each other—it is much easier to get started with insects. As with anyone who wants to create food for human consumption, insect farmers may need to comply with a variety of regulations to ensure that their products are safe for human consumption. Switzerland, for example, only legalized the sale and consumption of a small number of insects (crickets, locusts, and mealworms) in 2017.

Today, intensive insect farming is mostly confined to a few species that are easy to raise: crickets, locusts, and mealworms. According to Meticulous Research, a market research firm, the edible insect market is expected to continue to increase in size, with the bulk of the growth in Asia, where eating insects is already normalized. Because of the tiny size of insects, a single facility can raise hundreds of millions of insects at a time. Most of the companies that are growing insects today are startups and are not part of traditional agribusiness; the funding comes from venture capital firms with an interest in sustainable food production. Collectively, these companies have raised hundreds of millions of dollars in just the past few years.

One of the potential uses for insects is to create a protein-rich formula that can be used as a supplement for children and others suffering from malnutrition. According to the United Nations Children's Fund, about 50 percent of all children under five who die each year die from malnutrition. In fact, many of the insect farming startups were founded with the same idea: to use insects to fight hunger. (One company even makes a small mobile insect farm kit, which would allow people living in refugee camps to raise their own insects for food.) Another potential use of insects is to turn them into pet food and feed for fish and livestock, which will reduce the overall use of animals in agriculture. Because insects have no cholesterol or saturated fat, it is feasible that insect products can be used as a health food or as a protein supplement for body builders.

One of the most popular methods to turn insects into food today is grinding up the insects and turning their bodies into flour. The flour can then be combined with other ingredients and made into pasta, burgers, protein bars, and bread. Consuming insects in this fashion, where the bodies of the animals are fully disguised, may help increase consumption and decrease squeamishness. Some companies are even selling the waste of their insects, known as frass, to be used as fertilizer.

Today, insects have found their way onto the menus of a number of high-end restaurants, and baseball fans can even eat grasshoppers while watching the Seattle Mariners baseball team. However, for most Westerners who have tried insects, it is no more than a novelty snack. Widespread insect consumption in the West has a long way to go, given the deep taboo in many Western countries that eating insects holds.

See also: Geoduck Farmer.

Further Reading

Halloran, A., Flore, R., Vantomme, P., & Roos, N. (Eds.). (2018). *Edible insects in sustainable food systems.* Springer.

Loo, S., & Sellbach, U. (2013). Eating (with) insects: Insect gastronomies and upside-down ethics. *Parallax, 19*(1), 12–28.

Moscato, E. M., & Cassel, M. (2019). *Eating bugs on purpose: Challenges and opportunities in adapting insects as a sustainable protein.* SAGE Publications: SAGE Business Cases Originals.

Instagram Influencer (Global)

An Instagram influencer is a person who makes a living, or a part of his or her living, through posting on Instagram. Instagram is a photo sharing and social networking application that was founded in 2012. It allows users to upload photos—which can be altered using Instagram's filters—and videos to their accounts to share them with their followers. Users—which include people, corporate brands, and nonhuman animals—tag their photos, add captions and hashtags for them, and create "stories," which are collections of photos or videos that will then drop off the users' feed after twenty-four hours. Other users follow accounts, "like" and comment on photos and videos, and interact with each other via the app.

As of mid-2019, Instagram has one billion monthly users, with the majority of users being located in the United States, India, and Brazil. Unlike other social media giants, such as Facebook, Instagram is increasing in popularity among the young audiences; more teenagers are on Instagram than any other app. In addition, most Instagram users follow at least one brand account (far more than any other social media application), making it one of the best applications to use to promote one's company or products.

Although many Instagram influencers gain fame through the app, others, including athletes, actors, and musicians, use Instagram to increase the reach of their fame. Portuguese soccer star Cristiano Ronaldo, singer Ariana Grande, Dwayne "The Rock" Johnson, and singer and actress Selena Gomez are currently the most popular Instagram users, and all gained their fame outside of the application.

Instagram influencers typically choose a niche, an area of expertise that their photos, videos, and stories will rotate around. The most popular areas on Instagram include fashion and style, food, photography, travel, design, beauty, sports and fitness, and "lifestyle," which often includes all of the above.

Instagram is aspirational. Users follow other users to gain inspiration from those influencers' lifestyles as they are depicted on the platform. Travel influencers share impossibly glamorous photos of the exotic locations that they visit, food influencers share photos of the foods they have prepared or bought, and fashion influencers post their daily outfits; all do so with an eye toward influencing their followers to buy the products that they are promoting. In fact, this aspirational angle, which is what allows Instagram influencers to make money through the platform, also contributes to a decline in mental health according to a 2017 survey of users, as users compare their own lives to the perfectly curated lives of celebrities on Instagram.

Instagram users make money from the platform the way as YouTube users: through sponsored posts. As with YouTube, the price that an influencer can charge for a sponsored post rises as the number of followers rise. In 2019, a user with two thousand followers (which is about the minimum number needed for sponsored posts) can charge about $100–$125 for a post, but someone with over a million followers can charge well over $1,000 per post. Influencers who promote products (via photos, captions, and hashtags) that they are already using can approach those companies to look for sponsorships. Many businesses that appeal to young people have set aside a certain amount of advertising money to spend on influencers, and some companies actively search Instagram to look for influencers who are already interested in their products.

Influencers with large followings make money in other ways as well. Some offer (paid) meet-and-greets with fans, some offer online coaching, others charge speaking fees for events, and still others sell their own makeup, fitness, nutrition, or fashion lines. Many influencers are paid in free goods or services rather than cash; travel Instagrammers, for example, are typically comped their hotel stays in exchange for posts on the platform. Those travel Instagrammers who are paid to post are typically paid more than other influencers, as the value of the goods offered by travel companies tends to be high.

So, how does one become an Instagram influencer? It starts with having an interest or lifestyle that people want to follow and the skills to show it off to great effect. Because of the visual nature of the platform, the ability to take and edit beautiful photos is one of the major requirements for being an Instagram influencer. Investing in a good camera and editing software is critical for the job. Whether an influencer's area of expertise is food, nature, travel, fashion, or makeup, users want to follow accounts that feature high-quality photos with a well-thought-out aesthetic. Instagram influencers also need to post regularly to their page. To attract and retain a large audience, it is critical that users post high-quality content very frequently—at least a few times per week and often multiple times per day. In addition, it is not enough to simply post to one's page. Influencers need to engage with their followers; replying to their comments and engaging with other accounts is one of the most important ways of growing a following.

Most of all, an influencer must be able to influence other people to do something: wear an item of clothing, travel to a particular location, or eat at a specific restaurant. Instagram influencers must be willing to live part—or all—of their life in public, sharing intimate details about what they eat, wear, do, and even feel with their followers. It is this type of engagement, as well as the beautiful photos, that make users want to emulate an influencer. In fact, those Instagrammers who have been caught fabricating some or all of their lifestyle found that the price that they paid was a loss of their Instagram celebrity—and income.

See also: Animal Talent Agent; YouTube Celebrity.

Further Reading

Djafarova, E., & Rushworth, C. (2017). Exploring the credibility of online celebrities' Instagram profiles in influencing the purchase decisions of young female users. *Computers in Human Behavior, 68*, 1–7.

People, Y. (2017). *Instagram ranked worst for young people's mental health*. United Kingdom's Royal Society for Public Health.

Sammis, K., Lincoln, C., & Pomponi, S. (2015). *Influencer marketing for dummies*. John Wiley & Sons.

L

License Plate Blocker (Iran)

A license plate blocker is a person who is hired by a driver in the city of Tehran to block the driver's license plate.

Iran's capital city, Tehran, has a population of about nine million people and five million vehicles, including cars, buses, and taxis—in a city that was built to handle just three hundred thousand cars. The result is a crowded city with massive traffic and terrible air pollution. In fact, Tehran is one of the world's most polluted cities. To deal with this issue, in 1979, city managers began restricting traffic into the city center. Since 2003, the city has two special traffic zones. The Restricted Traffic Zone restricts all traffic into downtown between the hours of 6:30 a.m. and 5:00 p.m. to those private cars with a special pass, which is listed on their license plates. These passes must be purchased on a daily, weekly, or monthly basis and can cost as much as $10 per day. (Taxis, buses, and motorcycles can still drive freely downtown.) The second is the Odd-Even Zone, which controls traffic outside of the downtown Restricted Traffic Zone. In the Odd-Even Zone, cars with odd license plate numbers can only drive through the zone during the hours of 6:30 a.m. to 7:00 p.m. on Sunday, Tuesday, and Thursday, and even license plate numbers are able to drive on Monday, Wednesday, and Saturday. Friday and nights after 7:00 p.m. are open to all drivers.

The results of a 2017 study (Salarvandian, Dijst, & Helbich 2017) have shown that traffic has improved in the Restricted Traffic Zone, but people are continuing to drive in large numbers in the Odd-Even Zone, even though there are cameras throughout the city that are intended to monitor driver compliance by photographing vehicle license plates. There are a number of ways to get around the cameras so that drivers can drive in the restricted zones without the proper permissions.

Some residents may simply own two cars—one with an even number license plate and one with an odd number (all license plates in Iran end with a two-digit code). This option is only available to the wealthy, however. Another method is to cover one's license plate with a piece of paper or cloth to evade the cameras; some drivers even drive with their trunks open to conceal their plates. There are even electronic systems that automatically raise and lower a curtain over the license plate. All these methods are illegal, but traffic enforcement has been spotty. The city is planning on installing more cameras as well as a third restricted zone to further restrict traffic in Tehran.

Another method of evading traffic cameras is to hire someone to manually block one's license plate. This means finding someone who is willing to either run behind one's car, covering up the license from the traffic cameras, or to stand on the back of the car. Some license plate blockers will use a motorcycle driven closely behind the car to evade the cameras. It is unclear how much these human shields are paid to do this job, but given the level of poverty in the country (about a third of the country's population lives in absolute poverty), it is not difficult to find someone to do the work.

See also: Car Watchman.

Further Reading
Fotouhi, A., & Montazeri-Gh, M. J. S. I. (2013). Tehran driving cycle development using the k-means clustering method. *Scientia Iranica, 20*(2), 286–293.
Salarvandian, F., Dijst, M., & Helbich, M. (2017). Impact of traffic zones on mobility behavior in Tehran, Iran. *Journal of Transport and Land Use, 10*(1), 965–982.

Love Hotel Operator (Japan)

A love hotel operator is a person who owns or operates a love hotel (*rabuho* in Japanese), sometimes called boutique or fashion hotels, in Japan.

In some countries, hotel or motel rooms can be rented by the hour. In the United States, for example, hourly motels (also called no-tell motels) are typically very cheap. They are found in dangerous areas of town and are used by sex workers and others to have discreet sex. Many cities have regulations that prevent people from paying for a hotel room for less than a day as a way of discouraging the sex trade. (Some luxury hotels also offer these services, but hourly rates are rarely advertised nor promoted because of the stigma associated with hourly hotels. Some openly offer hourly rates but market them for business professionals who want to use the gym or pool for a couple of hours.)

In Japan, these establishments are called love hotels, after one of the earliest such businesses, Hotel Love, which opened in Osaka in 1968, although the practice of offering rooms for short-term rent is much older. In the Edo period, during the seventeenth century, teahouses and inns known as *tsurekomi* inns offered rooms for discreet sexual activity to clients. It was not until the twentieth century that people other than sex workers began using these businesses, which exploded in the 1960s. These hotels offer rooms that can be rented for an hour or two, and they are set up to make sexual transactions easier, with discreet entrances and unobtrusive staff. As a bonus, many Japanese love hotels are partly automated, allowing the customers to choose, pay for, and get the key for their rooms without having to deal with staff at all.

There are tens of thousands of love hotels in Japan, and they can be found in every major city. They are typically found near train stations and in urban entertainment districts that feature host and hostess clubs, restaurants, and bars. Most can be identified by the lack of windows, the hidden parking lots, and the discreetly located doors. In the past, they were distinguished by the sometimes garish architecture and the often obvious-sounding names, such as Naughty Kitten, Daytime Friend, and Hide and Seek Club. (It was once illegal for hotels to advertise that they offered rooms for sexual purposes, so the building's name and design served that purpose.)

Since 1985, love hotels have been regulated by special laws that mandate where and how these businesses must be operated. Legally, love hotels are defined by a set of features that are intended to distinguish them from regular hotels, such as no kitchen, no lobby, sex product vending machines, and mirrored ceilings. (Some hotels get around these laws, however, by presenting themselves as regular hotels with kitchens and lobbies while still offering hourly rates for sex.) But they are primarily defined by the fact that people can pay to "rest," which typically means "sex," for a few hours rather than to "stay."

By the 2000s, love hotels had experienced a renaissance. Today, they are not seen as seedy establishments offering couples quickie sex; instead, they have upgraded their image to appeal to women, young people, and couples. In fact, Japanese women are more likely to choose love hotels than men today.

Love hotels differ in terms of price (from about $30 per hour and up), decoration (some may offer features such as sex swings, hot tubs, or round beds, and many are themed), and architecture (some are still housed in garish buildings, but most today appear as regular buildings that do not attract attention). Amenities include televisions with adult channels, sex toys (which can be purchased in vending machines), stripper poles, and costumes for rent. In general, they are nicer establishments than similar businesses in, say, the United States. As in the United States, they serve both prostitutes and their clients as well as lovers and even married couples who want a little time without the children. But the need for privacy is much greater in Japan. As a very small but heavily populated country, many couples find that they do not have the opportunity to have sex in private. This was especially true prior to the 2000s, when young people tended to live with their parents until they got married themselves.

Those who operate love hotels today must do more than offer a cheap room for a few yen to customers wanting to have sex. Operators are updating their businesses, offering more amenities that appeal to middle-class women, and are marketing their services more thoughtfully to younger people who, because they do not live at home with their parents anymore, no longer need to visit love hotels as they did in the past. Hotel operators are also focusing on a new client pool: Chinese business and tourist travelers who are visiting Japan in large numbers. Many continue to offer hourly rates, but they are also offering other services to travelers who may not be interested in sex but are attracted by the concept of the love hotel.

So, what does it take to work at or run a love hotel? There are no real requirements for this job, other than discretion and a lack of prudishness around sex. (Cleaning staff in particular should not be squeamish.) Because there are so many love hotels in Japan today, there is no shortage of jobs. The pay is not great for those who work at these hotels, but for someone who wants to run his or her own establishment, there is no real limit to how much can be made.

Even as the industry is changing, love hotels are a lucrative business model, and the industry is worth an estimated $20 billion to $40 billion per year.

See also: Sex Worker.

Further Reading

Chaplin, S. (2007). *Japanese love hotels: A cultural history.* Routledge.

West, M. D. (2011). *Lovesick Japan: Sex, marriage, romance, law.* Cornell University Press.

M

Mahout (Southeast Asia, South Asia)

A mahout is a person who rides, cares for, and works with elephants in some Asian countries. (The word *mahout* is Hindi and is often used to describe elephant handlers in other Asian countries; however, many countries use terms from their own languages.) The practice of mahoutship is an ancient one and probably dates back to before recorded history, when members of tribal groups in South and Southeast Asia started catching and keeping elephants. Today, a number of tribal groups are still involved in elephant care, such as the Gwi of Thailand, the Jena Kuruba of India, and the Karen of Thailand, Laos, and Myanmar.

Asian elephants (as opposed to African elephants, which are a different genus and species) are native to India and many Southeast Asian countries and have played a significant role in many countries' economic, cultural, and social practices, especially Thailand's. Asian elephants are smaller and more trainable than their African cousins. This is one of the reasons why there is a long tradition of keeping elephants for work in Asia but not in Africa. In fact, we know that Asian elephants have been kept in captivity for at least five thousand years. Asian elephants are an endangered species. They are threatened by habitat destruction and fragmentation as well as poaching.

An elephant and mahout in Kerala, India. (Pindiyath100/Dreamstime.com)

The elephant is a sacred animal in Hinduism and is seen as the embodiment of one of its most important gods, Ganesh. That is why captive elephants live at many temples throughout India and play an important role in Hindu festivals. Buddhists, too, view elephants through a spiritual lens, comparing their thoughtfulness, deliberateness, patience, and intelligence to the Buddha himself.

Elephants have never been domesticated. Domestication involves the selective breeding over multiple generations of a species to produce physical and behavioral differences and, ultimately, speciation: a new species of animal. Although not all domesticated animals are proper species (dogs, for example, can still mate with wolves, as can domestic cats with some wild cats), for the most part, domesticated animals display enough physiological and behavioral changes from their wild counterparts to be seen as a totally new species.

Asian elephants, while not domesticated, have certainly been tamed and kept in captivity for thousands of years. One of the first uses of Asian elephants was for warfare: elephants were caught and used for war in ancient India, China, and Persia, but perhaps the most famous use of elephants during warfare was during the Punic Wars, when Hannibal brought dozens of elephants with him across the Alps into Italy to fight the Romans. Elephants were also once used in agriculture to drag plows, clear fields, and perform other tasks.

The most common use of elephants in Asia today is as a beast of burden. In particular, elephants have been a part of logging activities in Southeast Asia for hundreds of years. In Thailand, where this practice was most well known, elephants are classified, along with domesticated animals such as donkeys and horses, as draught animals; this means that they are not subject to laws intended to serve wildlife. When used in logging, elephants are trained to use their trunks and tusks to haul logs. However, because of the overlogging of Thailand's forests, the country banned logging in 1989, forcing thousands of Thai elephants—and their handlers—into other occupations. (Deforestation also destroyed much of wild elephants' habitat in Thailand.) Elephant loggers are still commonly used in Myanmar and India.

Other elephants are trained to give rides to tourists or to provide transportation for local people; still others perform in religious festivals. After the Indian Ocean tsunami in 2004, elephants were used to clear debris in Sri Lanka, Thailand, and Indonesia.

Working elephants are caught in the wild, as captive breeding of elephants is notoriously difficult. (In addition, Indian mahouts are sometimes hired by the government to capture "problem" elephants who cause damage to villages or farms.) In Thailand, because of the ban on logging, many captive elephants today work as street hustlers, performing tricks and begging for money and food from tourists. Once an elephant has been conscripted into working, he or she cannot easily be released back into the wild, so the animal must continue to be cared for. Feeding an Asian elephant involves hundreds of pounds of fruit, leaves, and other vegetation every day. (Mahouts in Nepal also make their elephants *kuchi*, which is a specialty food item made from grass that is formed into a bowl and filled with rice and other ingredients. More grass is used to wrap the kuchi into a ball; an elephant may eat ninety kuchi per day. Another word for kuchi is *dana*, which means "gift" in Nepali.)

Regardless of the type of work, working elephants in Asia are cared for by individuals called mahouts. The vast majority of mahouts are men; in fact, a woman in India named Parbati Barua is alleged to be the only female mahout in the world. Some mahouts own and care for their elephants by themselves. For others, ownership is through the family, and two to three individuals may actually be involved in caring for the elephant. The job of a mahout is fairly straightforward: he is responsible for caring for and overseeing the labor of a working elephant. But the reality is more complicated than the description.

Most mahouts begin their work as young boys, and they inherit and learn the job from older family members. As a boy, a mahout will get his first elephant, who he will live and work with for decades. (Asian elephants can live up to eighty years.) The mahout is responsible for training his elephant for the job that he will have, using tools such as chains, poles, and bullhooks. The process of training an elephant can take years, and it can be done gently or violently. Some mahouts use only positive reinforcement to train their elephants, but others use their tools to intimidate them into complying.

Mahouts form strong bonds with their elephants. Elephants are an extremely social species of animal: all female animals remain in their natal family units throughout their lives, while adult males live either alone or with other males. When living in captivity, without other elephants, these animals find their bond with their human caretaker. Mahouts bathe their elephants, massage them, and treat them when they are ill or injured. Many mahouts live in tourist or logging camps in the middle of the jungle and see their elephant more than their human family members.

The job of a mahout can be dangerous. Although deaths from working with elephants are rare, elephants are extremely strong, and accidents—or worse—can happen. In addition, male elephants periodically undergo musth, a period when their testosterone levels increase radically, causing the elephants to become aggressive. In fact, that is when most deaths attributed to elephant attacks occur. Catching an elephant is also dangerous. Whether the method is to lasso the elephant around the neck (the most common method used in Thailand, Vietnam, Laos, and Cambodia); use a female decoy elephant to attract a male; drive the elephant into a pen or corral (a practice called *khedda* in Hindi and the most common method of catching an elephant in India and Myanmar); conceal a noose on the ground (used in Sri Lanka to trap the elephant's leg), or cause them to fall into a hidden pit (the most dangerous method by far), elephant catching can be a risky endeavor for both the mahout and the elephant.

Mahouts typically do not undergo formalized training; they learn the job from more senior mahouts. But at least one organization, Elephants World, offers a one- to four-week course for foreigners to live and work with both mahouts and elephants at a cost of about $600 per week.

Some mahouts do not own their elephants. Instead, are hired by someone who owns elephants, usually a wealthy businessman, to care for his animals. This is common in the tourism industry today; a tour company owns a group of elephants and hires multiple mahouts to care for them. This modern relationship between a hired mahout and an elephant does not involve the lengthy learning process that mahouts who own their elephants traditionally undergo; it may involve only a few days of training. (According to a Food and Agriculture Organization (FAO) report (Lair 1997), the best-treated elephants are cared for by mahouts who own their animals, and the worst treated are those cared for by hired mahouts.) The work is hard, the hours are long, and the pay is low for these mahouts. Other mahouts work for the government, as in India, where many mahouts work for the state forest departments in logging operations.

Unfortunately, with tourism being the only viable industry for most working elephants and their mahouts today, there are now other problems that mahouts face. As Westerners become more sensitized to animal welfare issues, many animal welfare groups and advocates are demanding changes to the ways in which elephants are trained and used. At the same time, however, tourists still travel to Asia to see, touch, and even ride elephants, so the animals must be trained to handle this kind of work. Mahouts, then, must walk a tightrope between providing services to tourists, making a living for themselves and their elephants, and at least seeming to use humane methods of training to appeal to those same tourists.

In recent years, a number of international nongovernmental organizations (NGOs) have developed programs to work with mahouts and to provide them with equipment and tools that make their lives—and the lives of their elephants— easier. Because many mahouts are struggling to make a living, and because some of the training methods used include force, these organizations are attempting to help mahouts transition to more humane training methods. For example, Elephant Aid International encourages mahouts in Thailand and Nepal to give up the use of chains to control their elephants. Those who have done so are left with more work, because chaining makes caring for elephants easier. The organization is hoping to alleviate this problem with new equipment as well as positive reinforcement training methods. Elephant specialists today are not asking that elephants no longer be used in tourism, as doing so would cause serious harm to current working elephants and their mahouts. Instead, they recommend better treatment and training for the elephants and the mahouts as well as restrictions on catching wild elephants and a certification system for tourist camps to ensure minimal standards of welfare.

The tradition of the mahout no longer carries the prestige that it once did, as elephants' (and mahouts') roles in many cultures are reduced to simply tourism, causing the mahout-elephant relationship to change accordingly. The profession is dying out. The jobs that elephants can do are narrowing, especially because of logging bans. And while many working elephants today work in the tourist industry, rather than logging or agriculture, that work is limited. And, finally, as opportunities and respect for mahouts shrink, so does their pay, with the result being that most mahouts are struggling economically.

See also: Panda Nanny; Sloth Nanny.

Further Reading
Hart, L., & Sundar. (2000). Family traditions for mahouts of Asian elephants. *Anthrozoös, 13*(1), 34–42.

Hartle, D. (2019). *Giants of the monsoon forest: Living and working with elephants.* Norton.

Lair, R. C. (1997). *Gone astray: The care and management of the Asian elephant in domesticity.* RAP.

Namboodiri, N. (1997). *Practical elephant management: A handbook for mahouts.* Elephant Welfare Association.

Matchmaker (India, Pakistan, China, Japan)

A matchmaker is a person who is hired by parents in much of Asia to arrange prospective spouses for their children.

Marriage is one of the oldest social practices in the world and is found in every culture on the planet. It is one of the few cultural universals. It creates one of the oldest and most basic familial ties—what anthropologists call affinal ties or ties of affinity (with the second being consanguineal ties or ties of consanguinity, which are blood ties). Marriage is a culturally defined relationship between, usually, a man and woman from different families that provides for a set of important rights and responsibilities between each participant (such as the regulation of sex and the exchange of domestic duties), between the families involved (the creation of an important social and economic alliance), and between the participants and any children they have (marriage determines the legal parents of any children and creates, ideally, a fund of property for the children to inherit). Human children need care for many years, which necessitates coparenting and the formation of a pair bond. This pair bond was formalized into marriage during some time in our ancient past.

The most common form of marriage today unites one man and one woman as husband and wife. Prior to the rise of Christianity around the world through colonialism, however, the most popular form of marriage was polygyny, in which one man marries multiple women. In cultures around the world, there have also been cases where people of the same sex (but often a different gender) were able to marry, and today this is increasingly becoming more common among Western developed nations.

Because marriage is such an important social, cultural, and economic institution, every culture has rules that determine who is able to marry whom (such as laws of exogamy, which ensure that people do not marry close kin, or laws of endogamy, which may require that people can only marry within their religion, caste group, or race). Because marriage is so important, it has traditionally been the case that young people do not choose their marriage partners. Instead, marriages were arranged for most of human history by parents who looked at potential spouses from a variety of perspectives. Is the family good? Will they be a good family for us to align with? Will the woman be a good mother? Will the man be a good provider? Are there scandals in the family that would disgrace us?

Arranged marriages seem unusual to most Westerners today because the "love marriage" has taken over from the arranged marriage as the most typical form of marriage in the West. Westerners, and people around the world, want to fall in love and then marry the person with whom they fell in love. However, it appears that love marriages have, at least in some countries, much lower success rates than arranged marriages. Arranged marriages may last longer than love marriages because of the work that the parents put in to find the perfect partner or perhaps because the parents of both partners approve of the marriage (this may not always be the case in love marriages). And in countries with patrilocal postmarital residence, such as most Asian countries (where the newly married couple lives with, or near, the husband's parents), arranged marriages are most likely more successful because the young woman, who is now part of her husband's family, has been preapproved by them. If the family does not approve of the new wife, she may experience serious difficulties that could cause her to leave the marriage.

Arranged marriages are in decline around the world today, but they continue to be practiced most prominently in India, where Hindus see marriage as a sacrament and where the wedding industry is worth $50 billion. Many Indian parents used to advertise their son's or daughter's personal details (age, height, education, job, etc.) in the matrimonial section of the classified ads in the local newspaper, but many others use matchmakers to help extend the reach of their search.

Matchmaking is becoming increasingly common in India, as Indian society has undergone massive economic (India is one of the fastest-growing economies in the world) and cultural changes (such as the decline of the extended family) that have led to many families not having the vast social relationships they once had. This means the parents need help identifying potential spouses and brokering what can be a complicated marriage agreement. (In India, dowries are used, which means a woman's family pays her intended husband's family a certain amount of goods and cash, which must be negotiated in advance. The practice has been illegal since 1961, because of the potential for dowry violence if the dowry is not high enough, but the law is not enforced. Many families still demand dowries as part of the marriage agreement.)

Families who hire a matchmaker provide that person with photographs of their child, information about their child's personality, and as much information as they can provide on the family's (and perhaps the child's) expectations for a spouse. Some astrologers ask for the astrology chart of the child and will use that in finding a match.

After meeting with the family, the matchmaker starts looking for potential matches. Every family wants to be aligned with a family with a good reputation, and they want their future in-laws to be of good character. Most families specify that the match must be of the same religion, and many also require that the match's caste be either the same as the family seeking a spouse or a higher status. (While declining in India, caste is still an important part of Indian life. Caste position traditionally determines occupation, marriage, where one lives, and much more. Discrimination on the basis of caste was criminalized in 1950, and although it still does take place today, it appears that it is on its way out—at least in urban areas. Even intercaste marriage, which was once scandalous—especially to the family of the higher-caste spouse—is becoming more common.)

As caste begins to decline in importance, status remains a significant concern for most Indian families, so the profession, salary, and other indicators of social status will be extremely important to the matchmaker and the families involved.

Families will be asked to provide pay stubs and bank statements to prove their worth. Even what the family eats and how their food is prepared is important in seeking a match. If possible, the matchmaker will also use astrology or numerology to determine the best candidate. Finally, the appearance requirements for the spouse are also considered (especially when seeking a woman).

After the matchmaker has found a number of possible matches, either from within his or her own database or through his or her personal network, he or she will provide photos and information about those people to the family. The family, with the son or daughter, will then choose a few finalists to meet in person. If both families are interested after one such meeting, then the families will try to gather as much information about the other family, both with and without the matchmaker's help. (Some families hire private detective agencies that specialize in researching the history of potential partners.) Once both families have agreed on the marriage and the dowry, dates, and other issues have been negotiated, the wedding can proceed. Another reason for the use of matchmakers is that having a third party tell the families whose children were rejected that they were not chosen is easier on the family.

There is no training to become a matchmaker. Traditionally, matchmakers, known as *nayan*, were well-known figures within their local community whose social networks included a large number of families. Today, modern matchmakers may also be wedding planners, offering their services for every aspect of the wedding planning process. In fact, traditional matchmakers often helped with the weddings that they arranged. Traditional matchmakers were paid in goods, but modern matchmakers determine a cash fee for their services.

Matchmakers must be personable, knowledgeable, and attentive to their clients' needs. They also need to be discreet. They will be privy to a great deal of personal and financial information about the families they work with and must be trusted to not share that information outside of the matchmaking process. In addition, because matchmaking will result in a certain number of rejected would-be spouses, the matchmaker needs to be trusted to not share anything that will result in a family's disgrace.

Most matchmakers now advertise their services on the Internet to reach a larger audience, although some still find customers the traditional way—through word of mouth. Some matchmakers throw parties and host events for eligible singles, where potential partners can meet and talk. But unlike similar events in the West, parents attend these events as well, weighing in on the participants and helping to choose the people with whom their son or daughter might talk. The costs for services like this vary widely from country to country. Even within India, where matchmaking remains popular, the costs can vary; costs go up for families seeking wealthy spouses for their children.

Many people still prefer arranged marriages over love marriages. Entering an arranged marriage means not having to spend years looking for a potential mate. Leaving the work of finding a partner to their parents (and a matchmaker) takes the pressure off the young people so that they can focus on building their careers. Some people even think it is romantic to fall in love with your spouse after marriage.

Indians who have immigrated to other countries will often allow their families back home to hire a matchmaker on their behalf. Some matchmakers focus on providing matchmaking services for Indians living in the United States. Parents especially value arranged marriages, as it gives them control over who will become part of their family, and by ensuring that their son or daughter marries someone of equal or greater social status, the family's wealth is preserved within the family.

In many arranged marriages today, the partners have a chance to get to know each other prior to the marriage, and if the partners are adamantly opposed to the marriage, the marriage will not be forced. In fact, most families choose multiple partners for their children to meet and give them the right to refuse any of the partners who do not meet their own demands. This right of refusal is critical for young Indian men and women today, who may value different qualities, such as companionship and chemistry, than their parents, who tend to focus on financial stability and social status.

Today, online matchmaking is the fastest-growing area within the Indian marriage market. Thousands of sites are competing for the large market of Indian singles who want to arrange their own marriages but need helping finding partners. Just as singles in other countries use dating sites such as eHarmony, Match.com, and Plenty of Fish, Indians are now using their own online matchmaking services (which are distinguished from other dating sites by use of the term "matrimony sites"), such as Shaadi.com and BharatMatrimony.com, which extend the network of possible matches far beyond that of a single matchmaker. Unfortunately, many Indian users of these sites report some of the same problems as users of other matchmaking sites—many people who use these services are more interested in hooking up than finding a marriage partner. This is one reason why matchmakers are still so important in helping to arrange marriages in India.

See also: Wedding Guest.

Further Reading

Banerjee, D. C. (1995). *Arranged marriage.* Doubleday.
Jaiswal, T. (2014). *Indian arranged marriages: A social psychological perspective.* Routledge.

Mime or Clown (Global)

Mimes and clowns are performance artists. In many ways, they are similar to actors or other performers, but they are also quite different from other performers as well as from each other.

Mimes and clowns do not use their voices as part of their performances (in the case of clowns, they may do so only minimally); instead, they use their distinctive makeup and body movements to portray a character and tell a story. Both mimes and clowns commonly perform in public, at fairs, on public streets, and at community events, and while one can pay to see a clown or mime perform, in, say, a theater, this is less common. Instead, as street performers, most clowns and mimes perform for tips. (However, many can be hired to perform for private parties.) In

A mime inspects a small present during his act. (Svetlana Mihailova/Dreamstime.com)

addition, as street performers, both types of performers will interact with their audiences, bringing them into the show.

Mimes are performers who tell stories without speaking; instead, they act out, or mime, a story using their bodies, hand movements, and facial expressions. Miming is related to mummery, in that both are forms of street performance that date back hundreds of thousands of years. In the case of miming, clearly the use of gestures and hand signals to communicate predates human speech and is thus hundreds of thousands of years old. Expressive movements without speech also led to the many forms of dance seen around the world; classical Indian and Thai dances, for example, both share many stylistic features with mime.

The earliest known form of mime originated in ancient Greek theater. Telestes is the first actor that we know of who performed mime on the Greek stage. He interpreted, through gestures, the stories that were sung or recited by the chorus; his first documented mime performance was in the play *Seven against Thebes*. True pantomime, though, in which no speech or singing takes place—the action is entirely depicted through gestures—emerged with the performances of ancient Rome. Performers during this period performed short scenes of love, tragedy, comedy, and current events as well as literary works.

Miming later continued after the fall of the Roman Empire with the traveling performers of medieval Europe. Miming, singing, dancing, juggling, and performing acrobatics were some of the activities that these performers engaged in, entertaining commoners and royalty alike. At the end of the Middle Ages, a new

---

Funeral Clown

A funeral clown, called an *archimimus*, was a person who dressed up as a deceased person and attended that person's funeral in ancient Rome. The clown wore a mask made up to look like the deceased and danced and interacted with mourners. Funeral clowns were hired by the family of the dead to bring some levity to a sad situation, and it was believed that having a clown present would soothe the spirits of the dead.

The funeral clown was very similar to the court jester or fool who would emerge in European courts a few hundred years after the fall of the Roman Empire. Both funeral clowns and court jesters were expected to challenge authority and behave in ways that were socially unacceptable. The only reason that they were allowed to act this way was because the roles were very narrowly defined; for the court jester, he could get away with making fun of the king precisely because he was a fool and, thus, not someone to be taken seriously. The funeral clown, on the other hand, was never allowed to mock the dead—and especially such an important figure as an emperor—except within the very narrow circumstances of the funeral and while dressed up as the deceased.

The presence of a clown—who made jokes, mocked the dead, and behaved in ways that would otherwise be completely inappropriate—at an otherwise solemn occasion seems strange to us today. And yet the tradition of funeral clowns has reemerged in some countries. Ireland, for example, saw its first funeral clown company, Dead Happy Ireland, open in 2009, offering modern Irish people the opportunity to hire a clown (who does not dress as, nor mimic or mock, the deceased) for their loved ones' funerals.

Source: León, V. (2009). *Working IX to V: Orgy planners, funeral clowns, and other prized professions of the ancient world.* Bloomsbury Publishing.

---

form of improvisational performance emerged called *commedia dell'arte*. This new theatrical form involved actors, wearing masks with exaggerated facial features, who depicted stock characters and specific moods. It was derived from the tradition of masking during Carnival in Northern Italy. Stock characters included servants, lovers, masters, and clowns. Commedia dell'arte was unusual in that female performers acted alongside of men, and performers were highly physical, incorporating dancing, tumbling, and other activities into their performances. Miming also played a role in what were called dumb shows, plays or pieces of plays performed without dialogue in both the Middle Ages and the Renaissance.

During the nineteenth century, some of the conventions of the modern mime emerged: a silent figure wearing heavy white face makeup, combined with a more refined, less slapstick form of performance. In the twentieth century, Parisian mimes such as Jacques Copeau, who trained mimes with masks, and Marcel Marceau took the art form much further, creating new styles of miming that are still with us today. Modern-day miming is largely a form of street performance, and mimes are easily recognized by their distinctive white makeup with black touches around the eyes and other facial features. Even though some mimes spurn the traditional black-and-white makeup, it is still the most distinctive identifying feature of a mime to many.

In general, the term *clown* referred to any comic performer, such as court jesters, buffoons, mimes, and acrobats. These performers often used (and still use) their comedy to criticize and satirize existing social conditions; even court performers could sometimes get away with subtly or openly criticizing the king. Comic performers like these were found in professional acting troupes as well, such as in the commedia dell'arte in Renaissance Italy and in Shakespeare's plays in Elizabethan England.

Joseph Grimaldi was an English mime who created a character called Clown at the turn of the nineteenth century, and he created the conventions for clowns that we still have today: a white face, with colorful paint creating exaggerated eyes, cheeks, and mouth. His physical appearance and performances shaped clowns into the present day. On the other hand, not all clowns look like the classic white-faced, red-nosed, red-haired clown. One famous clown type is the Auguste clown, whose face is painted a flesh tone but with large white areas drawn around his eyes and mouth (which is painted black). The Auguste clown is one of the most buffoonish of all the clowns.

With the rise of the circus in the eighteenth century, clowns moved from the theater into this new venue. One of the most famous of all the circus clowns is the hobo or tramp. Dressed in rags, with the white face but a sad expression, he is one of the more widely recognized clowns today. (Even though the hobo clown has a sad face, his performances are still aimed at eliciting laughter.) Another famous American clown is the rodeo clown. He dresses like typical clowns but actively participates in rodeo events, but in a comic way.

Because of the exaggerated appearance and behavior of clowns, many people are afraid of them, and a number of horror movies (most notably Stephen King's *It*) have used the clown as a figure of fear. In addition, in 2016, a new trend emerged of people dressing up as clowns to harass or even terrorize people in a number of American cities, which added to the overall fear of clowns.

Mimes and clowns differ in that clowns are almost always comedic performers, which is clear from their colorful and flamboyant costumes, while mimes, who wear a neutral costume, can and do portray a number of different emotions in their performances. Mimes, too, may portray a variety of characters in their performances, using only their bodies and facial expressions to differentiate them for the audience. The clown, on the other hand, plays a single character that the performer has created. This specific character is used by the clown during all of his or her performances. And while clowns are often associated with circuses and other performative spaces popular with children (such as children's birthday parties), mimes often tell a more complex, adult-oriented story in their performances.

Clowns and mimes both typically go to school to learn their arts, although doing so is not strictly required. (Some of the better known traditional clown schools, such as Ringling Bros. and Barnum & Bailey Clown College, have closed down in recent years.) Clown education covers the creation of a character, costuming and makeup application, juggling, acrobatics, tricks and pratfalls, using props, building a routine, and more. Clown schools typically also offer job assistance, networking, and professional development. On top of the formal education, clowns must be funny, high energy, and physically fit. They must be able to improvise, be able to interact effectively with audience members (either children or adults), be able to use their bodies in their performances, and must be comfortable making a fool of themselves for a living.

Mimes can also go to school to learn their craft. There are schools of mime around the world, and many university theater programs have courses in miming. A number of performing companies, such as the Mime Theatre Studio in Los Angeles and the American Mime Theatre in New York, offer training to students as well. Mime training is heavily focused on using one's body and face to tell a story. Students learn the miming techniques of some of the most well-known mimes of the past, such as Marcel Marceau and Etienne Decroux. On top of learning the physical skills of miming, students learn how to improvise, create characters, and create narratives.

Most clowns and mimes are self-employed and must rely on hired gigs for their income, with hourly fees starting as low as $15 and going as high as several hundred dollars. Annual income can thus range radically, with an average clown income of $36,000 per year being reported by Indeed.com. Once a performer develops a reputation, he or she can get paying jobs at corporate events, parties, and other venues or even full-time work at a circus or amusement park. (Cirque du Soleil regularly hires clowns for their troupes.) However, much of the work that clowns and mimes do is not paid at all. For example, clowns may perform for free for patients at children's hospitals, rehabilitation clinics, and veterans' hospitals or at schools and community events. Experienced clowns and mimes can also teach clowning at a clown school or through a local adult education program.

Unfortunately, both clowning and miming—but especially clowning—are becoming less popular today. According to the World Clown Association, the biggest clowning organization in the world, there are fewer clowns performing today and fewer young people learning to be clowns. One reason for this is the decline in circuses in the past decade, but the change also reflects changing ideas about entertainment. Other reasons for the decline include the stigma associated with clowns, thanks to their portrayal in horror movies; the lack of opportunities; and the low pay.

See also: Rodeo Performer.

Further Reading

Lust, A. (2002). *From the Greek mimes to Marcel Marceau and beyond: Mimes, actors, Pierrots, and clowns: A chronicle of the many visages of mime in the theatre.* Scarecrow Press.

Radford, B. (2016). *Bad clowns.* University of New Mexico Press.

Mohel (Global)

A mohel is a traditional Jewish circumciser. Technically, in Judaism, the father is required to circumcise his own sons, but because most fathers do not feel equipped to do this, the profession of the mohel emerged.

Circumcision is usually defined as the surgical removal of the foreskin from the penis. Circumcision is currently performed in many countries soon after a baby is born, but it was traditionally part of a male coming-of-age ritual in cultures where circumcision was practiced and would take place at around the time when a boy transitions into a teenager.

Male coming-of-age rituals are used to usher men from childhood into adulthood and are found in virtually every culture. These rituals demand that young men demonstrate bravery, strength, heroism, or an accomplishment in hunting or some other highly valued but difficult activity. Many such rituals involve pain; circumcision ceremonies are a good example of this.

For instance, among the Okiek of Kenya, boys undergo a circumcision ritual between the ages of fourteen and sixteen, after which they are excluded from the world of adults and the opposite sex for weeks. During the ritual, the Okiek boys are first separated from the tribe and kept in isolation with members of their sex and age cohort (during which time they wear white body paint and are given secret tribal knowledge), and in the third and final part of the ritual, they are reintroduced to society as adult circumcised men. Because circumcision in these rituals is done without anesthesia, it is painful, which is one of the important aspects of a male initiation ceremony—to test or challenge the boys to ensure that they are strong enough to earn adulthood.

Among Australian aboriginals, circumcision is also used to mark male adulthood. For Australians, as with Africans, both pain and physical transformation are critical aspects of the ritual, and as in Africa, boys are expected to demonstrate strength and courage and not flinch under the pain. During the boys' separation from society, they witness secret religious ceremonies and are given information about the origins of the universe.

In both Africa and Australia, circumcision makes a boy into a man through physically transforming his body and, not coincidentally, shedding blood, which is often seen as symbolically female and, thus, polluting. The rest of the ceremony, including the isolation from the community (especially women), the bonding with other men, and the transmission of secret knowledge, all plays an important role alongside the circumcision in making a boy into a man.

Today, just over a third of all men are circumcised. Circumcision rates are highest in Africa and West Asia, where it continues to be an important rite of passage for boys in many tribal cultures, and where there is also a large population of Muslims. Muslims, like Jews, see circumcision as part of their religious practice, and the majority of circumcised men today are Muslim. Muslims are usually circumcised during childhood, sometime between the age of seven and puberty. Circumcision is also popular in the United States and South Korea, although circumcision rates in the United States have been on a steady decline since the 1980s.

Neonatal circumcision is practiced in many countries today and is usually done for nonmedical reasons. As circumcision became more popular in the twentieth century, it became a social norm, and many parents today continue to have their baby sons circumcised so that they will not be ostracized by their peers.

Among Jews, circumcision, known as *brit milah* or *bris*, is mandatory and is a visible sign of the Jews' covenant with God (to seal a covenant, in Hebrew, means "to cut"). In the Book of Genesis, God commanded Abraham to become circumcised and to have his male descendants (as well as servants and slaves)

circumcised as well on the eighth day after a child has been born. This requirement is maintained even when the eighth day falls on the Sabbath, during which
time Jews are typically not allowed to work. (Adult Jewish converts may also be
circumcised.) Jews have been practicing circumcision for three thousand to four
thousand years.

In the Jewish tradition, Jews are circumcised by a mohel, who is a man (or, in
the Reform tradition, a man or a woman) specially trained in the practice of circumcision. The mohel is usually a rabbi or other religious leader, but any Jewish
man can technically perform a circumcision. Because of declining rates of circumcision (even among Jewish parents), most mohalim (the plural of mohel) do
not do the job full-time but as a part-time gig.

Many Jews arrange for the bris before the child is born, as the process of locating a mohel and planning for the ceremony can take time. Mohalim are found
either through word of mouth within one's local Jewish community or through
online services such as Yelp. Jews who live in an area without a trained mohel
may instead use a Jewish pediatrician, although that means they must forego the
ritual.

Before the ceremony, which must take place before sundown, the mohel explains
to the family what will happen during the procedure and provides instructions so
that the parents can prepare the baby. Some circumcisions take place in a syna-
gogue, but others take place in the home of the family. Some mohalim also perform circumcisions at hospitals if they have been given privileges by the facility.

In a bris (rather than a hospital circumcision), a male relative of the child sits in
a chair and holds the baby on a pillow, and that is where the mohel performs the
circumcision. The mohel may apply a topical anesthetic to control the pain, but
most do not, as the procedure is supposed to be at least somewhat painful for the
child. However, most mohalim offer the baby sugar water or wine to calm him
during the procedure. The mohel then offers a blessing that acknowledges the
importance of the occasion. The actual circumcision is very quick; the mohel lifts
the foreskin and places a guard between the foreskin and the penis to protect the
penis. Then, using a special ritual knife called an *izmil*, he slices off the foreskin
in one cut. After the foreskin is removed, the mohel suctions any blood from the
wound. This is traditionally done by mouth, known as *metzitzah b'peh*, but many
mohalim today either use a tube placed on the wound (to eliminate mouth-to-
wound contact, which may be responsible for spreading disease) or refrain from
suctioning altogether. After the surgery is over, the parents recite a blessing, and
the mohel recites a prayer during which the baby's Hebrew name is revealed.
After the ceremony, the family has a celebratory meal featuring a number of traditional prayers and blessings.

Many mohalim do not set a specific price for their service but instead ask parents to pay what they can afford. Others, however, do set prices, which usually
range in the hundreds of dollars.

Some Jewish doctors train to become mohalim so that parents who are worried
about dangers associated with the procedure can feel better about the risks. They
can also provide circumcisions for Jewish families in areas where no mohalim
work. Traditionally, a mohel inherited the position from his father or another male

relative, from whom he learned the surgical and ritual components of the bris. Today, some mohalim learn by apprenticing with an experienced practitioner, and some organizations, such as the National Organization of American Mohalim, offer formalized training programs.

See also: Traditional Healer.

Further Reading

Glick, L. B. (2005). *Marked in your flesh: Circumcision from ancient Judea to modern America.* Oxford University Press.

Mazor, J. (2013). The child's interests and the case for the permissibility of male infant circumcision. *Journal of Medical Ethics, 39*(7), 421–428.

Thiessen, M. (2011). *Contesting conversion: Genealogy, circumcision, and identity in ancient Judaism and Christianity.* Oxford University Press.

Mourner (Sub-Saharan Africa, Great Britain, China, India, Ireland)

A mourner is, at its most basic, someone who mourns the death of someone else. But a professional mourner is a person who is hired to perform the acts associated with mourning at the funeral of someone they do not know. Mourners are paid to wail, moan, and cry as a way to show the importance of the deceased and to encourage other mourners to cry as well.

In many cultures around the world, it was not only common but expected that mourners would wail loudly during the funeral of a loved one or a respected member of the community. This ritualized form of mourning, known as a death wail, was practiced in cultures as diverse as Papua New Guinea, indigenous Australia, and Ireland. In Ireland, the practice was called keening, and it was performed by the women before and during the funeral.

Sometimes families also hired specialist keeners, known as *bean chaointe*, whose presence showed respect and honor for the deceased. The keener was paid with a glass of whiskey or a token amount of money; she certainly did not make a living from it. One of the interpretations of keening is that the keener enters a sort of trance while keening, and by doing so, she essentially channels the grief of the entire community through her keens. The practice of keening disappeared in Ireland in the mid-twentieth century, as more people began to see the practice as incompatible with belonging to the modern world.

Mourning practices in small tight-knit communities have always been more stylized and elaborate than those in contemporary industrial and postindustrial societies. Because the death of an individual in a tribal or village society could affect so many people, funerals and their associated ceremonies were community events, bringing people together, reinforcing social solidarity, and ensuring continuity after the loss. It should not surprise us, then, that mourning in those settings is, to modern eyes, so unusual. Death is, for many people today, highly bureaucratized and sanitized, with the death, the business of preparing the body, and the burial itself all handled by professionals from outside of the family. Because we live relatively atomized lives, surrounded by loved ones, friends, and workmates

---

Death Messenger

In Northern Europe, until about the nineteenth century, after a person died, a death messenger traveled around the village to let other villagers know about the death and invite them to attend the funeral. Death messengers were generally paid based on the distance that they had to travel, and they sometimes rang a ball while delivering the news; this practice evolved from the "dead bell" that was rung after a person's death in the Middle Ages to drive away evil spirits and summon prayers for the deceased. The death messenger was also linked to an Irish folkloric tradition in which a supernatural specter of a woman, often clothed in white, appeared and began to keen, or cry; the keening of this death messenger alerted all those who heard it that a death was soon to come. (She also appears in English folklore as a banshee.) The supernatural death messenger was linked to Irish funerary practices in which women—either friends or family of the dead or specialist keeners hired for this purpose—keened loudly over the dead body. A different version of the Irish death messenger was known as the *cóiste bodhar*, a coach that collected the soul of the dead and drove it to the afterworld. Korea, too, has a supernatural death messenger who was thought to appear at funerals to escort the soul of the dead to judgment in the underworld; family members of the deceased put out rice and shoes to help the death messenger for this journey.

Source: Butler, J. (2008). Symbolic and social roles of women in death ritual in traditional Irish society. In E. J. Håland (Ed.), *Women, pain and death: Rituals and everyday life on the margins of Europe and beyond* (pp. 108–121). Cambridge Scholars Publishing.

---

but not the larger community in which we live, there are fewer people to mourn us when we are gone, and many people today mourn in relative silence and privacy. Mourning is expected to be brief and relatively contained, and then we move on with our lives.

This modern mourning process is in great contrast to the ways in which people in small-scale societies have traditionally dealt with and demonstrated grief and mourning. In particular, the use of loud wailing, either by women or women and men, has long been present in the funeral practices of people in Africa, Asia, Australasia, and Latin America. This kind of wailing, often accompanied by seizure-like behavior, trances, and the rending of clothes and hair, seems uncontrollable but is actually culturally appropriate and prescribed. To outsiders from cultures in which mourning is expected to be private and contained, however, it seems crazy. In 2017, the president of Tajikistan, perhaps in an effort to make the country look more modern, banned the practice of loud wailing at funerals.

In cultures where this sort of ritualized grief was expected, the use of professional mourners—often women—developed. The Irish keeners were exclusively women, and in most cultures that employ professional mourners, women take on this role as well. In most of the world, it is women, after all, who are responsible for caring for the bodies of the dead—washing them, dressing them, and preparing them for burial—and it is women who are typically given greater latitude in expressing emotions.

The practice of hiring women to mourn for one's deceased loved ones goes back to at least the ancient cultures of the Near East. In Greece, women called moirologists were hired to perform a funeral dirge, and in Egypt, the families of important men would pay women to come in and supplement the family's wailing with their own as a way to show further respect to the dead. These women were specifically chosen for this duty and were there to represent the goddesses Isis and Nephthys. Roman families, too, hired women who not only wailed but also pulled out their hair and scratched their own faces as part of their performance. (Roman funerals also sometimes had mimes, dressed in black, who walked in the funeral procession and imitated the characteristics of the deceased.) The practice is also written about in both the Old and New Testaments. In all these cases, it was realized that a large number of mourners at the funeral was linked to a greater amount of respect for the dead.

This practice continued throughout much of the world, with cultures in East Asia, Central Asia, the Middle East, Africa, and Southern Europe all using the services of others to elevate the level of wailing in the ceremony and sometimes to aid the dead in their travels to the underworld. How these wails occur, of course, are culturally specific; in the Middle East, women ululate, while in Ireland, keening is a form of improvised poetry.

Rarely, the professional mourner did not wail or even make a sound. A mute was a man who participated in the funerals of the rich in England from prior to the seventeenth century through the Victorian era. Two mutes, clad in black suits, attended the ceremony, and both men did not speak a word but looked sad and somber while guarding the home where the body lay in state and then walking in the funeral procession behind the body. By the eighteenth century, mutes were provided by the undertaker, but before that time, they may have been hired by the family of the dead.

In Asian cultures, the hiring of professional or specialized mourners is a long tradition. The expectation that mourners will wail loudly at funerals of important citizens goes back to imperial China, at least to the Han Dynasty, when highly respected citizens were expected to have a funeral that demonstrated a high level of honor and respect. In particular, the children of the dead were expected to publicly demonstrate how much they mourned for their parents when they died. One way to demonstrate this was to host an elaborate, and expensive, funeral for the deceased and to invite professional mourners to lament loudly at the funeral. This practice not only demonstrated honor paid to the dead, but it also helped them to enter the afterlife more quickly. Many of the most ostentatious practices of mourning, including the hiring of professionals, was abolished during China's Cultural Revolution, but many have reemerged today. Professional mourners are once again used in China as well as Taiwan, where they continue to allow families to publicly display their love and affection for their parents.

Chinese and Taiwanese mourners engage in dramatic, and noisy, displays of grief at these funerals; they not only sing songs, lament, and cry loudly but also crawl, throw themselves onto the ground, and grab onto the coffin. They wear the traditional white satin robes and mourning hoods that the family wear, but the mourners (who usually attend a funeral in a troupe of seven members) have never met the family member before.

In India, in many regions, women are hired to perform the *oppari*, a traditional Indian funerary lament, at men's funerals. Oppari are always performed by lower-caste women because, in India, anything related to death tends to be stigmatized and done by members of the lower castes. In addition, the women who do this must be widowed themselves. The oppari is a mixture of singing and crying and is performed at the beginning and end of the sixteen days of mourning.

Besides singing, these women are responsible for attiring the new widow in the clothing that represents her new status and for removing and destroying any materials, such as jewelry, that represented her status as a married woman. They do other jobs as well, but their primary purpose is to mourn for the dead and help the widow to adjust to her new role in life. Unlike other parts of Asia, the Indian professional mourner tradition appears to be dying out as the older generation of women die and do not get replaced with younger women.

Finally, many African cultures have long employed professional mourners who are, as in most cultures, women. Professional mourners are used in the Côte d'Ivoire, South Africa, and Kenya, but there is a great deal of debate as to whether this practice is positive or negative.

Professional mourning has slowly entered the Western world as well. In 2012, the first company to offer such services in Great Britain, Rent a Mourner, opened, and it now offers mourners who attend funerals and wakes throughout the country. The company's website states, "We are typically invited to help increase visitors to funerals where there may be a low turnout expected." These mourners are not paid to wail; instead, they are expected to behave in ways that are consistent with other mourners at the ceremony, and the website uses the word "discreet" a number of times, indicating that the goal is to increase the number of mourners but to not let others know that they are paid participants. This deviates from the way in which professional mourners had long been used. In most cases, the mourners had particular skills that they provided to the ceremonies, and the fact that they were invited or paid to attend did not distract from this; in fact, it demonstrated their importance.

Western mourners, who are often paid actors, need to not only dress and behave appropriately at a funeral but must also have a convincing backstory if they hope to keep the fact that they have been paid to attend private. If the funeral is very small, the mourner will likely need to interact with other guests at the funeral. They also need to be able to show emotion effectively, although they are not expected to wail.

See also: Burial Bead Maker; Fantasy Coffin Maker; Wedding Guest.

Further Reading

Ashenburg, K. (2010). *The mourner's dance: What we do when people die.* Vintage Canada.

McCoy, N. P. (2009). Madwoman, banshee, shaman: Gender, changing performance contexts and the Irish wake ritual. In E. Mackinlay, B. L. Bartleet, & K. Barney, (Eds.), *Musical islands: Exploring connections between music, place and research* (pp. 207–220). Cambridge Scholars Publishing.

Mitford, J. (2000). *The American way of death revisited.* Vintage.

Mystery Shopper (Global)

A mystery shopper, also known as a secret shopper or an undercover shopper, masquerades as a shopper to test the level of service provided by the staff of a store. It is a form of market research, in that it allows businesses to test the quality of their services on actual customers.

The mystery shopping industry is represented by a few organizations. The largest of these is the Mystery Shopping Providers Association, which sets standards for the mystery shopping industry and works with companies in the Americas, Asia, Europe, and Africa. The Independent Mystery Shoppers' Coalition is the organization that represents shoppers rather than companies.

Mystery shoppers either work directly for large retailers or, more likely, work through mystery shopping agencies that collect job requests from retailers and other businesses and provide them to shoppers through their web portal. These websites provide information on any open jobs in the area, including what the job entails, how much it pays, and whether there will be any reimbursement for products purchased. (Some jobs ask the shopper to make a purchase using their own money, which the company may or may not cover.) It is helpful to sign up for multiple such websites to have access to as many jobs as possible.

Oftentimes, shoppers will not be asked to buy anything at all. Instead, they may be asked to try on clothing or ask questions about a product to evaluate the customer service of the salespeople. Shoppers may also be asked to return a product to gauge the salespeople's understanding of procedures.

There are also jobs for shoppers to purchase items online to test a company's procedures, the website's operations, and to find any trouble spots. Occasionally, retailers may also have a job for a customer to call into their customer service line with a problem or question. These phone calls must typically be made through an interactive voice response system so that the company can listen to the call afterward.

Not every job is in the retail arena. For instance, a health insurance company may have mystery shoppers call their customer service line to ask them a specific question about health care to test their employees' knowledge. Restaurant chains may hire shoppers to eat at their restaurants, or shoppers may have the opportunity to go to movies or amusement parks.

Mystery shopping often involves memorizing a script provided by the company, which may include very specific questions to ask salespeople or even an entire scenario involving a previous purchase, the problems the shopper had with that purchase, and why the shopper is returning to the store for help. After a job is complete, the shopper is expected to upload the details of the encounter to the shopper website, including receipts, observations, and details of the experience.

Anyone over the age of eighteen who speaks English can be a mystery shopper (bilingual shoppers are highly valued because they can also evaluate the ability of employees to handle non-English-speaking customers.) There is no training or certification of any kind. However, mystery shoppers must own or have access to a computer, transportation, a camera, something to take notes, and appropriate attire for the specific job. They must also be punctual and reliable and be able to follow directions and follow up after the job with a coherent report for the company.

Mystery shoppers should be on the lookout for scams or unsavory business practices. Some agencies ask applicants to pay them a fee prior to getting a job. This should be a red flag to anyone seeking a legitimate shopper job because shoppers should never have to pay to work. Legitimate mystery shopping companies will also not send e-mails to strangers offering them jobs (those companies also ask for a fee once the applicant signs up). It is recommended that anyone wanting to become a mystery shopper first check the website of the Mystery Shopping Providers Association to find out which agencies are legitimate.

If shopping is a fun activity for someone, mystery shopping may be a good way to make a little extra money or to receive free merchandise, especially if the person has a flexible schedule. But it is not a full-time job, and a shopper cannot even expect to get so much work that it would serve as a part-time job. In addition, the pay is low—it can range from $5 to $20 for a shopping trip, online purchase, or call to a customer service call center. If the customer is asked to purchase an item, and the contract does not stipulate that the shopper will be reimbursed, then the net pay can be even lower than these figures indicate. Shoppers must also realize that the fee covers their time spent on the actual task as well as reading about and preparing for the scenario beforehand and reporting what happened afterward. With all of this taken into account, the pay for these jobs is often well under minimum wage (and may even put the shopper into the red).

Mystery shoppers, like other gig workers, must be responsible for their own taxes and are expected to report any earnings, no matter how small.

See also: Standardized Patient.

Further Reading

Jankal, R., & Jankalová, M. (2011). Mystery shopping—The tool of employee communication skills evaluation. *Business: Theory and Practice, 12*(1), 45–49.

Wilson, A. M. (2001). Mystery shopping: Using deception to measure service performance. *Psychology & Marketing, 18*(7), 721–734.

Organic Harvester (Global)

Organ Harvester (Global)

An organ harvester, or organ procurer, is someone who harvests organs from recently dead bodies for a living.

The scientific use of bodies is not a new phenomenon. For centuries, doctors have been dissecting human bodies to understand anatomy and disease and to develop surgical techniques. The ancient Greeks practiced dissection and other techniques on animals as well as on living and dead human beings (mostly prisoners and slaves). Herophilus, for example, dissected both dead bodies and live criminals. Dissection of live humans was largely discontinued after the rise of Christianity in the Roman world, but the use of humans as test subjects in drug trials continued; in fact, it was common for doctors and inventors to test drugs on themselves and their families.

Although experimenting on live humans, even prisoners, was largely replaced by animal experimentation, it infamously reappeared during World War II, when Nazi scientist Josef Mengele experimented on human subjects, mostly Jews, Russians, and Gypsies housed at concentration camps, from 1941 through 1945, and when Japanese scientists experimented on Chinese prisoners of war from the

A protest against organ harvesting in Taipei City, Taiwan. (Tktktk/Dreamstime.com)

1930s into the 1940s. Also during the 1940s, the U.S. Army, in conjunction with the University of Chicago Department of Medicine, infected four hundred prisoners from a Chicago prison with malaria to test new drugs on them, and both the American military and the CIA have conducted numerous experiments on soldiers, prisoners, and other test subjects, many without their consent.

Perhaps most infamously, starting in 1932, American doctors at the Tuskegee Medical School in Alabama ran a trial on patients without their consent in the Tuskegee Syphilis Study. During this decades-long study, poor African American men who had syphilis were evaluated by doctors to see how syphilis would develop in an untreated patient. The men—many of whom died during the course of the study and whose wives and children were infected—were neither informed that they had syphilis nor offered treatment (penicillin was widely available as a cure for the disease as of 1947) until news of the study was leaked in 1972 and the study terminated.

After the end of World War II, once the Nazi atrocities came to light, the Nuremberg Code was developed, which established guidelines for human experiments, including the mandate for voluntary, informed consent for any test subjects; the absence of coercion; a lack of suffering and minimal risk for subjects; and a clear scientific gain for both the subject and society in general. Because of the Nuremberg Code, most medical testing on living humans is limited to clinical trials.

Dead humans, on the other hand, are an entirely different matter. Donated human heads are used to teach plastic surgery techniques to surgeons, and whole bodies are used in anatomy classes in medical school. Prior to the modern era of body and organ donations, doctors and anatomists also needed access to bodies, and when those bodies were not easily available, they hired men to dig them up from cemeteries.

Today, however, thanks to the Uniform Anatomical Gift Act in the United States, people can donate their bodies to science after death, where they can be worth up to $200,000. If their organs are in good enough shape, they can also donate their organs to the living who need them after their death. In 1983, cyclosporine, an immunosuppressant drug, was released, making it far easier for people to accept organs from people who are not related to them (before that time, these organs were generally rejected). Since then, the need for organ donations has skyrocketed, as more lives could be saved through organs from both living and dead donors. In the United States, where many people do donate their organs, a single dead donor can provide enough organs to save the lives of eight people. The knowledge that one's loved one has saved other people's lives is a major factor in encouraging survivors to let doctors remove their loved ones' organs.

Many organ recipients also want to find out about their donors, and some even reach out to the families of the donors to thank them for the "gift of life" that they have received. Additionally, some recipients even believe that they have received, alongside a heart or set of lungs, some of the personality or life force of their donor.

In the United States alone, 115,000 people are awaiting healthy hearts, livers, kidneys, lungs, corneas, and other organs, but there simply are not enough organs for all, or even most, of them. Sometimes it is because people do not believe in organ donation. In Japan, for example, cultural values preclude most Japanese from donating organs after death. On average, the waiting period for a kidney is ten years, and on average, eighteen people die each day waiting for organs. In addition, it has become clear that a kidney from a living donor can keep a person alive for twice as long as one from a corpse. That means that living organ donors are needed now more than ever. Consequently, there is a thriving black market in organ sales.

Selling organs is illegal in most countries, because of the obvious risk for exploitation, but it does continue to happen, primarily in the poorest countries on the planet, such as India. In general, organs—usually kidneys—in this black market move from south to north, from poor to rich, and from black or brown to white. Certainly, the kinds of people who sell their organs could not afford to get them themselves; they could neither afford the surgeries nor the immunosuppressant drugs to keep them alive afterward. The World Health Organization (WHO) estimates that perhaps one-fifth of all kidneys transplanted every year are illegally procured. It even occurs in the United States, where poor Americans sometimes try to sell their organs to the rich.

In India, which only prohibited the sale of organs in 1994, Indian "donors" sell their kidneys for about $2,000 (which are then sold for closer to $150,000) to pay off debts or to pay for a dowry for a daughter. Families with an "extra" daughter are often forced to sell a kidney to raise the funds for the dowry. The problem in India is so bad that, in 2008, several people were arrested in what has come to be known as the Gurgaon kidney scandal; kidneys were taken from as many as five hundred poor victims, some of whom were drugged and operated on without their consent, and transplanted into patients in other countries, including the United States.

In Brazil, organ transfers are done locally, and the buyer and seller pretend that they are friends or relatives, even though one is obviously wealthy and the other obviously poor. To stop the sale of organs, Brazil has recently passed a law mandating that all Brazilians, after death, are automatically organ donors unless they opt out of the requirement. In this way, there will be plenty of organs available, and no one will need to sell their organs. Unfortunately, poor Brazilians feel that they will be taken advantage of and killed for their organs; therefore, more people are opting out of the law than expected, and the poor continue to sell their organs to the rich.

In addition, the rich can locate, via brokers, organs taken from the dead—usually executed prisoners—from countries such as China or Singapore, a practice that has been banned by the World Medical Association but still continues today, especially in China. In fact, Chinese doctors remove organs from Chinese prisoners even before they are executed to be given to wealthy patients from Hong Kong or other countries, who travel to China for their surgeries, a practice known as medical tourism. Amnesty International has accused China of increasing the number of death penalty crimes in the country so that they can create a larger pool of organs for sale; Human Rights Watch estimates that 90 percent of all of the organs in China are from executed prisoners, at least two thousand per year.

What this means is that poor people and criminals (who are, after all, often the same) are often more valuable dead than alive. They are also more valuable as repositories of organs than they are as living, breathing human beings. In 2005, an e-mail circulated with the subject line, "Human parts processing factory in Russia." The e-mail included a number of very graphic photos that appeared to depict dozens of naked corpses piled on the floor and on tables in a filthy room; other photos showed men wearing bloody aprons hacking the bodies apart. The e-mail warned that this body processing factory in Russia was harvesting organs from unclaimed bodies and selling them to universities and pharmacies. The e-mail and the images within it are a hoax—to be medically viable, the harvesting of organs must be done in a sterile environment and must be taken from the very recently dead or the brain dead—but its believability points to the widespread social concerns surrounding organ donation.

In Brazil, these concerns manifested themselves in the widely held belief, beginning in the 1980s, that children were being kidnapped so that they could be killed and their organs sent to wealthy nations such as the United States and Japan. Anthropologist Nancy Scheper-Hughes (1993) heard these stories while working in Brazil. The stories led to many poor Brazilians staying away from hospitals (where they might be killed), opposing international adoption (as adopted children were believed to be used for the same purpose), and even attacking American tourists. While no proof of these mysterious organ abductions ever materialized, the reality is that there does exist an illegal trade in black market organs, and those organs do come largely from poor people such as those in Brazil's shantytowns. The reason for this black market has to do with both the rising need for organ donations around the world and economic realities. Those who can profit off the bodies of others will often do so, and the desperately poor will often sell their own bodies, or body parts, to alleviate some of their desperation. Bodies, then, carry economic value.

Legal organ harvesters must work within a complicated array of national and international regulations. In the United States, besides the Uniform Anatomical Gift Act, which regulates the donation of bodies and organs after death, there is also the National Organ Transplant Act of 1984, which outlaws the sale of organs; the goal of the act was to put an end to the growing black market in organ sales. Ironically, however, the result has been that people who wish to donate sperm, blood, plasma, or eggs can do so and be compensated for it, but people who wish to donate a kidney cannot be compensated for it. The United Network for Organ Sharing (UNOS), a U.S. organization, operates the Organ Procurement and Transplantation Network (OPTN), which maintains a database of those who need organs and matches those in need with potential donors, both alive and dead, who can provide organs. Finally, the United States has fifty-eight organ procurement organizations that operate throughout the country to determine locally who is eligible to donate organs; once that has been determined, they manage the procurement, or harvesting, process.

For deceased donors, once they have been designated as brain dead and they, or their family members, have given consent to have their organs donated, their body's basic functions are maintained through artificial means to allow the organs to remain viable. Once the deceased patient and his or her organs have been approved for transplantation by staff at the local organ procurement organization, all the information about the deceased is entered into the UNOS database to see whether a match with a live patient (or matches with multiple live patients, as donors may have multiple organs that can be used) can be found. If a match is found, doctors or other specialists will then remove the appropriate organs and transport them to a hospital where the patient needing the donation waits.

Living donors who wish to donate a kidney or other nonvital organ to either a stranger or loved one must also go through a lengthy screening process to make sure that they and their organs are healthy and to find a recipient who will match the donor. The surgery to remove the organ from the donor will typically be covered by the insurance of the organ recipient.

While it is always a medically trained surgeon who removes the organs from living or deceased donors, this is not the case when other body parts are needed for transplant or other medical use. For example, after the heart has stopped working and organs can no longer be used, other tissues in the body, such as skin, bones, heart valves, arteries, veins, and corneas, are still viable and able to be removed and transplanted into living people, and these parts do not need to be removed by surgeons. The American Association of Tissue Banks (AATB), for example, provides certifications for someone to become a tissue bank specialist (also known as a tissue recovery technician or surgical recovery technician), which allows the person to harvest, or recover, muscle, bone, tendons, ligaments, skin, and reproductive organs from dead bodies. (One does not need certification from the AATB, however, to do the job.) People who remove muscle, bones, and other tissues may remove these items from the deceased at hospitals, but they also work at funeral homes and coroner's offices, removing the materials that will be supplied to transplant surgeons. These people are on call twenty-four hours per day, and they must travel when someone dies to recover the tissues.

Surgical recovery technicians do not have medical degrees; the minimum qualification is usually an AS degree, and the bulk of the training in tissue removal is done by the companies that they work for. Tissue removal is not regulated by the organizations that regulate organ transplants.

See also: Crime Scene Cleaner; Pet Taxidermist.

Further Reading

Beard, T. R., Kaserman, D. L., & Osterkamp, R. (2013). *The global organ shortage: Economic causes, human consequences, policy responses.* Stanford University Press.

Scheper-Hughes, N. (1993). *Death without weeping: The violence of everyday life in Brazil.* University of California Press.

P

Pallet Recycler (Global)

A pallet recycler is a person who recycles wood pallets for a living. Wood pallets have been, for the past few decades, one of the most important items used in the distribution of goods around the world. There are billions of shipping pallets in every corner of the world that are used to carry every possible type of good. According to some estimates, 80 percent of all goods in the United States are carried on pallets.

Pallets started out as simple skids made of wood or metal with small legs underneath on which goods were loaded to be moved. Using skids like this made the job of loading and unloading quicker and easier for the longshoremen who were employed to load and unload ships. With the invention of the forklift in 1937, which made picking up goods loaded onto skids much easier, and the arrival of World War II, which necessitated massive logistical innovations to feed and supply millions of American soldiers, the modern pallet—made of two sets of deck boards connected by wooden support beams known as stringers nailed in between the top and the bottom decks—emerged, making loading and unloading even quicker.

The modern American pallet, known in the industry as a core, is forty-eight by forty inches (other countries have other standard sizes) and about six inches high; this allows the tines of the forklift to enter into the space between the top and bottom boards to safely lift and move the loaded pallet. Another innovation in pallet design was the invention of the four-sided pallet, with notches cut into the stringers to allow the forklift to lift the pallet from all four sides rather than just two.

One of the problems with the use of pallets to deliver goods is that once the goods have arrived at their destination, the retailer is left with a load of wooden pallets to dispose of. This dilemma, which first emerged in the 1970s, resulted in two new developments in the pallet industry: pallet repair and recycling and pallet rental.

Most pallets today are referred to by the term *whitewood*, which refers to unpainted pallets that are recycled after use and resold to pallet companies for reuse. This is contrasted to pallets that are typically painted blue (made by the company CHEP) or red (made by a company called PECO), which are not purchased and recycled but rented. The latest rental pallets are made by a company called iGPS, and they are plastic rather than wood.

Whitewood pallets are produced by pallet manufacturers and distributed to wholesalers and other distributors, who use them to ship their products. Once they arrive at their destination and are unloaded, they will move back into the system through the labor of a network of participants. On the bottom of the system are the pallet pickers, who are independent contractors who salvage used pallets from construction sites; the backs of large grocery, pet food, or hardware stores; and any business that gets goods delivered in large quantities. Pallets can also be found by pickers at dumps, at newspapers or magazines, and at large wholesale grocery markets. Pickers take their pallets back to their homes and then typically sort them into piles based on how dirty or damaged they are. They will then sell these to the people at the next stage of the ecosystem: the pallet recyclers.

Recyclers buy pallets from pickers, paying more for those in good shape, and then repair those that are damaged and disassemble those in terrible shape. Some recyclers work directly with large retailers that arrange to pick up their pallets directly. Reusable pallets are then sold, either directly to companies that need them or to brokers who manage larger deals, and the unusable pallets may be ground into wood fiber. Repaired pallets can sell for anywhere from $2 to $7 apiece, depending on condition. Recyclers are only supposed to work with white-wood pallets, as blue and red pallets (or other pallets that are specially marked) are part of the rental, rather than the recycle, market.

Rental pallets, on the other hand, are made differently from whitewood pallets. They use wooden blocks instead of stringers, which allows the forklift to pick them up from four directions instead of just two. Costco now only uses CHEP blue pallets because the difference in design allows for faster loading and unloading times as well as more efficient stacking. These kinds of pallets are more expensive to build than whitewood pallets, which makes them more appropriate

---

Chimney Sweep

A chimney sweep is a person who sweeps chimneys to remove the layer of creosote that develops over time. The job emerged as European houses went from single rooms with an open hearth to multiroom (and multistory) homes in which the fire was encased by a fireplace, with a chimney to expel the smoke, in the thirteenth century. Hiring chimney sweeps became a necessity as people shifted from wood fires to coal fires, which built up greater amounts of soot.

Children, from the age of six or so, were recruited to act as "apprentices" to a master chimney sweep. Although they were called apprentices, they actually did the chimney sweeping because they could fit into the narrow chimneys that adults could not manage. They crawled up the chimney and used a brush to sweep out the sides of the chimney; the removed soot was sold for fertilizer. The boys were not paid, but they were given basic room and board. Chimney sweeping was not only dangerous (suffocation and burning were common threats) but could also cause cancer of the scrotum from continued exposure to soot. The practice of using small boys was criminalized in 1840, but the practice continued nevertheless.

Chimney sweeps lost their usefulness with the development of wood-burning stoves and, later, central heating. However, many people today have fireplaces, and while they are no longer used to heat the house, they still need to be maintained; therefore, (adult) chimney sweeps are once again being used.

Source: Phillips, G. L. (1949). *England's climbing-boys: A history of the long struggle to abolish child labor in chimney-sweeping* (No. 5). Baker Library, Harvard Graduate School of Business Administration.

for the rental market. Because so many rental pallets inadvertently end up in the hands of whitewood recyclers, the rental companies must buy back their pallets from these recyclers, usually for not much more than a dollar apiece.

To enter the pallet recycling business, one needs a warehouse or large lot to store and sort the pallets, plus a forklift and pallet jack to move them around. A large truck with cargo straps is needed to pick up the pallets, and anyone who works in the business needs training to operate a forklift as well as the ability to do manual labor. Leather gloves and repair equipment will also be necessary. Construction skills are a benefit for those who will be repairing damaged pallets. Because of the financial requirements—to buy the forklift and to pay for the property on which to do business—becoming a recycler involves a substantial initial investment.

Many people enter the pallet business because their parents were involved in the industry. There is no formal training to work in the industry on any level, so recyclers (as well as pickers) learn the business from others who are working in it.

Pallet recycling is a competitive business that rises and falls according to the economy. When economic growth is high, the pallet industry, including pallet recyclers, do well. But when economic growth is slow, the whole industry struggles. According to a Fortune Business Insights report, the global pallet industry was worth almost $60 billion in 2018, with the majority of the industry still centered on whitewood pallets, of which 849 million were produced in 2016. This is good news for pallet recyclers, because they will be out of business if rental pallets end up replacing whitewood pallets, as some recyclers fear.

See also: Bike Fisherman; Golf Ball Diver; Scooter Charger and Retriever.

Further Reading

Fortune Business Insights. (2019). *Pallets market size, share and industry analysis by material type (wood, plastic, composite wood, and others), by application (pharmaceuticals, F&B, manufacturing, and others), and regional forecast, 2019–2026.* https://www.fortunebusinessinsights.com/industry-reports/pallets-market-100674

Hodes, J. (2013–2014). Whitewood under siege: On the front lines of the pallet wars. *Cabinetmaker Magazine, 52.* http://cabinetmagazine.org/issues/52/hodes.php

Levinson, M. (2016). *The box: How the shipping container made the world smaller and the world economy bigger.* Princeton University Press.

Richardson, S. (2003). *Pallets: A North American perspective.* PACTS Management.

Panda Nanny (China)

A panda nanny is an informal name for a person who cares for pandas in a breeding or conservation facility. It can also be used for someone who works with pandas in a zoo.

The panda, also known as giant panda or panda bear, is China's national animal. (It is distinct from a different species, the red panda, also native to China, which is not a bear.) It is one of the most charismatic of all the megafauna and has a variety of important symbolic connotations both in China and around the world. Pandas are distinctive looking, cute, and playful, and along with other charismatic

A panda caretaker with an infant panda.
(Hungchungchih/Dreamstime.com)

animals, such as whales and tigers, their image is used by conservation organizations around the world to attract support to their causes.

Pandas, like so many other animals today, are threatened by human activity. Since 2016, the panda has been reclassified by the International Union for Conservation of Nature as vulnerable; prior to that time, they were listed as endangered. They are in this precarious position because of habitat loss and fragmentation, their highly specific diet of bamboo, their low birth rate, and their difficulty breeding in captivity. They have only partially recovered their tenuous position because of the work of conservationists, especially in China, who have been working to both protect wild pandas and to breed more pandas to be reintroduced into the wild.

As of 2014, there are now 1,864 pandas in the wild and over 300 pandas in captivity at zoos around the world and at reserves and other facilities in China. Those pandas that live in zoos are on loan from China and remain part of China's breeding and conservation programs. In addition, zoos that would like to host a panda must pay the Chinese government, with the fees going to aid in conservation efforts. Zoo Atlanta, for instance, currently has four pandas, Lun Lun, Ya Lun, Xi Lun, and Yang Hang, but it has had a number of other pandas in the past, all of whom have been returned to China. The San Diego Zoo, which has had pandas for decades, returned its two most recent pandas, who had lived at the zoo for over twenty years, to China in 2019, after a trade dispute erupted between the United States and China. Pandas can still be found in the United States at the National Zoo in Washington, DC; the Memphis Zoo, and Zoo Atlanta.

Kings, queens, and other world leaders have long given out animals from their countries to other leaders to elevate their own status and to create ties between nations. These animals were typically held in private menageries where only elites could see them. The first public zoo, the Ménagerie du Jardin des Plantes, opened in Paris in 1794, and it allowed the public to view the animals. Like modern zoos today, these early zoos competed for the best and most exotic animals and displays. And like the ancient collections, the early European zoos were a place to put all the animals African and Asian rulers sent as gifts.

China took this ancient practice of giving gifts of animals to other countries and expanded upon it. *Panda diplomacy* is the term used today to refer to China's practice of giving out pandas to zoos around the world as a form of diplomacy.

The first time a panda was sent outside of China as a gift was in the late seventh century, when Empress Wu Zetian gave a pair of pandas to Japan. The United States received its first pandas in 1972, when China sent Ling-Ling and Hsing-Hsing to the United States after President Richard Nixon's historic visit to China. (There had been a previous panda who lived in the United States at Chicago's Brookfield Zoo; Su Lin, as she was called, was captured in 1937 as a baby by American fashion designer and socialite Ruth Harkness.) Those pandas were kept in the Washington Zoo, which has had pandas ever since that time. This resulted in England's first gift of pandas arriving from China in 1974. These panda gifts symbolized (and still symbolize today) friendly relations between China and the countries that received the pandas, making them important elements of diplomacy.

It was not until the 1980s, however, that China began restricting its panda gifts to temporary loans. And since 1988, American zoos can only keep pandas if they pay China millions of dollars, most of which must be earmarked for conservation projects. Finally, zoos (and by extension, the country in which they operate) must treat China with a certain amount of deference after receiving a panda; a country whose leaders criticize China or its leaders is at risk of losing its pandas.

Conservation of giant pandas began in the 1940s but did not really become successful until much later. The 1960s saw the development of the first panda reserves in China, and in the 1970s, the World Wildlife Foundation began working with the Chinese government to help bring the species back from the edge of extinction. Today, there are approximately forty centers within Southwestern China in which pandas are bred and studied or live in protected reserves. These reserves protect the bamboo that the pandas rely on and keep the pandas safe from poaching, logging, and other detrimental practices.

The first panda to be successfully bred in captivity was Li Li, who gave birth to Ming Ming in 1963 at the Beijing Zoo. Breeding pandas in captivity is extremely difficult, as there is just a short window of time during which females are fertile—only two to seven days per year—and many pandas lose the inclination to breed while in captivity. Since 2009, pandas have been bred by artificial insemination, which involves forcing an anesthetized male panda to ejaculate through the use of electrical stimulation and then inseminating an anesthetized female panda with the semen. Ironically, the keepers at Ocean Park, a theme park and zoo in Hong Kong, have been trying to mate two pandas, Ying Ying and Le Le, for the past 10 years. In March 2020, when the coronavirus pandemic shut down the zoo, the pandas finally mated.

Keeping pandas in captivity is extremely expensive. Countries that have been lucky enough to receive a panda "gift" from China are expected to pay at least a million dollars per year to the Chinese government, and most zoos that receive a panda spend additional millions of dollars in designing and constructing new enclosures to best display their new animals. In 2019, for example, the Copenhagen Zoo built a brand-new panda enclosure to house its new pandas at a cost of $24 million.

In China, the people who care for the pandas at the many reserves and breeding centers throughout the southwestern part of the country are known as panda nannies or panda keepers. Unlike zookeepers in many parts of the world, who must have at least a bachelor's degree in zoology, animal behavior, or a related field, panda nannies may not need a specialized education. While the people who are responsible for studying or breeding the pandas have scientific backgrounds appropriate for their duties (veterinarians, geneticists, biologists, nutritionists, or zoologists, for example), those who care for, feed, clean up after, and play with the pandas may not. Instead, they must have a passion for the animals and a willingness to get dirty and sometimes scratched or bitten. Because pandas are very sensitive to smell, panda nannies must use scent-free products The pay is not high—about what a waiter or waitress can expect to earn—but for those who love pandas, the job is fulfilling.

Many panda nannies are volunteers, often from other countries, who travel to China to experience caring for pandas for a short time. These volunteers work through a number of international organizations and must pay—typically around $100 per day—for the privilege of volunteering. One popular organization, the Great Projects, places volunteers at the Bifengxia Panda Center in Sichuan Province, which houses sixty pandas and operates a breeding program and research program. Because the panda centers are located in rural areas, often far from cities, workers, whether paid or volunteer, must live relatively isolated lives while caring for the pandas. Another drawback for volunteers is that some programs will not allow volunteers to touch the pandas, especially because the volunteers may only be there for a short time. In addition, many of the animals are being prepared to be released into the wild, and thus all human contact with them is limited.

Panda nannies are responsible for cleaning out the animals' habitats and preparing their food. These tasks involve a considerable amount of time, as pandas must eat for well over half their day, which means that a lot of food must be prepared (twenty to forty pounds of bamboo per day, plus vegetables, fruits, and specially made gruel or bread), and a lot of poop must be cleaned.

One of the best parts of the panda nanny job is caring for the babies. After they graduate from the breeding center where they were born, young pandas live in specialized areas within the panda centers known as kindergartens. Those nannies who care for the babies are responsible for the animals' safety, but they also get to play with them.

See also: Sloth Nanny.

Further Reading

Hartig, F. (2013). Panda diplomacy: The cutest part of China's public diplomacy. *The Hague Journal of Diplomacy, 8*(1), 49–78.
Lindburg, D. G., & Baragona, K. (Eds.). (2004). *Giant pandas: Biology and conservation.* University of California Press.

Pet Cemetery Operator (Global)

A pet cemetery operator is a person who runs a pet cemetery—a dedicated burial plot for nonhuman animals. The history of pet cemeteries derives, in part, from the history of human cemeteries.

Human bodies are disposed of in a variety of ways in cultures throughout the world. They may be buried in the ground (with or without items to accompany the deceased into the afterlife), they may be cremated, they may be left outside for animals to scavenge the body, or they may be donated to science. But bodies cannot be buried just anywhere. They are typically buried at cemeteries, which are locations that are set aside by the city or state as an exclusive area for bodies to be buried. In some cultures, however, bodies may be buried in the home itself, as in some parts of Africa. In Christian countries, these resting places are often associated with churches (in which case they are called graveyards) because bodies at one time had to be buried in consecrated ground. Today, they may still be associated with churches, but they can also be totally independent and secular as well. In fact, it is more common today to find cemeteries located outside of the bounds of cities. With the various plagues throughout European history, it was safer to keep the dead separated from the living.

In some cases, cemeteries are found outside of city limits because the land within the city was too valuable to give to the dead. That was the case in San Francisco in 1900, when the development of any new cemeteries was banned. From that point on, the city's dead were buried just south of the city, in a small town named Colma. Today, Colma has a living population of 1,514 (as of 2017), but because of its many cemeteries, its dead population is well over a million.

Human burial practices may be as old as humankind (with the oldest graves dating to at least one hundred thousand years ago, during the Paleolithic Period, or early Stone Age), but cemeteries—places set aside for the permanent interment of the dead—are more recent. The oldest known cemetery is probably Taforalt, a cave in Morocco that was used at the end of the Paleolithic Period, perhaps fifteen thousand years ago. Other ancient cemeteries began to emerge in Asia, in other parts of the Mediterranean, and in Europe over the next ten thousand to fifteen thousand years.

Cemeteries offered humans something new: the ability to not just bury a loved one but to commemorate the person with a grave marker. In addition, cemeteries allowed grieving family, friends, and community members to visit the grave after the burial for years into the future, giving us a way to remember our dead kin.

Animals have been found in burials—sometimes with humans, and sometimes alone—since the Neolithic Period, or the late Stone Age. Archaeologists and zooarchaeologists have recorded countless cases of dog as well as other animal burials (mostly livestock but occasional cats or even wild animals); some of these burials seem to indicate that the animals were intentionally buried because of a connection to the humans who buried them. Animals who were not killed and buried as part of a sacrifice, for food, for population control, to accompany a human to the afterlife, or as a grave offering for a human burial were sometimes buried because of a relationship between a human and that animal. Those animals were sometimes buried with their own grave goods, such as toys or food for the afterlife, and sometimes they were buried with their human companion. For example, there are a number of examples of companion animal burials found among pre-Natufian (23,000–11,500 BCE) and Natufian (13,000–9,800 BCE) sites throughout the Eastern Mediterranean; one pre-Natufian site, Uyun al-Hamman, included a man who was buried with what appears to be his fox companion.

With the rise of Christianity and the development of specialized church grave-yards, only humans could be buried in these consecrated spaces. Animals, even those that were beloved by their owners, had no real place to be memorialized. Although people with access to land still continued to bury animals, many animals were simply thrown out with the trash. This was especially common in cities, where opportunities to bury a dog, cat, or horse were limited. As the number of pets began to rise in European and American cities during the nineteenth century, the need for a place to put those animals after they died and to allow their owners an opportunity to grieve became unmistakable.

The world's first known pet cemeteries were founded within just a few years of each other, and both served two major urban populations. Founded in 1896, the Hartsdale Pet Cemetery and Crematory in Hartsdale, New York (outside of New York City), was the first pet cemetery in the United States, housing the bodies of over seventy thousand animals. Europe's first and still-operating pet cemetery, the Cimetière des Chiens et Autres Animaux Domestiques, was established in a Parisian suburb in 1899. With the rise of the pet cemetery industry, people had a way to deal with the bodies of their dead companions (which was a problem for urban residents who could not simply bury a dog in the backyard), and they had a way to permanently memorialize them as well.

It was not until the postwar period that Western Europe, North America, and Asia (especially Japan, but also Singapore, Taiwan, and other Asian countries) saw a rise in the number of pet cemeteries as pet ownership continued to rise. With the fall of the Iron Curtain in the 1980s, pet keeping and, with it, pet cemeteries exploded in Eastern Europe as well. Today, there are at least seven hundred pet cemeteries in the United States, over seventy-five in the United Kingdom, and at least nine hundred in Japan, with an unknown number around the rest of the world. Even the industry groups (in the United States, the International Association of Pet Cemeteries and Crematories is the major industry group, while the Association of Private Pet Cemeteries and Crematoria is the British group) do not know how many there are, but according to the American Pet Products Association, pet cemeteries, like all aspects of the pet industry, are growing.

At pet cemeteries, the grieving person can invite his or her family and friends to a funeral, and there, surrounded by those who knew the animal, people can reminisce. For those with religious sentiments, they can have a member of the (human) clergy present to lead the mourners in prayer.

Unlike most pet cemeteries, Hartsdale is unusual in that humans can elect to be buried along with their pets, and, indeed, the cemetery hosts hundreds of people who wanted to remain close to their companions after death. New York is one of a growing number of states and countries that are starting to allow what the industry calls "whole family burials," where humans and their pets can be buried in the

same grave. In some cases, that means that pets can be buried in a human cemetery; in other cases, that means that humans can be buried (or their ashes scattered) in a pet cemetery. Eventually, we will see the development of whole family
cemeteries that do not distinguish between pets and humans and that will allow a
grave to be dug up after the first partner in a human-pet relationship dies and has
been buried to bury the other partner.

Pet cemetery operators have far more complex jobs than human funeral home
operators. The human death care industry involves a wide variety of professions
and activities—from the funeral director who runs the business, to undertakers
and morticians who prepare the body for burial or cremation, to the gravediggers
who prepare the graves, to the sellers of gravestones and coffins, to cemetery
maintenance workers (or cemeterians), to the religious figures who officiate at
funerals—but many of these activities are done by the same person in the pet
cemetery industry.

A pet cemetery operator will typically own their own cemetery; sell the coffins,
urns, and other burial supplies; prepare the bodies for burial or cremation; run the
crematorium; and both organize and officiate the viewing and funeral. Some operators will even pick up bodies from homes or veterinary clinics. On the other
hand, larger pet cemeteries have a staff of more than one, with certain staff tasked
with specific jobs, such as cremation or gravedigging. Many pet cemeteries are
small, family-run operations that were often founded by families who owned land
and saw a need that they could fill.

While salaries for staff who work at a pet cemetery or crematorium are not
great (pet cremation technicians, for example, do not make much more than minimum wage in the United States), running one's own pet cemetery can be lucrative,
depending on the number of burials per year and the types and expenses of the
services that are sold. Many larger operations sell memorial jewelry and a variety
of urns and other receptacles for cremains, and they offer online memorials similar to those offered by human funeral parlors. Costs for services vary widely, with
cremations ranging from $50 (for a small pet who has been cremated commu-
nally) to many hundreds or even thousands of dollars (for larger pets or pets who
have been cremated individually), and there are additional costs for transportation, viewing, and a receptacle for the cremains. Patrons who wish to leave the
remains in a columbarium will pay extra for those costs, as will those who would
like a funeral prior to the cremation.

Burial costs start higher and include the cost of the burial plot, the digging of
the grave, the coffin, the headstone, the service, the preparation of the body, and
flowers for the service. Costs typically run in the thousands for these services,
although opting to buy a simple casket and headstone and having no service can
cost less. (Ground maintenance fees are an added annual cost that applies to burials as well.) Other providers may offer grief services and other forms of
aftercare.

Many of the earliest pet cemeteries were established with very little funding
and typically not much more than a plot of land, but today's operations are much
more complex, especially when cremation services are offered. The start-up costs
can be very high, as the equipment needed to store and cremate pets is expensive.

There is little to no education available for those who want to work in the industry, although the International Association of Pet Cemeteries and Crematories does offer limited training and accreditation to its members.

One of the problems that pet cemetery owners face that is rarely faced by human cemetery owners is what to do with the bodies if the cemetery land has been sold. Because pet cemeteries do not have any legal protections, if the land is sold to another party, there is no guarantee that the animals who are buried there will not be dug up and thrown away or that a building or parking lot will not be built over their bodies.

The pet cemetery and cremation industry is not nearly as heavily regulated as the human death care industry, but regulations do exist. For example, in the United States, operators must typically have a state- or county-issued permit to cremate bodies, and how and where bodies are disposed of is also regulated. Beyond that, though, pet owners are warned to do their due diligence and only work with a pet cemetery that has good reviews and owns the land on which the cemetery operates. The regulations that do exist generally protect the public from things such as groundwater contamination from burials or air pollution from the cremation furnace.

One exception to this is found in New York, which provides an extensive set of regulations governing the pet death industry in the state that aims to protect both the public as well as those who use the services of pet cemeteries and crematories. These regulations cover the licenses needed, the size of land needed for a cemetery, regular inspections (which must be funded by the pet cemetery operators), and record-keeping provisions, and they provide for a legal dedication of the property as a pet cemetery. This dedication ensures that the land cannot be sold without prior plans to relocate the bodies, with the consent of those who purchased burial plots.

See also: Fantasy Coffin Maker; Mourner.

Further Reading

Ambros, B. (2010). The necrogeography of pet memorial spaces: Pets as liminal family members in contemporary Japan. *Material Religion, 6*(3), 304–335.

Brandes, S. (2010). The meaning of American pet cemetery gravestones. *Ethnology: An International Journal of Cultural and Social Anthropology, 48*(2), 99–118.

Howell, P. (2002). A place for the animal dead: Pets, pet cemeteries and animal ethics in late Victorian Britain. *Ethics, Place & Environment, 5*(1), 5–22.

Pet Taxidermist (United States)

A pet taxidermist is a person who prepares deceased pets for display.

Taxidermy is the practice of professionally preparing the bodies of deceased animals to be displayed in a home, museum, or another context. Today, it is done by removing the skin from the deceased animal (in as large a piece as possible), preparing it, and stretching it over a mount made of wood, foam, or wire shaped like the animal's body. Prior to the development of professional mounts, skins were sewn together by upholsterers, and the skin would then be stuffed with cloth, sawdust, and other materials to achieve a semirealistic appearance.

The first step in the process of taxidermy is preparing the skin, which relies on the ancient practice of tanning. Tanning was first developed in the Neolithic Period, about seven thousand years ago in South Asia, and later in a variety of locations throughout the Middle East and Near East. By the first millennium, tanning was practiced in all the ancient and classical civilizations of the Old World.

Tanning originally involved soaking the skins in water, scraping away the flesh and eliminating the hair by using urine or lime. The skin was further softened by soaking it in animal brains or by rubbing and soaking the skin in animal dung

A taxidermied cat. (Owensmith/Dreamstime .com)

and water. The actual tanning process involved using the chemicals derived from plant tannins such as tree bark to make the skin elastic and strong.

Today, tanning uses modern chemicals to treat the animal skin after first curing the skin with salt to prevent decomposition, removing the flesh with a fleshing machine, and soaking the skin in brine. The skins are soaked in water to which lime is added to remove the hair along with a variety of toxic chemicals. After deliming the skin, it is treated with enzymes, salt, and sulfuric acid, after which it is soaked in water and biocides and then is ready to be tanned. During the tanning process, the skin is stretched and soaked in a concentration of either vegetable tannin, chromium sulfate, formaldehyde, or synthetic polymers for eight to twelve hours.

After the skin has been prepared, and the taxidermist has noted the dimensions of the body and the locations of features such as the eyes, the taxidermist stretches the skin over the mount and then works to ensure (especially on the face) the most realistic-looking appearance for the animal. Occasionally, the taxidermist will use the skull or leg bones of the animal to help make the mount more lifelike. Mounts today are much more lifelike than those of previous eras and are often positioned in "action poses" that are specific to the species of animal used.

Keeping taxidermied animals in one's home became popular during the Victorian era, and for trophy hunters, it is still extremely common to take the animals one has shot to a taxidermist to have them prepared for display. In fact, the United States is now the chief market for "trophy animals"; there are tens of thousands of

---

Tanner

A tanner is a person who transforms cow skins into leather via a labor-intensive and chemical-rich process. After an animal is slaughtered, the animal's skin must be prepared to keep the skin from rotting. After the domestication of animals, people invented methods of turning rawhide into a more long-lasting product, and those methods evolved into tanning about six thousand years ago. For thousands of years, tanners followed the same procedures: cleaning the skin, soaking the skin in urine or lime, pounding it to remove flesh and hair, washing it again, working animal brains or feces into the skin to make it supple, and, finally, after another rinse in the river, soaking the skin in a vat of tannin to preserve it, after which, about a year later, the skin was rinsed one more time. Because the work was so filthy and smelly, and because each time the skins were washed the river or stream became polluted, tanneries were located on the outskirts of towns, and the tanners themselves were some of the poorest members of society.

The tanning of buffalo hides during the great buffalo extermination of the nineteenth century was a primary factor in the destruction of forests and pollution of rivers on the East Coast through the intensive stripping of the bark of hemlock trees to produce tannin and the discharge of industrial runoff (including lime, animal hair, and animal flesh) into rivers, respectively. Even today, tanners around the world (but especially in the developing world where regulations and worker protections are limited) are exposed to so many toxins that they have increased risks of bladder, lung, and nasal cancer. Tanneries use chromium to tan leather, a known carcinogen that can also cause convulsions, liver and kidney damage, and ulcers. Because most leather production is now carried out in developing countries, the world's poor suffer the greatest risks from this industry.

Source: Thomson, R. S. (1991). A history of leather processing: From the medieval to the present time. In C. Calnan & B. Haines (Eds.), *Leather: Its composition and changes with time* (pp. 12–15). Leather Conservation Centre.

---

animals whom hunters kill from all around the world and bring back, as trophies, to the United States. Some hunters even call animals killed for trophies "wall hangers." The other major use of taxidermied animals has been, for the last three hundred years, to display wild animals in natural history museums or other public educational and entertainment venues. Cabinets of curiosity, dime museums, and traveling fairs were all examples of the types of spaces where one may have seen taxidermied animals in the past. These animals are usually displayed in dioramas, often with other animals, to show how the animals lived as well as what they looked like.

In recent years, we have seen the rise of pet taxidermy—the process of preserving the bodies of dead companion animals. This practice is actually very ancient, as the ancient Egyptians mummified not only people but also other animals as well. Many animals were mummified for religious reasons, but many wealthy individuals also had their pets mummified after their (natural or otherwise) deaths.

The practice of preserving the bodies of deceased pets reemerged in the Victorian era, which was, not coincidentally, also the era that saw the rise of the professional pet industry in the West. As middle- and upper-class Victorians began to keep pets in large numbers, it was inevitable that practices would emerge that demonstrated the love that many humans felt for their animals, and there was always the sticky question of how to deal with the bodies of their animals after death. This period also saw the rise of pet cemeteries for the first time in human history.

At this time, pets were taxidermied the same way as other animals: their skin was removed, tanned, and stretched and sewn over a mount. These animals were then displayed in the homes of their Victorian pet owners, often in glass cases or under bell jars (which helped to control insect infestations).

Today, pet taxidermy is again becoming popular, although the methods used are quite different from those of just fifty years ago. Most pets that are preserved after death are freeze-dried rather than taxidermied. Freeze-drying an animal involves cutting into the carcass and removing the organs and body fat of the animal (which is not usually done in regular taxidermy). Without the organs and fat, the hollowed-out body must be stuffed to regain its shape, after which it is posed and then inserted into the freeze-dryer. The body remains in the freeze-dryer at very low temperatures for up to a year, as it takes many months for all the moisture to be removed from the frozen body, which retains its shape thanks to the animal's muscles and bones as well as the artificial stuffing. The larger the body, the longer the body must stay in the freezer. After removing the body from the freezer, the taxidermist inserts glass eyes, artificial teeth, and often an artificial tongue as well.

Pet taxidermy is also different from the taxidermy of wild animals for another reason. As Jane Desmond (2002) notes, wild animal trophies are prepared and displayed to be an exemplar of their species. Taxidermied pets, on the other hand, are displayed as a representation of—or a continuation of the life of—a single individual animal, with his or her own personality, personal history, and relationship with the person or persons who had the animal preserved. In many ways, this makes the job more difficult for the pet taxidermist, who needs to ensure that the preserved animal not only looks lifelike after preservation but also captures the personality of that individual animal. In addition, anthropologist Garry Marvin claimed that hunting trophies do not really memorialize an animal's life. Instead, they capture "the process of how the hunter was able to bring about its death" (Marvin 2011, p. 203). Pet taxidermists, on the other hand, are charged with something much more difficult: how do you accurately represent the life of an animal? And, in particular, how do you capture an animal who has been embedded in an intimate social relationship with the person who will be displaying their body?

Someone does not display their preserved pet so that it will impress others, or act as a reminder of his or her hunting skills, or be able to be studied as a scientific specimen. Instead, the goal is to keep the animal who was once so loved with the owner after death to maintain even a bit of that relationship that was so important in life.

A taxidermist can make hundreds of dollars for small mounts and can command thousands of dollars for larger or more complicated mounts or for complicated poses. Those that work with pet owners can make more, but they also must work with very distraught and highly emotional people who are dealing with the death of something very important to them. This emotional aspect of the work is completely absent with taxidermists who only deal with wild animals. Most taxidermists do not offer pet taxidermy services because the costs are very high for the freeze-dryer and also because of the high degree of difficulty in ensuring a perfect representation of the animal and, thus, satisfying one's customers.

In recent years, pet taxidermy has become more popular in response to *American Stuffers*, a show that features a pet taxidermist named Daniel Ross, which debuted on the Animal Planet in 2012. Still, only a small percentage of pet owners use pet taxidermy, both because of the costs and because of other factors. Clearly, pet love is growing around the world, and we will probably not see a time when pet taxidermy is commonplace. Most people do not want to see the body of their deceased companions—human or animal—as it reminds them of their death, which, for many, remains an uncomfortable taboo. And no matter how well done the process of preservation, and how artistic and lifelike the result, the personality, behaviors, and individual quirks of an animal cannot really be captured in the new form. In addition, the idea that one's beloved pet will be cut into (even though the body itself is not removed) is also troubling to many who might otherwise want to have their animal preserved.

See also: Pet Cemetery Operator.

Further Reading

Desmond, J. (2002). Displaying death, animating life: Changing fictions of 'liveness' from taxidermy to animatronics. In N. Rothfels (Ed.), *Representing animals* (pp. 159–179). Indiana University Press.

Madden, D. (2011). *The authentic animal: Inside the odd and obsessive world of taxidermy.* St. Martin's Press.

Marvin, G. (2011). Enlivened through memory: Hunters and hunting trophies. In S. J. M. M. Alberti (Ed.), *The afterlives of animals: A museum menagerie* (pp. 202–217). University of Virginia Press.

Pirate (South America, Sub-Saharan Africa, South Asia, China, Caribbean)

A pirate is a person who steals from merchant (and sometimes other) ships and also operates from a ship. Pirates have been in existence for as long as there has been commercial sea travel, but it was not until the fourteenth century BCE that the first written reports of pirates emerged in the historical record. The first recorded pirate attacks were from a group known today as the Sea People, a late Bronze Age collection of pirates who attacked ships from the Eastern Mediterranean region. Piracy was also engaged in by sailors from other ancient civilizations, such as the Phoenicians, the Greeks (where it was once seen as an honorable profession), and other cultures from the Mediterranean, Southern Europe, and areas farther east.

After the end of the Iron Age, piracy continued in the Old World, and as naval technology progressed and the limits of the "known world" expanded, piracy expanded as well. Pirates were a common threat in medieval China, Korea, and Japan, and in Europe, the Vikings emerged as possibly the most well-known seafaring raiders of the era. Vikings did not just attack ships, as other pirates then and now do, they also raided towns, villages, and religious centers from the British

Isles to Greenland to Spain to North Africa and the Baltic region in search of both riches and slaves. Moorish pirates (i.e., Muslims living in the Iberian Peninsula) were active throughout Southern Europe, and Arab pirates patrolled the Mediterranean.

Another infamous pirate culture emerged from North Africa that attacked ships throughout the Mediterranean, down the West African coast, and northward as far as Iceland. Like the Vikings, these Barbary pirates, authorized by the Ottoman Empire, did not just attack ships but raided coastal villages and towns as well. Also like the Vikings, Barbary pirates became a major source of slaves, but they far surpassed the Vikings in this respect; they are thought to have captured hundreds of thousands of people from the sixteenth to the seventeenth centuries for the international slave trade. Other pirates who specialized in capturing people for the slave trade included Muslim slavers who operated in Southeast Asia (primarily modern-day Indonesia and Malaysia) from the eighteenth through the late nineteenth centuries.

As the age of exploration dawned in the fifteenth century, European piracy in particular continued to expand, as pirates followed explorers, colonizers, and merchant ships into the New World. This period—from the mid–seventeenth to the mid–eighteenth centuries—is sometimes known as the Golden Age of Piracy. The focus for these pirates was primarily merchant ships bringing back cargo from the rich colonies of the West Indies and Latin America—gold, silver, and other riches. These pirates were based in the Caribbean, and they sailed out of ports in Tortuga, Hispaniola (modern-day Haiti and the Dominican Republic), Trinidad, and, most notably, the Bahamas, among other places.

Pirates largely came from the ranks of sailors, as expertise in sailing was obviously one of the most important qualifications to be a pirate. Piracy was appealing because of the promise of wealth (pirates could make far more than they made as sailors with, for example, the Royal Navy), but pirates also enjoyed a life of relative freedom and, surprisingly, a relatively egalitarian lifestyle, with all ranks of pirates having a say in the running of the ship and the disbursement of booty. Because of the promise of freedom that a career as a pirate offered, many fugitive as well as former slaves became pirates—perhaps as many as one-third of all pirates operating in the Caribbean during the Golden Age.

Although piracy was illegal during the colonial era, as it was in antiquity, some states sanctioned piracy when the goods brought back were given to the state. For instance, Francis Drake (1540–1596), an English explorer and slave trader who had been sailing since he was a teenager, attacked Spanish merchant ships carrying cargo back to Spain. This was done under the blessing of Elizabeth I to capture some of the riches that the Spanish colonies were generating, as England had, at that time, relatively few (compared to Spain) overseas colonies and none as rich with resources as those of Spain (and, to a lesser extent, Portugal). Also known as a privateer, Drake was just one of a number of Englishmen (known collectively as "Sea Dogs") who took advantage of England's relative poverty and intermittent warfare with Spain to enrich themselves and the English Crown. France, too, sanctioned piracy in the sixteenth century, and as in England, French pirates targeted Spanish and Portuguese ship as well as English and Dutch ships. Even the

United States authorized pirates (or privateers) to attack the ships of specific named countries. As the trans-Atlantic slave trade expanded in the eighteenth century, pirates took advantage of the number of ships bringing slaves to the Caribbean.

European piracy began to decline in the eighteenth century (after a brief resurgence in the nineteenth century) as piracy lost its royal sanction in countries such as England and France and as the European superpowers increased the penalties for piracy (in England, hundreds of pirates were executed for their crimes in that century) and expanded their military presence in the Atlantic to better combat pirates. However, piracy never went away.

Today, the most notorious pirates operate out of Somalia. Somalia, a Muslim nation located in Northeast Africa, has experienced years of political turmoil since the nation broke out in civil war in 1991. Typically, individual nations police their own territorial waters. However, without any real central government and no navy or coast guard, and with constant warfare, Somalia was no longer able to do this. As a result, Somali piracy emerged as an international threat.

Somali piracy began with fishermen attacking fishing ships from outside of Somalia that were operating illegally off the coast of the country and posing a threat to local fishing activities. It expanded to become much broader in terms of the types of ships targeted (from fishing ships to merchant ships) and in terms of the areas in which the pirates operated, including the Somali Sea, the Gulf of Aden, and the Guardafui Channel. With no central government and very little law enforcement of any kind, piracy continued to expand and became a very costly—and potentially dangerous—threat to international vessels and their crews.

Somali pirates do not operate by stealing cargo. They take control of foreign ships, hold the crew hostage, and demand a ransom from the ship's owners for their return. They do this by confronting the ship's crew with weapons that range from AK-47s to machine guns to rocket-propelled grenade launchers. Somali pirates use a "mothership" as their base of operation. It carries the dozen or so crew members, weapons, and other provisions, and from that ship, they use speedboats to approach the targeted ship. After a few years, piracy became so lucrative that wealthier Somalis began funding pirate ships, splitting the proceeds of the ransom after the vessels had been returned to the owners. Besides fishermen, warlords and militia members have also gotten involved with piracy. Piracy today is a form of organized crime in Somalia.

Although the pirates are armed, most hijackings have not involved harm to those who have been attacked, although, according a report by Reuters, sixty-two sailors were killed in the four worst years of the crisis, from 2008 to 2011. (This figure does not include the number of pirates killed in the course of an attack or in gun battles with authorities.)

The money generated from hijacking has made many pirates rich, but it has also helped the communities from which the pirates operate, which is one explanation for why piracy has been allowed to continue. In Puntland, the region where most Somali pirates operate today, wealthy pirates essentially run the economy. In addition, the lack of jobs and opportunity in the country still provide plenty of incentive for pirates to operate. For poor young Somali men with no other options, and in particular for fishermen, piracy remains a viable form of work. In addition, many pirates maintain that they are not criminals but are simply protecting the waters off their own coast against foreign fishermen. Other pirates who have spoken to reporters acknowledge that they attack ships to get money, but they still justify their actions.

The costs of piracy can be enormous. According to the ICC International Maritime Bureau, a nongovernmental agency that tracks piracy, the worst years for pirates operating in Somali waters were 2009–2011. During that period, pirates attacked 379 ships, with the worst year, 2011, seeing a record 160 attacks, most in the Gulf of Aden, off the coast of Somalia. According to the One Earth Future Foundation, those attacks resulted in a loss of well over $6 billion, of which the international shipping industry paid over $5 billion. The rest of the costs were borne by government agencies. The costs for the ransoms that year, however, were relatively small, at $160 million, compared to money spent on insurance, security, rerouting, prosecution, counterpiracy activities, and other costs. (On the other hand, insurance companies have benefited from piracy, as they have been able to drastically increase their premiums.) Another reason for the enormous costs has to do with the types of vessels that the pirates started targeting—from small unprotected fishing ships to major chemical and oil tankers, often with armed guards aboard.

In addition, there can be other costs associated with piracy. For example, in 2008, Somali pirates attacked and took control of the *Sirius Star*, a Saudi-owned oil tanker carrying two million barrels of oil worth millions of dollars. The *Star*'s owners paid $3 million (down from the original request of $25 million), but on top of that, the global price of oil went up while ransom negotiations were being undertaken.

Starting in 2006, in an effort to combat the growth of Somali piracy, Combined Task Force 150, a multinational antiterrorist coalition, began to be used to patrol the waters off the coast of Somali. This action, along with antipiracy actions headed by a number of nations, including Russia, China, Iran, and India, has eventually resulted in a steep drop in the number of attacks. According to the One Earth Future Foundation, in 2017, piracy costs dropped to the lowest number in the past decade: $1.4 billion. These costs were associated with fifty-four total incidents by Somali hijackers that resulted in four hijackings and fifteen failed attacks. (There were, as with other years, additional pirate attacks in West Africa, Asia, and Latin America during 2017.)

However, 2018 saw an increase after years of declines, with 201 incidents (including successful as well as failed attacks). Whether this is a temporary bump in the statistics or the beginning of a new rise in pirate attacks is unclear. Many of the most recent attacks came from a semiautonomous region of central Somali known as Puntland, where government control is far weaker than in other regions.

Today, piracy is still a threat. According to the International Maritime Bureau, pirates operate in the waters around Bangladesh, China, India, Indonesia, Malaysia, Singapore, Vietnam, Benin, Guinea, the Ivory Coast, Nigeria, the Congo, the Red Sea region, Togo, and Somali as well as in South America, Ecuador, and Peru. Of those regions, Nigeria is becoming a dangerous new location, with the majority of kidnappings being committed by Nigerian pirates.

See also: Bounty Hunter.

Further Reading
Bialuschewski, A. (2008). Black people under the black flag: Piracy and the slave trade on the west coast of Africa, 1718–1723. *Slavery and Abolition, 29*(4), 461–475.
Murphy, M. N. (2011). *Somalia, the new Barbary? Piracy and Islam in the Horn of Africa.* Columbia University Press.
One Earth Future Foundation. (2012). *The Economic Cost of Somali Piracy 2011.* Oceans Beyond Piracy.
Palmer, A. (2014). *The new pirates: Modern global piracy from Somalia to the South China Sea.* I. B. Tauris.
Reuters. (2011, June 20). Deaths of seafarers in Somali pirate attacks soar. *Reuters.* https://www.reuters.com/article/somalia-piracy-seafarers/deaths-of-seafarers-in-somali-pirate-attacks-soar-idUSLDE75J1KA20110620
Thomson, J. E. (1996). *Mercenaries, pirates, and sovereigns: State-building and extraterritorial violence in early modern Europe.* Princeton University Press.

Polygraph Examiner (Global)

A polygraph examiner is a person who operates a polygraph, better known as a lie detector. A polygraph is a machine that is used to measure the blood pressure, respiration, and pulse of a person who is being asked a set of questions by the examiner. Polygraph examinations rely on the assumption that if a person is lying, his or her blood pressure, pulse, and respiration rate will increase, indicating to the examiner that the person is being untruthful. (There is no scientific proof that polygraphs actually work to detect lying. Even those who promote their use admit that guilty people can and do pass the test and that innocent people often fail it.)

A polygraph technician administers a polygraph test. (Lenar Nigmatullin/Dreamstime.com)

In many countries, polygraphs are used by law enforcement agencies during criminal investigations. While in some jurisdictions, the results of polygraph exams cannot be used in court, a passing score can help police eliminate a suspect, and a failing or inconclusive score can focus further attention on a suspect. In the United States, a suspect cannot be forced to take a polygraph. Corporations and government agencies may also use polygraph exams as part of their hiring practices, where the practice is not prohibited.

The polygraph process begins with the examiner conducting a pretest interview, whereby he or she gathers basic information about the person, some of which is used to develop the questions to be asked. After setting up his or her equipment and hooking up the subject to the sensors (which measure breathing rate, pulse, perspiration, and blood pressure), the examiner begins by giving the subject an overview of the process. Then the examiner asks a few control questions to see how the subject's body responds to simple questions that are not relevant to the issue being explored. As the test proceeds, the polygraph machine records the subject's signals on a long piece of moving paper. Throughout the exam, the examiner watches the subject and monitors the polygraph to see how the subject's vital signs are changing in response to the questions.

Because interpreting the results of a polygraph is so subjective, polygraph examiners need to use more than the responses to the machine to evaluate the subject's credibility. The examiner is responsible for developing the test questions, selecting the test methodology, and interpreting both what the suspect says and how he or she says it to determine whether the subject is being truthful. The examiner is also responsible for writing clear reports that document the session.

Some polygraph examiners work directly for a law enforcement agency, but others work independently and may be hired by law enforcement, probation officers, or attorneys as well as companies and government offices.

In the United States, polygraph examiners must be certified through the American Polygraph Association (APA), the governing body for the field. The APA requires that those wanting to become certified first get trained through one of the approximately twenty-five APA-accredited programs available in the United States, Canada, Israel, Great Britain, Peru, Columbia, Honduras, Mexico, Singapore, and South Korea. Completion of one of these programs typically takes eighteen months and ends with an internship during which the student must successfully complete between ten and twenty-five polygraph exams. The courses can cost thousands of dollars, and to remain certified, polygraph examiners must take continuing education courses throughout their career.

Basic requirements for an examiner include at least a bachelor's degree in a criminal justice, psychology, or a health-related field; experience in criminal justice; excellent communication and analytic skills; professional training and certification; and multiple years of experience. An examiner needs to pass a thorough background check and will typically be asked to take a polygraph as well. The pay is good, starting at about $50,000 per year.

See also: Crime Scene Cleaner.

Further Reading

Krapohl, D., & Shaw, P. (2015). *Fundamentals of polygraph practice*. Academic Press.

Raskin, D. C., Kircher, J. C., Honts, C. R., & Horowitz, S. W. (2019). A study of the validity of polygraph examinations in criminal investigation: Final report to the National Institute of Justice Grant No. 85-IJ-CX-0040. *Polygraph, 48*(1), 1–66.

Porn Star (Global)

A porn star, or adult film actor, is someone who has sex on film.

While the representation of human bodies and bodies having sex have long existed in likely every culture, it was not until the nineteenth century when European archaeologists uncovered the ruins at Pompeii, in Italy, that the term *pornography* first emerged. Pompeii was a Roman town that was destroyed by a volcano, and when it was uncovered in 1860, scientists found a vast array of paintings and sculptures of a sexual nature. They were so shocking that they had to be hidden away from view, and around that time, the world's first obscenity law was passed in England and Wales. For the first time, it became illegal to view material of an obscene nature, although, in reality, upper-class men continued to collect and view illustrations and other materials. Women and the working classes, however, were expected to be shielded from such materials.

As different forms of media developed, different forms of pornography developed as well. From the printing press, which allowed for the distribution of images of naked bodies and sexual activity; to photography, which allowed for the first photographs of naked bodies; to cheap paper, which led to dime novels, pulp fiction, and, of course, pornographic magazines, media has always spurred the development of new forms of pornography. These new technologies have also, without exception, made technology easier to access by wider populations.

With motion pictures came the first moving images of people having sex (as early as the late nineteenth century), and after decades during which pornographic films were consumed at the home, mostly during private male-only parties, the era of porn theaters was eventually ushered in the 1970s. During this era, known as the "golden age" of pornography, the first widely distributed and viewed pornographic films became available, such as *Deep Throat* in 1972. With cable TV came the first cable networks devoted to pornography; later, the VCR emerged, which allowed people to watch porn in the comfort of their own homes. The latest technological innovation, of course, is the Internet and with it online pornography in all its varieties.

In terms of pornography, there is an infinite variety of content available both on film and online: amateur pornography shot by nonactors in private spaces; every variety of fetish (feet, butts, dwarves, amputees, and the morbidly obese); professionally shot porn videos and pro-am porn (professionally shot porn that looks like amateur porn); and home webcams where you can direct the performer to perform according to your own desires. It can be softcore or hardcore, depending on whether sexual penetration and ejaculation occurs.

So, who acts in porn films? Besides the true amateur films, pornographic movies and videos feature actors who are paid for their work. For men and women, though, the path to becoming a porn star is often very different.

To be an adult film actor, there are a number of job requirements, some of which are obvious and some of which are not. In most countries, the minimum age to legally perform pornography is eighteen, even though many of those countries and jurisdictions may have lower ages of consent. (In those locations, having sex at, say, sixteen is legal, but filming it for public consumption is not.) Child pornography (whether print, film, or other) is illegal in most of the world, as minors are not legally able to consent. (This does not mean that minors are not in fact found in pornography or that the porn industry does not exploit many people's interest in such material, producing legal and semilegal categories of porn such as "jailbait" and "barely legal" to meet this demand.)

Beyond the age requirement, porn actors must, of course, be comfortable being naked in front of strangers and having sex with strangers in front of other strangers, often for hours at a time. Performers also tend to enjoy sex. In fact, studies have shown that porn actors usually had their first sexual experiences earlier than other people, and they often have had a larger number of sex partners outside of filming than the general population.

Many porn actors enter the field by contacting an adult talent agency. These agencies represent both print models and film actors, and they look for men and women who will appeal to either a broad audience or to very specific audiences. When applying to be represented by an agency, the would-be actors must provide information (including nude photos) about their physical appearance, including any special features (such as "big butt"); what types of porn they might be appropriate for ("Milf"); what they are willing to do (e.g., aggressive sex, interracial sex); and any special talents ("self-fisting"). Some agencies also ask what other activities actors would be willing to do, such as sign photos at events or perform in music videos or at live shows.

Many adult film production companies seek out their own performers and do not require that would-be porn stars go through an agent. Instead, they screen performers in the same way that the agencies do—via an online application process followed by an interview.

Once someone gets through the initial application process, the performer will be required to do an in-person interview. What happens at this interview differs by performer and type of work.

For men, the idea of acting in pornography can seem like a wish come true, but that does not mean that the job is easy to get or easy to maintain. One of the minimum requirements for a man is to have a large penis. Perhaps more important than the size of the penis is the performer's ability to control it; developing and maintaining an erection and controlling when to ejaculate are incredibly important parts of the job. At the interview, a would-be male porn star can expect to be asked to show his penis and must demonstrate his ability to attain an erection and ejaculate on command. Physical attractiveness is not as important in male actors than in women.

Most female porn actors are expected to be attractive, and large breasts are generally the norm in the business, with many performers having breast implants and other surgical procedures to meet these expectations. Others, however, have natural or small breasts, as there is such a wide market for porn today that almost any physical appearance can find an audience somewhere.

The pay can vary from a few hundred dollars per scene or even film, to thousands of dollars for a better known performer. Pay also depends in part on the type of acts that the actors will engage in. The "easier" or more common acts pay less than do those that are more extreme. Unlike most industries, men typically make less per scene and per movie than women. Top performers, especially women, can make hundreds of thousands of dollars per year.

So, who becomes a porn actor? It is a common perception that people who enter the porn industry (particular women) have been abused as children, are drug users, or have other emotional problems that may have led them into this career. According to recent research, however, this is not the case (see Griffith et al. 2012 and Griffith et al. 2013). Female performers are not more likely to have been abused as children or to use drugs, and they are, interestingly, more likely to report high self-esteem than other women; the same has been found to be true among men. Both male and female performers also overwhelmingly tend to enjoy sex more than the average person, both off and on camera. Interestingly, most male porn actors, even those who engage in gay porn, identify as heterosexual, but most female actors identity as bisexual.

Most porn actors, like athletes, have relatively short careers. They "age out" of the industry, usually in their thirties (unless they then start performing in fetish films that feature older actors), and the work can be physically and emotionally demanding and can conflict with a normal social and family life. There is also no job security, as actors only get paid when they are actively working on a film.

On set, male performers are expected to be able to easily attain an erection and to maintain it for a very long time (even during shooting breaks) while engaging in a number of sexual acts with the other performer or performers. Many will take erectile dysfunction or enhancement drugs to help with this. While on a shoot, the actors will often perform all the foreplay scenes in the morning and then, after lunch, the scenes involving orgasm and ejaculation are filmed.

Female performers also have a strenuous job. In any given shoot, they perform sexual acts for hours on end, sometimes with multiple other performers, and will be penetrated countless times during a day. Sometimes there is pain involved, especially because male performers are hired in part for the size of their penis. Unlike a male performer, the female performer's sexual performance and enjoyment of that performance are not judged by a visible erection, but she must nevertheless appear to be enjoying the sex throughout the shoot. Whether or not the actress has an orgasm is immaterial to most films, which are still largely geared to a male audience, unless it is a specialized film that features female ejaculation.

The higher ranked a female actor is the better her job pay will be and the better her experiences on set. Younger and newer actors, as well as those who are older, not as attractive, or not as well known as the big stars, often have to perform the least desirable and more extreme acts.

There is also a lot of behind-the-scenes work that the performers must engage in to be able to film their scenes. Whether it is prepping for an anal scene (which involves enemas as well as restricting food) or regaining an erection, the day is punctuated by a lot of activities that never make it on camera but are critical to the work. Finally, actors working with the better production companies will not just be paid better but will often have better working experiences, and female performers will have access to hair and makeup, which are not present on the cheaper sets.

Many female porn stars, once they have developed a measure of fame from their videos, begin a webcam career, called "camming," in which they can leverage that fame into a more lucrative area and control their own future. Performers can work out of their own homes, engaging in sexual practices (alone) in front of a webcam for paying customers, many of whom become devoted fans of particular performers. Being a cam girl can provide a performer with a much safer and more controlled environment to work, and it can bring in more income to those who work hard to develop a strong fan base.

The San Fernando Valley used to be the "Hollywood" of the porn industry, but since the 2012 passage of Measure B in Los Angeles County, which requires performers to wear condoms in all scenes that involve anal or vaginal penetration, many production companies have moved out of Los Angeles to places such as Las Vegas or Miami that do not have condom laws. Many production companies opposed the law because of their concerns that condoms would turn off viewers, and many performers opposed it as well; women in particular testified to how uncomfortable it is to perform sexual acts for hours with a condomed partner.

The adult film industry today is keenly interested in the health and safety performers. Since the rise of HIV in the 1980s and 1990s, protection from AIDs is a critical concern. This concern spurred the introduction of mandatory and regular HIV testing throughout the industry, beginning in 1998, and the passage of Measure B, the condom law, in Los Angeles in 2012. Today, performers are tested every two weeks, and if someone tests positive for HIV, they are banned from performing again.

See also: Animal Talent Agent; Sex Worker; YouTube Celebrity.

Further Reading

Escoffier, J. (2003). Gay-for-pay: Straight men and the making of gay pornography. *Qualitative Sociology, 26*(4), 531–555.

Griffith, J. D., Mitchell, S., Hammond, B., Gu, L. L., & Hart, C. L. (2012). A comparison of sexual behaviors and attitudes, self-esteem, quality of life, and drug use among pornography actors and a matched sample. *International Journal of Sexual Health, 24*(4), 254–266.

Griffith, J. D., Mitchell, S., Hart, C. L., Adams, L. T., & Gu, L. L. (2013). Pornography actresses: An assessment of the damaged goods hypothesis. *Journal of Sex Research, 50*(7), 621–632.

Professional Foreigner (China)

A professional foreigner, or *laowai*, is a Caucasian who works for a Chinese company to help that company project a modern global image.

China has the world's fastest-growing economy, and with its almost 1.5 billion residents, it is a major source of consumers for international companies. In addition, China is the world's biggest industrial economy with the world's largest labor force, and it hosts a large percentage of the world's largest multinational corporations. Chinese companies know that to compete in the global market-place, they must be able to effectively appeal to executives from other countries. One way for Chinese companies to do this is to ensure that their key executives speak other languages (especially English). Another way to do this is to have for-eigners on staff or to use them at specific events.

Some Chinese companies have found that having a European or American as part of their staff brings status to the company and makes it seem more legitimate to potential business partners from outside of China. Foreigners can also be used to attract international investors or government investment to a project by making it seem international.

To be a professional foreigner, one requirement is that the candidate speaks Chinese (in particular, Mandarin, China's official dialect) so that he or she can communicate with others in the company. The job also requires that the foreigner looks and behaves like a business professional. This person must be able to dress and act like an executive—but he or she is not. The foreigner may even have an official job title listed on his or her business card, but the title does not reflect the work that he or she does. (Foreigners have been hired to pretend to be lawyers, architects, and venture capitalists.)

Instead, these foreign workers are present at business meetings and social events that include foreigners. Their presence is used to help build the company's international profile and make it appear as if they are successful enough to have white workers. The workers do not necessarily need to know a lot about what the company does because they are not expected to actually represent the company's products. They are props that are used to represent the company's global reach and cosmopolitan qualities.

Foreigners are often used at promotional events in China; having white people present at these events makes the products seem more exotic and higher status for Chinese consumers. Some Chinese consumers think that products associated with or made by foreigners are better made than Chinese products. The foreign models do not need to speak Chinese, as the only thing required of them is their presence. (A derogatory term for these performers is "white monkeys.") They may be asked to pretend to play music, dance, or wear costumes.

Some companies advertise directly to hire foreigners, but others use foreigner rental agencies that represent foreigners and take a percentage of the fee that the worker is paid. Some businesses hire foreigners who are not legally allowed to work in China but have a student or tourist visas. These workers are typically paid with cash.

The most highly sought foreigners are tall and have light skin and blond hair, as these features are still very rare in China. Having foreigners like this at a business event can also bring more press, as photos that contain foreigners as well as Chi-nese people are thought to be more interesting. American workers can command more money, but Eastern European foreigners are more plentiful in China today. The pay varies based on the type of company, the event, and much more, but it can be $100 or more per event or occasion.

Westerners who live and work in China are often disdainful toward rent-a-foreigners, as they worry that their presence reflects badly on foreigners who hold legitimate jobs in the country. However, even Westerners with real jobs in China can end up playing the part of a professional foreigner. They may end up appearing in advertising campaigns or playing a part at business meetings that they would otherwise not attend.

See also: Mourner; Rental Boyfriend; Wedding Guest.

Further Reading

Bork-Hüffer, T., & Yuan-Ihle, Y. (2014). The management of foreigners in China: Changes to the migration law and regulations during the late HuWen and early XiLi eras and their potential effects. *International Journal of China Studies, 5*(3), 571.

Lee, C. K. (Ed.). (2006). *Working in China: Ethnographies of labor and workplace transformation.* Routledge.

Martin, D. (2008). *Live & work in China: The most accurate, practical and comprehensive guide to living and working in China.* Crimson Publishing.

Professional Line Stander (United States, Australia, Europe)

A professional line stander is a person who gets paid to stand in line for someone else.

No one enjoys standing in line, but sometimes a line is unavoidable. To get a seat at a good restaurant, to buy tickets to a hot Broadway show such as *Hamilton* or a Taylor Swift concert, or to buy the latest generation iPhone, sometimes standing in line is necessary. However, a new job has emerged over the last decade or so in which people get paid to stand in line for those who do not want to.

At this time, there are two ways to be paid to stand (or sit) in line. The first is by using a service such as Task Rabbit, which connects freelance workers with people who want to hire them for tasks such as gardening, shopping, running errands, or standing in line. The customer registers on the site and puts in details about the kind of work to be done. He or she will then be matched with individuals willing to do that work and shown their hourly rates. For line standers, the rates usually run from about $15 to $25 per hour. A similar service, but much more specific, is called Placerapp. This mobile app works the same way that Task Rabbit does, except that the only jobs being sought on this app are line standing jobs, called placer jobs by the app.

Another way to be a line stander is to start one's own company. In New York, for example, Same Ole Line Dudes offers its services for New York customers. The line standers are called waiters, and they are paid a minimum of $45 for two hours, with each additional hour costing another $20. Line Angel offers similar services for Los Angeles residents.

A line stander, once he or she has been given the instructions of where and when to queue up, stands in line until almost reaching the front of the line, at which point he or she will let the customer know that he or she is almost at the front. At that point, the paying customer relieves the line stander, who goes home. When using an app such as Task Rabbit or Placerapp, the line stander will be paid directly through the app.

There is no training for this job, nor are there any requirements, other than reliability and a willingness to stand or sit for hours. No matter the service that a customer uses, line standers are much easier to find in major metropolitan areas, where the need for line standers is great and where a large population of young people willing to stand in line for hours can be found.

See also: Car Watchman.

Further Reading

Kessler, S. (2018). *Gigged: The gig economy, the end of the job and the future of work.* Random House.
Prassl, J. (2018). *Humans as a service: The promise and perils of work in the gig economy.* Oxford University Press.

Professional Television Watcher (North America)

A professional television watcher is someone who makes money by watching television. One of the oldest ways that Americans could get paid to watch television was by becoming a Nielsen family. Since 1950, Nielsen Media Research has developed a technique to measure how many people were watching a particular show at a given time. The information compiled by Nielsen was then used to determine which shows had greater audiences so that advertisers could determine what shows to advertise on. From the earliest days of the Nielsen rating systems, families were recruited who kept diaries of what they watched and when. This manual system was only just recently discontinued in 2018. It has been replaced by electronic monitoring systems that automatically monitor the television watching habits of a given household and the individual members of that household, and they provide that information seamlessly to Nielsen. Nielsen still relies on viewers to generate their data, however.

As television watching technology changed, Nielsen's habits changed as well. In 2005, Nielsen began tracking the use of digital video recording devices (DVRs) to better understand how time-shifted viewing impacts ratings, and in 2017, they began tracking programs from services such as Netflix, Hulu, and YouTube TV. Even though Nielsen's ratings are based on a tiny minority of American viewers, and even though the Nielsen system is still inadequate to handle the large percentage of television that is watched outside of the household, on mobile devices, or on streaming services, the ratings collected by Nielsen can allow a television show to be renewed or cause a show to be canceled. Nielsen families, then, have exerted an unusually high level of influence over the fates of countless television shows since the 1950s.

Nielsen actively recruits households, which means that no one can apply or volunteer for the job. First, the company determines a geographic area for which they need coverage. From there, Nielsen narrows down that area to just a few blocks and then selectively recruits families and households on those blocks. Families who choose to work with Nielsen become Nielsen families and participate in Nielsen panels, which allow market researchers within the company to get more personal feedback from viewers on the shows that they watch. Working as a Nielsen family must be kept secret. Although Nielsen does compensate its families, either through cash or gifts, the amount of money that can be earned is minimal—perhaps $15 per month.

Once a family has been chosen as a Nielsen family, the company installs the monitoring equipment in the home. Each household member gets a different login so that each person's viewing patterns can be tracked separately, and no one can watch television without first logging in.

Besides becoming a Nielsen family, there are a few other ways that one can make money through television watching. A number of talk shows, for example, pay people to watch hours of their shows to find good clips to recommend that the show use for promotional purposes. There are also companies that pay small amounts to viewers to watch programs on their platforms; Swagbucks, for example, pays viewers in gift cards, cash, and points for watching television and doing other online activities such as shopping.

Finally, Netflix pays a very small number of people to work as Netflix "taggers," known as editorial analysts or content analysists. In these full-time positions, taggers watch Netflix shows and movies and help to categorize and rate those shows, and they help the company to enhance the use of metadata to better promote those shows. Taggers look for similarities in shows and movies so that the company can make suggestions to users based on their viewing habits. Someone who watches a lot of female-driven detective series, for example, will find that Netflix recommends other female-driven detective shows. This is thanks to the taggers, who tag all of those shows with multiple tags so that they will show up on lists like this.

Taggers work at Netflix offices in an environment that the company, in their job postings, calls "a high-volume, high-quality, deadline-driven environment." Although it involves watching a lot of television, the job also involves preparing reports, watching for any culturally sensitive issues that may come up, and working on projects with other team members. Unfortunately, the requirements are not limited to liking television. Instead, Netflix taggers should be fluent in a variety of data management systems; have experience in content analysis, preferably in a media environment; and possess good communication and presentation skills.

See also: Background Artist.

Further Reading
Basin, K. (2018). *The business of television*. Routledge.
Saxbe, D., Graesch, A., & Alvik, M. (2011). Television as a social or solo activity: Understanding families' everyday television viewing patterns. *Communication Research Reports, 28*(2), 180–189.

Psychic (Global)

A psychic is a person who has, or claims to have, psychic abilities. Psychic abilities could include the ability to communicate without words (telepathy), the ability to move objects with one's mind (telekinesis), and the ability to gain information through the mind alone (clairvoyance). Psychics are understood, by those who

---

Vestal Virgin

A vestal virgin was one of four to six Roman priestesses who served the goddess Vesta, who was associated with both the fires that burn in each household hearth as well as the central hearth in the Temple of Vesta. In this capacity, the virgins were responsible for maintaining the central fire; it was believed that if the virgins fell short on this important responsibility, or did not maintain their virginity, the existence of Rome itself would be threatened. Therefore, the cult of the vestal virgins, the only major state priesthood that allowed (and exclusively allowed) women, was central to Roman state religion and civic life.

The vestal virgins were chosen as young girls from among Rome's wealthiest patrician families. After being consecrated, they lived and served together for thirty years, after which they could rejoin secular life. The virgins had other responsibilities as well. They performed rituals related to the purification, storage, and preparation of the harvest and the preparation of the sacred grains used for sacrifice. In exchange for these important functions, they were given special rights, such as the right to make decisions about their own property. Virgins who failed in their responsibilities risked being buried alive, and many were blamed when Rome experienced significant defeats or hardships.

The cult of the vestal virgins began prior to the founding of the Roman Republic, in about 700 BCE, and lasted until the rise of Christianity as the state religion in the fourth century, when the College of Vestals was disbanded.

Source: Wildfang, R. L. (2006). *Rome's vestal virgins*. Routledge.

---

believe in them, to have extrasensory perception, or the use of an additional sense that is absent in most people, to see and understand the world. According to some estimates, a quarter of Americans believe in psychic abilities.

Psychics became popular in the West (especially in England, Australia, and the United States) in the nineteenth century during the spiritualism movement, which was based on a belief that spirits of the dead remain present in this world and can be communicated with by spirit mediums. A medium is someone with psychic abilities who can contact the spirit world and who acts as a vessel through which spirits can communicate to loved ones. Mediums, who conduct séances or use automatic writing, are a specialized form of psychic.

However, the presence of people who claim to have special abilities and who offer guidance and advice to those who pay them is an ancient one. Most cultures have had a type of spiritual practitioner, known as a diviner (sometimes also called a soothsayer), who uses divination to make sense of the unexplainable, to answer questions about the future or the past, and to make predictions and offer advice. Diviners use a variety of methods to do this; some undergo spirit possession, using the insight provided by the spirit to provide information to a client. Others use animal sacrifice as an offering to the gods or ancestors and to read the bones or entrails of the animal to find the answer to a question.

The Sisala of Ghana, for example, throw cowry shells, call fairies, and use spirit possession to divine the future. The Pythia of ancient Greece, who was the high priestess at the Temple of Apollo at Delphi, used fasting, holy water, the throwing of colored beans, and animal sacrifice to answer questions about the future. The druids of Celtic Britain, the use of oracle bones and the I-Ching in ancient China, the diviner priests known as *chilanes* in the Mayan civilization, and the Nechung Oracle of Tibet are all examples of such practices, as is the use of astrology, numerology, tarot, tea leaf reading, and palmistry. Today, psychics use most of these methods and more (such as the iconic crystal ball) as part of their consultations with clients.

While diviners were once used by royalty, military leaders, and everyday people, by the seventeenth century and the Age of Enlightenment, they had moved to the margins of society, and divination, now called fortune-telling, became associated with the Roma (better known as Gypsies) and the ignorant. Still, they reemerged in the nineteenth century, finding new audiences who were once again open to the idea of people having psychic abilities. This was also the period when psychic services moved into the commercial realm, and psychics and mediums could both charge willing customers for their services. In the early twentieth century, the use of psychics dropped again, but it emerged again in the 1960s, during what many in the paranormal world call the Age of Aquarius.

Psychics use their abilities and intuition to gain access to information about a client's past and present and to make predictions about their future. Some psychics work with tools such as tarot cards or runes to do this, while others read a client's palms, energy field, or aura. Some psychics also practice astrology, but practicing astrology (or tarot, runes, or numerology for that matter) does not require psychic ability.

Most psychics use either hot reading or cold reading, or a combination of the two, as part of their readings. Cold reading is a technique whereby the psychic asks careful questions and makes educated guesses based on the customer's appearance, manners, and facial expressions to solicit enough information from the customer to provide relevant information back to him or her. As the psychic learns more about the client, including information about any loved ones that he or she is concerned about, the psychic can respond more directly to the client's needs, and it can appear that the psychic intuitively know something about that person. When a client indicates that the psychic is on the right track, he or she can narrow the focus to that subject. Cold reading relies on clients who both believe in psychic abilities and are enthusiastic enough about the process to provide information to the psychic.

Hot reading, on the other hand, relies on information about the clients that has been gathered beforehand. For instance, psychics may research clients ahead of time to find out important information that will be used in their readings. Psychics who do demonstrations in front of crowds may have an assistant speak to audience members ahead of time to gather some details that they can use in their readings.

To be a psychic, one must either have psychic abilities; skills in tarot, palmistry, or another method of divination; or the ability to do cold readings. In addition, there are countless online and in-person programs and courses that teach people how to discover and use their own "hidden" abilities.

Today, psychics work in a few different realms. Some continue to operate private businesses where they advertise their services and accept clients off the street for readings. (Some psychics do not have to advertise because they use their buildings as a form of advertising. In the United States, the iconic indicator of a psychic business is a neon sign in the shape of a hand.) Some work at candle shops or botanicás, where they may offer spiritual readings, spells, cleansings, or spiritual products for home use. Psychics who live in some areas, such as New Orleans, for example, or Salem, Massachusetts, can make a good living from seeing tourists with an interest in the occult.

Customers who see a psychic tend to be concerned about a few different areas in their lives: love, money, career, and happiness. Ultimately, people who seek the services of a psychic, such as those who approach a bruja or sorcerer in other cultures, are looking for some control over their lives. Visiting a psychic who can provide information that a client is unable to gain elsewhere can give that person a sense of control and can relieve some of his or her anxiety over a situation that may feel untenable. Many psychics today see themselves as being personal coaches; they provide advice and guidance on the client's problems and sometimes give practical (as well as spiritual) feedback on how to solve them.

Some psychics operate or work at a psychic phone line. These began in the 1990s with the Psychic Friends Network, which advertised its services on late-night television in informercials featuring singer Dionne Warwick. The psychics employed at Psychic Friends Network worked in their homes, answering calls that were forwarded to them by the network. This model is still used today by a variety of psychic phone lines, which typically charge customers a few dollars per minute.

Working at a psychic hotline is the easiest way to make money as a psychic because there is no overhead and no work to set up one's own business. Some phone lines hire employees to work directly for them, but others use psychics as independent contractors who are paid a percentage of the fees; a phone psychic working for a company that charges $3 per minute may make only $1.50 per minute. Phone psychic jobs are plentiful, and most can be applied to online with a simple application in which the applicants state their background and what kind of psychic experience they have. Most companies provide training and will do a practice reading with the applicant to evaluate his or her skills. (This does not test whether the applicant is psychic but how well he or she can do a phone reading.) Employees may be trained to do cold readings (if they do not have experience working as a psychic) and to extend the phone call for as long as possible, ensuring the highest charge for the caller.

As with psychics who run their own businesses, phone psychics find that they will get repeat clients who ask to speak with them over and over; in fact, most customers are repeat customers. For both the phone and in-person psychic, building relationships with these clients is the best way to ensure long-term success.

Still other psychics work on television, where they are paid to do readings for celebrities or audience members at public demonstrations. Youree Dell Harris, known as Miss Cleo, was the first television psychic, even though she did not actually conduct psychic readings; instead, she was (along with singer Dionne Warwick) the public face of the Psychic Readers Network and was used to advertise their services. James Van Praagh was another early television psychic who appeared on the 1995 television show *The Other Side* before hosting his own shows in the 2000s. Tyler Henry, a contemporary television psychic, first gained notoriety by appearing in an episode of *Keeping Up with the Kardashians*, and he now has his own show that airs on the E! Network. Theresa Caputo, another TV psychic, has a different business model from the other television psychics. On her show, *Long Island Medium*, Caputo does formal readings for clients who have booked her ahead of time as well as informal readings with people on the street. Television psychics can also make money by writing books or offering group demonstrations in front of paying audiences.

Some psychics offer their services (either for free or for a charge) to law enforcement officials during missing person cases. Most police agencies will not openly work with psychics and very rarely pay them, but they sometimes accept their help on the sly. For a psychic who is seen to have successfully aided the police in finding a victim, this can result in substantial publicity and a boost to one's business.

Finally, some psychics specialize in doing readings for pets. Pet psychics (or animal communicators), who claim an ability to communicate with animals, tend to be self-employed and offer their services either in person or over the phone. Pet psychics advertise in animal-friendly publications and, like other psychics, gain customers by word of mouth. A typical charge for a pet psychic may range from $20 to $50 per short session, but fees can go up to hundreds of dollars for a longer session.

Psychics who run their own businesses must be prepared to do whatever they can to market themselves. Many operate their own YouTube channels or blogs to reach out to potential customers and educate the public about their business.

Psychics can charge $50 to $150 per session, with famous psychics commanding much higher fees. In addition, unscrupulous psychics can ask for, and receive, thousands of dollars from individual clients whom they have convinced must pay them to rid themselves of a problem. (A psychic may charge a low fee of $10 or $15 for the initial consultation followed by hundreds or thousands of dollars for services after the reading.) Sometimes customers who feel that they have been taken advantage of by a fraud can gain relief through the criminal justice system, but they often cannot if the psychic was operating under the conditions of the law.

Offering psychic services for pay is prohibited in some locations, such as in New Zealand and New York, unless the service is explicitly advertised as "entertainment." It is illegal in Saudi Arabia to be a psychic at all.

See also: Astrologer.

Further Reading
Edward, M. (2012). *Psychic blues: Confessions of a conflicted medium*. Feral House.
Stone, A. (2016). Rational thinking and belief in psychic abilities: It depends on level of involvement. *Psychological Reports, 118*(1), 74–89.
Wooffitt, R. (2017). *The language of mediums and psychics: The social organization of everyday miracles*. Routledge.

R

Ravenmaster (Great Britain)

The ravenmaster (officially the yeoman warder ravenmaster) is the person who cares for the ravens who live at the Tower of London.

The Tower of London, one of London's most popular tourist attractions, was built by William the Conqueror after his successful conquest of England in 1066 to demonstrate his control over the country and, in particular, over England's largest and most important city. The Tower, which includes not only the iconic White Tower but also an entire complex of structures within the Tower's walls, was initially built over the last centuries of the eleventh century, but it has been expanded many times since then and has served, over the centuries, as a royal palace, a prison, an armory, and a home for the mint, the Crown Jewels, and a royal menagerie.

The Tower has been guarded by the yeomen warders (popularly known as Beefeaters) since the end of the fifteenth century, when Henry VII first created the yeomen of the guard, the official bodyguards to the monarch. Because Henry VII

A raven and a guard at the Tower of London in England. (Erica Schroeder/Dreamstime.com)

lived at the Tower, the yeomen were responsible for, in part, guarding the interior of the palace.

When the last British monarch to live in the Tower of London, Henry VIII, moved to Westminster Palace in 1509, he brought most of his guards with him but left twelve, ultimately renamed yeomen warders, to guard the Tower. The job is largely ceremonial today, with the warders being responsible for welcoming visitors to the Tower, giving tours, and participating in state events.

All yeomen warders are retired officers from the British or Commonwealth armed services with at least twenty-two years of service and an award called the Long Service and Good Conduct Medal. In 2007, the first female yeoman warder was hired at the Tower. Yeomen warders, who live in accommodations at the Tower, are employed by the Historic Royal Palaces, which oversees all royal palaces in the United Kingdom.

One of the duties of the warders is to care for the ravens who live at the Tower. No one knows how long ravens have lived at the Tower of London, but they did not appear in the written record until the late nineteenth century. Therefore, the popular story that Charles II ordered seven ravens be kept in the Tower at all times, because without them the Tower (and presumably all of England) would fall, is most likely a Victorian-era myth that is maintained to create a sense of continuity with the past. (In fact, the Victorian era is responsible for the invention of a number of British traditions, just like the idea that the wearing of kilts in Scotland is an ancient practice, when it actually dates to the seventeenth century.)

Coin Stamper

A coin stamper is a person who stamps, or strikes, a blank coin (known as a *planchet*) with an image. Historically, this was done by first creating a coin die, which was made of two pieces (one for the front, or head, and one for the back, or tail, of the coin) of metal, originally bronze, that had a raised, inverted image engraved into them; engraving was later replaced with a process made by punches. The engraving of the die was done by a skilled artist known as an *engraver*, and the person who stamped the coin was the coin *stamper* or *striker*; they worked in teams of two. The upper, or pile, die was used for the tail, and the lower die, or trussel, was used for the head, which, not coincidentally, usually contained the head of a king, emperor, or god. The planchet was placed on the head die, which itself was inserted into a block of wood, and the tail die was placed on top of the coin that was originally heated. The die was then stamped, or "struck," onto the blank coin with a hammer; this also stamped the lower image onto the head side of the coin.

Dies eventually lost their image and had to be remade, with the old dies destroyed to prevent their use by counterfeiters. Trussels wore out first because they were directly struck by the hammer. Coins were most likely first developed about twenty-seven hundred years ago. The coin stamper originally worked out of his home workshop, but the process had moved to a building called a *mint* by the seventh century BCE. In the eighteenth century, ancient methods of coin stamping were replaced with steam-powered presses that used steel dies; today, the presses are electric.

Source: Balog, P. (1955). Notes on ancient and medieval minting technique. *Numismatic Chronicle and Journal of the Royal Numismatic Society, 15*(45), 195–201.

At least a half dozen ravens have lived continuously at the Tower since at least the late nineteenth century, with a short break after the end of World War II, when the two remaining ravens escaped. They were quickly replaced, and at the orders of Winston Churchill, the population was restored to six.

The ravens are a popular tourist draw. They are retained on the Tower grounds by keeping their wings clipped (but only partly, so they can still fly around the Tower), but during the day, they can do what they like—as long as they stay on the Tower grounds. All the ravens have been bred in captivity, with the most recent four babies being born at the Tower itself.

The ravenmaster title was first used in 1968, and it continues to be used to refer to the yeoman warder who has been assigned the task of raven care. Christopher Skaife is the current ravenmaster. He has held the title since 2011, and he cares for the current population (as of 2019) of Jubilee, Harris, Gripp, Rocky, Erin, Poppy, and Merlina (the "required" six plus a spare). In addition, a pair of breeding ravens, Muninn and Huginn, gave birth in 2019 to four babies, one of whom, George, will remain at the Tower.

The ravenmaster is responsible for letting the ravens out of their cages first thing in the morning, feeding the ravens twice a day (mostly meat purchased at the local Smithfield meat market), and putting them to bed at night. (Most of the ravens live either individually or in pairs in specially made cages, but Merlina lives in her own enclosure within the Queen's House (built for Anne Boleyn just prior to her execution).

The ravenmaster watches over the ravens during the day as they interact with tourists and each other, learning their personalities and individual behaviors (each bird has a different colored band on his or her leg for easy identification) and ensuring that they are safe and in good health. When the ravens do not fulfill the expectations of their role (by biting tourists, for example), they may be fired for "conduct unbecoming a Tower resident" and retired to a zoo or sanctuary.

See also: Mahout.

Further Reading

Sax, B. (2007). How ravens came to the tower of London. *Society & Animals, 15*(3), 269–283.
Skaife, C. (2018). *The ravenmaster: My life with the ravens at the Tower of London.* Farrar, Straus and Giroux.

Rental Boyfriend (Japan)

A rental boyfriend is a man who, through an agency, is rented out to a woman to act as her boyfriend.

Since the rise of Confucianism in Japan, gender roles have traditionally been extremely rigid, and expectations for men and for women have tended to be relatively fixed. Women's economic and political conditions have changed over Japan's long history, but some expectations remained: women were expected to be largely confined to the domestic sphere, and men were expected to engage in public life. This is not atypical for cultures around the world, especially prior to the twentieth century. Japan, however, is perhaps more extreme than other cultures in the extent to which women's behaviors and expectations have been so narrowly defined.

For example, Japanese women were traditionally held to very specific standards of behavior. They were expected to be modest, neat, compliant, quiet, and courteous. Service was (and is) highly valued. While men are expected to be breadwinners (in modern terminology, salarymen), women were raised to be wives and mothers. They were expected to be submissive to their fathers as children, then to their husbands, and, finally, to their sons (and to not marry or have children was unheard of). To the outside world, Japanese women appeared to be submissive in all aspects of their lives—an appearance that was, however, misleading, as even as homemakers women were in control of all aspects of domestic and family life.

According to Japan's Ministry of Internal Affairs and Communications, as of 2018, 51 percent of all women in Japan work outside of the home (in the United States, it is 57 percent). Japanese women still make less than men, however, although this gender pay gap is found throughout the world, and they are very underrepresented in corporate leadership positions. In addition, even in the past when women did work outside the home in significant numbers, most women still left work after the birth of their first child to become housewives. Those who do not leave the workplace are often subject to a kind of "mother harassment" known as *mata-hara*. As in other cultures, Japanese women still perform the vast majority of (unpaid) domestic work, even as more women join the paid workforce. Still, the expectations for a Japanese mother, whether or not she works outside the home, can be demanding: all moms, working or not, are still expected to prepare their children's boxed lunches (or *obentos*) in such a way that their love, maternal duty, and creativity are evident.

The expectations of Japanese motherhood are often incompatible with paid work, and the demands of working in Japan are notoriously high. Japan's workers work long hours and take fewer vacations than other developed countries (except for the United States), and they are expected to be fiercely loyal to their companies. Employers are also expected to socialize with their colleagues after work, making it even harder for working women with children to get ahead. And, finally, Japan ranks quite low in terms of the number of women who participate in political life, so they lack the opportunity to change the laws and practices that restrict women's participation in the workforce. Even with these limitations, however, the roles of women are clearly changing, and changing dramatically, in Japan.

Another important issue in Japan is the country's rapidly shrinking birth rate. Typically, birth rates in cultures shrink when a number of factors are present, including rising education rates for women, rising levels of female participation in the workforce, and access to contraception. In Japan, all of these factors are in place (as well as a decline in weddings among young people), leading to a recent, and drastic, decline in the nation's births to well below replacement rate. In addition, as the birth rate drops, the number of potential workers drops, which has led to a labor shortage in recent years. One of the responses to that shortage (on top of encouraging more births) has been to encourage more women to join the workforce, by, for example, providing more parental leave, flexible job hours, and day care centers in workplaces.

As more and more women are bucking tradition and joining the workforce (and remaining employed after childbirth), some new cultural traditions are emerging. One example of this is the rise of the rental boyfriend, or *rentaru kareshi*. For many young, urban, educated Japanese women today, getting ahead in a career is more important than marrying and having children. Just thirty years ago, women who elected to not marry or raise children would be referred to by a host of negative terms, such as "parasite single" (which refers to men or women, but mostly women, who still live at home with their parents) or "Christmas cake" (referring to a stale holiday cake that cannot be sold after Christmas). Today, that situation is changing as young women are choosing to delay marriage or forfeit it altogether.

The rental boyfriend derives from traditional hostess clubs, long popular in Japan, where Japanese men (sometimes accompanied by foreign visitors) can enjoy drinks and conversation with pretty young women. Men often visit these clubs with colleagues after work (which offers yet another way in which women's participation in the workforce is limited in Japan). These hostesses, who may be Japanese or foreign, are the modern version of the geisha. Today, there are host clubs (*hosuto kurabu*) as well as hostess clubs. At a host club, women pay to drink with young men who are employed by the club. These hosts, like the hostesses, are paid by commission; the more drinks that their customers buy, the more that they are paid. As with hostess clubs, hosts can be chosen by a customer to be their "named host," or personal host, who will then receive a percentage of all sales from that customer in the future. Although hosting is not about sex, some hosts do meet clients outside of the club for dates.

The rental boyfriend is slightly different from the club host. Women can rent a boyfriend from one of a number of Japanese agencies to accompany her to public and private events, such as weddings, business affairs, or even just a day out on the town. There are a number of rules that govern the exchange: clients cannot engage in sexual activities with the boyfriend, they cannot spend the night with them, and they cannot be with them in a private home or car.

Boyfriends are chosen via a boyfriend rental website. A potential client first chooses the man that she wants and then she fills out an application listing the date(s) required, the activities, and the location(s) of the date. Once the application is accepted, the boyfriend contacts the customer via email and makes the arrangements—the date is set. The customer is expected to pay the boyfriend in person at the beginning or end of the date. The cost is set by the number of hours of the date. Each agency and each boyfriend have different rates; they can range from $50 to $100 per hour, plus all costs associated with the date, including the date's transportation.

So, what does it take to be a rental boyfriend? Most are young, in their early twenties, and they are chosen in part for their good looks. (There is also one company that specializes in providing older men, or *ossan*, for rent, mostly for older women.) The men must be good companions, good conversationalists, polite, and attentive to their dates. Because the women who hire them can range from young working women to older married women, the men must be able to entertain women from all different backgrounds. Many women report that they were treated like princesses by their boyfriends, who will often ask for money from their clients at the beginning of the date so that they can be seen paying for all the activities on the date. Many women are so taken by their boyfriends that they have repeat dates with them.

For young working women who are delaying (or foregoing) marriage, rental boyfriends are a good way of having a relationship with a man that lacks all the complications (and ultimate ending) of a real relationship. But for many women, young and old alike, they report that rental boyfriends are much more attentive to them than their "real" boyfriends or husbands, as so many Japanese men are focused on their work. Having a man focused entirely on her, without making any demands whatsoever, is a welcome change for many Japanese women.

A related type of service to the rental boyfriend is the cuddler. As relationships become scarcer in Japan, cuddle cafés, or *soineya*, have emerged to provide men and women the chance to receive physical contact from an attractive stranger. Like the rental boyfriend, which offers women a facet of the boyfriend relationship for as long as she is willing to pay for it, the cuddle café offers men or women a small part of the physical contact that comes with a normal relationship—again, for as long as someone is willing to pay $100–$200 for it.

Finally, another related service to the rental boyfriend comes from a Tokyo company called Ikemeso, which provides young men to anxious and stressed working women for one purpose: to wipe away their tears.

The rental boyfriend phenomenon is similar in many respects to what some scholars call romance tourism, where women in the middle to upper middle class travel to foreign destinations to engage in romantic (and often sexual) relationships with local men. The primary destinations for romance tourism are Southern Europe (mainly Italy, Turkey, Greece, and Spain), the Caribbean (Jamaica, Barbados, and the Dominican Republic), Hawaii, parts of Africa, and beach areas in Thailand. Unlike sex tourism, where men go to bars to pay women to have sex, in romance tourism, women meet men on the beach or in other tourist locations. Women do not pay men for sex but instead buy them gifts, pay for meals, and take them out. Women are attracted to the men not only because they are exotic but also because the men are romantic, pay attention to the women, and talk sweetly to them in ways that American, Japanese, or Northern European men often do not. As for the men, they benefit economically, and the very lucky men may end up in a permanent relationship whereby they can relocate to the woman's country as her new husband.

See also: Mourner; Wedding Guest.

Further Reading

Robins-Mowry, D. (2019). *The hidden sun: Women of modern Japan*. Routledge.

Xiao, L. E. I. (2017). "What we want is to be happy rather than marrying": Exploring Japanese single women's perceptions on marriage. *Journal of International and Advanced Japanese Studies, 9*, 15–29.

Yamaguchi, K. (2000). Married women's gender-role attitudes and social stratification: Commonalities and differences between Japan and the United States. *International Journal of Sociology, 30*(2), 52–89.

Rental Paparazzo (United States, Great Britain)

A rental paparazzo is a person who pretends to be a paparazzo to make someone appear famous. A paparazzo (the plural is paparazzi) is a freelance photographer who takes photographs of celebrities and sells them to magazines, newspapers, and online media outlets. Many celebrities view the activities of paparazzi—who use telephoto lenses, follow celebrities down the street, sometimes antagonize them to get a good photo, and otherwise harass people—as a nuisance and an invasion of privacy. On the other hand, paparazzi can help to make a young star or would-be celebrity famous; it has long been rumored that celebrities such as Lindsay Lohan, Paris Hilton, and Kim Kardashian have called paparazzi to let them know where they will be and at what time to ensure that they will be photographed.

Now regular people can enjoy this benefit as well. There are at least a dozen companies that offer rental paparazzi in the United States and at least one in England. Most operate in only one city, but one company, Famous for a Day, founded in 2006, operates in thirty American cities. Famous for a Day offers three different packages for customers to choose: the A-List package, which provides four paparazzi to take photos for a period of a half hour; the Superstar package, which includes four paparazzi and a bodyguard for an hour; and the Megastar package, which lasts for up to two hours and includes six paparazzi, a bodyguard, a publicist, and a limousine. All of the company's packages include digital photos after the event. The fees start at $549 for the lower-end package and go up to over $3,000. Another company, Party with the Paparazzi, offers services in multiple cities as well. Besides providing paparazzi, Party with the Paparazzi will provide "scene starters" to start trouble, police officers to arrest a client, celebrity impersonators, and other party guests.

The rental paparazzi are actually models and actors, and although they use real cameras and take real photos, they are not photographers. Like other actors and models, these fake photographers must apply to the rental companies to be considered for work. Once a company has a booking from a client who wants paparazzi at a party, the company will take a look at the actors in its network and offer the work to candidates who meet the client's criteria.

If someone wants to hire a paparazzo to photograph a birthday party, dinner date, or bachelorette party, the person contacts one of the rental agencies for a quote. Once the agency has the information about the event and the needs of the client and has collected a deposit, it will choose who will attend the event. The company provides the equipment, which includes cameras equipped with flash bulbs, microphones, and video cameras. The "paparazzo" will then show up at the appointed time and place and be provided with information about who hired them and what the client wants. Besides taking photos, the assignment may also involve calling out the client's name, shouting questions at the client, or following the client as he or she travels from location to location. Actors can also be hired to play bodyguards, publicists, or even fans.

Becoming a rental paparazzo involves signing up with any rental companies that operate in one's city. Most agencies do not require acting training or experience, but it is a bonus. Rates are hourly and are similar to those offered for other short-term modeling or acting jobs.

See also: Background Artist; Rental Boyfriend; Wedding Guest; YouTube Celebrity.

Further Reading
Howe, P. (2005). *Paparazzi.* Artisan Books.
Murray, R. (2011). Stalking the paparazzi: A view from a different angle. *Visual Communication Quarterly, 18*(1), 4–17.
Ferris, K. O., & Harris, S. R. (2011). *Stargazing: Celebrity, fame, and social interaction.* Routledge.

Rickshaw Driver (Global)

A rickshaw driver is a person who drives a rickshaw, which is either a small two-wheeled passenger cart, which typically holds two passengers, that is pulled by someone on foot (this is known as a pulled rickshaw) or one of the more modern variants of the rickshaw, which may be operated by a bicycle or, the newest style, use a motorized vehicle.

The original pulled form of the rickshaw was first used in Japan in the mid–nineteenth century, and by the end of the century, this was the most common form of transportation, as using human-driven rickshaws was cheaper than the use of horse-driven carts. Rickshaws emerged from litters, which were once used throughout much of the world to carry elites from place to place. Wealthy families owned their own rickshaws and employed their own drivers, but most people hailed rickshaws on the street.

By the late nineteenth century, the use of rickshaws had become popular in other areas of Asia, such as Singapore, China, India, and Korea, and later spread

A rickshaw puller navigates his rickshaw through the city streets. (Saurav Purkayastha/Dreamstime.com)

to Africa. Traditionally, rickshaw drivers were always male, in part because of the strength needed to pull a fully loaded cart around.

By the mid–twentieth century, the use of pulled rickshaws started to decline because they were seen by politicians and business leaders keen to modernize their nations as a visible sign of poverty, exploitation, and a lack of modernity. They were largely replaced by bicycle rickshaws (also known as pedicabs) and, later, motorized vehicles, including motorized rickshaws (called tuk tuks), cars, and motorcycles. With the rise of urban trains and subways, the use of rickshaws declined even further.

As in the past, rickshaw drivers—but especially those who operate the hand-pulled rickshaws—are poor and go into the job with no education or training. Many rickshaw drivers are migrant workers without a place to live in the city and are so poor that they sleep in, or even under, their rickshaws; others share cheap lodging with other pullers. The job is physically demanding (especially in the tropical heat), dangerous, and stressful, and many drivers do not even own their own rickshaws; they pay rent for the privilege of using one each day.

Today, the use of the traditional hand-pulled rickshaw is still found in a handful of countries, including Bangladesh, Madagascar (where they are called *pousse-pousse*, which means "push push"), and India (especially in Kolkata, where the pullers are called *wallahs*), where it is a primary mode of transportation for many urban residents. Rickshaw pullers may make deliveries for business owners, transport children to school, and are often the only reliable form of transportation during the country's notorious monsoons, which flood the streets, making car traffic untenable. They also serve as a cheap ambulance, transporting the sick or injured to hospitals.

Other forms of rickshaws are still used, primarily to transport tourists, but the use of the rickshaw as regular transportation has declined with the rise of cars and motorcycles. Even Bangladesh is considering retiring these once ubiquitous vehicles. In 2019, Dhaka, the capital of Bangladesh and its largest city, banned the use of rickshaws on its most populous roads, and it plans to eliminate all rickshaws from the city by 2021, putting thousands of poor Bangladeshis out of work. Dhaka is the world's most densely populated city, and the hundreds of thousands of rickshaws on the city's streets, according to city leaders, are a major contributor to the city's traffic and accidents. Another reason that the country's leaders would like to see rickshaws eliminated is that they remain a sign of poverty, lack of development, and human exploitation. On the other hand, eliminating the rickshaws from Bangladesh's streets will put hundreds of thousands of men into even deeper poverty. It also means the end of the unique tradition of decorating one's rickshaw with colorful and elaborate paintings, a practice that emerged in the 1950s.

Today, either bicycle rickshaws or motorized rickshaws can be found in most major cities, where they are mostly used to give tours to tourists but also serve as a form of public transportation for middle-class commuters in countries such as India (where the poor cannot afford to pay for rides and the wealthy have other ways to move from place to place).

See also: Gondolier.

Further Reading

Islam, M. S., Hakim, M. A., Kamruzzaman, M., Safeuzzaman, H. M., & Alam, M. K. (2016). Socioeconomic profile and health status of rickshaw pullers in rural Bangladesh. *American Journal of Food Science and Health, 2*(4), 32–38.

Rahim, M. A., Joardder, M. U. H., Houque, S. M., Rahman, M. M., & Sumon, N. A. (2013, February). Socio-economic & environmental impacts of battery driven auto rickshaw at Rajshahi city in Bangladesh. In *International Conference on Mechanical, Industrial and Energy Engineering 2012*, Khulna, Bangladesh.

Roadkill Cleaner (United States, Great Britain)

A roadkill cleaner is a person who cleans up roadkill either for a living or as part of their job. *Roadkill* refers to animals, wild or domesticated, who have been hit by a vehicle and killed. Once they are dead on the side of the road, they are considered "roadkill." The term *roadkill* is, of course, a modern invention, only emerging with the invention and popularity of cars. Because animals killed on the side of the road, with the exception of those animals who were pets, are unknown to human passersby, they tend to elicit very little in terms of mourning or sadness by most people.

The frequency of these deaths also serves to desensitize even animal lovers to the sight. Approximately one million animals are killed by cars in the United States alone every day (Huijser et al. 2009), and four hundred million are killed per year (Seiler & Helldin 2006), making vehicles the second greatest cause of death for animals (after meat production). In addition, after death by vehicle,

A dead raccoon, waiting to be retrieved by a roadkill cleaner. (Jim Delillo/Dreamstime .com)

the animals' bodies are often irreversibly harmed, so the response from drivers and others who see roadkill bodies is often disgust rather than sadness. Their deaths, then, not only go unmarked (even though their deaths are so public), but the people who are charged with disposing of their remains also see them as simply trash.

Large animals' bodies are usually removed from traffic by state transportation or wildlife authorities, but they are still left at the side of the road until someone else, usually hired by the state, can pick them up. Most animals who make up the category of roadkill, however, are small animals and birds, whose bodies do not pose a big problem for traffic and are typically not removed. However, the exception to this, at least in municipalities, is pets. People tend to resist the idea of seeing a dog or a cat slowly disintegrate on the side of the road—especially in urban and suburban areas in Western countries—so they call the authorities and request that those animals be removed. Some municipalities mandate that people who hit animals with their cars, or certain types of animals (such as horses, dogs, and other domesticated animals), must call the city or state to report it. The agency will then get someone to pick up the animal and will try to locate the owner to notify them of the death.

For pets, most are picked up by animal control agencies that have been called by individuals who reported them, and some are picked up by someone with the local sanitation agency. When animals are picked up by animal control officers, there is a good chance that they will scan the animal for a microchip or look for a collar and tag to contact the owner to inform them of the death. Sanitation agencies may not do this.

Some roadkill collectors are private contractors who are paid by the state wildlife department per animal or sometimes per hour. These are the people who are called to pick up the large animals or who may work a regular schedule, driving around the region to which they are assigned, looking for bodies. These contractors may earn as much as $40 per deer, which may not sound like much, but according to a report on CNN, one roadkill collector in Pennsylvania retrieves about eighteen hundred deer per year, which adds up to $72,000 per year.

There are also private companies that pick up and remove dead animals from private properties for a fee that they charge to the homeowner. These companies will typically remove animals who died under houses or in walls or who simply died in a private yard. These are often the same pest control companies that can be called to trap and remove wild animals who have made a home inside of or near a person's house.

About half of U.S. states allow individuals to pick up roadkill animals to take home and eat, although for large game animals, the individuals must get a permit or tag from the state first. Other states do not allow the removal of roadkill for food because they do not want to encourage people to use their vehicles as an easy way to hunt animals. Another concern is that people will cause traffic risks by stopping to remove animals from the road. Some states that do not allow people to pick up roadkill do allow unprotected or "nuisance" animals, such as porcupines, skunks, and coyotes, to be picked up by anyone.

Gong Farmer

A gong farmer, or night soil man, was a person who cleaned out latrines, privies, and cesspits in medieval England. This was a job left to the very poor and desperate and was typically done at night so that the person doing it, and the activity itself, would not be seen. Because of this, the waste that they collected was known as *night soil.*

Gong farmers typically employed small boys to help them because it was easier for them to fit into the small spaces of the privy. The waste was sold to farmers, who used it as fertilizer. Gong farming was both a dirty job—and bathing was a luxury that gong farmers could not afford—and a dangerous one, as the risk of asphyxiation, disease, and even drowning was high. Because of the smell, gong farmers were restricted to living in certain areas.

In the nineteenth century, as privies were replaced by water closets, gong farmers became far less prevalent in developed countries, but they are still used in some parts of the world today.

Source: van Oosten, R. (2016). Nightman's muck, gong farmer's treasure: Local differences in the clearing-out of cesspits in the Low Countries, 1600–1900. In D. Sosna & L. Brunclíková (Eds.), *Archaeologies of waste: Encounters with the unwanted* (pp. 41–56). Oxbow Books.

Roadkill collectors wear protective clothing because they are picking up bodies that may be oozing with blood or other bodily fluids, which can transmit infection in addition to being gross, and sometimes the bodies are infested with maggots or other bugs. The bodies will smell after decomposition begins, so some may wear something to keep the smell down as well. Their jobs are not only disgusting but also dangerous, as they are picking up animals on roads.

Collectors use a variety of tools to scrape up the animals, including shovels, picks, and other common tools. Workers who remove large animals may use a winch or other system, such as a lift gate, to pick up the animal and place it into a truck. Many roadkill collectors work at night, when traffic is expected to be lighter than in the day. No matter what type of animal or what type of person picks up the animal, they all go to the same place: the local landfill.

Road ecologists have looked at the ways that highways are designed and provided suggestions on how to protect animals from being killed. Some cities and states have constructed wildlife crossings, such as bridges and tunnels, that allow wild animals to pass safely; these are especially effective if the wildlife crossing is placed on the path that migrating animals normally use. Solutions like this cost money, however, and are typically only used when the animals being killed are a threatened species or when the animal is large enough to constitute a danger to drivers.

See also: Crime Scene Cleaner; Pet Cemetery Operator.

Further Reading
Coffin, A. W. (2007). From roadkill to road ecology: A review of the ecological effects of roads. *Journal of Transport Geography, 15*(5), 396–406.

Huijser, M. P., Duffield, J. W., Clevenger, A. P., Ament, R. J., & Cost-Benefit, P. M. (2009). Analyses of mitigation measures aimed at reducing collisions with large ungulates

in the United States and Canada: A decision support tool. *Ecology and Society,*
14(2), Article 15.

Seiler, A., & Helldin, J. O. (2006). Mortality in wildlife due to transportation. In J. Davenport & J. L. Davenport (Eds.), *The ecology of transportation: Managing mobility for the environment* (pp. 165–189). Springer.

Simmons, J. R. (1938). *Feathers and fur on the turnpike.* Christopher Publishing House.

Rodeo Performer (United States, Argentina, Australia, Brazil, Canada)

A rodeo performer is a man, woman, or child who performs in a rodeo. Rodeos are sporting events in which performers perform tricks using animals, typically horses and cattle, to demonstrate their skills against other performers.

The rodeo is a historical legacy from the days of the frontiersman and the American cowboy, combining traditions borrowed from nineteenth-century cattle ranching with more modern activities. At one time, working cowboys held contests to see who was the best calf roper or who could best "break" wild horses into saddle horses, and these informal contests eventually formed the rodeo.

Another influence on the rodeo was the Wild West shows that were popular at the turn of the century, such as Buffalo Bill's Wild West Show and Exhibition.

A rodeo clown. (Esego/Dreamstime.com)

These shows combined reenactments of historical cowboy scenes with shooting and racing competitions, and they involved the use of horses and cattle as well as Native Americans. Finally, modern rodeos are influenced by the Spanish and Mexican *vaqueros* who worked with cattle in the Southwest. Although rodeos are strongly associated with the American Southwest, any country with a ranching culture, such as Argentina, Australia, Mexico, Brazil, and Canada, has rodeo events.

Veterinarian and rodeo scholar Elizabeth Lawrence called rodeos ritual events that serve to "express, reaffirm, and perpetuate certain values and attitudes characteristic of the cattle herders' way of life" (Lawrence 1984, p. 211). In this interpretation, the rodeo borrows the main themes from the cowboy's life and exaggerates them through performances with horses, who are viewed as the cowboy's primary work partners. In this sense, rodeos, like alligator wrestling events, are cultural performances that are enacted to display and maintain traditions associated with the culture—in this case, the culture of cowboys.

Rodeos include two types of competitions: roughstock events and timed events. Most also give an award for best "all-around cowboy." Roughstock events involve the cowboy riding a bull or a bucking bronc to demonstrate his dominance over the animal. For instance, bareback riding is an event in which the cowboy subjugates a "wild horse" by riding him bareback. It is a dangerous sport, both for the riders—bareback riders suffer more injuries than all other rodeo cowboys—and for the animals, who endure the pain of the bucking strap, a leather belt that is tightened around the animal's flank and can cause painful, bloody sores. Timed events, on the other hand, are those that involve riders using horses to perform traditional cowboy tasks in a set amount of time. Additional events include barrel racing (in which a rider on a horse races around barrels) and trick and clown performances, many of which include horses.

Traditionally, roughstock competitions used wild mustangs because the subjugation of the wild Spanish mustang was a part of the cowboy's life during the frontier days and symbolized the conquering of the American West. Successful cowboys were able to catch wild horses and not only subdue them but also eventually tame them to the extent that they could be trained, even for specialty activities such as cattle roping and dressage, a form of training that results in a ballet-like performance. Saddle bronc riding is similar to bareback riding, except that the cowboy uses a saddle, but the horse still wears a bucking strap. In both riding styles (as well as in bull riding, which has no traditional origin but rodeos still use it to demonstrate the cowboy's fearlessness), the rider must remain on the animal for at least eight seconds while only using one hand. Bronc riding is the centerpiece of a rodeo performance.

Because there are few wild horses left, broncs are now purpose bred to jump, kick, and flip around their riders. So, while the sport is supposed to be symbolic of the conquering of the wild horse by man, the modern way the sport is carried out—selectively breeding domesticated broncs to look and act wild so that they can be ridden and subdued for show—represents a powerful irony. In addition, today, many broncs are former saddle horses who "went bad," or started to buck riders off. As broncs are not confined in a pen or stall for most of the year, in that sense at least, it is less inhumane than other types of horse events, where horses have very little freedom to roam.

Timed events such as calf roping not only demonstrate the cowboy's ability to rope the calf but also how well the cowboy's horse has been trained. This particular task is a difficult one for the horse to learn, as he must move backward, pull against the rope, stand firm without moving, and perform other difficult tasks. In calf roping, the cowboy must compete against the clock and rope the calf as quickly as possible. Steer wrestling is a similar event in which the cowboy, known as a "bulldogger," wrestles a steer to the ground as quickly as he can by grasping the animal's horn while still hanging on to his moving horse. Team roping is another timed event that involves two cowboys riding two horses. They first chase the steer; then rope him around the horns, head, or neck; and then rope both hind legs, throwing him on the ground in the process.

All of these events are dangerous to the riders—which only adds to their appeal and the size of the prize that riders can win—but they are also dangerous to the horses, bulls, and calves. No government entity oversees the hundreds of professional and amateur rodeo events that take place every year. Instead, the Professional Rodeo Cowboys Association (PRCA) sets up standards that rodeos sponsored by the association (but not amateur rodeos or rodeos sanctioned by other organizations) and its ten thousand members must abide by. The sixty animal care regulations include a mandate that veterinarians be present for every performance; that animals cannot be transported for a period of more than twenty-four hours without food and water; that team-roped steer are protected by horn wraps; that cattle in timed events are not used two years in a row; that spurs on boots be dulled; and that animals be inspected for health prior to events.

Rodeo performers are generally one of two types: those who participate and compete in the roughstock and timed events mentioned above or rodeo clowns, who participate in "special events." Both types of rodeo performers are a kind of cultural specialist, in that they are responsible for the performing events that allow for the transmission of cultural traditions. In the case of the rodeo, rodeo performers continually reenact the activities, now ritualized, of the cowboy, and without the affection that rodeo audiences hold for the cowboy and what he (or sometimes she) represents, the rodeo would not survive, especially in the face of animal rights criticism.

Rodeo performers can be contestants who enter rodeos to compete and win prizes, or they can be contract entertainers who, typically like the rodeo clowns, are hired to perform in the rodeo for a set fee. This includes, for example, trick performers who are skilled in performing a number of tricks and exclusively perform those for the crowd.

Like other clowns, rodeo clowns are performers who dress up in clown costumes, complete with makeup and wig, and perform a humorous routine to make the audience laugh. Rodeo clowns often perform with some of the same animals that other rodeo performers use, and they also participate in regular rodeo events. For example, many rodeo clowns participate in bull riding competitions, where their job is to distract the bull after the rider has fallen off the animal, sometimes by jumping into a barrel to hide. In this role, the clown essentially takes on the role of the bullfighter, in that the clown's job is to provide a new target for the bull to chase. Rodeo clowns must be funny, athletic, used to working with bulls, and brave.

In the United States, rodeo clowns rarely take on this job anymore, as it is now done by people known as rodeo protection athletes or bullfighters. But in other countries, and in smaller rodeos in the United States, the clown continues to perform this dangerous function alongside his more entertaining functions. Whether or not the bullfighter is also a regular rodeo clown, he dresses up in colorful, loose clothing (or a full clown outfit) with protective gear underneath the costume. In recent years, bullfighting has become an activity in its own right, with its own competitions and performances.

Outside of bullfighting, rodeo clowns are expected to entertain the crowd at rodeos in between the main events; they tell jokes, act in foolish ways, and often satirize cowboys and the cowboy lifestyle for laughs. The fee for a rodeo clown ranges from $100 to $500 per event, and clowns, like other rodeo performers, make more money when they are more talented or well known than others.

Rodeo performers and clowns can enter the business in a number of ways. Traditionally, one learned the skills of rodeo through one's work as a cowboy or cowgirl. Today, some performers continue to learn in this on-the-job way. On the other hand, there are a number of rodeo schools or clinics around the country, where would-be performers learn to ride bulls and broncs, rope calves, and race wild horses. Rodeo clowns, too, can learn their skills in these short programs. Another way to learn is simply to begin entering small amateur events. At these events, athletes without a lot of experience in working with animals can learn from their own participation as well as by watching more experienced competitors.

To make a living, performers and clowns both travel, generally by driving, from rodeo to rodeo. Depending on their level of experience, they may compete in amateur rodeos, professional rodeos, or semiprofessional rodeos. They can compete as individuals or as part of a team. If they are not contract performers, they must pay an entry fee at each event in which they perform, but they hope to win that back with the prize or purse, assuming that they win an event. Rodeo performers typically specialize in one or two events, and they travel around the country (American performers often perform in both the United States and Canada) to enter and compete in those particular events. There are over six hundred professional events in the United States per year run by the largest rodeo association in the United States, the Professional Rodeo Cowboys Association (PRCA), and hundreds of semiprofessional and amateur events organized by smaller associations as well. Traveling from event to event, in what is called the rodeo circuit, is known as "riding the circuit."

If a performer performs badly at an event, he or she loses the entry fee and gets no money at all. Many events pay the winner as well as the top six or eight performers, however, so there are a few chances to earn money. The size of the purse varies by event and typically includes money from the entry fees plus additional prize money. Prizes can range from $1,000 to $70,000 per event at the top competitions. The National Finals Rodeo in Las Vegas, which is the championship event for the PRCA, gives away millions of dollars in prizes each year for all its events.

Performing well in a rodeo depends on the athletic skill of the performer, but it also takes a bit of luck—performers cannot choose the animal that they ride or work with at the event; the animals are matched with the performers by random draws. Performers must pay for their own travel, and they often travel and stay together to save on costs. Well-known performers can also get sponsors that help to pay some of their expenses. To participate in the top professional events, performers must qualify for those events by performing well at lower-level events throughout the year. Amateurs can only become professionals and compete at the higher-paid professional events (which in the United States are primarily sanctioned by the PRCA) after purchasing a permit from the PRCA, which involves earning at least $1,000 in PRCA-sanctioned events. (There are also non-PRCA events that professionals can compete in, such as those sponsored by the Professional Bull Riders and other organizations.) Only top-ranked performers can compete in championship events such as the National Finals Rodeo (NFR), and ranking is based on money; in the case of the NFR, the top fifteen money winners from the previous year are invited to compete. Because so much of a rodeo performer's earnings is based on luck, as well as how many and which events one participates in each year, it is difficult to give an average earning for a year. But according to the Cowboy Lifestyle Network, amateurs may only make $10,000–$15,000 per year. Besides the prize money, competitors also compete for a belt buckle, which is the primary nonmonetary trophy in the rodeo world.

Women have been competing and performing in rodeos since the nineteenth century, when stars such as Annie Oakley performed around the world in such events as Buffalo Bill's Wild West Show and Exhibition. They performed alongside men in amateur and professional rodeos until they were banned from roughstock events in the 1930s and 1940s, which led to the formation, in 1948, of the Girl's Rodeo Association, known today as the Women's Professional Rodeo Association (WPRA).

Today, women can perform in events sponsored by the major rodeo associations as well as in female-only events held by the WPRA or the Professional Women's Rodeo Association (PWRA). But top-ranked female rodeo performers, like the male performers, aim to compete in the PCRA-sponsored events, where the prizes are much higher. However, qualifying for the top events is still difficult for women, who must earn a certain amount of money to qualify. It was not until 2012 that Kaila Mussell became the first woman since the 1940s to earn a spot in the PRCA as a bronc rider.

Because earning money through rodeos is such a gamble, many rodeo performers, except for the top-level performers, work outside of the rodeo as well, often in livestock- or cowboy-related jobs, such as horse training.

See also: Alligator Wrestler; Bullfighter.

Further Reading

Fredriksson, K. (1993). *American rodeo: From Buffalo Bill to big business.* Texas A&M University Press.

Lawrence, E. A. (1984). *Rodeo: An anthropologist looks at the wild and the tame.* University of Chicago Press.

Lawrence, E. A. (1990). Rodeo horses: The wild and the tame. In R. Willis (Ed.), *Signifying animals: Human meaning in the natural world* (pp. 222–235). Routledge.

Meyers, M. C., & Laurent, C. M. (2010). The rodeo athlete. *Sports Medicine, 40*(10), 817–839.

Westermeier, C. P. (2005). *Man, beast, dust: The story of rodeo.* University of Nebraska Press.

Rose Parade Float Builder (United States)

A Rose Parade float builder is a person who builds floats for the annual Tournament of Roses Parade. The Tournament of Roses Parade, or Rose Parade, is an annual parade held in Pasadena, California, on January 1. It has become a New

A lion float in the Rose Bowl Parade, Pasadena, California. (Joe Sohm/Dreamstime .com)

Year's tradition for millions of Americans to wake up and watch the parade, which is immediately followed by the Rose Bowl, a college football bowl game that is aired immediately after the parade (and which was first held in 1902 as a way to raise funds for the parade).

First held in 1890, when it was called the Battle of Flowers, because it was intended to highlight California's winter-blooming flowers, the parade features flower-covered floats, high school and college marching bands, equestrian teams, a parade queen (and her court), a grand marshal, and other officials. Each January, the Tournament of Roses president picks a theme for the next year, and all floats must in some way reflect that theme. The 2019 theme, for example, was the Melody of Life, and the 2020 theme was the Power of Hope. Members of the Tournament of Roses, which oversees the parade, are responsible for setting the rules, choosing the parade participants, inspecting floats, and helping to ensure that the event runs smoothly on parade day.

One of the most unique aspects of the Rose Parade are the floats. The rules for the parade mandate that all floats be entirely covered with plant material, including flowers, seeds, bark, grasses, and leaves. The first floats used in the earliest years of the festival were flower-covered horse-drawn carts, but with the popularity of motor vehicles, the carts were replaced by vehicles, which were then covered with flowers.

The floats that participate in the parade each year are typically owned by corporations, which use the parade as a way to advertise their products and services, and nonprofits, who also use the parade get their message across to thousands of in-person viewers and millions of television viewers. Some of the companies and organizations that are regularly represented at the parade include the U.S. Marine

Corps, Honda, Donate Life (which promotes organ donations), the City of Hope (a medical research organization), Farmers Insurance, Cal Poly Universities, and Trader Joe's.

Applicants who want to enter a float into the parade must apply in January via the Tournament of Roses website, and the winning applicants are chosen by the members of the Tournament of Roses organization, usually in early February. The applicants are judged by how well the preliminary design meets the year's theme. (By March, the final plan must be submitted and approved.) Floats are accepted in two categories: the large commercial floats and the floats entered by smaller companies, nonprofits, cities, or other entities. There are anywhere from forty to fifty floats accepted each year (out of about two hundred that apply). Past floats have included replicas of the Statue of Liberty, cruise ships, working volcanos and waterfalls, alien spaceships, a giant bottle of milk, and massive tigers, puppies, eagles, and insects.

Once an organization or company is accepted into the tournament, they must either hire a company to design and build their float or do so themselves, often with volunteer assistance from their own employees or community members who volunteer through a number of community organizations that support the parade, such as the Downey Rose Float Association or the Burbank Tournament of Roses Association. Most big corporations have their floats built by professional float builders, whereas the smaller organizations tend to use volunteer labor. Most floats today, which are bigger and more elaborate than ever before, are built by professional float makers, who also win the most prizes each year.

Cal Poly Universities' floats, however, which represent California State Polytechnic University, Pomona, as well as California Polytechnic State University, San Luis Obispo, and have appeared in the parade each year since 1949, still build their floats entirely with (unpaid) student labor from design ideas contributed by members of the community. Students who work on the float come from a variety of backgrounds, including welding, robotics, electronics, fiber optics, animation, hydraulics, and more. In fact, the Cal Poly entries have been responsible for introducing a number of new technologies into float design. The Cal Poly floats have received over fifty awards since they first began participating in the parade.

Whether commercially produced or not, the construction of a float takes about a year and will start as soon as possible after the previous year's parade. It begins with a chassis, typically taken from an old (but operational) truck, and by adding steel, chicken wire, wood, and a coating of liquid polyvinyl, it will be transformed into Mt. Rushmore, a pirate ship, or an African jungle. Many floats are now equipped with computer technology that not only allows moving parts but animation and other special effects as well. After the major building is completed, the decorating begins with the nonperishable plant items, such as bark or seeds. Finally, just prior to the event (typically right after Christmas), it will be decorated with thousands of flowers, seeds, and leaves. It takes thirty roses to cover just one square foot of surface area, so the average float can require as many as 250,000 flowers or parts, or ten thousand pounds of material, some of which is donated by flower farmers but most of which must be purchased. This is the part of the process when the most volunteers are needed, as decoration is a time-consuming activity, but it requires no real skill to do. Even the commercial float builders use volunteers to help with decoration.

Roses and other delicate flowers are not glued onto the float; rather, they are affixed to the float in individual vials of water to keep them fresh. (Although the parade began as a way to showcase California's flowers, in recent years, the majority of flowers and plants used for the floats have come from out of state and typically outside of the United States.)

After it has been completed, the float is driven down the parade route by a driver, who communicates with float riders and observers who help him or her navigate. Prior to the parade, a team of volunteers judges the floats, awarding twenty-five different prizes, including the top prize, the Sweepstakes Award, which is given to the most beautiful float of the year. In 2019, twenty of the twenty-five prizes went to commercially built floats (built by just three builders), and only five were given to self-built floats.

To volunteer to help with float decoration, most organizations only require that the volunteer be at least thirteen years old, work a full shift, and sign a waiver for insurance purposes. Volunteers participate in float building because they enjoy being a part of such an important American tradition and to help community organizations shine in the parade. Some volunteer because they support the mission of the organization, while others do so as part of an organized group of volunteers, such as the Boy Scouts.

To get work at one of the Rose Parade float construction companies, one needs to have a varied background that could include design, architecture, computer modeling, engineering, or sculpting. Many people gain experience on different aspects of the float-building process by working on set design at community or college theaters. The other big events that use floats—New Orleans' Mardi Gras Parade and the Macy's Thanksgiving Day Parade—use floats that are constructed very differently than Rose Parade floats, although experience working in any float-making capacity is certainly helpful.

See also: Sugar Painter.

Further Reading

Adams, L., & M. Riffey. (2007). *More than a parade: The spirit and passion behind the Pasadena Tournament of Roses.* Stephens Press.

Hoefferle, M. M. (2012). Floats, friendship and fun: Exploring motivations for community art engagement. *International Journal of Education through Art, 8*(3), 253–269.

Lawrence, D. (1982). Parades, politics, and competing urban images: Doo dah and roses. *Urban Anthropology, 11*(2), 155–176.

S

Saturation Diver (Global)

A saturation diver is a deep-sea diver who temporarily lives and works at very great depths. Saturation divers are typically employed to do underwater construction and often work for oil companies, repairing oil rigs in the middle of the ocean. The vast majority of saturation divers are men because of the very difficult nature of the work and also because divers live together in small habitats for weeks at a time with no privacy.

Humans cannot live underwater; they need oxygen tanks, at a bare minimum, to survive. On top of that, divers must worry about pressure. The deeper a diver dives underwater, the more the water will press down on his or her body, causing the natural gases in the body to compress. Scuba divers must equalize their ears while descending to help alleviate this pressure. When the diver is ascending to the ocean surface, the process reverses itself; the pressure declines, and, the gasses in the body expand. Divers must then ascend slowly, to give the body enough time to release the additional trapped gases. If a diver does not do this after a deep dive, he or she can experience what are colloquially called the bends (decompression sickness), which may involve burst eardrums or even lungs and when severe can cause death.

Saturation divers work at depths far deeper than a regular diver goes (up to one thousand feet below the service) and thus need special protection for their work. They work in such deep depths that ascending safely to the surface takes many days. For instance, diving to just 650 feet mean that it will take eight days to travel back to the surface. For that reason, divers who are employed to work under the sea live there as well, in small underwater compression chambers, usually with other members of the crew. The divers are safe living in these extreme conditions because once they have descended, and after about twenty-four hours, the gases in the body reach equilibrium with the pressure at the depth; in other words, the tissues of the body have been so saturated with gases that the body cannot take on more. And because the divers do not need to return to the surface daily, there is no risk of decompression sickness. Where recreational scuba divers do not stay underwater so long that their bodies become saturated (so that they can quickly ascend to the surface if necessary), that is the goal of the saturation diver.

Depending on the job, divers may stay underwater for two weeks or up to a month, which includes the time that it takes to descend and the multiple days that it will take to ascend again. During the time under, they work daily on their assigned tasks and eat, drink, sleep, use the toilet, shower, and enjoy leisure time within the chamber, which is pressurized to match the pressure at the depth that the crew is working and may only be as big as a master bedroom.

Saturation divers are not just divers. They not only have extensive training in saturation diving but must also be trained in basic medical techniques, as they will be so isolated that they will be out of reach of medical aid. (There will also be a team above water to monitor the divers and communicate with them.) Of course, the divers must also be trained in the actual work that they will be doing: welding, drilling tunnels, laying pipe, or any other work required by the company. Skilled divers can earn anywhere from $50,000 to $100,000 per year.

Saturation diving is extremely dangerous work and very hard on the body. It takes highly trained individuals to do this work, and they must be willing to live and work in conditions that most people could not handle. Even "going to work" each day involves a complicated process. To leave their underwater home to work outside, they must be transferred, while still pressurized, from the chamber to a personnel transfer capsule, known as a closed diving bell, which will lower the diver to the working location, where he will exit to begin work. (A fellow diver remains in the bell to assist if something goes wrong.) The diver is connected to the bell via his umbilical, which is a set of up to eight different hoses that supply

hot water to course through his hot water suit (similar to a wetsuit but hot water runs through tubes in the suit), a communications cable, a video cable, and more. There is also a hose that provides breathing gas (a mixture of oxygen and helium) to the diver as well as another hose that removes gas.

When the work is done and the divers are ready to ascend, they do so in the closed diving bell—the same one that they use while working—which is also how they descended in the first place. The bell ascends very slowly with breaks in between ascents.

Saturation divers are trained the same way as other commercial divers, at accredited commercial diving schools. Not all diving schools are equipped to train saturation divers, however, but those that do provide the student who has completed the program with a certificate demonstrating his training.

See also: Bike Fisherman.

A commercial offshore diver wearing an anticontamination suit and helmet. (Erik Ihlenfeld /Dreamstime.com)

Ice Cutter

An ice cutter or ice harvester is someone who cuts ice from the surface of frozen rivers or ponds for sale. Prior to the development of ice-making machines in the mid–nineteenth century and, later, refrigerators, which allow food to stay cold without the use of ice, perishable food needed to be preserved through the use of ice or snow or through other methods, such as salting or canning. For thousands of years, people have been harvesting ice and snow to store food or to cool beverages, and in the early nineteenth century, iceboxes were developed, which made it easier to store food and ice together. This led to the commercialization of ice cutting and the development of the ice trade, whereby individuals in cold and northern climates harvested surface ice, via saws and axes, to ship to warmer areas, where the ice was sold to the public by icemen.

Ice cutting was done at night, when the ice was thicker, and involved a dozen different jobs, all physically demanding and many dangerous. During the height of the ice trade, ice was harvested in New England, stored in a variety of icehouses along the way, and shipped as far as India. With the development of the horse-drawn ice cutter in 1825, the job became easier, and as the cost of ice dropped, more people could afford to purchase it. With the development of the home refrigerator at the beginning of the twentieth century, the need for ice cutters evaporated.

Source: Rees, J. (2013). *Refrigeration nation: A history of ice, appliances, and enterprise in America.* Johns Hopkins University Press.

Further Reading

Brubakk, A. O., Ross, J. A., & Thom, S. R. (2011). Saturation diving; physiology and pathophysiology. *Comprehensive Physiology, 4*(3), 1229–1272.
Swann, C. (2014). *The history of oilfield diving: An industrial adventure.* Oceanaut Press.

Scooter Charger and Retriever (United States)

A scooter charger or scooter retriever is a person who tracks down rental scooters after they have been rented and either charges them and returns them to the street or returns them to the rental company. Most retrievers are independent contractors who are paid by the scooter rental companies.

Shareable electric scooters emerged in the United States in 2017, when Bird and Lime introduced their scooters to Santa Monica and San Francisco, and they quickly spread to most major cities in the United States as well as many countries around the world. After the success of ridesharing services such as Lyft and Uber, shareable bikes and scooters emerged as the latest transportation innovation. Led by Bird and Lime, plus newer companies such as Jump (owned by Uber), Razor, Spin, Skip, and Voi, this new industry is already worth billions of dollars and can be found today throughout Europe, Asia, and South America.

Tourists, commuters, and anyone who wants a relatively quick way to travel in any of the hundreds of cities with scooter-sharing services first starts by downloading a smartphone app from one of the companies. The app provides the user with the locations of any nearby scooters; the user then pays to rent one of the scooters through the app and is given a code to unlock it. After the rider gets to where he or she is going, he or she is expected to park the scooter in a designated

Two Spin scooters on the sidewalk in Detroit, Michigan. (Smontgom65/Dreamstime .com)

area. Then the rider uses the app to lock the scooter so that it cannot be stolen or used for free.

Rental scooters, or e-scooters (for electric scooters), are an example of a micro-mobility solution that is intended to be used for short-distance travel and are ideally suited to get people from public transportation centers, such as metro stations, to either home or work. Ultimately, it is hoped that scooters will help to get more people to use public transportation.

Because most e-scooters are dockless, they will have to be recharged after they have been used so that the next person can rent them. This is done by an army of workers known as chargers, who typically work at night, returning the scooters early in the morning.

Bird and Lime, the two largest companies, are constantly hiring chargers. The hiring process is mostly done online, with a phone interview after the online application. Chargers must use their own transportation, be eighteen or older, and have a driver's license, but beyond that, there are not a lot of requirements.

Most companies pay their chargers about $5 per scooter that is picked up, charged, and put back on the street (some companies pay more for hard-to-locate scooters). Once they have been hired, the chargers log onto a special app that indicates where the scooters are located. Once they have decided which scooters to claim, they pick them up and return to their homes, where they will charge the scooters using special chargers provided by the company, a process that takes from three to five hours. The scooters are charged using the worker's home electricity. The more chargers and cables that a charger has, the more scooters that can be charged at one time. Most chargers work at night and return the charged scooters back to the street by the next morning. Once a job has been completed, the charger is paid through the app.

Chargers need to be reliable, and they must work very early in the morning, when the scooters must be brought back to the street. (Many chargers collect their scooters at night and charge them overnight, but this is not required.) Some chargers buy additional chargers and cables so that they can charge more scooters at once. Other equipment that some chargers purchase include gloves, a flashlight, a reflective vest, and a surge protector. There is a great deal of competition for charging jobs in major cities; the most successful chargers develop a clear strategy to maximize their profit.

One of the many problems caused by e-scooters is that many users simply abandon their scooters after use wherever they like rather than at the charging stations that riders are supposed to use. This has resulted in city sidewalks, parks, and other public areas (especially in high tourism areas) becoming littered with abandoned scooters, sometimes hundreds in one location, which causes visual pollution as well as a hazard to walkers, joggers, and wheelchair users. In addition, some people intentionally dump scooters in strange places so that the companies cannot find them.

The dumping of scooters on city streets has resulted in cities either restricting or prohibiting the use of e-scooters until the problem is resolved. Many cities now require scooter companies to provide plans for how they will deal with the problem of abandoned scooters, and others only permit scooters in specially approved zones. In recent months, both France and Singapore have banned scooter sharing outright.

One system that has developed to help solve the problem of abandoned scooters is the scooter retrieval industry. In San Diego, for example, ScootScoop is a private scooter retrieval company that picks up scooters that have been abandoned on private property and then returns them to the companies that rent them for a fee, which the scooter rental companies see as a form of ransom. In reality, companies such as ScootScoop, which fields calls from business owners looking to have scooters removed from their property, operate a bit like bounty hunters or repo men, finding and locating scooters (instead of skips) and returning them for a fee (ScootScoop charges $30 per scooter). The employees, known as "scoopers," are then sent out to retrieve the scooters, which are held in a warehouse until the companies pay to get their property back.

In response, the largest scooter-sharing companies are now providing their own scooter retrieval services. For instance, besides paying workers to charge scooters, Lime also pays workers to pick up scooters that are parked illegally and move them (within four hours) to a designated location. These workers use an app to locate scooters, just like the chargers use, to locate the scooters and verify that they have been moved.

See also: Bounty Hunter; Car Jockey; Pallet Recycler.

Further Reading

Hollingsworth, J., Copeland, B., & Johnson, J. X. (2019). Are e-scooters polluters? The environmental impacts of shared dockless electric scooters. *Environmental Research Letters, 14*(8), 084031.

Yang, C. J. (2010). Launching strategy for electric vehicles: Lessons from China and Taiwan. *Technological Forecasting and Social Change, 77*(5), 831–834.

Sex Worker (Global)

A sex worker is a person who works in the sex trade, although the term typically
refers to those who engage in sex for pay, or prostitutes. *Sex work*, however, is the
preferred term by those who work in the industry because it emphasizes that it is
work, and as work, it should be protected and respected like other forms of work.
And like all forms of work, there are positive and negative aspects to sex work.
Opponents of prostitution, however, dislike the term *sex work* because they feel
that it sanitizes the practice, erasing all the harms inherent in it.

In prostitution, often called "the world's oldest profession," women, or men,
sell sexual access to their bodies for a price. Among the ancient Greeks and Sumerians, prostitution was once practiced both recreationally and in a ritual context,
known as sacred prostitution, which took place within the temple. Although
sacred prostitution did not survive the rise of Christianity, prostitution was often
tolerated by the church; in medieval Europe, prostitutes were given a location to
ply their trade outside of city walls because buying and selling sex was seen as
less sinful than masturbation or sodomy.

Sander Gilman (1985) points out that during the nineteenth century, the era
during which racialized groups were being measured and classified, prostitutes
were subject to the same types of analysis. Freud, for instance, said that certain
women have an "aptitude for prostitution" based on the anthropological studies of
the time, which focused on the women's weight, skull size, facial abnormalities,
and family background.

In some countries (and some counties in Nevada) today, certain kinds of prostitution are legal. Generally, where prostitution is legal, as in much of Europe, Australia, and New Zealand, it is regulated and occurs in brothels, where prostitutes
are regularly checked for sexually transmitted diseases and the clients must wear
condoms and shower before sex. The conditions in brothels are considered to be
safe, and the prostitutes are, ideally, paid a living wage. Street prostitution, however, is typically illegal, as is pimping, because it involves coercion and the control of one person over another person's body. (In Japan, oddly, vaginal prostitution
is illegal but fellatio is legal.)

Where street prostitution occurs, women and men (called hustlers or rent boys)
tend to be young, they are often runaways, they are often addicted to drugs, and
they have often been coerced into becoming prostitutes. They live dangerous
lives. Street prostitution is the most dangerous job in the United States in terms of
occupational mortality than any other female-dominated profession, and the prostitutes are at risk of being abused or killed by pimps, clients (most of whom are
married men), and others who prey on the vulnerable. They are also at very high
risk of sexually transmitted diseases.

Sex workers offer a variety of reasons as to why they began working in the
industry. For many, the choice was not entirely their own, as they may have been
victims of domestic or sexual abuse, or both, or may be struggling with drug use.

For others, however, they see the work as something that could bring them financial independence and the freedom to set their own hours and not report to a boss. Many enjoy sex and like the work. But after working for a couple of years, many prostitutes, no matter how voluntary their employment, try to get out and reintegrate into mainstream society with a regular job. One of the reasons for this is because it is so difficult to maintain a romantic relationship with someone while working as a prostitute. For sex workers who lie to their family and friends about what they do, this often gets to them, driving them to eventually leave. And even when they are open about what they do, they must deal with the stigma associated with the job. But leaving the industry is difficult because even when the money is not great, it is more reliable than finding a low-paying job somewhere else, especially as sex workers may not have many marketable job skills or a college education.

Some sex workers work for an agency instead of a brothel, and others are freelancers, marketing themselves online and through word of mouth to customers, who are called clients, within the part of the industry known as escort services. The fees that the clients pay are typically much larger than those paid in brothels (and certainly more than paid to a street prostitute), and although the agencies take a cut, the worker makes more money at the end of a "date." When an agency is involved, it is responsible for finding clients, screening them, advertising, and even transporting the escort to the hotel for her work.

Prostitutes, whether working on the street, in a brothel, for an agency, or for themselves, engage in multiple forms of labor. The work is physical, but it also involves a huge amount of emotional labor. The prostitute must behave as if she is turned on, no matter what she feels, and she is responsible for getting the customer aroused as well. She must also be able to talk to her customers, and listen to them, and must be able to emotionally connect with them (or at least appear to do so).

But even where prostitution is voluntary and relatively safe, many people argue that it should still not be allowed because, by its very nature, it exploits women (or the men who work in the industry) by turning them into objects who exist to provide sexual pleasure to men. In addition, many feminists argue that the whole notion of "voluntary prostitution" is illusory because no woman (or man) would become a prostitute if she (or he) were not desperate to start with. In addition, although regulated brothel prostitution often results in women being able to make good money and exercise a great deal of control over their bodies and their working conditions, as in the Netherlands, this is not always the case.

German brothel workers, for example, are not paid a wage at all. Instead, they work on commission, earning a portion of each customer's fee. They must also pay the brothel a set fee to work for the day or night. On busy days, they can potentially make a lot of money, but on slow days, they may make no money at all or, worse, find themselves in the red after paying their brothel fee. And all brothel workers are responsible for buying the different outfits that they wear on the job, and they must endure being selected, or passed over, by customers, which can be a demeaning experience.

In other countries, the situation is much worse. In Thailand, for example, where prostitution is technically illegal but extremely common, young girls and women work in brothels where they service multiple men per day for very little money, most of which goes to pay off a debt that their family owes as well as their food and other living expenses. These girls are often trafficked from other countries, such as Burma, and they are at the mercy of the people who own them, the clients who have sex with them, and the police who also victimize them. Virgins are sold for as much as $1,000 (money that the girls never see), but after that, their rate drops as they become used up.

Trafficking is an ancient practice that involves forcing women and children into forced labor and often sexual servitude. It is often associated with war; conquering armies may kill men in conquered nations, but they often bring women and children back as spoils of war and force them to become slaves. During World War II, hundreds of thousands of Korean and Japanese women and girls were kidnapped and enslaved by the Imperial Japanese military and forced to serve soldiers as unpaid prostitutes known as comfort women. This practice is an example of wartime rape, a common practice in which conquering armies use rape as both a reward for soldiers as well as a tactic to terrorize the population and humiliate the enemy, destroying family bonds in the process. It is also a method of ethnic cleansing, as in the Bosnian War, when over twenty thousand Muslim women and girls were raped, and many impregnated, by Serbian soldiers as a program of ethnic and cultural genocide. But it is also an example of the ways in which prostitution and war have also long been linked.

Brothels are often set up near military bases during wartime, often with the explicit support of the military, to service the needs of soldiers. This was the case in the Korean War, when Korean women served as prostitutes, or comfort women, to American GIs; the brothels were set up as part of the mutual defense treaty signed by South Korea and the United States. During the Vietnam War, American officials set up sites in nearby Thailand for soldiers to get away from the war for R & R (rest and recreation), which was expected to include sex with local women. The United States provided financial investments in cities such as Bangkok in exchange for Thailand creating the "recreational" opportunities for American soldiers.

This was the origin of the modern sex trade in Thailand today. As with the comfort women in the Korean War, the women who served as prostitutes in the Vietnam War were desperately poor and, for many, were hoping for an opportunity to marry a soldier and go to the United States. Some of these women, called "minor wives," did get to come to the United States after the war, but many more were left behind, sometimes with children. Because the children were of mixed race, they were often ostracized and sent to orphanages, where they were raised by nuns or adopted internationally. After the end of the Vietnam War, the prostitution infrastructure set up to serve the soldiers was converted to serve the international sex trade.

Today, human trafficking is the fastest-growing form of slavery, and according to the U.S. State Department, it is the second-largest and fastest-growing criminal industry in the world, particularly in Southeast Asia and Eastern Europe. Traffickers prey on the poor and desperate who are looking for a way out of poverty and believe that they will get a better life by going with the men who offer their families money. These women are transported to other countries, sorted by beauty and age, and sent to their destinations, where they will be purchased and used. Some of the women think they will become domestic servants or even models, but they instead become prostitutes. Once they realize their new situation, they are threatened with violence or their family is threatened if they attempt to escape.

Child prostitutes are very popular with Western tourists who come to places such as Thailand on sex tourism vacations. They have an especially difficult life, having sex with a dozen or more men per day, often without condoms, and they experience pregnancy and disease with alarming frequency. Approximately 1.2 million children are trafficked each year, most for prostitution, according to UNICEF (2006). In 2011, the U.S. Department of Justice produced a report showing that 82% of all trafficking victims are used for sex, with half of those victims being under age 18 (Larsen 2011).

For men who participate in sex tourism, according to sociologist Jacqueline Sanchez Taylor (2000 and 2006), the appeal lies in that the women and girls are foreign and exotic, preferably Asian. Many customers apparently do not even consider the practice that they engage in to be prostitution; instead, they think that the women or girls simply want to have sex with them. The sexual exchanges are driven by sexual and racial stereotypes that suggest that white women are stuck up, too independent, or sexually conservative, but Asian women are submissive, ready to please, and sexually voracious. These men are blind to the fact that poverty and desperation underlie one side of the international sex trade.

Today, most women's groups take the positions—thanks to activism by sex worker rights groups—that all prostitution is not necessarily exploitative, that prostitution that is truly voluntary should be decriminalized and regulated so that women who engage in sex work can be protected, and that all forms of forced prostitution should be eliminated.

See also: Porn Star.

Further Reading

Gilman, S. L. (1985). Black bodies, white bodies: Toward an iconography of female sexuality in late nineteenth-century art, medicine, and literature. *Critical Inquiry*, *12*(1), 204–242.

Kempadoo, K., & Doezema, J. (Eds.). (2018). *Global sex workers: Rights, resistance, and redefinition*. Routledge.

Larsen, R. (2011, May 20). U.S. Human Trafficking Incidents, 2008–2010. *Journalist's Resource*. https://journalistsresource.org/studies/government/criminal-justice/human-trafficking.

Taylor, J. S. (2000). Tourism and 'embodied' commodities: sex tourism in the Caribbean. In S. Clift and S. Carter (Eds.), *Tourism and sex: Culture, commerce and coercion* (pp. 41–53).

Taylor, J. S. (2006). Female sex tourism: A contradiction in terms? *Feminist Review*, *83*(1), 42–59.

UNICEF. (2006). *Child Protection Information Sheet: Trafficking*. https://www.unicef.org/protection/files/Trafficking.pdf.

Sideshow Freak (United States, Great Britain, Australia)

The term *freak* refers to individuals who are physically and visually different from other people, and it generally refers to those who are put on display in a freak show. Although the term was once used as an insult, modern freaks who perform in sideshows embrace the term. Types of freaks include *born freaks* (those with disfiguring diseases or disabilities), *made freaks* (such as tattooed or heavily pierced people), and *novelty acts*, such as sword swallowers and fire eaters.

Traveling shows in which human oddities were displayed alongside exotic animals, deformed animals, musicians, jugglers, and other attractions have been popular throughout the Western world, going back to the Middle Ages. In the West, freaks were displayed as single attractions in inns, taverns, and at local fairs throughout medieval Europe. Early documented attractions included a woman from New Guinea displayed in Europe in 1738 and Chang and Eng, the first conjoined twins, who were displayed starting in 1829.

The first freak to be displayed

A carnival stilt performer at the Tauranga Art and Tattoo Show in New Zealand. (Jon Paul /Dreamstime.com)

in the United States was Miss Emma Leach, a dwarf who was shown in Boston in 1771. One of the saddest and most notorious of the early freaks was Saartjie Baartman, a Kung San woman with steatopygia, a condition marked by large fatty deposits in the buttocks; she was purchased for display as the "Hottentot Venus." She was displayed in 1810 and 1811 in a cage in London, where customers were invited to pinch her buttocks. After her death in 1815, her body was dissected, her body parts were preserved for future study, and plaster molds of her body and genitals were displayed in a French museum until the 1980s.

In the mid–nineteenth century, human oddities joined what became known as the freak show or ten-in-one, in which multiple attractions were combined into one show, as part of a stationary or traveling exhibit. In the United States, these exhibits were primarily found in the dime museums popular in the nineteenth century.

Although the human oddities were not originally the main attractions in these early museums, they quickly became more popular than the stuffed birds and dusty artifacts and provided acceptable entertainment (disguised as education) in an era in which the church frowned upon frivolous fun. From 1870 to 1890, the freak show was the king of dime museum attractions. At the end of the nineteenth century, the dime museum began to decline as the forms of entertainment previously granted legitimacy by their scientific cover now expanded into other venues, such as circuses, carnivals, street fairs, and world's fairs. In 1880, the first freak show appeared at Coney Island.

Dime museums were urban, but circuses went to rural areas where they, along with the county fair, were often the only entertainment. Single freak attractions joined circuses in the early 1800s, but the organized sideshow did not get started until midcentury. The earliest traveling freak shows were traveling museums, and some museums joined traveling circuses as concessions. By the 1840s, though, the museum part of the circus finally became the circus sideshow and was no longer independently owned and operated.

Around 1840, however, human oddities became joined into what is now known as the freak show, the sideshow, or, in circus and carnival parlance, the ten-in-one, meaning ten separate acts in one location, especially because of the endeavors of P. T. Barnum, who established the American Museum in 1842 and brought a number of exotic attractions together into one place. Dime museums such as the American Museum gave birth to the freak show as we know it, and freak shows later moved into world's fairs, circuses, carnivals, and amusement parks.

When being displayed in a sideshow, freaks are what the talker, manager, or showman makes them. Born freaks were rarely in charge of their own careers or destinies; indeed, they usually joined circuses or carnivals because that was the only way they could make a living for themselves. The "exotic" presentation is one form of displaying a freak, appealing to people's interest in the exotic, the native, and the primitive. In this way, most freaks were also frauds or "gaffes," in that the showman created extraordinary stories that typically went well beyond the individual's personal history or capabilities. For example, Tom Thumb was displayed as an eleven-year-old English boy but was actually a four-year-old American, and the original Wild Men of Borneo were actually mentally disabled brothers from Ohio.

Born freaks included hairy ladies such as Leonine the Lion Faced Lady, Alice Bounds the Bear Lady, and Annie Jones; giants such as Patrick O'Brien the Irish Giant and Sam Taylor the Ilkeston Giant; fat men and women; dwarves and little people, such as Tom Thumb, Major Mite, Harold Pyott, and Anita the Living Doll; albinos; conjoined twins such as Chang and Eng or Daisy and Violet Hilton; parasitic twins; animal-human wonders, such as lobster boys; human torsos; pinheads; and hermaphrodites.

Made freaks and novelty acts (which often overlapped in the individual performers) included sword swallowers, tattooed men and women, fire eaters, contortionists, regurgitators, snake charmers, and other performers.

In the twentieth century, with the rediscovery of Mendelian genetics, the rise of modern science, and the eugenics movement, the disabled began to be understood from a biological and cultural perspective, and this began to adversely affect the attendance at freak shows. Notions of pity, humane impulses, and the desire to lock away all undesirables led to its decline, as well as the rising middle class and their aversion to corporeal entertainment such as this. The eugenics movement of the twentieth century, which saw abnormal births in the same light as racial minorities, influenced the elimination of the physically disabled from the public eye in places such as Germany. There, freak shows were restricted or banned as early as 1911 and especially after World War I, when clean-cut showgirls emerged as a new form of entertainment.

The use of the physically disabled in freak shows in the United States finally ended in the 1960s when the American Civil Liberties Union (ACLU) brought attention to the situation of displaying the physically disabled in circus freak shows and caused their demise; many U.S. states now prohibit the exhibition of deformed or disabled people for entertainment. Many former sideshow freaks ended up in institutions or on welfare once the freak show had died. But even before that time, the display of freaks began to die out as early as the 1930s, partly due to the effects of the Great Depression on American's spending habits.

Today, the term *freak* is rarely used to refer to people with disabilities, and the disability rights movement has created opportunities for the disabled that allow for a range of careers that do not depend on the display of one's condition for money. On the other hand, there are still a number of people who willingly undergo multiple tattoos, piercings, implantations, and other body modification procedures to transform themselves into modern freaks. Katzen, the Enigma, the Leopard Man and the Lizardman are all examples of modern freaks, many of whom perform in sideshows or other venues today.

The first modern version of the old circus and carnival freak show was the Jim Rose Circus Sideshow, which during the 1990s employed performers who took old sideshow acts such as sword swallowing and fire eating and blended them with modern physical oddities such as heavily pierced, tattooed, and implanted people. Many of the acts were geared to shock the audience, including Mr. Lifto, who lifted heavy weights from his piercings; the Enigma, who ate slugs and could put a power drill up his nose; and the Tube, who swallowed tubes and pumped liquids into and out of his stomach. Another modern incarnation of the sideshow is the Coney Island Circus Sideshow, the last permanent, nontraveling, ten-in-one sideshow in the United States, which features fire eaters, snake charmers, contortionists, human blockheads, razor blade eaters, strong men, sword swallowers, and tattooed attractions.

One modern freak show that still shows born freaks, or people born with physical abnormalities, is the 999 Eyes Freakshow, founded by Ward Hall, which includes a half girl, an elephant man, a giant, a lobster girl, and a dwarf as well as bug eaters, fire eaters, a man tattooed like a leopard, deformed animals, and the like. Finally, the Internet has created an entirely new audience for freaks through websites that display (either for fetishistic purposes or for shock value) photos of human abnormalities.

Another contemporary sideshow freak is Chayne Hultgren, who calls himself the Space Cowboy, a tattooed and pierced performer who is a sword swallower, knife thrower, juggler, and human blockhead, among other acts. He travels with his Mutant Barnyard, a collection of animal freaks and gaffes, and performs at musical events and festivals around the world.

Other modern sideshow acts include Strange for Hire, the Monster Sideshow, the Pickle Brothers Circus, the Circus of Horrors, Hellzapoppin Circus Sideshow Revue, the Wreckless Freeks, and FreakShow Deluxe.

Because most modern sideshow performers are made freaks, rather than born freaks, having a serious disability is no longer required to become a freak. Instead, sideshow performers today build up their skills, learning such traditional sideshow acts as sword swallowing, fire eating, knife throwing, laying on a bed of nails, and contortionism. Many have also modified their bodies, sometimes extensively, via tattoos, piercings, cutting, and implants, as did sideshow performers in centuries past.

Historically, sideshow performers have either been self-taught or have learned from experienced sideshow performers. This is still largely the case, although there is now one opportunity for students who want to learn to be a sideshow performer: the Sideshow School held through Coney Island, USA, which runs the Coney Island Circus Sideshow. Students can learn sword swallowing, fire eating and breathing, glass walking, human blockhead, the bed of nails, the blade box, and a variety of other classic sideshow acts. Students will even learn to care for snakes!

Becoming a freak today, as in the past, is no simple matter. This type of profession takes a major commitment, especially because so many modern freaks have modified their bodies so extensively that they are unlikely to be hired for most regular jobs. In addition, jobs are not easy to get, and the same performers are often competing for the same jobs. But well-known sideshow performers with unique skills can be hired for a variety of different jobs, including movie and television appearances, and they can develop quite a substantial following.

The good news for those who would like to embark on a career as a freak is that freak shows are experiencing a bit of a resurgence right now, thanks in part to the publicity generated by television shows such as *American Horror Story: Freakshow* and *Carnivale* and movies such as *The Greatest Showman* and *The Vampire's Assistant*.

See also: Mime or Clown.

Further Reading
DeMello, M. (2007). *Encyclopedia of body adornment: A cultural history.* Greenwood Press.
Durbach, N. (2009). *Spectacle of deformity: Freak shows and modern British culture.* University of California Press.

Sloth Nanny (Costa Rica)

A sloth nanny, more formally known as a sloth caretaker or technician, is a person who cares for sloths, typically at a sloth sanctuary.

Sloths are slow-moving arboreal animals native to the rainforests of Central and South America. They are herbivores and are divided into two families: two-toed sloths and three-toed sloths. Sloths are related to both anteaters and armadillos, and relatively little is known about them, compared to many other well-studied animal species. Because of their unhurried nature, sloths are often thought of as dull-witted, sluggish, and lazy; in fact, the animal was named after one of the

A baby sloth in an animal sanctuary in Costa Rica. (Ingalin/Dreamstime.com)

seven deadly sins, and *sloth* comes from the word *slow*. Yet, the deliberate movements of sloths are a beneficial adaptation, making them very successful animals in the rainforest environment.

Sloths spend most of their days hanging from trees by their claws. From there, they eat, sleep, mate, and give birth, only returning to the ground weekly to use the bathroom. On the ground, they cannot walk, so they must use their claws to drag themselves along if they need to travel. They are surprisingly strong and (relatively) quick swimmers, however. Because of sloths' inability to move quickly on the ground (about four meters per minute), they are subject to injury from other animals, cars, or people when they are out of the trees.

There are currently six species of sloth, and two of those species are classified as either vulnerable or critically endangered because of deforestation and climate change. They have very few natural predators; and their greatest dangers come from people. They are poached by locals, hit by cars, electrocuted by electrical lines, and are stolen as pets. After birth, sloths need to spend many months with their mothers to learn everything they need to be independent adults. They even learn from their mothers what and how to eat. When a sloth with a dependent baby dies, usually due to a human cause, that baby will also die without someone to help it learn to be a sloth.

This is where sloth sanctuaries come in. Because these animals are so vulnerable, and because their care needs are so specific, sloth sanctuaries have emerged to care for injured, orphaned, and ill sloths. The oldest of these sanctuaries—and for twenty years the only sloth sanctuary—is the Sloth Sanctuary of Costa Rica, founded in 1992, which has cared for hundreds of sloths since its founding. It is also the most well-known sloth sanctuary in the world thanks to its adorable You-Tube videos and the 2013 Animal Planet television show *Meet the Sloths.*

Sloth sanctuaries such as the Sloth Sanctuary of Costa Rica nurse sick and injured sloths back to health and care for young sloths until they can be released back into the wild. This involves teaching the babies the skills that should have been taught to them by their mothers. Sloth sanctuaries depend heavily on volunteers to help with the care of the animals, as staffs are small and budgets are limited.

To become a sloth caretaker, one must first and foremost be passionate about sloths. For general caretaking, specialized degrees or training may not be necessary, although for research- or conservation-related jobs, a degree in zoology, wildlife ecology, or a related field will typically be required. Because the work is done in the areas where sloths live, the ability to speak Spanish is a plus along with the willingness to travel to and live in an often isolated jungle location. There are a number of international organizations that offer opportunities to volunteer with sloths, and some organizations, such as the Sloth Institute, offer their own volunteer and internship programs.

The job of being a sloth nanny, whether paid or volunteer, involves a number of tasks. Sloth caretakers tend to work very long days—including nights—with limited time off. (Two-toed sloths are nocturnal, and while three-toed sloths are both diurnal and nocturnal, they are still relatively inactive during the day.) As with caretakers for other animal species, sloth nannies must not be afraid to get dirty, to get very tired, or to get scratched. Working in the tropical rainforests of Central or South America means being hot, sweaty, sticky, and bug-bitten. Caretakers prepare food, feed the sloths, clean their environments, assist with medical treatment and releases, provide enrichment materials to the resident sloths, and help to not only raise the babies but also teach them how to be a sloth. Caring for babies involves syringe feeding the youngest babies every two hours, around the clock, which is one reason why the job can be so demanding (and exhausting). Older babies only need to be fed five times per day (including overnight). Because sloths eat so many leaves (mostly from the *Cecropia* genus of trees), workers need to collect leaves and other plant matter multiple times per day.

Besides caretaking tasks, other employees and volunteers with sloth organizations may be involved in releases, in monitoring wild released sloths, in analyzing data, or in other research-related tasks. As with other animal care jobs, but especially those at sanctuaries, the job of a nanny caretaker can be emotionally difficult as well when these delicate, vulnerable animals die.

See also: Panda Nanny.

Further Reading

Garcés-Restrepo, M. F., Pauli, J. N., & Peery, M. Z. (2018). Natal dispersal of tree sloths in a human-dominated landscape: Implications for tropical biodiversity conservation. *Journal of Applied Ecology, 55*(5), 2253–2262.

Vaughan, C., Ramírez, O., Herrera, G., & Guries, R. (2007). Spatial ecology and conservation of two sloth species in a cacao landscape in Limón, Costa Rica. *Biodiversity and Conservation, 16*(8), 2293–2310.

Snake Milker (United States)

A snake milker is someone who extracts the venom from venomous snakes.

According to the World Health Organization (WHO), about six hundred snake species, or about 20 percent of all snakes, are venomous, which means they produce venom in their saliva. The snakes inject the venom into their prey via their teeth, which in most venomous snakes are hollow, either killing or disabling the victim. Venomous snakes, such as deadly cobras, mambas, vipers, moccasins, and rattlesnakes, are found throughout the majority of the world, except the far northern regions.

When someone has been bitten by a venomous snake, the person may require antivenom to save his or her life. Antivenom binds to the toxins in the snake venom, stopping further damage (but not reversing the damage already done). Most snake bites are not fatal, but even so, they can cause severe pain and injury, including internal bleeding, local tissue necrosis, or damage to the heart, the muscles, or the nervous system. And while most bites are not fatal, anywhere from 80,000 to 138,000 people still die from snake bites every year, with three times that many bites resulting in amputation. In comparison, there are around five deaths per year in the United States.

This uneven distribution has to do both with the geographic spread of venomous snakes (the thirteen most dangerous venomous snakes are found in tropical and subtropical regions in Melanesia, East Asia, South Asia, Southeast Asia, and sub-Saharan Africa) and the distribution of health care access around the world. Snake bite victims are more likely to die in countries with uneven access to health care. In addition, antivenom is expensive. In the United States, a vial of antivenom can cost around $4,000, and most bites will require multiple courses of treatment using multiple vials of antivenom. Outside the United States, the cost is much

A cobra being milked for its venom. (Ali Cobanoglu/Dreamstime.com)

Rat Catcher

A rat catcher was a man or a boy (or more rarely a girl) who caught rats for pay in Victorian England. During the reign of Queen Victoria, as industrialization brought thousands of new residents to the big cities, the resulting overcrowding and disease posed major health problems to city residents. Rat catchers emerged at this time to provide a civic service. Although rat catching was a job that attracted the poor, and rats were seen to symbolize poverty, savagery, and criminality (and only later disease), rat catchers worked in every walk of life: Queen Victoria had in her employ a flamboyant rat catcher named Jack Black.

Because rats are extremely cunning, rat catchers had to come up with ingenious ways to outwit them. They either caught the rats live and then killed them, or they killed them in situ, typically by poisoning. Rat catchers created their own poisons, which they sold on the street, and to gain more business, they often poisoned their rats in front of a crowd. To catch live rats, they attracted the animals by rubbing sweet-smelling substances on their hands (which also disguised their own scent), and when the rats approached, they grabbed them. Many rat catchers kept, and often bred, terriers and ferrets to help them with their work.

Rat catchers were paid by the rat, and it has been argued that some rat catchers ensured that their income would remain high by breeding rats that they could then kill and provide for payment. Sometimes the rats were not killed but instead sold to people who used them in public rat-killing spectacles; other rats were, ironically, sold as pets. Rat catching became such an important job in Victorian England that rat catchers formed their own guild.

Source: Mancoff, D. N., & Trela, D. J. (Eds.). (1996). *Victorian urban settings: Essays on the nineteenth-century city and its contexts* (Vol. 1889). Taylor & Francis.

---

less—about $100 per vial for wholesale distribution—but that cost, while low, is still too expensive to be practical. Even where health care is available, that does not mean that antivenom is available, thanks to its high costs and a declining number of antivenom producers. In fact, with the exception of Australia, the countries with the most dangerous snakes tend to be countries where antivenom is least available—especially to rural residents.

When someone has been bitten by a venomous snake, and can get access to medical care, the doctor, nurse, or EMT will clean out the wound and ensure that the area of the bite is kept below the heart to keep the venom from quickly spreading. Depending on how severe the bite is, the patient may need assistance with breathing, intravenous fluids, antibiotics, or even a blood transfusion. If it is available, antivenom will also be given to the patient, but only if the patient knows what kind of a snake caused the bite, as antivenom is generally specific to a snake species (some antivenoms can be used to treat the bites of a number of related snakes within a region).

Antivenom is made by milking a venomous snake and then injecting that venom into a horse or sheep, whose blood produces antibodies to the venom; these antibodies are then processed into the antivenom. The antivenom is then administered to the patient via an injection.

Antivenom technology has changed little since it was developed in the late nineteenth century and still requires the hand milking of live snakes to gather the venom. (Venom is also used to treat heart attacks and blood clots and is being studied to see whether it is a viable treatment for other conditions such as cancer.)

Snake milkers are men or women who work—and often live—with snakes. For the most part, snake milkers are either private entrepreneurs and hobbyists without formal training in snake care or milking or professional herpetologists with a degree in biology, herpetology, or a related field. With more hobbyists buying, keeping, and breeding snakes, many realized that they could make money, and save lives, by milking their venomous snakes for antivenom.

So, how do you milk a snake? Snakes are not mammals, so they do not have teats. Instead, they must be milked via their fangs.

Snake milkers typically keep (or work with) dozens, if not hundreds, of snakes. Each day, a milker will carefully remove each snake from his or her tank with a long-handled hook, and just as carefully, by holding the head of the snake, the handler opens its mouth, placing the fangs over a receptacle (sometimes covered with rubber for the snake to bite into), and massages the venom glands on its head, which stimulates the snake to eject a small amount of venom into the receptacle. Another way to extract venom is by harassing the snake enough to get it to bite the rubber voluntarily. Each milking only produces a tiny amount of venom, so milkers must milk multiple snakes, sometimes multiple times per day, to gather enough venom to sell. The venom is then freeze-dried and sold to manufacturers who will use it to produce antivenom.

The job is extremely dangerous, and even highly experienced snake milkers can and do get bit. To make it even more dangerous, snake milkers may not wear protective gloves because it is more difficult to feel the snake's movements while wearing them. In addition, many milkers develop an allergy to snake venom by handling it daily, which makes the risk of a bite especially lethal.

To become a snake milker, one can either go the amateur route or the professional route. To be a professional snake milker, the requirements include a college degree in a field related to reptiles as well as the ability to knowledgably and safely handle dangerous snakes. Professional snake milkers will typically work in labs at universities, pharmaceutical companies, or toxin research centers, where the snakes are housed. Independent venom producers often work out of their homes, where they may keep their snakes. (Some will also milk snakes caught at, for example, rattlesnake roundups; the snakes are killed afterward.) Most snake milkers have spent a lifetime with snakes, and many report that they are obsessed with them, making the job an especially good fit.

While the pay can be good—a gram of venom can sell for anywhere from $100 to $4,000 to an antivenom manufacturer—it takes a lot of work to generate enough venom to make a good living. In addition, especially for those who work as freelancers, there is a huge amount of startup costs associated with the job. The freelance snake milker needs to own the property to house the snakes and the facilities to keep them, and he or she must invest in the snakes, the freeze dryer, and other specialized equipment. All snakes are carnivores, so the animals must be fed with either live or freeze-dried animals, which is another cost.

See also: Alligator Wrestler.

Further Reading

Goswami, P., Samant, M., & Srivastava, R. S. (2014). Snake venom, anti-snake venom & potential of snake venom. *International Journal of Pharmacy and Pharmaceutical Sciences, 6*(5), 4–7.

World Health Organization, & Regional Office for South-East Asia Staff. (2016). *Guidelines for the management of snakebites* (2nd ed.). World Health Organization.

Standardized Patient (United States)

A standardized patient, also known as a simulated patient, is a person who pretends to be a real patient seeking medical help. The term *standardized* is often used to reinforce the idea that the patient must be consistent in repeating his or her history and symptoms to numerous students. Medical and nursing students first train on standardized patients before moving to real patients.

Most American medical schools, and many nursing programs, employ people to serve as teaching tools for students. This practice began in the 1960s and has become common in teaching hospitals since that time, as it provides students a safe and controlled environment in which to practice their clinical skills, encounter new or rare conditions, and gain self-confidence.

These fake patients (who may be dressed in street clothes or, with prior notification, a hospital gown) will be provided with information about the patient that they will portray: the person's history, medical condition, and any symptoms (physical or otherwise) that they would present with such a condition. The standardized patient will provide his or her history and sometimes act out those symptoms to medical (or nursing) students. A typical training scenario takes place either in a real hospital or in a simulation center that is set up with fake exam rooms and operating rooms. Multiple patients are set up in different stations, all with a different case to present, and the students move from patient to patient, collecting histories, testing his or her communication skills, conducting physical exams, taking notes, and attempting to diagnose the patient. If the patient presents with a serious or life-threatening (simulated) condition, the student will also have an opportunity to practice delivering bad news and dealing with an emotionally charged situation. Some patients may be asked to dislike their doctor or to react emotionally during the exam, testing the student further. Each encounter may take about fifteen minutes, and one patient may undergo anywhere from four to eight different exams in one day.

Patients should expect to undergo a physical exam in each encounter, which may involve the students listening to the patient's heart and lungs; looking into the eyes, ears, and nose; checking the pulse or blood pressure; checking reflexes; or checking the body for tenderness, pain, or lumps. Some female patients may be chosen to undergo breast or pelvic exams, and some male patients may be asked to undergo prostate or rectal exams. Patients who volunteer to do this undergo additional training, and any intimate exams are conducted in the presence of a faculty member.

Another responsibility of the patient is to provide feedback to the medical students who are evaluating them. Most will use a checklist or form to note how well the student performed, but they will also give the student verbal feedback.

Ultimately, the faculty determine whether the student has completed the training satisfactorily. Standardized patients are used in the classroom, in conference talks, in teaching videos, and in other educational settings. Sometimes they are used outside of the teaching environment: a standardized patient may be hired to visit a doctor's office to evaluate the practices there.

Anyone can be a standardized patient, but those with acting experience are in greatest demand because they are trained in memorization and can realistically portray a variety of different characters. Actors are also trained in improvisation, which is an important skill for patients. Typically, a standardized patient applicant must be over twelve years of age and have no criminal record. They need to have transportation and must be both flexible and punctual. (The work is part-time, and they may be called at any time for a class or demonstration.) Most hospitals also test all job applicants for drug use. Patients must have excellent communication skills, both to present their history to the students and to provide constructive feedback afterward. They also need to be consistent. Each patient will speak to multiple students and needs to present his or her case exactly the same way each time. Hospitals seek people from all walks of life to serve as their teaching patients as well as the patients' family members, as doctors must be able to communicate effectively with both patients and their loved ones.

Most teaching hospitals have an online application that potential patients can fill out. Applicants must be willing to provide information on their ethnic or racial background, their gender orientation and identity, their physical measurements, any languages they speak, and any disabilities or preexisting health conditions. Hospitals are always on the lookout for people of different ethnic backgrounds and gender identities so that students will gain experience working with more than, for example, white heterosexual cisgender men (who were, until recently, the "normative" patients for medical training). After filling out an application, if the applicant is suitable, they will be called in for an in-person interview.

Standardized patients will be trained after they are hired in a process that can take weeks or even months (for which they will be paid). Once hired, they will typically be given cases that match their own background, age, gender, and more so that they can more realistically perform their roles. Sometimes they may be made up to simulate victims of a traumatic accident.

There is no real way to make a living as a standardized patient, as most patients only get called for a job a few times per month or year. (However, those who live in major metropolitan areas with multiple medical programs may work more often.) The work is temporary, part-time, and seasonal. The pay is above minimum wage, with many hospitals paying in the range of $15–$20 per hour; some hospitals pay patients who must portray difficult cases more. Those who perform well and work well with the students and professors will tend to get hired again, but there is still no promise of regular work.

See also: Background Artist.

Further Reading
Anderson, M. B., Stillman, P. L., & Wang, Y. (1994). Growing use of standardized patients in teaching and evaluation in medical education. *Teaching and Learning in Medicine: An International Journal, 6*(1), 15–22.

Jee, S. H., Baldwin, C., Dadiz, R., Jones, M., & Alpert-Gillis, L. (2018). Integrated mental health training for pediatric and psychology trainees using standardized patient encounters. *Academic Pediatrics, 18*(1), 119–121.

Sugar Painter (China)

A sugar painter is an artist who paints with melted caramelized sugar. Sugar painting, known as *tánghuà*, is a traditional folk art that has been practiced by Chinese artisans since at least the Ming Dynasty, which makes the craft at least four hundred years old. It is most well-known in the Sichuan Province in the southwestern part of the country, but it is practiced elsewhere as well.

Sugar painters set up shop in public spaces: on the street, at markets, at fairs, or any place where the public and tourists may see their work. They make their paintings in public and immediately sell them to customers. Because the final paintings are so delicate, it is not a craft that lends itself, for instance, to mail order or even to having a permanent shop from which to sell one's work. Instead, these ephemeral objects are made, sold, and usually eaten or destroyed in the very same day. The paintings are popular with children and tourists. Some sugar painters also hire themselves out to work at private parties.

A sugar painter only needs a few basic tools to do his or her work: a table from which to work, a wok, a stove or source of fire, a marble or steel board, a ladle to stir the caramel and paint the picture, and a few simple steel tools that are used for tweaking the design and, finally, scraping the picture off the board.

The sugar painter begins his or her process by caramelizing the sugar. There are a variety of different recipes for this, and many artists use their own recipe; it basically involves melting sugar (sometimes combined with honey) and water into a thick, caramel-colored syrup. Traditional sugar painters do this in a wok over an open flame. The painter can use the syrup right after making it, but many people do their prep work ahead of time. In this case, after melting the sugar, the artist pours the syrup out onto the marble board, waits for it to harden, and then breaks the caramel into pieces so that it can be stored. When the artist then sets up his or her workspace on the street, he or she can remove pieces of hardened caramel and remelt them in the wok until they reach the right consistency for painting.

With the caramel at the right consistency, the artist can begin painting. To do this, he or she ladles up a small amount of melted sugar and begins carefully drizzling it onto the marble into a shape. The paintings are intricate, made by swirling thin lines of caramel carefully across the board until the figure is complete. What makes these paintings even more extraordinary is that they are created without a pattern, drawing, or mold. They are made entirely freehand and with a ladle and caramel, rather than a brush and paint. Sometimes the artist will affix candies onto the design to make it more festive, but many sugar paintings include nothing but sugar. The final step is to attach a bamboo stick to the painting, using the melted sugar as glue, before carefully removing the finished painting from the marble. The process only takes a few minutes. It must be done quickly because it only takes a few minutes for the sugar to harden.

Chinese astrological signs are a popular item for sugar paintings, as are other animals, flowers, and trees, but many artists create paintings of famous figures from history or art or even contemporary pop culture images such as cartoon characters. Some painters will offer a variety of designs for customers to choose from in the form of a board or plate painted with the artist's designs and overlaid by a pointer; by spinning the pointer, the customer chooses his or her image. Customers who request a different or more intricate design may pay more.

Sugar painting requires a steady hand, artistic talent, and the ability to work quickly in a hectic public space. Many sugar painters learn the skill from their parents and then go on to teach their children the art. After learning some basic designs, many artists will continue to challenge themselves by learning new designs, which they practice at home so that they can do them quickly and accurately for a customer.

Sugar painting is related to another traditional Chinese folk art called sugar people. Here, the sugar is combined with other ingredients and cooked into a Play-Doh-like consistency. The sugary ball is used to create figurines of animals, mythological creatures, and everyday objects, which can be kept as decorations. As with sugar painting, artists create their figures at markets, fairs, and other public spots, where they sell them directly to the public. Today, pastry chefs around the world use a technique similar to sugar painting to create spun sugar decorations on cakes and other pastries.

As with so many traditional crafts around the world today, there is a danger that sugar painting will die out; fewer members of the younger generation want to follow their parents and grandparents into what is a poorly paid field. After all, each drawing only sells for a few yuan (a few cents). To make matters worse, automatic sugar painting machines can now be bought for a few hundred dollars online and can be used to make paintings with no skill at all. What may help to preserve this ancient art is the fact that the Sichuan government of China has recently listed it on the Provincial Intangible Cultural Heritage List.

See also: Ear Cleaner.

Further Reading
Jin, Z., & Jin, B. (2004). *Chinese folk arts.* China Intercontinental Press.
Wang, Y. F., & Zhou, Z. K. (2016). The details exploration of intangible cultural heritage from the perspective of cultural tourism industry: A case study of Hohhot City in China. *Canadian Social Science, 12*(7), 30–36.

Surrogate (Global)

A surrogate is someone who gives birth to a baby on behalf of someone else.

In the twenty-first century, thanks in part to the delay in childbearing for many women in the West, infertility rates have skyrocketed, with approximately one in eight American couples experiencing infertility, and along with them the use of assisted reproductive technologies to get pregnant. Where infertility was once seen as a personal failing, reflecting poorly on either the maternal qualities of the woman or the virility of the man (both of whom each bear about 30 percent of the problems in infertility), today, much of the moral judgment has disappeared as infertility has become increasingly medicalized in the West. In addition, with the rise of single parenting and gay and lesbian families, there is an increased need for fertility options for couples who may not have fertility problems but still need help with conceiving or bearing a child.

Today, there are a variety of treatments available for infertility, or for singles or gay couples who want to raise a child, including artificial insemination with donor semen if the male partner is infertile or for single women or lesbian couples; in vitro fertilization (IVF), where an egg and sperm are fertilized in a petri dish and then the embryo is placed inside the mother's uterus; in vitro fertilization or artificial insemination with a surrogate womb; gamete intrafallopian transfer (GIFT), where the egg and sperm are mixed in a test tube and then placed into the fallopian tubes to fertilize; and intracytoplasmic sperm injection (ICSI), where sperm is injected directly into the egg. All of these procedures, and many more, can utilize either the mother's egg, a donor egg, the father's sperm, or a donor's sperm.

Wet Nurse

A wet nurse is a woman who nurses another woman's baby for pay. Wet nurses were commonly employed by European nobility as well as members of the upper and even middle classes, from antiquity through the Victorian era and from China through Europe. Typically, wet nurses were women from poor (but not desperately so) backgrounds, and, at least in Europe, the kinds of women who were most often hired were married, with children of their own, and were young, healthy (with good breasts and nipples), clean, and well behaved. Some people believed that the mother, or the wet nurse, would transmit her anxieties and "passions" to her baby via her breast milk, so the emotions of the wet nurse needed to be tightly controlled as well.

Wet nurses could be hired by orphan hospitals as well as by private families; nurses who worked for families were paid more than those who nursed orphans. Women could employ a full-time wet nurse to live in the family home, but many women sent their children to live with the wet nurse for up to three years; the children were returned to the home once they were eating solid food. Once a wet nurse weaned one child, if she wanted to remain employed as a wet nurse, she needed to find another baby soon to keep her milk from drying up. Compared to modern standards, in premodern Europe, poor families had fewer children than wealthy families; this fact only makes sense when one realizes that the babies of those wealthy families were nursed by other women, freeing the wealthy women up much earlier to become pregnant again.

Wealthy and, when they could afford it, middle-class women did not want to breastfeed their own children for a variety of reasons. Some women could not physically breastfeed their own babies, but for most women, it was social, rather than physical, issues that prevented them from doing so. Many women feared that their figures would suffer, and many men did not want their wives to breastfeed, in part because of taboos restricting sex during lactation. There was also, briefly, a belief that the colostrum in breast milk was dangerous. The result was that some new mothers not only hired wet nurses but used dogs to suckle their breasts to relieve the pressure of milk. In Europe, wet nursing was at its peak of popularity during the seventeenth century; after this, attitudes toward breastfeeding and child-rearing began to change, leading to an eventual decline in the practice.

Source: Fildes, V. (1988). *Wet nursing: A history from antiquity to the present.* Basil Blackwell.

According to the U.S. Society of Assisted Reproductive Technologies, there were a million babies born from 1987 to 2015 in the United States from using assisted reproductive technologies.

These procedures have been a godsend to many individuals and couples who have been unable to conceive or bear a child naturally. But they have also created a whole new set of social, ethical, and economic concerns. In addition, the whole concept of mother and father has shifted with these new technologies, which often produce distinctions between social and biological mothers and fathers.

Surrogacy is one form of assisted reproductive technology that is combined with one or more other forms. The simplest way for surrogacy to work is for a surrogate to be inseminated with the sperm of a man. The surrogate then gives birth to a baby who carries the genetic material of the surrogate mother as well as the donor father. The intended father and his partner, if there is one, then raise the child as their own. This is known as traditional surrogacy, and it is the oldest form of surrogacy.

Heterosexual couples who want their baby to have DNA from both parents will instead opt to use gestational surrogacy combined with IVF. In this case, the intended father provides a semen sample, and the intended mother has a handful of her eggs removed. A reproductive specialist then combines the two to produce a number of embryos, some of which are implanted into the surrogate, or gestational carrier. The surrogate then carries the baby to term, and the couple raises the baby. This form of surrogacy has only been possible since the mid-1980s, when an anonymous woman carried the first baby conceived this way to term.

A couple can also elect to get an egg donation from a stranger or a sperm donation from a stranger (or both), and, again through IVF, they can have the resulting embryo or embryos implanted into the surrogate's uterus. Finally, the intended parents can use an embryo donated from someone else, which is then implanted into the surrogate using, again, IVF. Often. the choice that is made at this point depends on what, if any, infertility problems plague the intended parents; for example, perhaps the mother can produce viable eggs but cannot carry the baby to term.

Although the surrogate is sometimes either a relative (often a mother or sister of one of the parents) or friend of the people who want the baby, the surrogate is usually a stranger. In this case, there is compensation involved in the process. In the former case, known as compassionate or altruistic surrogacy, the couple or intended parent still signs an agreement with the surrogate outlining the duties and responsibilities of each party. For instance, the intended parents generally agree to cover all costs associated with the pregnancy, and the surrogate agrees to surrender the baby after birth.

For couples who would like to use a surrogate but are not going to use a friend or family member, most go through a surrogacy agency. The agency then acts as the go-between for the intended parents and the surrogate and ensures that there is a legally binding contract in place that not only covers the costs and obligations of the parents and surrogate but also provides compensation for the surrogate herself. This is known as commercial surrogacy. (Whether or not compensation is involved, most fertility clinics who work with surrogates will require that both the surrogate and the intended parents undergo some psychological screening before the process begins.)

In commercial surrogacy, a surrogate is technically not paid to have a baby, as buying and selling babies is illegal around the world. However, because the costs paid to a surrogate include not just medical and legal costs but also costs associated with lost wages, being a surrogate can and does become a form of paid labor throughout the pregnancy. Many surrogacy agencies are not shy about advertising the amount that they pay for surrogates; one agency's online tagline is "Earn up to $86,000." Some agencies provide a base compensation amount, ranging from $42,000 to $58,000, and then offer a number of add-ons, such as an extra $10,000 for each additional child carried (i.e., twins, triplets, etc.), additional fees for a C-section, compensation for travel, and more. First time surrogates typically earn less than those who have successfully been a surrogate before.

Surrogacy is regulated very differently around the world, and even in the United States, each state has a different set of laws related to the legality and regulation of surrogacy. Some U.S. states, and some countries, do not allow commercial surrogacy at all, while others do. Still other locations have no regulations in place. Those countries and states that allow commercial surrogacy ensure, through legislation, that surrogacy contracts are enforced and provide some legal protections to the parties involved. If a couple engages in a contract with a surrogate in a state or country that does not allow commercial surrogacy and then something goes wrong, there is no legal recourse whatsoever, and the surrogate is awarded custody of the child.

Many couples travel overseas to countries with very liberal surrogacy laws to find a surrogate. This is known as fertility tourism, and it involved couples from the United States, Europe, and other wealthier locations traveling to India, Thailand, Cambodia, or Mexico to find a surrogate. Those countries that became popular surrogacy destinations offered couples complete packages that included the surrogate, the clinic where the child would be born, and even a location where all the pregnant surrogates lived throughout their pregnancies. In the past few years, these countries have banned commercial surrogacy, moving fertility tourism to other locations, such as Eastern Europe.

One of the reasons for these new prohibitions is the concern that these practices lead to the exploitation of third-world women at the hands of wealthy parents from other countries, turning some of the women into baby-producing factories. Ironically, the United States (specifically the states in which commercial surrogacy is legal) has become a surrogacy travel destination, not because it is cheaper than other places or the laws more lax, but because the children born to American surrogates on American soil will automatically become American citizens. The cost to parents in the United States who work with surrogacy agencies is over $100,000, which includes matching the parents with a surrogate; all legal, medical, and administrative costs; and the costs paid directly to the surrogate.

There are a number of requirements for becoming a surrogate. Most agencies look for women who are in their reproductive prime, in their twenties or thirties, who are very healthy, who do not smoke, and who have had at least one successful, uncomplicated childbirth. Surrogates must undergo strenuous physical, mental, and emotional testing to make sure that they are prepared for the process, as well as a criminal background check, and if they have a partner, that partner must also go through at least some form of background check.

Being a surrogate can be both physically and emotionally difficult. Physically, a surrogate, whether gestational or not, undergoes all the same physical challenges that other pregnant women experience. However, for gestational surrogates, when IVF is used, multiple embryos are often implanted at once because the risk of some of those embryos failing is quite high. (Even then, only 20–30 percent of all implantations will result in a successful birth, so the process is often repeated multiple times to achieve a baby.) That means that if all the embryos do survive to term, the surrogate must carry and deliver multiple babies, which often involves a Caesarian section and carries additional risks to the surrogate. It also means that the surrogate must often undergo multiple cycles of IVF, which involve injections of Lupron, which carries its own set of risks. When there are complications, the surrogates may not feel adequately compensated or even cared about, and some have found that they were left with unpaid medical bills after the birth.

Surrogacy can also be emotionally difficult. Although many surrogates report having had a positive experience with both the pregnancy and childbirth and see providing a baby to someone who cannot bear one to be incredibly fulfilling, other surrogates may struggle with the difficulties of the pregnancy or childbirth, with a difficult or strained relationship with the intended parents, or with the emotional strain of having to give away a baby that they had carried for nine months.

One of the most important legal cases surrounding surrogacy emerged in the earliest days of the practice of gestational surrogacy, when a New Jersey woman named Mary Beth Whitehead, who was acting as a surrogate to William and Elizabeth Stern, refused to give the baby to the Sterns after delivering her in 1986. The case resulted in the awarding of the baby to the Sterns and in the creation of new laws to deal with the ethical and financial issues associated with surrogacy.

Surrogacy is also subject to other ethical concerns. How much should a woman be allowed to do with her body, and how much she should be forced to do? Can a surrogate be forced to abort a baby who is not healthy? Surrogacy is an interesting type of labor contract in that what is being paid for—the birth of a baby—is a very different kind of a product or service than that involved in other kinds of legal contracts. One of the legal questions to emerge from surrogacy is whether commercial surrogates are selling their own children to other people. Selling babies is illegal, and yet, as defined in surrogacy contracts and legislation, it is not.

Another interesting implication of these technologies is the separation of sex from reproduction. In surrogacy, babies are conceived thanks to the skills and equipment of medical specialists, and the moment of conception may happen in the uterus (as with artificial insemination) or in a petri dish (as with IVF). When, then, does life begin? And what do we do with the millions of leftover embryos produced through these practices, which may have been intended for use in surrogacy but were ultimately not needed? These embryos are currently sitting in freezers in doctors' offices around the world.

Other questions relate to who gets to have children via these technologies and practices. Should very old women be allowed to get pregnant and give birth, even if they are giving birth for a family member? (In 2016, a sixty-seven-year-old Greek grandmother acted as a surrogate for her own daughter, becoming the world's oldest surrogate.) Should doctors or fertility agencies be able to deny treatment to gay men or lesbians? Should the number of embryos implanted be restricted, and should doctors force women to abort "surplus" embryos?

Finally, surrogacy challenge us to think about what is "natural" when it comes to conception, pregnancy, and parenting. Surrogacy allows for the creation of children outside of the womb and for multiple "mothers" and "fathers" to have played a role in producing and then raising a child. These questions are confounding to medical ethicists, theologians, and pro-life and pro-choice advocates alike.

See also: Sex Worker.

Further Reading

Rudrappa, S. (2015). *Discounted life: The price of global surrogacy in India.* New York University Press.

Twine, F. W. (2015). *Outsourcing the womb: Race, class and gestational surrogacy in a global market.* Routledge.

T

Traditional Healer (Global)

A traditional healer, or ethnomedical practitioner, is a person who uses nonscientific methods and theories to make sense of, and to treat, illnesses. Traditional healers have been found in all cultures until the development of modern biomedicine in the nineteenth century, and they are still found in many traditional cultures today. The methods used by traditional healers include rituals (some religious), the use of herbs and minerals, exercises and bodily practices, and more.

Understanding how different cultures understand and treat illnesses through what anthropologists call "ethno-etiologies" is critical to health care providers and policy makers who work in non-Western cultures around the world. Without understanding how people think illnesses develop and how they can be cured, Western-trained doctors and nurses are at a considerable disadvantage because it is not easy to provide a form of health care to a people who do not believe in the principles on which it is based.

A culture's understanding of health and illness, and of any illnesses that are unique to their culture (culture-specific or culture-bound illnesses), is often linked with that culture's religious views and with its general view of the relationship between humanity, the natural world, and the supernatural world. While the Western biomedical view of illness sees illness as being spread by bacteria or viruses (an approach known as germ theory) that may be treated by a variety of antibiotics and other drugs combined with modern surgical techniques, there are other ways of looking at health and illness that focus on more than the physical causes and symptoms of illness. For the most part, Western doctors see the body and the mind as separate components and treat physical illnesses as separated from the physical, spiritual, and social environment in which they exist.

Personalistic disease theories, on the other hand, are very common approaches to illness; they view sickness and health as being connected to a person's relationship with external entities, such as sorcerers, ghosts, or the spirits of ancestors. In cultures in which this theory is common, an individual's relationship to others, living and dead, is primary. This makes a degree of sense given that this approach is found in small-scale societies, such as foraging bands or pastoral and farming tribes.

In these types of cultures, where people know everyone else in the culture, maintaining good relationships with others is the keystone to having a successful life. Experiencing a negative relationship with another person could result in illness because that person may seek out a witch, for example, to cause harm to the person with whom there is conflict. Another example is blaming one's illness on having neglected or insulted one's ancestors, who in many cultures are seen to exert a continuing influence on the lives of their kin. In shamanistic cultures, shamans are individuals who communicate directly with the spirit world and can intervene in the case of illnesses that derive from such spirits. On the other hand, if a witch or a sorcerer is thought to be behind one's illness, the patient or his or her family must turn instead to a witch doctor who can prescribe a form of counter magic. People can try to prevent illness by wearing amulets that ward off spiritual harm and by maintaining positive relations with members of the community as well as with the ancestors.

Another theory used to explain illness is known as emotionalistic disease theories. These theories understand illness as being caused by some sort of emotional harm. Susto, for example, is a culture-bound illness found in Latin America that is thought to be caused by an individual either witnessing or experiencing a traumatic event. (In modern psychiatric terms, we may assign posttraumatic stress disorder (PTSD) as an explanation for this type of occurrence.) Quite literally, *susto* is understood as "fright sickness," and in the worst cases, known as *espanto* (which means "intense fright"), a person's soul has separated from his or her body as a result of the fright. Susto often manifests itself in the victim with nervousness, lack of appetite, diarrhea, and insomnia. It is often seen in people who are suffering from what Westerners would call stress. Susto can be cured by a *curandero*, a traditional Latin American healer, who frightens the victim's soul back into his or her body with an elaborate ritual involving the application of herbs, prayers, and other ritual activities.

A type of disease theory that is common in Asia is known as disharmony theory. In this theory, the body is normally thought to exist in a state of balance; if this balance gets disrupted, illness will develop. In cultures with this type of belief system, to cure an illness, balance must be restored through changes in diet, activity, or through practices such as acupuncture or acupressure.

Barber-Surgeon

Barber-surgeons were barbers who cut hair and often performed surgery in medieval Europe. At this time, surgery was largely separate from health care. Health care was performed by a variety of local healers with limited education, but surgery was undertaken by people with no medical training whatsoever. Instead, butchers and, primarily, barbers used their training with knives to perform crude surgeries without anesthesia, such as limb removals on people who needed it.

A barber-surgeon worked under the auspices of the local barbers' guild and trained through an apprenticeship with a master barber. The bulk of the job involved cutting hair and pulling teeth, but barber-surgeons also worked on battlefields, performed bloodlettings, and performed surgeries, large and small. It was not until the eighteenth century that the professions of surgeons and barbers split, with surgery coming firmly under the rubric of medicine.

Source: Jütte, R. (1989). A seventeenth-century German barber-surgeon and his patients. *Medical History, 33*(2), 184.

And, finally, anthropologists and other scholars have posited another theory to account for illness. A structural explanation focuses on the structural conditions in the culture that may be causing people to suffer rather than looking at an individual person or the symptoms of his or her illness. The focus is on poverty and inequality and the ways in which these problems affect people's minds and bodies through illness. It is not uncommon, by the way, for the sufferers themselves to point toward this type of explanation for their condition. For example, *sufriendo del agua* (translated as "suffering from water") is a disease suffered by poor people in Mexico who do not have access to clean water. It manifests in conditions such as anxiety and nervousness (similar to susto), but it is clearly caused, in the minds of its sufferers, by the lack of clean water and the underlying inequalities that cause this lack. Structuralist explanations help explain why some cultures, or some populations, tend to suffer certain kinds of illnesses while other groups do not. We know, for example, that the conditions that tend to cause mortality and morbidity in poor countries (communicable diseases, childbirth, and malnutrition) are very different from those of wealthy nations (cancer, heart disease, and conditions related to obesity and aging). With a structural understanding of disease, health care officials may want to focus on treating illnesses as well as trying to find solutions to the poverty and inequality that underlie so many illnesses in poor nations.

Traditional healers operate within cultures with any, or all, of the above medical theories of illness. As such, they are holistic, in that they focus on more than just the physical illness; instead, they diagnose the whole patient to detect whether the disturbance is physical, emotional, mental, spiritual, or social (or all of the above). Instead of using charts, machinery, or X-rays, healers use their senses. The cure, too, is multifaceted and may involve the patient ingesting herbs, having hands laid on him or her, and wearing a talisman or amulet. Patients in traditional healing play a role in their own healing and are not just acted upon. In addition, rather than treating the patient in isolation, traditional healers often work with the family as well as members of the wider community.

Sometimes healers do not take on all the functions of a healer as we are defining it here. Some people are specialists. In many parts of Africa, for example, diviners (sometimes called *sangoma*) are people who use rituals and often trances to diagnose illness (diviners can also uncover the reasons for other types of misfortune and can sometimes see the future or the past). Herbalists are people who focus on healing; their specialty is herbal cures. Midwives help mothers to deliver their babies. There may also be those healers who specialize in the treatment of bone and muscle disorders, known as *hueseros* or *sobadores* in Latin America. And faith healers are Christian healers who heal people of illness through a combination of laying hands, prayer, or the use of holy water and other blessed substances. The healing itself is intended to heal the patients' illnesses, protect them from spirits who would do them harm, and prevent future illnesses.

Healers typically do not attend formal schooling for their education; instead, they train with an experienced practitioner, often a parent or grandparent, and the knowledge is orally transmitted. In some cases, as with shamans, the person may undergo a spiritual transformation that demonstrates to the person and the community that he or she has the special knowledge or skills to be a shaman. This may take the form of a serious illness or disability that is interpreted as being spiritual in nature. Once the person overcomes this condition and learns to accept and control the spirits, he or she can use that knowledge to help other people. There is typically still a period of training or apprenticeship, but this is to supplement the abilities that the person is seen to naturally possess. Others consider themselves born with the inherent ability to heal, although they may or may not recognize that ability until later in life. Like shamans, traditional healers tend to be past middle age, both because a good healer depends on experience and wisdom and also because it may not be until later in life that the person has the calling revealed to him or her. In many cultures, the traditional healers are, or were, often women or people from other marginalized groups (such as people with disabilities).

A *curandero* is the Spanish term for a folk healer who operates in Latin America or among Latin Americans in the United States, and it is sometimes used to refer to folk healers in Southern Europe. In the Americas, curanderos use knowledge and techniques from indigenous American populations combined with folk practices and beliefs as well as a strong commitment to Catholicism, which was brought over from Spain and Portugal. Curanderos use both personalistic and emotionalistic theories of disease in their practices, and they look at the relationship between the ill person and the persons, spirits, and experiences that may be affecting him or her. Like a shaman, curanderos are thought to be able to enter the supernatural realm, via trance, to diagnose an illness and effect a cure. Curing is done with herbs, with rituals using healing objects, and through spiritual means; one of the most well-known types of cures is known as *limpiadas* or *limpieza* (which means "cleaning" in Spanish) and is a way to cleanse the spirit of an ill person. Curanderos, like other traditional healers, may or may not be paid with money for their services; sometimes services are provided for free, in exchange for goods or services from the patient's family, or with a promise of some future gift. When they do charge a monetary fee, it is generally much less than that charged by Western doctors.

Today, traditional healers continue to work around the world, and they may be the only health care workers to whom many people have access. They often practice alongside Western-trained health practitioners, who recognize that working with traditional healers is often the most effective way of providing Western medicine to people with traditional beliefs. Other Western doctors, however, do not work with nor have respect for traditional healers, seeing the services they offer as being rooted in ignorance and potentially dangerous.

Even when they have access to Western doctors, people continue to use traditional healers for a variety of reasons: traditional healers are far less expensive than biomedical doctors; the healing deals with psychological and emotional problems as well as physical problems; many people distrust modern doctors or practices associated with white people, the West, or the United States; the recognition that Western medicine cannot effectively treat culture-bound illnesses; and, for many, the belief that the source of many illnesses is spiritual in nature. For all these reasons, traditional healers remain popular today. In fact, some patients choose between visiting a traditional healer or a Western doctor, and they may see some illnesses as being better treated by one or the other. Traditional healers tend to be more popular among older people (one study showed that the median age of curandero patients is over seventy-six years; see Applewhite 1995); however, this situation may change in the future.

See also: Bruja; Witch Hunter.

Further Reading

Adams, J., Andrews, G., Barnes, J., Broom, A., & Magin, P. (Eds.). (2012). *Traditional, complementary and integrative medicine: An international reader.* Macmillan International Higher Education.

Applewhite, S. L. (1995). Curanderismo: Demystifying the health beliefs and practices of elderly Mexican Americans. *Health & Social Work, 20*(4), 247–253.

Connor, L., & Samuel, G. (Eds.). (2001). *Healing powers and modernity: Traditional medicine, shamanism, and science in Asian societies.* Greenwood Publishing Group.

Stepan, N. L., Nouzeilles, G., & Coutinho, M. (2003). *Disease in the history of modern Latin America: From malaria to AIDS.* Duke University Press.

Torres, E., & Sawyer, T. L. (2004). *Curandero: A life in Mexican folk healing.* University of New Mexico Press.

Train Pusher (Japan, China, Spain)

A train pusher, or *oshiya* in Japanese, is someone who works for a Japanese rail company and pushes people onto crowded trains. First used at the Shinjuki subway station, where they were called "passenger arrangement staff," the position is now part of the job duties of railway attendants at the busiest stations in the Tokyo metropolitan region. Some stations also hire part-time workers to supplement the staff during peak commute times who are only responsible for shoving people onto trains.

Japan is a small yet heavily populated nation, with 126.7 million people living in a country about the same size as California (with a population of less than forty million). Tokyo is not only Japan's largest city but also the largest city on earth with a population of over thirty-seven million. Most people who live in Tokyo do not use cars but instead travel on the train, which serves forty million passengers daily. The train system is one of the most crowded in the world.

Because of the level of crowding on the trains and in the train stations of Tokyo, a new job emerged in the 1960s, when Japan was undergoing a period of massive economic growth. During the morning and evening rush hours, pushers, who wear railway uniforms and white gloves, stand outside of the doors of train cars, and as people push to get onto a crowded train, they help by pushing everyone inside so that the door can close. When crowding is especially severe, it sometimes takes multiple pushers to get everyone safely inside the car. The pay for a part-time pusher in Tokyo is about $10 per hour.

China, too, uses train pushers in the most crowded subways in the country, including those in Beijing, Chongqing, and Shanghai, and train pushers are being used in the Madrid subway system and the Frankfurt train station, where they are called *Einstiegslotsen*. New York subways also used staff members to push passengers onto trains in the early decades of the twentieth century.

See also: Car Jockey.

Further Reading

Freedman, A. (2011). *Tokyo in transit: Japanese culture on the rails and road.* Stanford University Press.

Iwata, O. (1992). Crowding and behavior in Japanese public spaces: Some observations and speculations. *Social Behavior and Personality: An international journal, 20*(1), 57–70.

U

Ufologist (Global)

A ufologist is a person who studies unidentified flying objects, or UFOs. Although the term UFO refers to anything in the sky that is not easily identified, it typically refers to spacecraft from outer space. Captain Edward Ruppelt of the U.S. Army Air Forces, a now defunct branch of the American military, came up with the term UFO in 1953 to describe what many people were calling "flying saucers" or "spaceships." Today, many people who do not believe in interplanetary space travelers prefer the term UAP, for unidentified aerial phenomena, which lacks the alien baggage of UFO.

How long people have been seeing UFOs is unknown, but people have certainly been observing the movements of the heavens for thousands of years and have provided a variety of scientific and fantastical explanations for the presence and movement of entities in the sky. Some of these reports made it into written accounts, which means we can read about people from hundreds of years ago who reported seeing unusual objects in the sky. It was not until the nineteenth century,

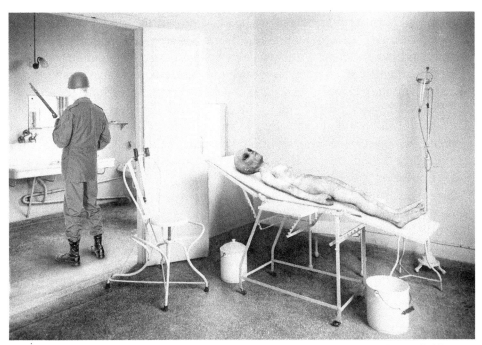

A scene from the International UFO Museum and Research Center in Roswell, New Mexico. (Wisconsinart/Dreamstime.com)

however, and the rise of both a widespread interest in science and a corresponding explosion in science fiction writing that the idea emerged that some of these unexplained objects may be entities from another planet, solar system, or universe. This was also, not surprisingly, the era that saw the development of airships, such as zeppelins and blimps, so it was the first time in history that humans could look up and see something in the sky that was manmade. As the nineteenth century turned into the twentieth century, more sightings occurred, and by World War II, thousands of people (many from the militaries of the various combatants in the war) had reported seeing UFOs.

The idea of visitors or invaders from outer space visiting Earth became popularized in the early 1950s thanks in part to the release of almost fifty science fiction films (and countless books and magazine articles, including an influential 1952 *Life* magazine story titled "Have We Visitors from Outer Space?") about spaceships, extraterrestrials, and alien invasions. This era, just as the Cold War with the Soviet Union was escalating, was also characterized by widespread anxiety and fear about technological change and nuclear destruction as well as a deepening fear of being invaded. One of the first major flying saucer reports emerged at this time as well; a reported sighting occurred in Washington State in 1947 that gained widespread media coverage. There were also a number of less popularly reported incidents.

The year 1947 was also the same year as the "Roswell UFO Incident," when a rancher found the remains of a high-altitude balloon used by the military that had crashed just north of Roswell, New Mexico. This incident, however, did not get the same media attention as the Washington sighting at the time, as the public believed the Air Force's story that the object was a weather balloon. In fact, the balloon had been used as part of a classified project to detect the presence of Soviet nuclear tests. It was not until the 1970s that this incident developed into a major conspiracy, with many ufologists believing that not only did a crash occur in Roswell but that at least one dead alien was also recovered that was then subjected to a military autopsy, which was covered up by the government.

Although there are people with an interest in UFOs, UFO sightings, and ufologists all over the world, the ufology movement took off in the United States and remains focused there today. Half of all Americans believe in UFOs, and according to a 2019 Gallup News Poll (Saad 2019), 68 percent of Americans believe the U.S. government is hiding information on UFOs.

Since the 1940s, various world governments have implemented a number of programs (some confidential) to investigate the veracity of UFO claims. For instance, Sweden had a program to investigate "ghost rockets" from 1946 to 1947; Brazil ran a program called Operation Saucer in 1977; the Soviet Union ran Institute 22, which investigated UFOs from 1978 until the end of the Cold War; Canada operated a program called Project Magnet from 1950 to 1954; and the United Kingdom ran two programs, the Flying Saucer Working Party, which ran from 1950 to 1951, and Project Condign, which ran from 1997 to 2000. France and Uruguay (and most likely other countries) run similar programs today. The United States has spearheaded at least ten different investigations since the first such program in the 1940s, with the latest known program, the Advanced Aerospace

Threat Identification Program, having been run out of the Pentagon from 2007 to 2012. It is not known whether there are any UFO programs in the U.S. government today.

Many ufologists work under the rubric of one of the major organizations devoted to ufology. These include the Mutual UFO Network, founded in 1969; the Center for UFO Studies, founded in 1973 by Josef Allen Hynek, an astronomer and scientific adviser to three U.S. government–sponsored investigations into UFOs from 1947 to 1969; and the latest, To the Stars Academy of Arts & Science, founded by musician Tom DeLonge, former U.S. military counterintelligence officer Luis Elizondo, and Chris Mellon, the former deputy assistant secretary of defense for intelligence and former deputy assistant secretary of security and information operations. Another new group is the Scientific Coalition for UAP Studies (SCU), which held its first conference in 2019; it has attempted to differentiate itself from other UFO organizations by emphasizing the scientific caliber of its members and research projects. In regard to its members, the organization's website states, "SCU is an organization composed of affiliate members from science, engineering, astronomy, psychology, chemistry, military and other disciplines with many holding PhDs, BS, BA degrees" (SCU 2019).

So, what does a ufologist do? Ufologists engage in the "scientific" study of UFOs. They track UFO sightings (which are now easily compiled online by the various organizations in the field) and research both contemporary and historical sightings to find out whether a sighting was legitimate or whether there were other explanations to account for the phenomena. They also investigate reports of alien encounters and alien abductions (when a person has reportedly been kidnapped by aliens and taken aboard a spaceship, where they typically underwent scientific experiments until they were released).

Ufologists must have an open mind, but they also must be open to the idea that many UFOs can be explained by other nonextraterrestrial explanations. Having a working understanding of astronomy and meteorological events is useful. An investigator conducting research into a sighting will, first, need to investigate any witnesses. They need to use interview techniques that try to get at the substance of the witnesses' experiences, as they may be confused, traumatized, or perhaps just unreliable. (Some investigators use hypnosis or cognitive interview techniques borrowed from law enforcement.) The investigator must also examine the physical location of the sighting—especially if the spacecraft landed on earth. This involves making careful observations at the scene of the landing, taking measurements and notes, using photography or video to document the scene, and, finally, collecting evidence to be analyzed later. Evidence could include debris from a spacecraft, mutilated animals, crop circles, footprints, or what some witnesses have referred to as "angel hair," a jellylike substance that is said to be released by spaceships as they fly. If the sighting was in the sky, and the craft did not land, the investigator analyzes any photographic or video evidence of the craft, if it exists, and interviews witnesses to understand the appearance and movements of the craft.

When investigating an abduction, or any other personal encounter between a witness and an extraterrestrial, the investigator may look for indications of surgical scars on the witness, as that could be an indication of an alien surgery. Another

feature that an investigator may look for (or ask the witness to identify on themselves) is a scoop mark—a small indentation on a person's skin that is known to
ufologists as indicative of a "punch biopsy." Finally, many abductees have claimed
to have had an electronic implant inserted under their skin, which are understood
to control the mind of the abductee, to erase his or her memory, or perhaps to track
the subject. Some women report after their abduction experiences that their men-
strual cycles have become irregular, and both men and women often report head-
aches or sinus problems (which are sometimes explained by use of the implant).
All these physical signs could indicate to the researcher that an abduction has
taken place. (It should be noted that there is not a single documented case in the
scientific or medical literature of an alien abduction.)

UFO investigators must assemble a kit for their investigations that includes the
tools they may need when looking into a UFO sighting or alien encounter. The kit
includes a still and video camera, a tape recorder, cameras with night vision technology, binoculars, gloves, a Geiger counter (and sometimes other specialized
equipment, such as a spectrometer), something to take notes with, containers for
evidence collection, a compass, measuring equipment, and knives, tweezers,
shovels, and other tools.

Until recently, there was no formalized training for a ufologist. Both hobbyists
and those who make a living through UFOs spend years reading books and articles and attending conventions and local meetings where ufologists get together.
Many belong to the major UFO organizations, which offer newsletters, other publications, and conferences, such as the annual UFO symposium organized by
MUFON, the National UFO Conference, which has been held every year since
1963, and the International UFO Conference, which according to its website is the
Guinness World Record holder for largest UFO conference. Others mentor with
an experienced ufologist. Many of the most well-known ufologists come to the
field through law enforcement or the military, although that background is not
required. MUFON now operates a training program called MUFON University,
which uses its own manual, *The MUFON Field Investigator's Manual* (Chapter 4:
Misinterpretation of Slime Molds as UFO Physical Trace Evidence) to teach students; students who successfully complete the program as well as a background
check can get certified through the organization. Courses can also be taken at a
handful of other (nonaccredited) organizations, such as the U.K.-based Center of
Excellence, and the IMHS Metaphysics Institute offers a PhD in ufology.

Unlike ghost hunters, who may be paid by customers seeking help with a haunting, there are no such revenue streams for ufologists. In fact, most ufologists are
not paid for their investigative work. However, well-known figures in the field can
command lucrative fees through speaking at conferences and conventions, writing books, teaching courses, or consulting on movies, podcasts, and other media
projects. And like ghost hunters, they may also be featured on their own television
shows.

Most scientists view UFO sightings as being misperceptions or misunderstand-
ings of natural phenomena such as clouds, birds, or comets or man-made phenomena such as airplanes, balloons, military crafts, or satellites. In fact, ufologists and
skeptics alike will agree that most sightings can be explained without using UFOs.

But that does not mean that an interest in UFOs has gone away, nor have we seen a drop in interest in scientifically studying UFOs. However, ufologists differ from scientists in that they believe that there are some cases that have never been satisfactorily explained, and cannot be satisfactorily explained, without alien spacecraft. One thing that seems to be common to all ufologists is a mistrust of government (and scientific) authorities and an assumption that when they deny the existence of aliens, this denial is simply part of a decades-long coverup.

There is also a new surge in movies and television shows about UFOs, aliens, and even ufologists. In recent years, we have seen a number of shows by and about ufologists: the History Channel's *Ancient Aliens* and *In Search of Aliens*, featuring alien hunter Giorgio Tsoukalos; History's *Project Blue Book* (which covers one of the U.S. government secret programs); and the Travel Channel's *UFOs: The Lost Evidence*. This year, there is History's *Unidentified: Inside America's UFO Investigation*, featuring Luis Elizondo, formerly of the Advanced Aerospace Threat Identification Program, and the Travel Channel's latest, *Alien Highway*, featuring ufologist Chuck Zukowsky.

UFOs are back in the news in 2019, as are ufologists, after reports and videos of UFOs (or UAPs, as the government calls them) by five credible navy pilots were uncovered from 2014 and 2015. These latest sightings are yet to be identified or explained; therefore, the navy is investigating them because they may indicate a breach of national security.

See also: Ghost Hunter.

Further Reading

Devereux, P., Brookesmith, P., Keen, M., & Watson, N. (1997). *UFOs and Ufology: The first 50 years*. Blandford.

Eghigian, G. (2017). Making UFOs make sense: Ufology, science, and the history of their mutual mistrust. *Public Understanding of Science, 26*(5), 612–626.

Glenday, C. (1999). *The UFO investigator's handbook: The practical guide to researching, identifying, and documenting unexplained sightings*. Running Press.

Saad, L. (2019). Americans skeptical of UFO's, but say government knows more. *Gallup Poll*. https://news.gallup.com/poll/266441/americans-skeptical-ufos-say-government-knows.aspx.

SCU. (2019). *AAPC 2019*. https://www.explorescu.org/aapc-info.

V

Victim Advocate (United States, Europe, Australia)

A victim advocate is a person who either works within the criminal justice system or outside of it to help crime victims cope with the aftermath of the crime and to negotiate the criminal justice system. Victims' advocates are increasingly seen in the United States, especially for victims of domestic violence and sexual assault, and are starting to emerge in Europe and Australia.

In countries such as the United States, which inherited the basis of its legal tradition and criminal justice system from the British, criminal defendants are guaranteed a number of basic legal protections to ensure that people who are accused of a crime are not convicted without the opportunity to fully defend themselves in open court. British courts have relied on the jury system to handle criminal prosecutions since the Middle Ages. But until the nineteenth century, a person's guilt could be determined with very little evidence (or in the case of the witch trials, with forms of evidence known as "spectral evidence" being legally acceptable) and little opportunity for the accused to defend himself or herself in court. Trials in the premodern era were heavily favored against the defendant, and because death was a common penalty for crimes such as poaching, arson, treason, rebellion, and, of course, murder, the outcome for the defendant, even for crimes that we consider trivial today, could be substantial. Trials during this period were also strongly focused on the victim of the crime, who was encouraged to play a major role in the process of gaining justice.

From the seventeenth through the early nineteenth century, England was governed by what is known as the "Bloody Code," which mandated death (generally by hanging) for over two hundred offenses, including pickpocketing and shoplifting. The stakes for defendants, then, were very high, and as far back as the eighteenth century, lawyers and others were pushing for reform to ensure that the innocent and those who committed petty crimes were not sentenced to death.

It was not until the nineteenth century that British courts began to develop many of the procedures that we are familiar with in courts today: the right for the defendant to have an attorney, the right to be free from excessive fines or bails, the right to be free from cruel and unusual punishments (including torture as a means of gaining information from a defendant), and the right of defendants to not incriminate themselves. With these rights, a system that had been heavily weighted towards crime victims and the state shifted slightly toward a more balanced system, although these rights were, and still are, geared to favor wealthy defendants over the poor. At the same time, court procedures began to focus less on the victim and more on the dangers to society that crime and criminals pose. That is why court cases are now organized around two parties: the accused and the state (rather than the victim).

In the United States, the first ten amendments to the U.S. Constitution (ratified in 1788), the Bill of Rights, are based in part on these English rights (drawn in part from the Magna Carta and the English Bill of Rights), and they encode some of the most basic protections for those accused of crimes. For instance, the right of the defendants to remain silent and not incriminate themselves as well as the right to not be tried twice for the same crime (double jeopardy) are found in the Fifth Amendment; the right for the accuser (or their lawyer) to confront witnesses, the right to a "speedy" jury trial, and the right to be represented by an attorney are found in the Sixth Amendment; and the right to be free from unjust search and seizures is found in the Fourth Amendment. These basic rights have been expanded upon over the years, primarily by court cases, to ensure that the innocent are not wrongfully convicted and are given every opportunity for a fair trial.

Because of these protections, which are encoded in both English and American law (as well as other legal systems throughout the world), many people feel that victims have fewer rights than defendants. It was not until the late twentieth century that organized efforts emerged to legally encode rights for crime victims and to provide resources to help victims of crime.

The crime victims' rights movement has had a number of important successes, including the creation of a set of legally binding victims' rights for citizens of the European Union, and in the United States, the Crime Victims' Rights Act was passed in 2004, which grants victims eight basic rights. Another development has been the creation and expansion of the victims' right advocate position. In fact, over two-thirds of U.S. states have also passed their own victims' rights laws, some of which, such as that in Oregon, mandate that victims have a right to an advocate.

A victim advocate has a variety of responsibilities, and these differ by the location around the world where such positions appear. They differ by the type of offense (victims of sexual assault, child abuse, and domestic violence may have specific needs that are addressed differently by advocates in various locations), and in the United States, they differ based on whether the crime is a property or violent crime and whether the crime is a misdemeanor or a felony.

Typically, a victim advocate's job is to advocate for the victim's rights and to guide the victim through the criminal justice system. Some victim advocates have their first contact with a crime victim when they are called to a hospital to help a victim of a sexual assault. The advocate's job begins at the hospital, as he or she is expected to provide comfort to the victim in a scary situation, to explain about the sexual assault exam and process, to outline the victim's rights, to protect the victim's confidentiality, to help the victim come up with a safety plan, and to assist the victim in identifying whatever immediate needs he or she may have—for example, regarding safety, childcare, finances, or housing. This first contact with the victim involves multiple forms of crisis intervention, without which many victims would be retraumatized.

After that initial encounter, and for other victims who are not first met at a hospital, the victim advocate works with the victim through what can be many months, or even years, as the case winds itself through the criminal justice system. Advocates attend hearings, grand juries, and trials with victims, they participate in meetings with attorneys, they help prepare victims for testifying or delivering a victim impact statement, and they generally help ensure that the victims' rights are being met. They may work with the victim to gain restitution from the offender or compensation for the crime from the state. When the victim is a child, the advocate works with the parents or responsible party to ensure, again, that the victim's rights are met.

Some victim advocates work with the state—typically the position is found within the district attorney's offices in the United States—but others work with nonprofit organizations that help victims, usually those who are victims of domestic violence or sexual assault. Victim advocates must understand the legal system, and they must be able to adequately explain that system to victims. They operate as a go-between for the criminal justice system and the victim, ensuring that— while the police and prosecutors focus on prosecuting the crime—the victim is not forgotten. Some victim advocates have a degree in criminal justice or a related field, but others may come from social work or other helping professions.

The position of a victim advocate is not an easy one. The position demands compassion, empathy, an ability to listen, problem-solving skills, no victim blaming, an understanding of the criminal justice system, the dynamics of sexual assault and domestic violence, and confidentiality. In addition, the position can become overwhelming to some, as they are exposed to both physical and emotional trauma.

See also: Bounty Hunter; Crime Scene Cleaner.

Further Reading

Funk, T. M. (2015). *Victims' rights and advocacy at the International Criminal Court.* Oxford University Press.

Roach, K. (1999). *Due process and victims' rights: The new law and politics of criminal justice.* University of Toronto Press.

Wedding Guest (Korea, Japan)

A professional wedding guest is a person who attends weddings of strangers for a fee. The practice originated in the 1990s in Japan and Korea but is found in China as well.

Although the idea of a "love marriage," in which each partner falls in love with the other and they marry voluntarily, has become the norm in most of the world today, this idea is a relatively new phenomenon. In fact, marriages were traditionally contracts between two families, in which the husband and wife (who may or may not have even known each other) were chosen by elder family members to create or maintain an alliance between the respective families. The wedding ceremony—including the exchange of gifts between bride and groom or the bride's family and groom's family—is used to publicly mark the new relationship between both families as well as to reinforce the many rights and responsibilities of the married couple to each other. In some cultures, having an extravagant wedding with many guests acts as a sign of status; it demonstrates the wealth and resources of the families involved. This is certainly the case in Asia today.

A Chinese wedding. (Drserg/Dreamstime.com)

In East Asian cultures, as in other cultures around the world, wedding traditions are in flux, and they include both traditional elements as well as modern elements—such as the use of the white wedding dress for the bride, which was first popularized in the West by England's Queen Victoria in the nineteenth century. Traditional arranged marriages are in steep decline, replaced by love marriages, and the rights and responsibilities of the spouses have changed as well, given the number of women who work outside of the home alongside men.

Because status is so important in Asian cultures, whether the marriage is traditional or modern, it still must reflect the social and economic status of the families involved. Having a small wedding, or a wedding with poor food or decorations, or too few guests can mean a loss of face for all those involved. And while this concern about status is common in many non-Western cultures as well (such as the United States), it is especially a problem in Asia.

Western cultures that are more individual oriented (what are known as low-context cultures) tend to be less concerned about losing face, and cultures that focus more on groups than individuals (high-context cultures) tend to be more face conscious. People in low-context cultures engage in more direct communication and think less of other people's feelings, and people in high-context cultures, such as in Asia and the Middle East, care more about group harmony and tend to favor indirect communication techniques such as evasion.

Indeed, the term *face* first arose in China, where there are dozens of Chinese terms that refer to face, such as "selling face," which means to gain popularity, or "ripping up face," which means to stomp on someone else's feelings. "Having no face," on the other hand, means being without shame. In China, faces can be lost, borrowed, given (to show respect), stolen, or fought for through competition with others. Chinese languages have multiple words for face, including *mian*, *lian*, and *yan*. All these terms essentially refer to a person's social face and include respect, honor, prestige, and social standing, although *lian* refers more toward the bearer's moral character and trustworthiness and *mian* is more closely related to social standing and prestige.

Japan and Korea, both of which inherited many of China's cultural traditions, also have a strong cultural concern about losing or gaining face. It may even be more important in Japan, perhaps because it is a small country with a large population that must live cooperatively together. This may explain why the practice of hiring professional wedding guests began in Japan and Korea and remains extremely popular there today.

To ensure that one's wedding is as well attended as possible, to demonstrate to the other guests the status and importance of the families throwing the wedding, many East Asians will hire wedding guests to attend their wedding alongside their friends, business associates, and family. Sometimes this will just be done to replace a guest who had RSVP'd but could not attend, but wedding guests are typically hired in advance.

In Japan, the idea of hiring wedding guests is perhaps not that unusual, given contemporary Japan's large "rent-a-professional" industry, which offers everything from boyfriends and cuddlers to friends and whole families for rent. Japanese families can hire wedding guests through the larger rental companies or through smaller wedding-specific companies. The cost for someone to attend a wedding in Japan is about $100–$200, but it can go up depending on any additional requests, such as making a speech or a toast.

Korean weddings are especially large, as both families invite everyone they know to their children's weddings. Therefore, the expectation is that Korean weddings will have hundreds of guests. Professional wedding guests can help to meet that expectation if either of the families has fewer contacts but still needs to impress the other family. Korean guests command less money than the Japanese equivalent, and can be hired for as low as $20. Sometimes the bride and groom do not know that there are hired guests at their wedding, as many of the guests are associates of the families rather than the couple anyway.

To become a wedding guest, there is no real training involved. However, those who have acting talent or experience will have an advantage in this field because the job essentially involves pretending to be someone else. Sometimes a wedding guest is given a specific title and backstory—perhaps the person is impersonating the boss of the bride or groom—and needs to act it out throughout the ceremony and reception. This is especially common in Japan.

When the practice of hiring strangers to attend weddings was first reported internationally, in the last twenty years or so, Western reporters and readers first saw it as a strange, exotic tradition, using language such as "fake guests" and "desperate" to highlight the unusual nature of the practice. In the last few years, however, the practice of hiring wedding guests—bridesmaids in particular—has emerged in the West as well.

In many European and American weddings, the bride chooses a small number of women—usually drawn from her family, her fiancé's family, and her group of friends—to act as her bridesmaids. Bridesmaids assist the bride on the day of the ceremony and accompany her as she walks down the aisle during the wedding. They may also participate in the planning of the reception, bridal shower, or bachelorette party. In addition, they must wear (and purchase) a dress of the bride's choosing and pay for all her own costs associated with the wedding, reception, and any pre-wedding events. (It is said that one reason bridesmaids wear a similar dress to the bride is because, in ancient Roman weddings, it may confuse any malicious spirits that might be present.) Given how close a bride is expected to be with her bridesmaids, why would anyone ask a stranger to do the job?

Having a large bridal party is a sign of status for many, but at the same time, expectations for bridesmaids are increasing. For many brides, this has resulted in the decision to hire bridesmaids to help with the planning of the wedding and associated events. For some couples, hiring a professional bridesmaid is akin to hiring a wedding planner, in that her role is not to impersonate a bridesmaid so much as to handle much of the work that the friends of the bride traditionally do for free. Professional bridesmaids, at least in the West today, are often a practical choice that takes some of the work off the bride and the "real" bridesmaids. Hiring a bridesmaid in this capacity could cost hundreds or even thousands of dollars.

Contemporary Chinese weddings also use bridesmaids; historically, they acted to protect the bride from harm. This has evolved into a tradition in China today in which bridesmaids, who are still expected to protect the bride by, for example, drinking alcohol on her behalf, are subject to abuse (which is often sexual) by the wedding guests. In addition, Chinese weddings are judged in part by the number and beauty of the bridesmaids, so the families who put on the weddings have a stake in which women can be bridesmaids and participate in the ceremony. For these reasons, some families hire professional bridesmaids to elevate the status of the wedding and to save the bride's friends from doing what is sometimes a thankless and unpleasant task. Luckily, these bridesmaids are easy to hire, as they are offered by Chinese wedding planners as part of the wedding package.

See also: Mourner.

Further Reading

Kendall, L. (2014). Marriages and families in Asia: Something old and something new? In S. M. Tam, W. C. A. Wong, & D. Wang (Eds.), *Gender and Family in East Asia* (pp. 226–240). Routledge.

Monger, G. (2004). *Marriage customs of the world: From henna to honeymoons.* ABC-CLIO.

Tsuya, N. O., & Bumpass, L. L. (Eds.). (2004). *Marriage, work, and family life in comparative perspective: Japan, South Korea, and the United States.* University of Hawaii Press.

Witch Hunter (Papua New Guinea, Sub-Saharan Africa)

A witch hunter is a person who hunts witches.

In cultures around the world, there are beliefs in either sorcery, witchcraft, or both. Anthropologists typically distinguish between what they call *witches* and what they refer to as *sorcerers*. Sorcerers are regular people who have learned how to use herbs and other tools to harm or heal other people and to benefit themselves or their clients. In most cultures that have both a witch figure and sorcerers, sorcerers do not have inherent supernatural powers, but they have developed abilities that they can use to cause harm. They can be hired by someone who wants to have someone harmed. Most sorcerers use folk magical practices, herbs, and folk remedies to harm and to help people. The category of sorcerer, then, often overlaps with the categories of folk healer, wise woman, bruja, and cunning folk.

Witches, on the other hand, are thought to be individuals who are typically born with the supernatural ability to harm others; sometimes this skill is involuntary, and sometimes the alleged witch does not even know that they possess such a skill. These people are thought to be able to cause bad luck, deaths, illnesses, and accidents by either cursing another person or, sometimes, by simply looking at them. Witches in most cultures in which this belief system is found can reportedly shape-shift, especially into animals; can often fly; and are said to do such things as eating the entrails of living people as well as live babies. They are thought to have their organs organized backward or upside down, and they have a mark that is known in European lore as a "witch's teat" on their bodies.

Witchcraft accusations have been common throughout history in cultures around the world. Witches are a regular aspect of life in those cultures and typically arise when a misfortune arises; when people are harmed and do not understand why, it is natural to look toward a supernatural explanation for the misfortune. In societies with witch beliefs, when someone is accused of being a witch, the infliction of harm on the supposed with or his or her loved ones is a common result. Social deviants or outcasts are the people who often end up being accused. When they are found guilty of witchcraft, the result is that they are punished with a variety of punishments, from ostracism to death in the most extreme cases.

In early modern Europe and colonial North America, the fear of witchcraft was very real. Starting in the fourteenth century, the fear of witches began to rise and ultimately turned into a form of social hysteria that impacted people from Southern Europe to the north of the British Isles. At this time, witches were not just people who were able to supernaturally harm others; in the European context, these people were working with the devil and thus provided a major threat in this heavily religious context. This was also a period of time when religious minorities of all kinds were being heavily persecuted, including Jews, Cathars, and other heretics. This resulted in large-scale witch hunts and the persecution of countless thousands of men and women who were accused of witchcraft. As in tribal societies in Africa, Asia, and Latin America, accused witches tended to be social outcasts and the most vulnerable members of society. In addition, because of the categorical overlap between sorcerer and folk healer and the conflation of these categories with demonic witchcraft, healers and wise women often found themselves accused of being both witches and in league with the devil.

Because witches were thought by Europeans to work in groups, or covens, an accused witch was expected to name her (or his) fellow witches. The accused were tortured to extract this information, so it was very common for them to name other witches. By doing so, they might be spared execution or, at the very least, would no longer be tortured. Thanks to these practices, a single accused witch could, through her confessions and the confessions of those she named, result in dozens of prosecutions of witches.

During this time, there were people who exploited this fear and became witch finders or witch hunters; they were paid by villages and towns to hunt for and prosecute the alleged witches in their midst. Matthew Hopkins, who traveled from village to village finding witches in England in the mid–seventeenth century, was one of the most famous of these witch hunters. One of the methods that Hopkins and other witch hunters used to detect whether an accused was really a witch was to have them undergo a trial by ordeal.

The most infamous of such trials was the ordeal by water, which was known as "swimming." Because witches were thought to be made of wood, an accused witch was thrown into a body of water. If she floated to the surface, she was a witch, and she would be fished out and executed. But if she sank, she was not a witch. Others thought that witches floated because water was pure and would repel the witch. Another method was pricking, whereby Hopkins or one of his assistance pricked the accused with a knife; if they did not bleed, this was taken to be proof that they were a witch. Hopkins's methods, which he included in his book *The Discovery of Witches*, were also used in the American colonies, including during the Salem witch trials.

The European and Northern American witch hunts died down in the eighteenth century because of public and legal protests Anywhere from forty thousand to sixty thousand men and women had been killed. Although mass witch hunts no longer occur, witchcraft accusations and executions do still occur in some places today.

Most modern-day cases of witch hunts and accused witches are found in Latin America, India, Saudi Arabia, Melanesia, and sub-Saharan Africa—especially Tanzania, Cameroon, Gambia, Zambia, Ghana, Uganda, Kenya, and the Democratic Republic of Congo. In many of these countries, accusations and the killings of the suspected witches have been on the rise in recent years. In Africa, for example, twenty-two thousand to twenty-three thousand people were killed for being witches from 1991 to 2001 (Petraitis 2003), and in Papua New Guinea, witch killings increased by 400 percent from 2005 to 2010 (Urame 2008). As in the past, accused witches tend to be the socially marginalized, and as in the European cases, a witch hunter or witch finder is often called in and paid to participate in locating the witch.

The modern witch hunter sometimes claims to have a supernatural ability that allows the hunter to see witches. Some are priests or preachers, but others are laypeople who claim to have a special gift. Men almost always take this role (although among the Bantu-speaking tribes of Southern Africa, "witch smellers" are women), and in recent years, it has become a somewhat lucrative occupation for young men. More often than not, women tend to predominate as the accused. Witch hunters today use trials by ordeal, just as witch hunters in the past did, such as forcing the accused to retrieve a bracelet from a pot of boiling water (innocent people should not be burned or scarred as a result). Other methods are drawn from traditional divination techniques, such as cutting the throat of a chicken and watching to see which way the dying chicken lands on the ground. Some witch hunters go into a trance and are able to "smell out" witches while in the trance.

As in the past, witchcraft accusations today tend to emerge after a misfortune, often the death of a family member. Even in a world in which many (but not all) people have access to modern Western medicine, it is still the case that witchcraft is the most common explanation for an otherwise unexplained illness or calamity. With witchcraft accusations, the victim (or relative of the victim) gains some relief by calling in a witch finder and seeing the accused witch be punished. In addition, because the targets of accusations are often the socially inferior, the community is "cleansed" of a potentially troublesome individual. Witchcraft accusations also provide for social solidarity, as the others in the community rally together to demand justice against the witch. One explanation for the rise in witch killings in recent years is that the kinds of people killed—older women and, increasingly, children—are considered to be unproductive members of the family (Miguel 2005). The fact that witchcraft accusations and killings tend to be found in areas suffering extreme poverty provides some credence for this theory.

One of the differences between modern witchcraft accusations and those of the past is that many accused witches in Africa actually admit to being witches or at least having magical powers or having used magic to harm someone. These confessions, true or not, enable the belief systems to continue. In addition, sorcerers, who continue to operate in Africa, sometimes engage in deadly behaviors such as using the bones of people with albinism in spells; a number of albinos have been killed in recent years because of this market. Here again, beliefs about witchcraft and the practices of sorcerers are being conflated, with the result being a hardened determination to hunt witches in many countries. Ironically, some of the same people who fight witches use magical means to protect themselves from witches; Mai-Mai fighters in Uganda, for example, kill suspected witches without trial, but they also use magic water from a witch doctor to protect themselves from bullets.

And while witchcraft beliefs have been present in these communities since long before the introduction of Christianity, witch hunting has been especially fearsome in Pentecostal churches in Africa, where traditional beliefs blend with conservative Christianity. In these churches, witchcraft beliefs blend with beliefs about devil possession. Nigerian Pentecostal preacher Helen Ukpabio preaches that children who scream at night are servants of Satan; her prescription for these children is a particularly brutal form of exorcism that sometimes results in death for these children.

Witches today are killed in especially brutal ways; burning, being beaten or hacked to death, and being buried alive are not uncommon forms of death. Sometimes the victim is tortured before death to elicit a confession. Besides the witch hunter who leads the hunt against accused witches, another difference from the past is that local gangs of young men will band together to administer "justice" to the accused. This is the case in both Africa and Melanesia. Because witch hunters tend to be relatively well-respected men, and because local police and public officials often share the same belief systems, the police often take no action against those involved with killing accused witches. Other times, however, it is recognized that the behavior of these young men, especially if they were drunk or under the influence of drugs or if they killed a respected member of the community, is intolerable, and the public will demand that the police arrest and prosecute the men involved.

Some governments are now fighting witch hunters and witch killers. Papua New Guinea, for example, repealed the 1971 Sorcery Act in 2013, which allowed for the (legal) targeting of alleged witches, and Nigeria prohibits accusing someone of being a witch (at the same time, however, Nigeria still considers witchcraft to be a crime). South Africa is currently considering repealing the Witchcraft Suppression Act of 1957 and replacing it with one that bans witchcraft accusations and violent acts against accused witches; it would also criminalize violence associated with the supposed witches themselves.

See also: Bruja; Exorcist; Traditional Healer.

Further Reading

Briggs, Robin (1996). *Witches and neighbours: The social and cultural context of European witchcraft*. Penguin.

Knauft, B. M. (1985). *Good company and violence: Sorcery and social action in a lowland New Guinea society*. University of California Press.

Mair, L. (1969). *Witchcraft*. McGraw-Hill.

Middleton, J., & Winter, E. H. (Eds.). (2013). *Witchcraft and sorcery in East Africa*. Routledge.

Miguel, E. (2005). Poverty and witch killing. *Review of Economic Studies, 72*(4), 1153–1172.

Petraitis, R. (2003). *The witch killers of Africa.* The Secular Web. https://infidels.org/lib rary/modern/richard_petraitis/witch_killers.html.

Urame, J. (2008). Media reports and public opinion: Sorcery and witchcraft in Papua New Guinea. In F. Zocca & J. Urame (Eds.), *Sorcery, witchcraft and Christianity in Melanesia* (pp. 67–136). Melanesian Institute.

World of Warcraft Gold Farmer (China, South Korea)

A World of Warcraft gold farmer is someone who earns gold through playing World of Warcraft (WoW). WoW is a massively multiplayer online role-playing game (MMORPG), which means that it is an online game played by thousands of people using the same server in which users play the role of a character and inter-act with other users' characters as part of game play. First released in 2004, it is one of the most popular games of its type, with over ten million players around the world.

WoW players occupy a world known as Azeroth, created by gods known as titans, which is filled with creatures such as gnomes, orcs, dwarves, trolls, and elves. Players adopt a character and follow quests, earn gear, gain more skills, level up, fight each other, and gain "pets." Players must buy a subscription to play and can spend real money in the game through making in-game purchases such as the purchase of WoW tickets, which allow users to buy and sell in-game gold at a special auction house.

Players can earn gold in the game by completing quests, defeating enemies in battle, or through the sale of items within the game; certain professions within the game also earn gold. The gold is used to buy items within the game's auction house; to buy better armor, spells, and amulets; or even to pay other players to work for you. Because some players cannot earn enough gold within the game to progress as quickly as they would like, a black market system emerged that allowed for the purchase of gold with real money outside of the game.

Blizzard, the company that makes WoW, considers using gold purchased out-side of the game to be a form of cheating, but it happens anyway. As more people, and even companies, began doing so, the black market quickly turned into a viable way for some enterprising entrepreneurs to make money from the game.

For instance, Internet Gaming Entertainment (IGE) is a company that offers virtual currency for real money for dozens of online multiplayer games, but espe-cially for WoW gold. Until it was banned by Blizzard, these companies advertised within the game and by sending spam e-mails to millions of users. The explosion of companies like IGE has impacted the game by contributing to the inequality of the players, allowing some players to accumulate massive amounts of wealth. (Players can also buy whole accounts, often for thousands of dollars, allowing new players to immediately jump to the highest levels in the game.) In addition, too much gold in the game has created inflation, ironically lowering the value of the gold.

In 2015, as a response to the rising levels of gold sales that were impacting the game, Blizzard released new WoW tickets; these cost $20 and allowed players to

Conquistador

The term *conquistador* is typically used to describe Spanish and Portuguese explorers and military men who conquered much of Central and South America as well as parts of Asia and Africa from the sixteenth through the nineteenth centuries. It may also be used for conquerors from other countries. Conquistadors received permission from the crown or colonial officials to explore, conquer, and settle areas of the New World and either funded their expeditions through private financiers, the crown, or by themselves; any spoils would have to be shared with the crown as well as any financiers. After receiving royal permission, the conquistadors had to not only share the profits with the crown but also to follow any instructions they were given and to send in regular reports.

One did not have to have any special training or skills to become a conquistador, although they were often professional soldiers whose main motivations were profit. Hernán Cortés, the conqueror of Mexico, said, "I and my companions suffer from a disease of the heart which can only be cured by gold." Originally, the conquistadors were seeking gold and other precious metals, but they eventually began to extract other commodities from their new colonies and to establish plantations, using native people and, later, African slaves as laborers.

Expeditions were usually small, with no more than a few hundred people, and included soldiers, members of the clergy, horses, attack dogs, and livestock. The soldiers on the expedition were paid with a share of the treasure and sometimes with land grants, called *encomiendas*, which allowed the owner to use the native people living there as laborers. The expedition leaders received a greater share of both money and land. Conquistadors used a combination of diplomacy and violence to pacify the people and were aided by the use of horses and dogs, their technological superiority (especially with guns and steel weapons), and via the diseases that they unwittingly introduced into the New World.

Source: Stone, S. Z. (1990). *The heritage of the conquistadors: Ruling classes in Central America from the conquest to the Sandinistas.* University of Nebraska Press.

legitimately exchange gold for cash with other players. This has reduced the number of outside gold sellers somewhat, but it is still very easy to buy gold through them. In addition, the tokens have also impacted the virtual economy of WoW, as they have also contributed to the devaluation of gold within the game.

So, how do gold sellers accumulate the gold that they sell? Some do so by simply hacking into players' accounts and then stealing the gold (and other virtual goods) that the players have accumulated. However, large quantities of gold are typically accumulated through gold farming. Companies pay workers in developing countries to play the game full-time, accumulating gold or "power" leveling up players who paid for that service. Prior to the introduction of the WoW tokens in 2015, there were perhaps as many as one million people farming gold for pay in China alone. Gold farming became such a big business that facilities known as gaming or play-money workshops were developed in China to allow for large numbers of gold farmers to work in one place, and it has been reported that some Chinese prison officials have used inmates to farm for them.

Gold farmers can work up to eighteen hours per day for no more than a few hundred dollars per month. They must meet quotas that determine how much gold they are expected to harvest in a shift, and many live with other gold farmers in dorms. Most players are young, in their teens or early twenties; love playing computer games; and are experienced in WoW. Even though it takes skill to play a game like WoW, the farmers are treated and paid as if it is an unskilled job.

Gold farming is only possible in a world in which vast degrees of inequality exist. An American WoW player who earns the median monthly income of $3,714 (as of 2017) can earn enough money in ten hours to pay a Chinese worker to farm gold for a full month.

See also: Ethical Hacker.

Further Reading

Corneliussen, H., & Rettberg, J. W. (Eds.). (2008). *Digital culture, play, and identity: A World of Warcraft reader.* MIT Press.

Heeks, R. (2008). Current analysis and future research agenda on "gold farming": Real-world production in developing countries for the virtual economies of online games (Development Informatics Working Paper No. 32).

Nardi, B. (2010). *My life as a night elf priest: An anthropological account of World of Warcraft.* University of Michigan Press.

Y

YouTube Celebrity (Global)

A YouTube celebrity, or YouTuber, is a person who makes a living—or a partial living—by making videos for YouTube. YouTube, the world's most popular video sharing site, was founded in 2005, and since that time, and especially after its purchase by Google in 2006, it has grown into one of the world's major media companies, with an annual revenue of over $13 billion.

According to Omnicore Agency, as of September 2019, there are thirty million daily users on YouTube and two billion monthly users, and over five billion videos have been shared since 2005. It is the second most visited website in the world (after Google). And although all YouTube videos could originally be streamed for free, since 2007, there are a variety of ways for users, known as content creators, to make money from their YouTube content.

YouTubers develop fame (and thus income) by having a specialty that viewers find interesting. Some of the most popular YouTube categories include cooking, makeup (tutorials and reviews), travel, education, fitness, nutrition, technology, pets, and comedy (much of which is prank videos), and YouTubers who specialize in those areas can make a great deal of money. Other popular YouTube videos include unboxing videos (where viewers will watch a YouTuber open up the boxes of electronics that they just purchased), haul videos (where fashion or beauty bloggers will show off and describe their recent purchases), challenge videos (where users are encouraged to engage in and film challenges such as the Ice Bucket Challenge from 2014), and product review videos. According to Forbes, in 2016, the highest earning YouTubers earned over $70 million.

So, how does one earn money through YouTube? The most common way is to allow YouTube to run ads on one's videos through its YouTube Partner Program. (Since 2017, this is only available to content creators who have amassed at least ten thousand overall views on their channel.) A portion of that ad revenue (typically 55 percent) goes to the content creator. Another way to make money is to get corporate sponsorships. With sponsorships, a company pays a content creator a certain amount of money to use its product in his or her videos; the payment will be based on how many viewers the YouTuber has. YouTubers can make hundreds of dollars per video at the low end, and with over a half million followers, they can see their per video income rise to thousands of dollars per video. Other YouTubers sell merchandise (often their own product lines), develop apps, write books, or do live tours or personal appearances where fans pay to see them in person. (Another revenue source is paid subscriptions: any channel can ask for subscriptions, but paid subscriptions are only available to accounts with over one thousand free subscribers and four thousand hours of views in the past year.)

Becoming a YouTuber involves no real training whatsoever. Videos can be simply and inexpensively made with a smartphone and simple video editing software, although experienced professionals use much higher quality technology, including lighting, specialized mics, and more, to produce their videos.

One of the most appealing aspects of making a living through YouTube is the way that becoming famous on this platform differs from the old media model. Prior to the development of YouTube and other social media platforms, people became celebrities by having a talent, such as acting or singing, and then working with the gatekeepers of celebrity—talent agents, record producers, film studios, and the like. With YouTube, one can become a star based only on the strength of one's videos and the charisma of the producer.

Some YouTubers have niche audiences, and others have wide audiences that appeal to multiple demographics. One example of a niche video type is the autonomous sensory meridian response (ASMR) videos that became popular in 2015. ASMR refers to the pleasurable tingly sensation that some people get from hearing specific triggers, such as whispering or tapping, or seeing certain things, such as watching someone perform repetitive mundane tasks. Although many people can experience this sensation through, for example, watching the old Bob Ross painting shows or listening to Richard Attenborough's narration in a BBC nature documentary, many now visit YouTube to watch videos specially produced by YouTubers known as ASMRtists (or ASMR artists). These YouTubers use highly sensitive microphones and sometimes two microphones to best capture the sounds made by the creator. Some ASMRtists engage in role play, where they pretend that they are providing an intimate service to the viewer, such as doing one's makeup. Others will film themselves eating, massaging someone's head, or pretending to be a doctor. Many people watch ASMR videos to fall asleep.

Popular YouTubers, such as Instagram influencers, typically spend a lot of time interacting with their followers. This is one element of what makes a YouTuber popular—the level of intimacy and connection that their followers experience.

Youtubers, as well as other "new media" celebrities, such as Instagram influencers, can achieve extensive global fame, but they can also lose it very easily. YouTube has policies, known as community guidelines, that restrict certain types of "offensive" content (the definition of which is rapidly changing), but even content creators who abide by YouTube's rules can see their channels being demonetized if they do something offensive enough. For example, in 2018, popular YouTuber Logan Paul uploaded a video of a human body hanging from a tree in Aokigahara—known as "Suicide Forest"—in Japan, leading to his channel being temporarily demonetized. Other content creators, such as right-wing radio talk show host Alex Jones, had their YouTube channels removed after violating YouTube's community guidelines. Another prominent former YouTube channel, known as DaddyofFive, which posted videos of family activities and pranks, was removed by YouTube after the couple that ran the channel, Michael and Heather Martin, were accused of harming their children in the videos.

YouTube celebrities can potentially see their incomes continue to rise as YouTube becomes a more important site for millennials and younger generations to consume much of their media (including television shows and music videos). On the other hand, there is more content being created today than ever before (three hundred hours of video were uploaded every minute in 2018), which means You-Tubers have to do much more to stand out among all the content.

See also: Animal Talent Agent.

Further Reading

Bärtl, M. (2018). YouTube channels, uploads and views: A statistical analysis of the past 10 years. *Convergence, 24*(1), 16–32.

Berg, M. (2016, December 5). The highest-paid YouTube stars 2016: PewDiePie remains no. 1 with $15 million. *Forbes Magazine.* https://www.forbes.com/sites/maddie berg/2016/12/05/the-highest-paid-youtube-stars-2016-pewdiepie-remains-no-1-wi th-15-million/#1e0ae3837713.

Bibliography

Adams, J., Andrews, G., Barnes, J., Broom, A., & Magin, P. (Eds.). (2012). *Traditional, complementary and integrative medicine: An international reader.* Macmillan International Higher Education.

Adams, L., & Riffey, M. (2007). *More than a parade: The spirit and passion behind the Pasadena Tournament of Roses.* Stephens Press.

Allen, R. C. (2009). *The British industrial revolution in global perspective* (Vol. 1). Cambridge University Press.

Ambros, B. (2010). The necrogeography of pet memorial spaces: Pets as liminal family members in contemporary Japan. *Material Religion, 6*(3), 304–335.

Amorth, F. G. (2015). *An exorcist tells his story.* Ignatius Press.

Amott, T. L., & Matthaei, J. A. (1996). *Race, gender, and work: A multi-cultural economic history of women in the United States.* South End Press.

Anderson, M. B., Stillman, P. L., & Wang, Y. (1994). Growing use of standardized patients in teaching and evaluation in medical education. *Teaching and Learning in Medicine: An International Journal, 6*(1), 15–22.

Anguelov, D., Dulong, C., Filip, D., Frueh, C., Lafon, S., Lyon, R., . . . & Weaver, J. (2010). Google Street View: Capturing the world at street level. *Computer, 43*(6), 32–38.

Applewhite, S. L. (1995). Curanderismo: Demystifying the health beliefs and practices of elderly Mexican Americans. *Health & Social Work, 20*(4), 247–253.

Arndt, S. W., & Kierzkowski, H. (Eds.). (2001). *Fragmentation: New production patterns in the world economy.* Oxford University Press.

Ashenburg, K. (2010). *The mourner's dance: What we do when people die.* Vintage Canada.

Atkins, G. G. (2014). *Modern religious cults and movements* (Routledge Revivals). Routledge.

Auerbach, L. (2010). *Ghost hunting: How to investigate the paranormal.* Ronin Publishing.

Austin, J., & Hobbs, C. H. (2001). *Taking the train: How graffiti art became an urban crisis in New York City.* Columbia University Press.

Baigent, M. (1994). *From the omens of Babylon: Astrology and ancient Mesopotamia.* Arkana.

Bailey, J. B. (1896). *The diary of a resurrectionist, 1811–1812: To which are added an account of the resurrection men in London and a short history of the passing of the Anatomy Act* (Vol. 1). Library of Alexandria.

Balog, P. (1955). Notes on ancient and medieval minting technique. *Numismatic Chronicle and Journal of the Royal Numismatic Society, 15*(45), 195–201.

Banerjee, D. C. (1995). *Arranged marriage.* Doubleday.

Barbier, P. (1996). *The world of the castrati: The history of an extraordinary operatic phenomenon.* Souvenir Press.

Bärtl, M. (2018). YouTube channels, uploads and views: A statistical analysis of the past 10 years. *Convergence, 24*(1), 16–32.

Basin, K. (2018). *The business of television.* Routledge.

Beard, T. R., Kaserman, D. L., & Osterkamp, R. (2013). *The global organ shortage: Economic causes, human consequences, policy responses.* Stanford University Press.

Beck, R. (2008). *A brief history of ancient astrology* (Vol. 4). John Wiley & Sons.

Beckett, S. (2017). *Florida Seminole casinos generating massive revenues for tribe.* Casino.org. https://www.casino.org/news/florida-seminole-casinos-generating-massive-revenues-for-tribe.

Behar, R. (1987). Sex and sin, witchcraft and the devil in late colonial Mexico. *American Ethnologist, 14*(1), 34–54.

Benedetti, J. (2012). *The art of the actor: The essential history of acting from classical times to the present day.* Routledge.

Bennett, J. M. (1986). The village ale-wife: Women and brewing in fourteenth-century England. In Barbara A. Hanawalt (Ed.), *Women and Work in pre-industrial Europe* (pp. 20–22). Indiana University Press.

Berg, M. (2016, December 5). The highest-paid YouTube stars 2016: PewDiePie remains no. 1 with $15 million. *Forbes Magazine.* https://www.forbes.com/sites/maddieberg/2016/12/05/the-highest-paid-youtube-stars-2016-pewdiepie-remains-no-1-with-15-million/#27b6dc357713.

Bialuschewski, A. (2008). Black people under the black flag: Piracy and the slave trade on the west coast of Africa, 1718–1723. *Slavery and Abolition, 29*(4), 461–475.

Blau, F. D., Ferber, M. A., & Winkler, A. E. (2013). *The economics of women, men and work.* Pearson Higher Ed.

Bogdan, R. (1988). *Freak show.* University of Chicago Press.

Bohm, R. M. (2010). *Ultimate sanction: Understanding the death penalty through its many voices and many sides.* Kaplan.

Bork-Hüffer, T., & Yuan-Ihle, Y. (2014). The management of foreigners in China: Changes to the migration law and regulations during the late HuWen and early XiLi eras and their potential effects. *International Journal of China Studies, 5*(3), 571.

Brandes, S. (2010). The meaning of American pet cemetery gravestones. *Ethnology: An International Journal of Cultural and Social Anthropology, 48*(2), 99–118.

Briggs, R. (1996). *Witches and neighbours: The social and cultural context of European witchcraft.* Penguin.

Brubakk, A. O., Ross, J. A., & Thom, S. R. (2011). Saturation diving; physiology and pathophysiology. *Comprehensive physiology, 4*(3), 1229–1272.

Burns, R., Kinkade, P., & Leone, M. C. (2005). Bounty hunters: A look behind the hype. *Policing: An International Journal of Police Strategies & Management, 28*(1), 118–138.

Burton, B. (1990). *Bail enforcer: The advanced bounty hunter.* Paladin Press.

Butler, E. (2018). Tasting off-flavors: Food science, sensory knowledge and the consumer sensorium. *Senses and Society, 13*(1), 75–88.

Butler, J. (2008). Symbolic and social roles of women in death ritual in traditional Irish society. In E. J. Håland (Ed.), *Women, pain and death: Rituals and everyday life on the margins of Europe and beyond* (pp. 108–121). Cambridge Scholars Publishing.

Caldwell, T. (2011). Ethical hackers: Putting on the white hat. *Network Security, 2011*(7), 10–13.

Chagnon, N. A. (1983). *Yanomamö: The fierce people.* Holt, Rinehart and Winston.

Chagnon, N. A. (2013). *Noble savages: My life among two dangerous tribes—The Yanomamö and the anthropologists.* Simon and Schuster.

Chaplin, S. (2007). *Japanese love hotels: A cultural history.* Routledge.

Clinton, M., Haines, L., Belloir, B., & McBride, D. (2001). Sexing chick embryos: A rapid and simple protocol. *British Poultry Science, 42*(1), 134–138.

Coffin, A. W. (2007). From roadkill to road ecology: A review of the ecological effects of roads. *Journal of Transport Geography, 15*(5), 396–406.

Colas, A. (2018). *Food, politics, and society: Social theory and the modern food system.* University of California Press.

Connor, L., & Samuel, G. (Eds.). (2001). *Healing powers and modernity: Traditional medicine, shamanism, and science in Asian societies.* Greenwood Publishing Group.

Corneliussen, H., & Rettberg, J. W. (Eds.). (2008). *Digital culture, play, and identity: A World of Warcraft reader.* MIT Press.

Cressy, D. (2013). *Saltpeter: The mother of gunpowder.* Oxford University Press.

Crittenden, A. (2002). *The price of motherhood: Why the most important job in the world is still the least valued.* Macmillan.

Curry, P. (1989). *Prophecy and power: Astrology in early modern England.* Polity Press; B. Blackwell.

Dalby, C., & Carranza, C. (2019). InSight Crime's 2018 homicide round-up. *InSight Crime.* https://www.insightcrime.org/news/analysis/insight-crime-2018-homicide-roundup.

Davis, D. S. (1984). Good people doing dirty work: A study of social isolation. *Symbolic Interaction, 7*(2), 233–247.

Davis, R. C., Marvin, G., & Garry, M. R. (2004). *Venice, the tourist maze: A cultural critique of the world's most touristed city.* University of California Press.

Dawson, L. L. (2006). *Comprehending cults: The sociology of new religious movements.* Oxford University Press.

De Stefano, V. (2015). The rise of the just-in-time workforce: On-demand work, crowdwork, and labor protection in the gig-economy. *Comparative Labor Law & Policy Journal, 37,* 471.

Deane, P. M. (1979). *The first industrial revolution.* Cambridge University Press.

DeMello, M. (2007). *Encyclopedia of body adornment: A cultural history.* Greenwood Press.

DeMello, M. (2012). *Animals and society: An introduction to human-animal studies.* Columbia University Press.

Denny, R. M., & Sunderland, P. L. (Eds.). (2016). *Handbook of anthropology in business.* Routledge.

Desmond, J. (2002). Displaying death, animating life: Changing fictions of "liveness" from taxidermy to animatronics. In N. Rothfels (Ed.), *Representing animals* (pp. 159–179). Indiana University Press.

Devereux, P., Brookesmith, P., Keen, M., & Watson, N. (1997). *UFOs and ufology: The first 50 years.* Blandford.

Devine, M. V. (1982). *Brujeria: A study of Mexican-American folk-magic.* Llewellyn Publications.

Djafarova, E., & Rushworth, C. (2017). Exploring the credibility of online celebrities' Instagram profiles in influencing the purchase decisions of young female users. *Computers in Human Behavior, 68,* 1–7.

Dray, P. (2018). *The fair chase: The epic story of hunting in America.* Basic Books.

Dunkle, R. (2013). *Gladiators: Violence and spectacle in ancient Rome.* Routledge.

Durbach, N. (2009). *Spectacle of deformity: Freak shows and modern British culture.* University of California Press.

Edward, M. (2012). *Psychic blues: Confessions of a conflicted medium.* Feral House.

Eghigian, G. (2017). Making UFOs make sense: Ufology, science, and the history of their mutual mistrust. *Public Understanding of Science, 26*(5), 612–626.

Emmins, A. (2009). *Mop men: Inside the world of crime scene cleaners.* St. Martin's Griffin.

Endredy, J. (2011). *The flying witches of Veracruz: A shaman's true story of indigenous witchcraft, devil's weed, and trance healing in Aztec Brujeria.* Llewellyn Worldwide.

Escoffier, J. (2003). Gay-for-pay: Straight men and the making of gay pornography. *Qualitative Sociology, 26*(4), 531–555.

Evans, E. P. (1906). *The criminal prosecution and capital punishment of animals.* William Heinemann.

Fagone, J. (2006). *Horsemen of the esophagus: Competitive eating and the big fat American dream.* Crown Books.

Fildes, V. (1988). *Wet nursing: A history from antiquity to the present.* Basil Blackwell.

Fine, A. (Ed.). (2000). *Handbook on animal-assisted therapy: Theoretical foundations and guidelines for practice.* Academic Press.

Firth, R. (Ed.). (2013). *Themes in economic anthropology.* Routledge.

Fortune Business Insights. (2019). *Pallets market size, share and industry analysis by material type (wood, plastic, composite wood, and others), by application (pharmaceuticals, F&B, manufacturing, and others), and regional*

forecast, 2019–2026. https://www.fortunebusinessinsights.com/industry
-reports/pallets-market-100674.

Freckelton, I. (2018). *The trauma cleaner: One woman's extraordinary life in death & disaster.* St. Martin's Press.

Fredriksson, K. (1993). *American rodeo: From Buffalo Bill to big business.* Texas A&M University Press.

Freedman, A. (2011). *Tokyo in transit: Japanese culture on the rails and road.* Stanford University Press.

Frembgen, J. W. (2011). Itinerary ear-cleaners: Notes on a marginal profession in urban Muslim Punjab. *Anthropos, 106*(1), 180–184.

Ganz, N. (2004). *Graffiti world: Street art from five continents* (T. Manco, Ed.). Thames & Hudson.

Gao, Y., Colby, R., & Ikeda, G. (2014). The feasibility and economic potential of geoduck aquaculture in Neah Bay, Washington. *Journal of Agricultural Science and Technology A, 4*(4A), 291–299.

Garcés Restrepo, M. F., Pauli, J. N., & Peery, M. Z. (2018). Natal dispersal of tree sloths in a human dominated landscape: Implications for tropical biodiversity conservation. *Journal of Applied Ecology, 55*(5), 2253–2262.

Garland Thompson, R. (Ed.). (1996). *Freakery: Cultural spectacles of the extraordinary body.* New York University Press.

Geluardi, J. (2016). *Cannabiz: The explosive rise of the medical marijuana industry.* Routledge.

Giles, D. C. (2013). Animal celebrities. *Celebrity Studies, 4*(2), 115–128.

Gilman, S. (2008). The hottentot and the prostitute: Toward an iconography of female sexuality. In C. Malacrida & J. Low (Eds.), *Sociology of the body: A reader* (pp. 76–107). Oxford University Press.

Glenday, C. (1999). *The UFO investigator's handbook: The practical guide to researching, identifying, and documenting unexplained sightings.* Running Press.

Glick, L. B. (2005). *Marked in your flesh: Circumcision from ancient Judea to modern America.* Oxford University Press.

Global Justice Now. (2016). *Controlling corporations: The case for a UN treaty on transnational corporations and human rights.* https://www.globaljus
tice.org.uk/sites/default/files/files/resources/controlling_corporations_brie
fing.pdf.

Godelier, M., & Strathern, M. (1991). *Big men and great men: Personifications of power in Melanesia.* Maison des Sciences de l'Homme.

Gollaher, D. L. (2001). *Circumcision: A history of the world's most controversial surgery.* Basic Books.

Goodman, F. D. (1988). *How about demons? Possession and exorcism in the modern world.* Indiana University Press.

Gordon, D. G. (1996). *Field guide to the geoduck.* Sasquatch Books.

Goswami, P. K., Samant, M. A. Y. U. R. I., & Srivastava, R. S. (2014). Snake venom, anti-snake venom & potential of snake venom. *International Journal of Pharmacy and Pharmaceutical Sciences, 6*(5), 4–7.

Griffith, J. D., Mitchell, S., Hammond, B., Gu, L. L., & Hart, C. L. (2012). A comparison of sexual behaviors and attitudes, self-esteem, quality of life, and drug use among pornography actors and a matched sample. *International Journal of Sexual Health, 24*(4), 254–266.

Griffith, J. D., Mitchell, S., Hart, C. L., Adams, L. T., & Gu, L. L. (2013). Pornography actresses: An assessment of the damaged goods hypothesis. *Journal of Sex Research, 50*(7), 621–632.

Griffiths, H. R. (2000). *Diverted journeys: The social lives of Ghanaian fantasy coffins* (No. 83). Centre of African Studies, Edinburgh University.

Hale, T. A. (1998). *Griots and griottes: Masters of words and music.* Indiana University Press.

Halloran, A., Flore, R., Vantomme, P., & Roos, N. (Eds.). (2018). *Edible insects in sustainable food systems.* Springer.

Halvorsen, B. (2012). Effects of norms and policy incentives on household recycling: An international comparison. *Resources, Conservation and Recycling, 67,* 18–26.

Hanks, M. (2016). *Haunted heritage: The cultural politics of ghost tourism, populism, and the past.* Routledge.

Hanna, R., Kreindler, G., & Olken, B. A. (2017). Citywide effects of high-occupancy vehicle restrictions: Evidence from "three-in-one" in Jakarta. *Science, 357*(6346), 89–93.

Hart, L., & Sundar. (2000). Family traditions for mahouts of Asian elephants. *Anthrozoös, 13*(1), 34–42.

Hartig, F. (2013). Panda diplomacy: The cutest part of China's public diplomacy. *The Hague Journal of Diplomacy, 8*(1), 49–78.

Hartle, D. (2019). *Giants of the monsoon forest: Living and working with elephants.* Norton.

Heeks, R. (2008). *Current analysis and future research agenda on "gold farming": Real-world production in developing countries for the virtual economies of online games* (Development Informatics Working Paper No. 32).

Hoak, D. (1987). The secret history of the Tudor court: The king's coffers and the king's purse, 1542–1553. *Journal of British Studies, 26*(2), 208–231.

Hodes, J. (2013–2014). Whitewood under siege: On the front lines of the pallet wars. *Cabinetmaker Magazine.* http://cabinetmagazine.org/issues/52/hodes.php.

Hoefferle, M. M. (2012). Floats, friendship and fun: Exploring motivations for community art engagement. *International Journal of Education through Art, 8*(3), 253–269.

Hollingsworth, J., Copeland, B., & Johnson, J. X. (2019). Are e-scooters polluters? The environmental impacts of shared dockless electric scooters. *Environmental Research Letters, 14*(8), 084031.

Horlyck, C., & Pettid, M. J. (2014). *Death, mourning, and the afterlife in Korea: Ancient to contemporary times.* University of Hawai'i Press.

Horsey, R. (2002). *The art of chicken sexing* (University College London Working Papers in Linguistics No. 14).

Howe, P. (2005). *Paparazzi.* Artisan Books.

Howell, P. (2002). A place for the animal dead: Pets, pet cemeteries and animal ethics in late Victorian Britain. *Ethics, Place & Environment, 5*(1), 5–22.

Hughes, E. C. (1962). Good people and dirty work. *Social Problems, 10*(1), 3–11.

Hughes, V. (1977). *Ladies' mile*. Abson Books.

Huijser, M. P., Duffield, J. W., Clevenger, A. P., Ament, R. J., & Cost-Benefit, P. M. (2009). Analyses of mitigation measures aimed at reducing collisions with large ungulates in the United States and Canada: A decision support tool. *Ecology and Society, 14*(2), Article 15.

Islam, M. S., Hakim, M. A., Kamruzzaman, M., Safeuzzaman, H. M., & Alam, M. K. (2016). Socioeconomic profile and health status of rickshaw pullers in rural Bangladesh. *American Journal of Food Science and Health, 2*(4), 32–38.

Iwata, O. (1992). Crowding and behavior in Japanese public spaces: Some observations and speculations. *Social Behavior and Personality: An International Journal, 20*(1), 57–70.

Jaiswal, T. (2014). *Indian arranged marriages: A social psychological perspective*. Routledge.

Jankal, R., & Jankalová, M. (2011). Mystery shopping—The tool of employee communication skills evaluation. *Business: Theory and Practice, 12*(1), 45–49.

Jee, S. H., Baldwin, C., Dadiz, R., Jones, M., & Alpert-Gillis, L. (2018). Integrated mental health training for pediatric and psychology trainees using standardized patient encounters. *Academic Pediatrics, 18*(1), 119–121.

Jin, Z., & Jin, B. (2004). *Chinese folk arts*. China Intercontinental Press.

Jindra, M., & Noret, J. (Eds.). (2013). *Funerals in Africa: Explorations of a social phenomenon*. Berghahn Books.

Johnson, A. R. (2011). The magic metabolisms of competitive eating. In P. Williams-Forson & C. Counihan (Eds.), *Taking food public: Redefining foodways in a changing world* (pp. 279–292). Routledge.

Johnston, C. E. (2013). *Beware of that cup! The role of food-tasters in ancient society* [master's thesis]. University of Otago.

Jordan, A. T. (2012). *Business anthropology*. Waveland Press.

Kastenbaum, R. (2001). *Death, society, and human experience* (7th ed.). Allyn & Bacon.

Kellett, O. (2017). *Hand jobs: Life as a hand model*. Hoxton Mini Press.

Kempadoo, K., & Doezema, J. (Eds.). (1998). *Global sex workers: Rights, resistance, and redefinition*. Psychology Press.

Kempadoo, K., & Doezema, J. (Eds.). (2018). *Global sex workers: Rights, resistance, and redefinition*. Routledge.

Kendall, L. (2014). Marriages and families in Asia: Something old and something new? In S. M. Tam, W. C. A. Wong, & D. Wang (Eds.), *Gender and family in East Asia* (pp. 226–240). Routledge.

Kessler, S. (2018). *Gigged: The gig economy, the end of the job and the future of work*. Random House.

Kirkpatrick, D. (2011). *The Facebook effect: The inside story of the company that is connecting the world*. Simon and Schuster.

Knauft, B. M. (1985). *Good company and violence: Sorcery and social action in a lowland New Guinea society.* University of California Press.

Krapohl, D., & Shaw, P. (2015). *Fundamentals of polygraph practice.* Academic Press.

Lair, R. C. (1997). *Gone astray. The care and management of the Asian elephant in domesticity.* RAP.

Laurence, J. (1963). *A history of capital punishment.* Citadel Press.

Lawrence, D. (1982). Parades, politics, and competing urban images: Doo dah and roses. *Urban Anthropology, 11*(2), 155–176.

Lawrence, E. A. (1984). *Rodeo: An anthropologist looks at the wild and the tame.* University of Chicago Press.

Lawrence, E. A. (1990). Rodeo horses: The wild and the tame. In R. Willis (Ed.), *Signifying animals: Human meaning in the natural world* (pp. 222–235). Routledge.

Lee, C. K. (Ed.). (2006). *Working in China: Ethnographies of labor and workplace transformation.* Routledge.

Lee, D. (2015). Absolute traffic: Infrastructural aptitude in urban Indonesia. *International Journal of Urban and Regional Research, 39*(2), 234–250.

León, V. (2009). *Working IX to V: Orgy planners, funeral clowns, and other prized professions of the ancient world.* Bloomsbury Publishing.

Levinson, M. (2016). *The box: How the shipping container made the world smaller and the world economy bigger.* Princeton University Press.

Lewis, J. R. (2003). *The astrology book: The encyclopedia of heavenly influences.* Visible Ink Press.

Light, M., Orens, A., Rowberry, J., & Saloga, C. W. (2016). *The economic impact of marijuana legalization in Colorado.* Marijuana Policy Group.

Lim, G. D. J. T. (2017). *Feng shui and your health: A guide to high vitality.* Partridge Publishing Singapore.

Lindburg, D. G., & Baragona, K. (Eds.). (2004). *Giant pandas: Biology and conservation.* University of California Press.

Liu, H. (2015). *From Canton restaurant to Panda Express: A history of Chinese food in the United States.* Rutgers University Press.

Loo, S., & Sellbach, U. (2013). Eating (with) insects: Insect gastronomies and upside-down ethics. *Parallax, 19*(1), 12–28.

Lust, A. (2002). *From the Greek mimes to Marcel Marceau and beyond: Mimes, actors, Pierrots, and clowns: A chronicle of the many visages of mime in the theatre.* Scarecrow Press.

Machat, U., & Dennis, L. (2000). *The golf ball book.* Sport Images.

Madden, D. (2011). *The authentic animal: Inside the odd and obsessive world of taxidermy.* St. Martin's Press.

Mair, L. (1969). *Witchcraft.* McGraw-Hill.

Mancoff, D. N., & Trela, D. J. (Eds.). (1996). *Victorian urban settings: Essays on the nineteenth-century city and its contexts* (Vol. 1889). Taylor & Francis.

Martin, D. (2008). *Live & work in China: The most accurate, practical and comprehensive guide to living and working in China.* Crimson Publishing.

Marvin, G. (1994). *Bullfight*. University of Illinois Press.

Marvin, G. (2011). Enlivened through memory: Hunters and hunting trophies. In S. J. M. M. Alberti (Ed.), *The afterlives of animals: A museum menagerie* (pp. 202–217). University of Virginia Press.

Mazor, J. (2013). The child's interests and the case for the permissibility of male infant circumcision. *Journal of Medical Ethics, 39*(7), 421–428.

McCormick, A., & M. McCormick. (1997). *Horse sense and the human heart: What horses can teach us about trust, bonding, creativity and spirituality.* Health Communications.

McCormick, J. (2017). *Bullfighting: Art, technique and Spanish society.* Routledge.

McCoy, N. P. (2009). Madwoman, banshee, shaman: Gender, changing performance contexts and the Irish wake ritual. In E. Mackinlay, B. L. Bartleet, & K. Barney (Eds.), *Musical islands: Exploring connections between music, place and* research (pp. 207–220). Cambridge Scholars Publishing.

McNamee, R. (2019). *Zucked: Waking up to the Facebook catastrophe*. Penguin Press.

McPhee, C. C., Orenstein, N. M., & Orenstein, N. (2011). *Infinite jest: Caricature and satire from Leonardo to Levine*. Metropolitan Museum of Art.

Meldrum, T. (2014). *Domestic service and gender, 1660–1750: Life and work in the London household*. Routledge.

Merback, M. B. (1999). *The thief, the cross, and the wheel: Pain and the spectacle of punishment in medieval and Renaissance Europe*. University of Chicago Press.

Meyers, M. C., & Laurent, C. M. (2010). The rodeo athlete. *Sports medicine, 40*(10), 817–839.

Middleton, J., & Winter, E. H. (Eds.). (2013). *Witchcraft and sorcery in East Africa*. Routledge.

Miguel, E. (2005). Poverty and witch killing. *Review of Economic Studies, 72*(4), 1153–1172.

Mintz, S. W. (1986). *Sweetness and power: The place of sugar in modern history*. Penguin.

Mitford, J. (2000). *The American way of death revisited*. Vintage.

Molotch, H., & Norén, L. (Eds.). (2010). *Toilet: Public restrooms and the politics of sharing* (Vol. 1). New York University Press.

Monger, G. (2004). *Marriage customs of the world: From henna to honeymoons*. ABC-CLIO.

Moscato, E. M., & Cassel, M. (2019). *Eating bugs on purpose: Challenges and opportunities in adapting insects as a sustainable protein*. SAGE Publications, SAGE Business Cases Originals.

Murphy, M. N. (2011). *Somalia, the new Barbary? Piracy and Islam in the Horn of Africa*. Columbia University Press.

Namboodiri, N. (1997). *Practical elephant management: A handbook for mahouts*. Elephant Welfare Association.

Nardi, B. (2010). *My life as a night elf priest: An anthropological account of World of Warcraft*. University of Michigan Press.

Nerz, R. (2006). *Eat this book: A year of gorging and glory on the competitive eating circuit.* St. Martin's Griffin.

Nutini, H. G., & Roberts, J. M. (2019). *Bloodsucking witchcraft: An epistemological study of anthropomorphic supernaturalism in rural Tlaxcala.* University of Arizona Press.

Ogden, L. A. (2011). *Swamplife: People, gators, and mangroves entangled in the Everglades.* University of Minnesota Press.

Okagbue, O. (2013). *African theatres and performances.* Routledge.

Oldland, J. (2014). Wool and cloth production in late medieval and early Tudor England. *Economic History Review, 67*(1), 25–47.

One Earth Future Foundation. (2012). *The economic cost of Somali piracy 2011.* Oceans Beyond Piracy.

O'Neil, B. (2010). *Acting as a business: Strategies for success.* Vintage.

Osofsky, M. J., Bandura, A., & Zimbardo, P. G. (2005). The role of moral disengagement in the execution process. *Law and Human Behavior, 29*(4), 371.

O'Sullivan, S., Watt, Y., & Probyn-Rapsey, F. (2019). Tainted love: The trials and tribulations of a career in animal studies. *Society & Animals, 27*(4), 361–382.

Palmer, A. (2014). *The new pirates: Modern global piracy from Somalia to the South China Sea.* I. B. Tauris.

Parkes, M. B. (1991). *Scribes, scripts and readers: Studies in the communication, presentation and dissemination of medieval texts.* Hambledon Press.

People, Y. (2017). *Instagram ranked worst for young people's mental health.* United Kingdom's Royal Society for Public Health.

Pereira, N., Ribeiro, F., Lopes, G., Whitney, D., & Lino, J. (2012). Autonomous golf ball picking robot design and development. *Industrial Robot: An International Journal, 39*(6), 541–550.

Petraitis, R. (2003). *The witch killers of Africa.* The Secular Web. https://infidels.org/library/modern/richard_petraitis/witch_killers.html.

Pew Research Center. (2013). *On pay gap, millennial women near parity—For now.* http://www.pewsocialtrends.org/2013/12/11/on-pay-gap-millennial-women-near-parity-for-now.

Pfaffenberger, C. J., Scott, J. P., Fuller, J. L., Ginsburg, B. E., & Biefelt, S. W. (1976). *Guide dogs for the blind: Their selection, development, and training.* Elsevier Scientific Publishing Company.

Phillips, G. L. (1949). *England's climbing-boys: A history of the long struggle to abolish child labor in chimney-sweeping* (No. 5). Baker Library, Harvard Graduate School of Business Administration.

Picard, L. (2005). *Victorian London: The tale of a city 1840–1870.* Macmillan.

Pilcher, J. M. (2017). *Food in world history.* Routledge.

Pink, S. (1997). *Women and bullfighting: Gender, sex and the consumption of tradition.* Berg Publisher Ltd.

Potter, N. N., & Hotchkiss, J. H. (2012). *Food science.* Springer Science & Business Media.

Potts, J. (2004). Ghost hunting in the twenty-first century. In J. Houran (Ed.), *From shaman to scientist: Essays on humanity's search for spirits* (pp. 211–232). Scarecrow Press.

Prassl, J. (2018). *Humans as a service: The promise and perils of work in the gig economy.* Oxford University Press.

Prébin, É. (2012). Cremation's success in Korea: Old beliefs and renewed social distinctions. In N. Aveline-Dubach (Ed.), *The invisible population: The place of the dead in East Asian megacities* (pp. 138–164). Lexington Books.

Pschera, A. (2016). *Animal internet: Nature and the digital revolution.* New Vessel Press.

Pucher, J., & Buehler, R. (2008). Making cycling irresistible: Lessons from the Netherlands, Denmark and Germany. *Transport Reviews, 28*(4), 495–528.

Quick, H. (1997). *Catwalking: A history of the fashion model.* Hamlyn.

Radford, B. (2016). *Bad clowns.* University of New Mexico Press.

Radziwill, N., Romano, J., Shorter, D., & Benton, M. (2015). *The ethics of hacking: Should it be taught?* arXiv preprint arXiv:1512.02707.

Rahim, M. A., Joardder, M. U. H., Houque, S. M., Rahman, M. M., & Sumon, N. A. (2013, February). Socio-economic & environmental impacts of battery driven auto rickshaw at Rajshahi city in Bangladesh. In *International Conference on Mechanical, Industrial and Energy Engineering 2012*, Khulna, Bangladesh.

Raskin, D. C., Kircher, J. C., Honts, C. R., & Horowitz, S. W. (2019). A study of the validity of polygraph examinations in criminal investigation: Final report to the National Institute of Justice, Grant No. 85-IJ-CX-0040. *Polygraph, 48*(1), 10–39.

Rees, J. (2013). *Refrigeration nation: A history of ice, appliances, and enterprise in America.* Johns Hopkins University Press.

Reuters. (2011, June 20). Deaths of seafarers in Somali pirate attacks soar. *Reuters.* https://www.reuters.com/article/idINIndia-57804820110620.

Richardson, S. (2003). *Pallets: A North American perspective.* PACTS Management.

Richmond, T. (2011). *The mad art of caricature: A serious guide to drawing funny faces.* Deadline Demon Publishing.

Roach, K. (1999). *Due process and victims' rights: The new law and politics of criminal justice.* University of Toronto Press.

Robbins, T., & Palmer, S. J. (Eds.). (1997). *Millennium, messiahs, and mayhem: Contemporary apocalyptic movements.* Psychology Press.

Robins-Mowry, D. (2019). *The hidden sun: Women of modern Japan.* Routledge.

Roncaglia, S. (2017). *Feeding the city: Work and food culture of the Mumbai Dabbawalas.* Open Book Publishers.

Ross, J. I. (Ed.). (2016). *Routledge handbook of graffiti and street art.* Routledge.

Rudrappa, S. (2015). *Discounted life: The price of global surrogacy in India.* New York University Press.

Sahlins, M. D. (1963). Poor man, rich man, big-man, chief: political types in Melanesia and Polynesia. *Comparative Studies in Society and History, 5*(3), 285–303.

Said, E. W. (1978). *Orientalism.* Pantheon.

Salamone, F. A. (Ed.). (2012). *The Native American identity in sports: Creating and preserving a culture.* Scarecrow Press.

Salarvandian, F., Dijst, M., & Helbich, M. (2017). Impact of traffic zones on mobility behavior in Tehran, Iran. *Journal of Transport and Land Use, 10*(1), 965–982.

Sammis, K., Lincoln, C., & Pomponi, S. (2015). *Influencer marketing for dummies*. John Wiley & Sons.

Sanchez Taylor, J. (2006). Racism and child sex tourism in the Caribbean and Latin America. *Revista SER Social, 18*, 189–208. University of Brasilia.

Sanchez Taylor, J., & O'Connell Davidson, J. (2009). Unknowable secrets and golden silence: Reflexivity and research on sex tourism. In R. Ryan-Flood & R. Gill (Eds.), *Secrecy and silence in the research process: Feminist reflection* (pp. 42–53). Routledge.

Sax, B. (2007). How ravens came to the Tower of London. *Society & Animals, 15*(3), 269–283.

Saxbe, D., Graesch, A., & Alvik, M. (2011). Television as a social or solo activity: Understanding families' everyday television viewing patterns. *Communication Research Reports, 28*(2), 180–189.

Scheper-Hughes, N. (1993). *Death without weeping: The violence of everyday life in Brazil*. University of California Press.

Seiler, A., & Helldin, J. O. (2006). Mortality in wildlife due to transportation. In J. Davenport & J. L. Davenport (Eds.), *The ecology of transportation: Managing mobility for the environment* (pp. 165–189). Springer.

Shay, A. (2005). *Belly dance: Orientalism, transnationalism and harem fantasy*. Mazda Publishers.

Sillitoe, A. (2016). *Leading the blind: A century of guide book travel*. Open Road Media.

Simmons, J. R. (1938). *Feathers and fur on the turnpike*. Christopher Publishing House.

Simpson, R. (Ed.). (2012). *Dirty work: Concepts and identities*. Palgrave Macmillan.

Skaife, C. (2018). *The ravenmaster: My life with the ravens at the Tower of London*. Farrar, Straus and Giroux.

Smith, A. (2016). *Gig work, online selling and home sharing*. Pew Research Center. https://www.pewresearch.org/internet/2016/11/17/gig-work-online-selling-and-home-sharing.

Stepan, N. L., Nouzeilles, G., & Coutinho, M. (2003). *Disease in the history of modern Latin America: From malaria to AIDS*. Duke University Press.

Stokes, R. G., Köster, R., & Sambrook, S. C. (2013). *The business of waste: Great Britain and Germany, 1945 to the present*. Cambridge University Press.

Stone, A. (2016). Rational thinking and belief in psychic abilities: It depends on level of involvement. *Psychological Reports, 118*(1), 74–89.

Stone, S. Z. (1990). *The heritage of the conquistadors: Ruling classes in Central America from the conquest to the Sandinistas*. University of Nebraska Press.

Strathern, M. (1988). *The gender of the gift: Problems with women and problems with society in Melanesia* (Vol. 6). University of California Press.

Swann, C. (2014). *The history of oilfield diving: An industrial adventure*. Oceanaut Press.

Swedberg, R. (2009). *Principles of economic sociology.* Princeton University Press.

Tang, P. (2007). *Masters of the sabar: Wolof griot percussionists of Senegal.* Temple University Press.

Terkel, S. (2011). *Working: People talk about what they do all day and how they feel about what they do.* New Press.

Thiessen, M. (2011). *Contesting conversion: Genealogy, circumcision, and identity in ancient Judaism and Christianity.* Oxford University Press.

Thomke, S., & Sinham, M. (2010). *The dabbawala system: On-time delivery, every time.* Harvard Business School.

Thomson, J. E. (1996). *Mercenaries, pirates, and sovereigns: State-building and extraterritorial violence in early modern Europe.* Princeton University Press.

Thomson, R. S. (1991). A history of leather processing: From the medieval to the present time. In C. Calnan & B. Haines (Eds.), *Leather: Its composition and changes with time* (pp. 12–15). Leather Conservation Centre.

Toohey, J. V., & Dezelsky, T. L. (1980). Curanderas and Brujas—Herbal healing in Mexican American communities. *Health Education, 11*(4), 2–4.

Torres, E., & Sawyer, T. L. (2004). *Curandero: A life in Mexican folk healing.* University of New Mexico Press.

Trotter, K. S. (Ed.). (2012). *Harnessing the power of equine assisted counseling: Adding animal assisted therapy to your practice.* Taylor & Francis.

Tsuya, N. O., & Bumpass, L. L. (Eds.). (2004). *Marriage, work, and family life in comparative perspective: Japan, South Korea, and the United States.* University of Hawaii Press.

Twine, F. W. (2015). *Outsourcing the womb: Race, class and gestational surrogacy in a global market.* Routledge.

United States Department of Labor. (2016). *BLS report: Labor force characteristics by race and ethnicity, 2015.* https://www.bls.gov/opub/reports/race-and-ethnicity/2015/home.htm.

United States Department of Labor. (2017). *BLS report: Employment status of the civilian population by sex and age.* https://www.bls.gov/news.release/emp sit.t01.htm.

Urame, J. (2008). Media reports and public opinion: Sorcery and witchcraft in Papua New Guinea. In F. Zocca & J. Urame (Eds.), *Sorcery, witchcraft and Christianity in Melanesia* (pp. 67–136). Melanesian Institute.

U.S. Fish & Wildlife Service. (Eds.). (2018). *2016 national survey of fishing, hunting and wildlife-associated recreation.* U.S. Fish & Wildlife Service.

Vallerani, F., & Visentin, F. (Eds.). (2017). *Waterways and the cultural landscape.* Routledge.

van Oosten, R. (2016). Nightman's muck, gong farmer's treasure: Local differences in the clearing-out of cesspits in the Low Countries, 1600–1900. In D. Sosna & L. Brunclíková (Eds.), *Archaeologies of waste: Encounters with the unwanted* (pp. 41–58). Oxbow Books.

Van Wyhe, J. (2017). *Phrenology and the origins of Victorian scientific naturalism.* Routledge.

Vaughan, C., Ramírez, O., Herrera, G., & Guries, R. (2007). Spatial ecology and conservation of two sloth species in a cacao landscape in Limón, Costa Rica. *Biodiversity and Conservation, 16*(8), 2293–2310.

Wallerstein, C. (2010). *Culture shock! Costa Rica: A survival guide to customs and etiquette.* Marshall Cavendish International Asia Pte Ltd.

Wang, D. (2000). The idle and the busy: Teahouses and public life in early twentieth-century Chengdu. *Journal of Urban History, 26*(4), 411–437.

Wang, Y. F., & Zhou, Z. K. (2016). The details exploration of intangible cultural heritage from the perspective of cultural tourism industry: A case study of Hohhot City in China. *Canadian Social Science, 12*(7), 30–36.

Ward, H. D. (2017). *Egyptian belly dance in transition: The raqs sharqi revolution, 1890–1930.* McFarland.

Weber, E. (2000). *Apocalypses: Prophecies, cults, and millennial beliefs through the ages.* Harvard University Press.

Weissmann, A., Reitemeier, S., Hahn, A., Gottschalk, J., & Einspanier, A. (2013). Sexing domestic chicken before hatch: A new method for in ovo gender identification. *Theriogenology, 80*(3), 199–205.

West, M. D. (2011). *Lovesick Japan: Sex, marriage, romance, law.* Cornell University Press.

West, P. (1998). *The enduring Seminoles: From alligator wrestling to ecotourism.* University Press of Florida.

Westermeier, C. P. (2005). *Man, beast, dust: The story of rodeo.* University of Nebraska Press.

Whitaker, I. S., Rao, J., Izadi, D., & Butler, P. E. (2004). *Hirudo medicinalis*: Ancient origins of, and trends in the use of medicinal leeches throughout history. *British Journal of Oral and Maxillofacial Surgery, 42*(2), 133–137.

Wildfang, R. L. (2006). *Rome's vestal virgins.* Routledge.

Wilkie, R. (2015). Academic "dirty work": Mapping scholarly labor in a tainted mixed-species field. *Society & Animals, 23*(3), 211–230.

Wilson, A. M. (2001). Mystery shopping: Using deception to measure service performance. *Psychology & Marketing, 18*(7), 721–734.

Wooffitt, R. (2017). *The language of mediums and psychics: The social organization of everyday miracles.* Routledge.

World Health Organization, & Regional Office for South-East Asia Staff. (2016). *Guidelines for the management of snakebites* (2nd ed.). World Health Organization.

Wu, Shih-Jung (2019). *Feng shui: A comparison of the original concept and its current Westernized version* [thesis]. Rochester Institute of Technology. https://scholarworks.rit.edu/theses/10226.

Xiao, L. E. I. (2017). "What we want is to be happy rather than marrying": Exploring Japanese single women's perceptions on marriage. *Journal of International and Advanced Japanese Studies, 9*, 15–29.

Yamaguchi, K. (2000). Married women's gender-role attitudes and social stratification: Commonalities and differences between Japan and the United States. *International Journal of Sociology, 30*(2), 52–89.

Yang, C. J. (2010). Launching strategy for electric vehicles: Lessons from China and Taiwan. *Technological Forecasting and Social Change, 77*(5), 831–834.

Yin, J., & Miike, Y. (2008). A textual analysis of fortune cookie sayings: How Chinese are they? *Howard Journal of Communications, 19*(1), 18–43.

Yin, L., Cheng, Q., Wang, Z., & Shao, Z. (2015). "Big data" for pedestrian volume: Exploring the use of Google Street View images for pedestrian counts. *Applied Geography, 63*, 337–345.

Young, F. (2016). *A history of exorcism in Catholic Christianity.* Palgrave Macmillan.

Zavaleta, A., & Salinas A., Jr. (2009). *Curandero conversations: El niño fidencio, shamanism and healing traditions of the borderlands.* AuthorHouse.

Index

Note: Page numbers in **bold** indicate the location of main entries. Page numbers in *italics* indicate photos.

Printed in the USA
CPSIA information can be obtained
at www.ICGtesting.com
LVHW011032220224
772552LV00003B/57